FUN WITH THE FAMILY™ SERIES

FUN WITH THE FAMILY™

in ILLINOIS

HUNDREDS OF IDEAS FOR DAY TRIPS WITH THE KIDS

THIRD EDITION

By LORI MEEK SCHULDT

The Globe Pequot Press

Guilford, Connecticut

Cover and text design by Nancy Freeborn
Cover photograph by Julie Bidwell
Clothing on cover provided courtesy North Cove Outfitters, Old Saybrook, Connecticut
Maps by M. A. Dubé

Library of Congress Cataloging-in-Publication Data
Schuldt, Lori Meek.
Fun with the family in Illinois : hundreds of ideas for day trips with the kids / by Lori Meek Schuldt. — 3rd ed.
p. cm. — (Fun with the family series)
Includes index.
ISBN 0-7627-0757-7
1. Illinois—Guidebooks. 2. Family recreation—Illinois—Guidebooks. I. Title. II. Series
F539.3.S37 2001 00-050360
917.7304'44—dc21

Manufactured in the United States of America
Third Edition/First Printing

To Michael and Rachel, who put the fun in my family

Acknowledgments

I would like to thank Michael K. Urban, vice president and associate publisher of The Globe Pequot Press, for asking me to write this book and the staff at Globe for all their work. Special thanks to Liz Taylor. Thanks also to the many others who have aided me, both professionally and personally, in the journey from idea to printed page. I appreciate all the suggestions and support I have received from friends and family, especially my parents, Bill and Dian Meek; my sister, Cindy, and her five-year-old, Tyler, who accompanied us on some of our "field research"; my loving sisters in P.E.O. Chapter KY; the Studzinski family for providing a welcome refuge for Rachel while Mom was chained to the computer; and all the others whom I may not have named specifically but who made their own unique contributions.

In the grand tradition of saving the best for last, I would like to thank Rachel P. Schuldt, my darling 11-year-old daughter, for her spirit of adventure in all our little family "vacations" (since 1995, when we began work on the first edition of this book) and her patience during the long process of writing about them, and Michael B. Schuldt, my sweet husband and partner in life, for his willingness to play pilot to my navigator during our travels, for his experienced editorial eyes in reading the manuscript, and for his constant love and reassurance in this and every other endeavor.

Rockford
Schaumburg
Chicago
NORTHERN ILLINOIS
CHICAGOLAND
Quad Cities
WESTERN ILLINOIS
Peoria
CENTRAL ILLINOIS
Springfield
Vandalia
SOUTHERN ILLINOIS
ILLINOIS

Contents

Introduction

During presidential campaigns you often hear the saying "Whoever wins Illinois, wins the White House." It's true that since 1820, with few exceptions, every winning presidential candidate has carried the state of Illinois. Have you ever wondered why? Probably because no other state serves as such a microcosm of the United States. Illinois is a marvelous melting pot of people—descendants of immigrants from Europe, Africa, Asia, and Latin America, plus a few Native Americans—whose homes are big cities, sprawling suburbs, small towns, and isolated farmsteads. The state's topography includes rivers, bluffs, hills, flatlands, forests, and a Great Lake as wide as an ocean. For those of us who live in Illinois, it's a great place to visit somewhere different without ever leaving the state: Downstaters can get energized by the hustle and bustle of the greater Chicago area, while city dwellers can escape to the south and reconnect with nature. Illinois is the perfect state for all kinds of family adventures.

This book is designed to help you find places throughout the state that are of special interest to families, from educational attractions such as children's museums and zoos to recreational facilities such as water parks and miniature golf courses, keeping in mind that having fun is the number one goal. The guide is divided into six geographically based chapters: Chicago, Chicagoland, Northern Illinois, Western Illinois, Central Illinois, and Southern Illinois. The sections within each chapter also are arranged geographically so that you can find attractions that are close to one another. A regional map appears at the beginning of each chapter to help you get a better feel for the lay of the land. At the end of the book are a Restaurant Appendix and a Lodging Appendix that will familiarize you with some of the more family-friendly chains. And beyond the general index is an activities index that will help you find attractions by type, such as children's museums or water parks—plus one index of all the free attractions listed in this book.

Here are a few general guidelines to keep in mind. First, always call ahead to double-check that what you want to see is still there; some places may change location or shut down between the time this book goes to print and the time you want to visit. For family travel it's safest to stick with chain hotels and motels and to make your reservations in advance. This book places special emphasis on properties that have a swimming pool, because this amenity tends to keep the kids happier and gives them a place to burn off some of the energy that built up during the trip getting there. When possible, motels that allow pets are also pointed out for families who want to bring along four-legged members. In a similar vein, most of the restaurants mentioned are geared toward middle-of-the-road tastes: buffets, burgers, pizza, and meat-and-potatoes sorts of places. One last note: When admission to an attraction is by donation, you can usually gauge what the real expectation is by whether a specific dollar amount is suggested. If it is, you'll be more comfortable if you plan to pay that amount; if not, they'll be grateful for whatever you give.

In the sections "Where to Eat" and "Where to Stay," dollar signs provide an idea of the price range at those establishments. The following table illustrates what those ranges are.

Rates for Lodging	
$	$49 or less
$$	$50 to $74
$$$	$75 to $99
$$$$	$100 or more

Rates for Restaurants	
$	most entrees $9 or less
$$	most entrees $10 to $14
$$$	most entrees $15 to $19
$$$$	most entrees $20 or more

Many of the individual regions, towns, and sites included in this guide have a phone number you can call, an Internet Web site you can look up, or an address to which you can write to obtain more information.

For general information covering the whole state, you can contact the following:

Illinois Bureau of Tourism, (800) 226-6632; www.enjoyillinois.com

Illinois Restaurant Association, (312) 787-4000 or (800) 572-1086; www.illinoisrestaurants.org

Hotel-Motel Association of Illinois, (217) 522-1231; www.hotel-motel-illinois.com

Illinois Campground Association, (217) 279-3396

Illinois Association of Park Districts, (217) 523-4554; www.ilparks.org

Illinois Department of Transportation, (800) 452-4368; www.dot.state.il.us

Illinois Tollway, (630) 241-6800 or (800) 865-5394; www.illinoistollway.com

Note: With the exception of an unsolicited press pass at one amusement park, the author and her family spent their own money for all the attractions they visited. The author did not identify herself as a writer; the Schuldts wished to be treated the same way as any other family so that a realistic experience could be reported. No one paid the author or the publisher to appear in this book.

The prices and rates listed in this guidebook were confirmed at press time. We recommend, however, that you call establishments to obtain current information before traveling.

Attractions Key

The following is a key to the icons found throughout the text.

 Swimming

 Animal Viewing

 Boating / Boat Tour

 Lodging

 Historic Site

 Camping

 Hiking / Walking

 Museums

 Fishing

 Performing Arts

 Biking

 Sports/Athletic

 Amusement Park

 Picnicking

 Horseback Riding

 Playground

 Skiing/Winter Sports

 Shopping

 Park

 Nature Viewing

Chicago

Where does one start in describing the city of Chicago? There's so much to say. There's the history: the Fort Dearborn massacre of 1812, the incorporation of the city in 1833 with a white population of 150 and the subsequent ouster of more than 3,000 indigenous Indians, the industrial expansion in the mid-1800s that created the Union Stock Yards and the Chicago Board of Trade, Mrs. O'Leary's cow and the Great Chicago Fire of 1871, the World's Columbian Exposition of 1893, Al Capone and the gangster era of the 1920s, race riots throughout the 1900s, the political empire of Mayor Richard J. Daley. There's the architecture: Risen from the ashes of the Great Chicago Fire by pioneers who created the Chicago School, it today includes what we Illinoisians consider the world's tallest building (the Sears Tower) and other skyscrapers that make the downtown skyline one of the most distinctive in the world, especially since the lakefront has been deliberately spared from development so that everyone may enjoy the beauty of its parks and beaches. There's the culture: an ethnic mixture that includes the largest Polish population of any city outside Poland, plus descendants of wave after wave of immigrants from Europe, Africa, Asia, and Latin America, giving the city a vitality in music, art, and food that few other places can match. There are the sports: professional baseball, basketball, football, and hockey teams. It's no wonder that singers have made the city famous as "Sweet Home Chicago" and "My Kind of Town"—whatever you're looking for is probably here.

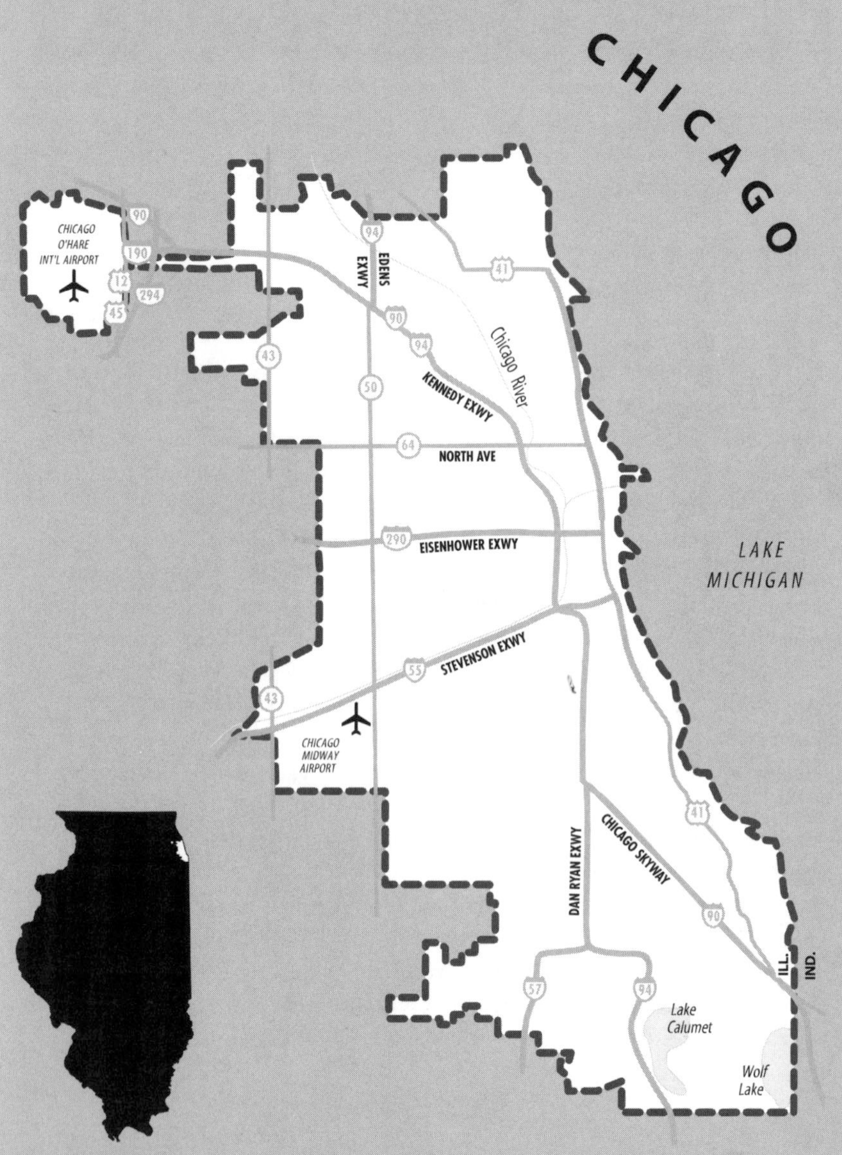
CHICAGO
CHICAGO O'HARE INT'L AIRPORT
90
190
12
294
45
94
EDENS EXWY
41
Chicago River
90
94
KENNEDY EXWY
43
50
64
NORTH AVE
290
EISENHOWER EXWY
LAKE MICHIGAN
55
STEVENSON EXWY
43
CHICAGO MIDWAY AIRPORT
41
CHICAGO SKYWAY
DAN RYAN EXWY
90
ILL.
IND.
57
94
Lake Calumet
Wolf Lake

But you may need help finding it. The Illinois listings for tourism, hotels, and restaurants in the introduction to this book include Chicago, but the city has two resources of its own to contact as well:

Chicago Office of Tourism
Chicago Cultural Center
78 East Washington Street
Chicago 60602
(312) 744-2400
(800) 487-2446 (outside Chicago area)
TTY (312) 744-2947
Internet: www.ci.chi.il.us/tourism

Chicago Convention and Tourism Bureau
2301 South Lake Shore Drive
Chicago 60616
(312) 567-8500
Internet: www.chicago.il.org

Getting to Chicago is no problem; there are so many choices. If you live in the suburbs, you can enjoy a comfortable ride in on a commuter train; the Metra rail system has about a dozen lines radiating outward from the city in all directions. You can reach Chicago from as far out as Fox Lake, Harvard, Elgin, Geneva, Aurora, Joliet, or University Park. For schedules, fares, and other information, contact Metra, 547 West Jackson Boulevard, Chicago 60661; (312) 322-6777. Internet: www.metrarail.com. The downtown Metra passenger terminal, officially called the Richard B. Ogilvie Transportation Center and formerly the Chicago and Northwestern Station before Union Pacific took over, was remodeled in the early 1990s and today is an eye-catching gray-blue architectural work of glass, steel, and marble. The food court on the lower level rivals that of many shopping malls, and there are useful stores on the upper level where you can grab a newspaper and a cup of coffee, get your shoes shined, or buy flowers, candy, or other gifts.

Train service is available from other parts of the state and from out of state via Amtrak; call (800) 872-7245 or check the Web site www.amtrak.com for information on routes, schedules, and fares. Another economical choice for transportation is Greyhound bus lines; call (800) 231-2222. Both Amtrak and Greyhound have passenger terminals in downtown Chicago.

You can fly in and out of Chicago's two major airports. On the northwest side, O'Hare—one of the world's busiest airports—handles flights from all over the globe; the general airport number is (773) 686-2200; for the hearing impaired, TTY (773) 601-8333. Smaller Midway, on the south side, services more domestic and regional carriers and is less congested; call (773) 838-0600; TTY (773) 838-0758. The Chicago Transit Authority (CTA) operates trains that can get you to and from either airport as well as trains and buses that go all around the city; call (312) 836-7000 or check the CTA Web site www.transitchicago.com for information on service. Shuttle services and taxicabs also provide transportation from either airport to the city and suburbs.

Coming by car affords travelers the greatest degree of independence and flexibility, but unless you live somewhere bigger (for example, New York or Los Angeles—the only two larger U.S. cities—or London, Tokyo, or Mexico City, among about two dozen urban centers in the world that exceed Chicago's size), you'll be appalled at the traffic. No matter what thoroughfare you take, you'll have plenty of other vehicles whizzing around you, cutting you off, riding your bumper, and generally paying little heed to many rules of the road, including speed limits—all this while your kids are screaming in the backseat. Downtown amid the congested streets, you'll have to deal with aggressive cabs resenting your very existence, harried couriers on bicycles darting out in front of you, delivery vehicles suddenly double-parking, and maybe even an overzealous young entrepreneur giving your windshield an unsolicited washing for a solicited tip. Parking is hard to come by on the streets and expensive in the lots. For the amount of aggravation incurred, driving may not be your top choice.

If you nonetheless opt to drive, here's a little assistance with the expressway lingo. The major north-south thoroughfare of I–94 is known as the Edens Expressway. Another interstate, I–90, which starts out being called the Northwest Tollway and changes its name around Rosemont to the John F. Kennedy Expressway, heads in from the northwest. In the north around Irving Park Road, I–94 joins with I–90, and at about that point the joint interstate is called the Dan Ryan Expressway. I–90/94 splits off again south of downtown, where I–90 continues east into Indiana as the Chicago Skyway and I–94, which is still called the Dan Ryan, continues south to a junction with I–80, at which point I–80/94 becomes known as the Kingery Expressway. A couple of key spurs off I–94 are I–294, also called the Tri-State Tollway, and I–394, also known as the Bishop Ford Freeway, formerly the Calumet Expressway. I–90's western spur, I–290, is called the Dwight D. Eisenhower Expressway. A major artery coming into Chicago from the southwest is I–55, which is known as the Adlai E. Stevenson Expressway. It has a spur, I–355, which was built in the late 1980s to connect western suburbs from south to north and has yet to receive an official alternate name. Also lacking additional nomenclature is I–57, which enters from the south. U.S. Highway 41 becomes concurrent with Lake Shore Drive as it skirts Lake Michigan. Farther out, U.S. Highway 30 has been dubbed Lincoln Highway, and Illinois Highway 50 is called the Dixie Highway. All this jargon is helpful to know if you have to ask directions, because a native may well say, "Take the Stevenson down to . . ." or "Get on the Dan Ryan and . . ." or "Head out the Kennedy to . . ." and not even be sure which number goes with which name. Radio traffic reporters also use the names more than the numbers.

One other thing you should know about Chicago: Its many neighborhoods have their own names, which can be a bit confusing to visitors from outside the metropolitan area who don't know the difference between a neighborhood name and a suburb name. If you hear about something in Uptown, Bucktown, Austin, Bridgeport, Englewood, Lakeview, or Pullman, you're still in Chicago. Many neighborhoods have *Park* as part of their name: Hyde Park, Rogers Park, Wicker Park, Jefferson Park, Norwood Park, Portage Park, Brighton Park, and Morgan Park, for example. (Unfortunately, many suburbs also use the word: Oak Park, Franklin Park, Schiller Park, Melrose Park, Bedford Park, Evergreen Park, Park Ridge, and Park Forest, to name a few.) You can lock in more easily on street addresses, because all the numbers radiate outward from the intersection of State and Madison Streets downtown. State Street runs north-south, so street addresses with East will be east of State, although not more than a mile or two because you run into the lake, and those with West run all the way to the city limits on the West Side. Madison Street runs east-west through the middle of the Loop, as the heart of downtown is called, so all the North and South addresses are relative to this point.

Now that you're finally here, let's examine what there is for families to see and do within the city limits of Chicago. We'll start downtown, then branch out to the North, West, and South Sides.

Downtown

CHICAGO TROLLEY COMPANY (all ages)

Pickup at various downtown locations; (312) 663–0260. Tours operate daily. First tour begins at 9:30 A.M.; last begins at 4 P.M. A one-day pass costs $18 for anyone age 12 through 64, $15 for seniors age 65 or older, and $8 for kids age 3 through 11. Children age 2 or younger ride free. Internet: www.chicagotrolley.com.

You can get an overview of the downtown area aboard a red sightseeing trolley. The Chicago Trolley Company offers a narrated tour a bit more than an hour long, and you can get on or off at any number of key spots, such as Water Tower Place, Navy Pier, Sears Tower, the Art Institute, and the Field Museum. The refurbished trolleys have rubber wheels and drive on the streets like a bus; the original trolley tracks and lines are long gone. Each trolley has an interior furnished with oak and brass trimmings and can hold 34 passengers at a time. The all-day pass allows an unlimited number of reboardings.

Hit the Beach The Chicago Park District manages the **Free** public beaches along the city's 29 miles of lakefront. You can swim (in certain supervised areas at designated times), play volleyball, or go jogging, roller-skating, or biking. It's a pleasure just to sit and watch the waves roll in, even during winter. For general information about the lakefront areas, call the park district at (312) 747–2200; for the hearing impaired, TTY (312) 986–0726. Internet: www.chicagoparkdistrict.com. The park district also oversees the dozens of local swimming pools throughout the city. Just north of the downtown area is the popular Oak Street Beach. Find out about its seasonal hours by calling (312) 747–0829.

HANCOCK OBSERVATORY (all ages)

875 North Michigan Avenue, Chicago 60611; (888) 875–8439. Open from 9 A.M. to midnight daily. Admission costs $8.75 for anyone age 13 through 64, $6.75 for seniors age 65 or older, and $6 for young people age 5 through 12. Children age 4 or younger get in free. Internet: www.hancock-observatory.com.

The John Hancock Center Observatory tower offers a panoramic view of the city from the 95th floor. Hang onto your stomach for the 40-second elevator ride that takes you to the top. You may want to give kids a piece of gum ahead of time or babies a pacifier to help keep their ears from popping. It's worth it once you get up there. It's true: On a clear day you can see forever.

WATER TOWER PLACE (all ages)

835 North Michigan Avenue, Chicago 60611; (312) 440–3165. Hours are 10 A.M. to 7 P.M. Monday through Saturday and noon to 6 P.M. Sunday. Hours may be extended around Christmastime. Internet: www.shopwatertower.com.

At the north end of the Magnificent Mile, as the famous shopping district is called, is Water Tower Place. Lord & Taylor and Marshall Field's anchor this six-level enclosed shopping center. The 125 or so stores encircle a central atrium, with lighted glass elevators and crisscrossing escalators to transport shoppers up and down. The original light brick water tower for which the mall was named stands at Michigan Avenue and Pearson Street, across the street. It looks rather puny compared to the skyscrapers that now surround it.

PEACE MUSEUM (age 5 and up)

314 West Institute Place (1 block north of Chicago Avenue and 1½ blocks west of Wells Street), Chicago 60610; (312) 440–1860. Hours are 11 A.M. to 5 P.M.

Tuesday through Saturday (open Saturday only in July); closed Sunday and Monday. Admission costs $3.50 for adults and $2 for students age 12 or older and seniors. Kids age 11 or younger are free. Internet: www.peacemuseum.org. Inquire about current exhibits.

Worth a detour a bit west of the Magnificent Mile is the Peace Museum, reportedly the only museum in the United States dedicated to promoting peace through the arts and humanities.

JAZZ SHOWCASE (age 5 and up)

59 West Grand Avenue (between Dearborn and Clark Streets), Chicago 60610; (312) 670–2473. Shows run Tuesday through Sunday evenings plus a Sunday matinee. Admission usually costs $15 to $20 per person. Call for current schedule.

Although Joe Segal's venerable downtown jazz club is generally geared toward adults, children are encouraged to attend the Sunday afternoon concerts. The venue is intimate enough that they'll get an up-close look at some of the finest jazz musicians in the business. Ellis and sons Branford, Delfeayo, and Wynton Marsalis have all played here; so have talented young trumpeters Roy Hargrove and Nicholas Payton, and numerous veterans, including saxophonists James Moody and Johnny Griffin, pianist McCoy Tyner, and drummers Elvin Jones and Roy Haynes. Portraits of Charlie Parker, Dizzy Gillespie, and other jazz greats adorn the walls, and the seating is at tables around the room.

NAVY PIER (all ages)

600 East Grand Avenue, Chicago 60611; (312) 595–7437 or, outside the Chicago area, (800) 595–7437. Open daily. **Free**, *except for rides and Children's Museum.Carousel rides cost $2.50 for anyone age 12 or older and $2 for kids age 2 through 11. Ferris wheel prices are $3.50 and $3, respectively. Babies age 1 or younger ride free. (See next entry for information on the Children's Museum.) The pier is accessible for wheelchairs; rentals are available on-site. Parking fees start at $6.50 for one hour. Internet: www.navypier.com.*

The 1995 grand reopening of the renovated Navy Pier was big news for Chicago—and it will be good news for you too, because there are lots of things here of interest to visiting families. The 80-year-old facility, which had fallen into disrepair after decades of disuse, now has a vibrant atmosphere that promises to attract city dwellers and tourists alike for years to come. The pier extends a total length of about 3,300 feet, but most of the family attractions are at the closer end. The first building you come to after passing the Gateway Park fountain is called the Family Pavilion. It houses the Chicago Children's Museum (see next entry), a large-screen theater, and a couple dozen retail shops and restaurants. At the west end of the pavilion is the spacious, glassed-in Crystal Gardens, which is filled with palm trees, exotic plants, and fountains. There are benches you can sit on to soak up the ambience. Just east of this building is a shallow reflecting pool that turns into an ice rink in winter. Nearby is a colorful musical merry-go-round. Next comes the most obvious new feature at Navy Pier: the 150-foot-tall Ferris wheel. Even people who have trouble with motion sickness could safely ride it: One revolution takes almost eight minutes. Passengers travel in 40 glass-enclosed gondolas that each can hold up to six people (sit on the right side for the best view of the city; the Ferris wheel is accessible for wheelchairs). In summer the carnival atmosphere is enhanced by vendor carts and authorized street performers. Continuing east, the soaring white rooftop of the Skyline Stage is reminiscent of the famous Sydney Opera House in Australia, but you probably won't see much opera here (the gorgeous Lyric Opera building on Wacker Drive has the corner on that market). The 1,500-seat outdoor theater does host a variety of performances, including music, dance, theater, and films. The remainder of the pier houses a fine-dining restaurant, a festival hall, a beer garden, and the Grand Ballroom. You can get to Navy Pier aboard the sight-seeing trolley or double-decker bus or ride one of six Chicago Transit Authority (CTA) public bus lines that stop here (numbers 29, 56, 65, 66, 120, and 121). If you drive, there is a parking garage underground that can hold more than a thousand cars.

CHICAGO CHILDREN'S MUSEUM (ages 1–12)

700 East Grand Avenue, Chicago 60611; (312) 527–1000. Open year-round. Hours are 10 A.M. to 5 P.M. daily. Admission costs $6.50 per person age 1 through 59, $5.50 for seniors age 60 or older, and is free for babies younger than 1. Admission is **Free** *during family time, from 5 to 8 P.M. Thursday. The facility is accessible for wheelchairs. Internet: www.childrensmuseum.org.*

Natural light pours in from the arched glass ceiling of the Great Hall to enhance the open, airy feel of this place. The centerpiece of the museum is a white three-story replica of a schooner, with rigging that kids can climb all the way up to the crow's nest. The lower level gives the impression of being underwater, thanks to aquariums filled with live freshwater fish. A black steel staircase wraps around the ship. The museum takes advantage of the building's twin-towered Headhouse with exhibits that use the full 50 feet of space from floor to tower ceiling. One tower has pipes, pumps, locks, and all manner of water

Won't You Let Me Take You on a Sea Cruise? A unique way to tour the city is by boat. Two sight-seeing cruise lines operate from the lower level of Michigan Avenue at Wacker Drive, near the white Wrigley Building with its jutting clock tower. The cruising season runs from mid-April to mid-October. Each boat plies the Chicago River, then heads out into Lake Michigan to give you a truly panoramic view of the city skyline and lakefront before returning one and a half hours later to where you started.

Wendella Sightseeing Boats. *400 North Michigan Avenue (north side of the Michigan Avenue Bridge), Chicago 60611; (312) 337–1446. Internet: www.wendellaboats.com.* This is arguably the more well known of the two cruise lines. Cruises sail daily at 10 and 11:30 A.M. and 1:15, 2, 3, 4:30, 7, and 8:30 P.M. Tickets cost $14 for anyone age 12 through 61, $12 for adults age 62 or older, and $7 for kids age 11 or younger. A two-hour cruise, which includes a stop at Buckingham Fountain, sails at 7:30 P.M. daily. Tickets cost $16, $14, and $8 for the respective age categories.

Mercury Cruiseline. *Across the river from Wendella; (312) 332–1368.* Cruises sail daily and depart on the hour from 10 A.M. to 7 P.M. Tickets cost $14 for anyone age 12 or older and $7 for children age 4 through 11. Tots age 3 or younger sail free.

A newer entry into the Chicago cruise business operates out of Navy Pier and puts a twist into the standard excursion by using a giant yellow speedboat:

Seadog Cruises. *Navy Pier; (312) 822–7200.* Operates from April through October; call for current schedule. These half-hour cruises technically are narrated, but it's hard to hear the guide over the noise of the twin 12-cylinder diesel engines. Bathing suits are welcome, although you are advised to bring a sweatshirt or jacket in case of cool lake air, and you may very well get wet, especially if you're seated near the outside. The 70-foot boat can carry up to 149 passengers and reach a top speed of 45 m.p.h., which is a pretty good clip when skimming across the water. Tickets cost $15 for anyone age 12 or older and $14 for kids age 3 through 11. Children age 2 or younger ride free, but they'd better be the daredevil type or everyone will be unhappy.

propulsion. The other tower houses the Inventing Lab, where kids make their own flying machines and then test their creations' aerodynamics by cranking up a conveyor belt to hoist the machines to the top of the tower and letting them go. One of the more popular exhibits is the hospital. Youngsters can handle medical instruments, X rays, kid-size crutches, and a model skeleton. The cab of a real ambulance features a flashing light and a dispatch radio. In the excavation pit you can dig for dinosaur bones. A special play area called PlayMaze is reserved for kids age 6 or younger (plus accompanying parents). Its wooded rural setting contains a log cabin, with cast-iron stove and other furnishings, and a tree house. Nearby is a "baby pit" filled with soft toys and encircled by 2-foot-high padded walls, restricted to children no older than 18 months. An urban setting lets kids pretend to be shopkeepers.

DISNEYQUEST INDOOR INTERACTIVE THEME PARK (age 8 and up)

55 East Ohio Street,Chicago 60611 (corner of Rush and Ohio Streets); (312) 222–1300. Hours are 11 A.M. to 10 P.M. Monday through Wednesday, 11 A.M. to midnight Thursday and Friday, 10 A.M. to midnight Saturday, and 10 A.M. to 10 P.M. Sunday. All kids age 12 or younger must be accompanied by an adult. Admission costs $16 per person for a limited-play card or $34 for an unlimited-play card, and each person entering must have a card. Strollers are not allowed inside. Elevators make the facility technically accessible for wheelchairs, but the mazelike layout is such that navigation would not be easy. Rest rooms on the second and fourth floors include "companion" facilities for families. Internet: www.disneyquest.com.

If Florida or California is too far away to travel, you can get a taste of the Disney experience in downtown Chicago. It's everything you would expect from Disney: busy, loud, and expensive. Whether it's worth it depends largely on your taste. This facility definitely is a better value for older kids and teens, for several reasons. First, some attractions have height restrictions. Second, many of the features are just too complicated for small children to handle. Third, teenagers may go in without adult accompaniment, saving Mom and Dad the entry fee if they're not all that interested in playing.

The minimum per-person cost of $16 for a limited-play card comes with 70 points. The plastic card has a magnetic strip like a credit card, and you swipe the card through a scanner, which deducts points for each game or "ride." The major attractions take 20 points each, so the limited-play card really fits its name. Spring for the unlimited-play card if you plan to stay more than an hour.

The facility has five floors connected by elevators and narrow circular staircases; signs point the way to various attractions, but it's easy to get turned around and very easy to lose a child who is not closely supervised. The only ride that actually moves is Buzz Lightyear's AstroBlaster, a set of wacky bumper cars with the twist of shooting out basketball-size rubber balls. Flashing lights, loud music, and canned laughter and merriment add to the mayhem. Other rides use virtual-reality technology, some with giant screens and others with helmets that fit over the eyes so that only the wearer sees the "action." The Jungle Cruise has perhaps the most successful blend: Riders sit in a mock yellow life raft puffed up with air, facing a big screen showing a river path; paddles with electronic sensors control the picture, while the raft seats rock to simulate the corresponding motion. Sometimes a splash of real water comes at the end. The most popular attraction is the virtual-reality roller coaster, for which you design your own course before being strapped into a seat that will simulate the plunges and actually roll full circle for loop-the-loops.

Arcade games at two points apiece are the same kind you can find at other, less pricey places. In the arts-and-crafts area, kids can design their own CD or a caricature portrait—the catch is that it costs an extra $10 if you want to keep it.

In the Food Quest dining area, you pick up your food at the counter and carry it to a table. Prices are on the high side—$1.75 for the smallest soda, about $2 for french fries, and nearly $4 for a kids' burger, regular hot dog, slice of pizza, or "melted cheese" sandwich. And just in case you have any money left, you must pass through the gift shop to reach the exit.

CHICAGO CULTURAL CENTER AND MUSEUM OF BROADCAST COMMUNICATIONS (age 3 and up)

78 East Washington Street (at Michigan Avenue), Chicago 60602; (312) 346–3278 for the current Chicago Cultural Center schedule of events or (312) 629–6000 for the Museum of Broadcast Communications. Museum hours are 10 A.M. to 4:30 P.M. Monday through Saturday and noon to 5 P.M. Sunday; closed state and national holidays. Admission is **Free**. *Internet: www.mbcnet.org.*

The Chicago Cultural Center is a National Historic Landmark. It's worth stopping in just for a glance at the golden Byzantine mosaic tiles on the curving arches. There are four galleries of art exhibitions, and you often can catch a **Free** musical performance. You can also see a free informative multilingual video show called *Round and About the Loop*.

Also housed within the Chicago Cultural Center is the popular Museum of Broadcast Communications. Your kids will be amazed to discover how television developed over the not-so-distant past (like, when we were kids, some of us parents didn't even have a TV, or only had a black-and-white one, and there was no cable—wow, dark ages) to become the megachannel giant it is today. There are thousands of audio- and videotapes from the "golden age" of radio and television. Chicago-area parents will get a nostalgia kick from the old *Garfield Goose* TV puppet shows. Many visitors are amused by the collection of award-winning TV commercials you can see here.

Taste the Taste Taste of Chicago, or "the Taste," is one of the city's biggest and most popular annual events. It runs from late June through the Fourth of July and features about 70 booths that represent the city's finest foods (restaurateurs compete fiercely for a spot here). The food booths line Columbus Drive from Monroe to Balbo Drives, which are all blocked off from vehicular traffic. You buy tickets at a booth near the entrance and then exchange them with the vendors for food and drink. Individual tickets cost about 60 cents, and most dishes require two to eight tickets, so you'll spend about $1.20 to $4.80 per item. You can find safe bets like pizza and corn on the cob, but this food fair also gives you a wonderful opportunity to sample ethnic cuisine you might not be willing to gamble on at a regular restaurant, such as Ethiopian beef, Thai chicken satay, Polish potato pierogies, or Jamaican jerk chicken. Save room for dessert—for example, Italian ice, fried dough, chocolate-dipped strawberries, or Eli's famous Chicago cheesecake. There are all sorts of music and dance performances to entertain you while you eat. Taste of Chicago does get pretty crowded, so if you can flex your schedule to come during the week in the late morning or midafternoon, you'll avoid competing with downtown office workers who come at lunchtime or after 5 P.M. during the week and with the throngs that surge in all weekend. On the evening of July 3, there is an Independence Day concert emanating from the Petrillo Music Shell and climaxing with a spectacular fireworks display to the *1812 Overture*. For information on this year's Taste, call (312) 744–3370.

ART INSTITUTE OF CHICAGO (age 5 and up)

Michigan Avenue and Adams Street, Chicago 60603-6110; (312) 443–3600. Hours are Monday through Friday from 10:30 A.M. to 4:30 P.M. (until 8 P.M. Tuesday) and 10 A.M. to 5 P.M. Saturday and Sunday; closed Thanksgiving and Christmas. Except for the **Free** *day, Tuesday, a monetary donation is required to enter. The suggested amount is $8 for anyone age 15 through 55 and $5 for kids* *age 6 through 14, students age 15 or older with an ID, and senior citizens age 56 or older. You can give less than these amounts, but you must give something. Children age 5 or younger are not expected to pay. Backpack-style baby carriers, large bags, and video cameras are not allowed; you must check such items at the service desk or stow them in a pay locker near the entrance. Internet: www.artic.edu.*

The Art Institute of Chicago is one of the city's most famous attractions, easily recognizable by the mammoth twin lions guarding the white building's pillared facade. It's also one of the world's finest art museums, with what's widely recognized as the finest collection of French impressionist paintings outside Paris. Georges Seurat's giant tableau *Sunday Afternoon on the Island of La Grande Jatte* holds a prominent place on display. Other galleries house fine collections of Oriental and "primitive" art. Medieval buffs will enjoy the glass cases filled with suits of armor and related paraphernalia. Most of the viewing rooms are spacious, and you can navigate a stroller through fairly easily, but please exercise good judgment in deciding whether to bring children younger than school age here. A quiet baby in a stroller is fine, but a chronically fussy one will disrupt others' peaceful enjoyment of these great art-

State Street, That Great Street State Street has long history and a variety of stores. The area regained some of its long-ago vitality in 1996 after a renovation that basically undid all the changes made in 1979, when the street was turned into more of a pedestrian mall and closed to all vehicular traffic except buses. That idea was a flop—why come to the city for a mall-like atmosphere when there are so many nice malls in the suburbs? No, you come to the city for the hustle and bustle, the traffic noise and smog, the crowded sidewalks, the gritty urban reality that makes you feel so alive! And if you buy stuff in the meantime, so much the better for the merchants. The renovation added some lovely old-fashioned touches that hark back to the street's heyday in the 1920s through 1950s, such as wrought-iron ornamental tree grates and fencing, historic lampposts, and art deco–style subway canopies.

Winter is a special time along State Street. The Marshall Field's window in this area has elaborate Christmas displays during the holiday season, and you can buy hot chestnuts from a nearby pushcart vendor. Skate on State is a **Free** outdoor ice-skating rink on State between Washington and Randolph Streets. It's open from 9 A.M. to 7:15 P.M. daily from late November through February, weather permitting. Bring your own skates or rent them at the rink for $2 to $3. For more information about Skate on State, call (312) 744–3370.

works. Likewise, the average toddler will have little interest in the art and simply think the open spaces look like a great place to run, causing distraction to other patrons and also depriving you of the opportunity to appreciate what the museum has to offer. For older children, however, a visit to the Art Institute can open up a whole new world.

SEARS TOWER (all ages)

233 South Wacker Drive (at Adams Street), Chicago 60606; (312) 875–9696. The entrance is on Jackson Boulevard between Wacker Drive and Franklin Street. Hours are 9 A.M. to 11 P.M. daily. Admission costs $9.50 for anyone age 13 through 64, $7.75 for seniors age 65 or older, and $6.75 for kids age 5 through 12. Children age 4 or younger and military personnel in uniform are admitted free. The last tickets of the day are sold at 10:30 P.M. Visitors must sit through a short movie presentation before boarding the elevator. Internet: www.the-skydeck.com.

The preschoolers you opted not to take to the Art Institute are more likely to be happy riding the elevator up to the Sears Tower Skydeck and looking out at the vast expanse of the city below from what is reportedly the highest observation deck in the world, on the 103rd floor. Renovation in 2000 made the skydeck more family-friendly. The *Knee-High Chicago* diorama is only 4 feet high and covered with colorful pictures to appeal to young children. Changes in sound and lighting also enhanced the ambience, and new viewing telescopes allow a better look at the world outside. New InfoVision kiosks offer information on the building and the city in your choice of English, Spanish, French, German, Polish, or Japanese.

Until recently, Sears Tower was universally recognized as the world's tallest building. The Petronas Towers building in Kuala Lumpur, Malaysia, was completed in 1996 and declared the world's tallest building, as measured from the sidewalk to the "structural top" of the building. Sears Tower representatives, not about to give up the title without a fight, argued that the only reason Petronas Towers measured taller was because it has a decorative spire atop each tower. In terms of occupied space, Petronas is only 88 stories high; both Sears Tower and New York's World Trade Center are 110 stories high, Sears Tower barely edging out the World Trade Center by a difference of 82 feet. So the Council on Tall Buildings, the organization that makes these official designations, then split the "tallest building" category into two categories, one for "structural top" and one for number of floors. Thus, Sears Tower remains, in at least one sense, the world's tallest building. Many of us would argue that there was never a doubt.

BUCKINGHAM FOUNTAIN (all ages)

Lake Shore Drive at Congress Parkway, Chicago; (312) 747–2200. Operates daily from May through October 1. **Free**.

Some of Chicago's best-known family attractions are clustered along Lake Shore Drive. One, at the intersection with Congress Parkway, is this huge outdoor fountain. The water shoots up and cascades down the ornate 1927 structure between 10 A.M. and 11 P.M. daily, the last two hours with a dazzling display of colored lights added. And there's no charge to enjoy all this aquatic magic.

FIELD MUSEUM (all ages)

Roosevelt Road and Lake Shore Drive, Chicago 60605-2496; (312) 922–9410. Hours are 9 A.M. to 5 P.M. daily. Admission costs $8 for adults age 18 through 64 and $4 for young people age 3 through 17, students age 18 or older with school ID, and seniors age 65 or older. Admission is **Free** *on Wednesday. Visitors in wheelchairs may be dropped off at the west door. Wheelchairs and strollers are available for rent. Internet: www.fmnh.org.*

The star attraction at this Chicago institution was unveiled May 17, 2000. It is Sue the dinosaur, the largest and most complete *Tyrannosaurus rex* skeleton ever found. Named after Sue Hendrickson, the fossil hunter who unearthed the prehistoric treasure in South Dakota in 1990, the skeleton was painstakingly cleaned and reassembled from more than 200 bones. No one knows for sure whether Sue was female or male, because the dinosaur's organs and soft tissue were not preserved. Alive, Sue would have weighed about 7 tons—nearly a ton of that weight resting in the 5-foot-long skull that remains. The skeleton is about 45 feet long and 13 feet high at the hips. It is the centerpiece of an informative display that kids and adults alike will enjoy. The museum also has an extensive collection of Native American artifacts, including a re-created Pawnee earth lodge you can walk around in and authentic carved totems. Another fascinating structure is the Maori meetinghouse in the Pacific section. Other permanent exhibits focus on ancient Egypt and other parts of Africa. The Egyptian exhibit includes a replica of the tomb of Unis-ankh, a pharaoh who lived around 2200 B.C. It includes real mummies of people, cats, and falcons, all dating from 3100 B.C. to A.D. 323. The other Africa exhibit takes visitors on a tour of the continent, both chronologically and geographically, using pictures, artifacts, music, and videos. It includes some hands-on features that make the information more relevant to kids. For example, they can operate a hand-pump bellows for an iron-smelting furnace or use a pulley to "draw" water from a deep well. There are lots of fascinating interactive question-and-answer displays as part of the exhibit. A section you could easily skip contains glass cases of taxidermy; these seem rather stale and dated in an era when many zoos have a wide variety of animals in live displays that imitate their natural habitat. Unless you just have to see the now-extinct passenger pigeon, spend your time elsewhere in the museum. Special displays periodically join the regular collection; call for details.

SHEDD AQUARIUM (all ages)

1200 South Lake Shore Drive, Chicago 60605; (312) 939–2438. Open year-round. Hours from Memorial Day through Labor Day are 9 A.M. to 6 P.M. daily. Hours the rest of the year are from 9 A.M. to 5 P.M. Monday through Friday and 9 A.M. to 6 P.M. Saturday and Sunday. The last entry is allowed 45 minutes before closing time. Admission to the aquarium section alone costs $8 for anyone age 12 through 64 and $6 for kids age 3 to 11 and adults age 65 or older. To include the Oceanarium in your visit, pay the rates of $15 and $11 for the respective age categories. Chicago residents get a discount. Oceanarium admission is limited, so your ticket will be stamped with the time you are allowed to enter that section—sometimes an hour or two from when you arrive. Children age 2 or younger always get in free for everything. There is a special entrance south of the main one for visitors in wheelchairs. Programs and services also are available for people with vision or hearing disabilities. Internet: www.sheddnet.org.

Kids of all ages will enjoy the Shedd Aquarium. The aquarium galleries branch off in all directions from a glass-domed central hall containing a huge circular tank that houses a living coral reef, big, colorful tropical fish, gray-brown nurse sharks, and sea tortoises that swim floatingly by. The galleries are divided by regions of the world, but be forewarned that while the tanks are well lit, the overhead lighting is very dim and the walls and vaulted ceilings are painted dark–hang onto your little ones. There are some really neat specimens in these tanks, however, so do take the time to look. An appealing new permanent exhibit featuring creatures of the Amazon River opened in 2000.

The bilevel Oceanarium section at the Shedd is spacious, airy, and light. A beautiful glassed-in arena overlooks Lake Michigan. From a certain angle it's hard to see the demarcation point between the water tank and the lake. This is where the dolphin shows are held, but you can see the dolphins and beluga whales in the water even without the show. A space on the upper level is reserved for special exhibits. Downstairs you can see penguins frolicking in a glass-enclosed colony. You also can see the bottom half of the tanks you viewed on the upper level as well as some hands-on exhibits. There are two restaurants and a gift shop on the premises.

SHORELINE SIGHTSEEING AND CHARTERS (all ages)

Office is at 474 North Lake Shore Drive, Suite 3511, Chicago 60611; (312) 222–9328. Operates from May through September. Departs from Shedd Aquarium every half hour from 10:15 A.M. to 6:15 P.M. daily. Tickets cost $8 for anyone age 12 through 64, $7 for seniors age 65 or older, and $4 for kids age 11 or younger.

The Shedd Aquarium overlooks Monroe Harbor, one of downtown Chicago's most picturesque locations. You can see both the city skyline and the boats in the harbor, with Lake Michigan beyond. Some people bring a picnic basket and just hang out on the grassy slopes. Docked at this spot is the boat for Shoreline Sightseeing and Charters. You can hop aboard this double-level excursion boat for a narrated half-hour jaunt around the lake. The company has several other pickup spots.

ADLER PLANETARIUM AND ASTRONOMY MUSEUM (age 4 and up)

1300 South Lake Shore Drive, Chicago 60605; (312) 922–7827. Open from 9 A.M. to 6 P.M. Saturday through Wednesday and 9 A.M. to 9 P.M. Thursday and Friday from June 1 through Labor Day. Regular hours the rest of the year are 9 A.M. to 5 P.M. Monday through Thursday, 9 A.M. to 9 P.M. Friday, and 9 A.M. to 6 P.M. Saturday and Sunday. Closed Thanksgiving and Christmas. Sky Shows start at 10 A.M. daily and continue on the hour until an hour before closing time. Museum admission costs $5 for adults age 18 through 64 and $4 for young people age 4 through 17 and adults age 65 or older. Children age 3 or younger are admitted free. Admission is **Free** *for everyone on Tuesday. Sky Show tickets are an additional $5 per person, all ages. Buildings are accessible for wheelchairs. You can park at Soldier Field and ride the trolley to Adler at no extra charge. Downtown CTA bus number 146 stops at Adler. Internet: www.adlerplanetarium.org.*

The Adler Planetarium is a pleasing combination of old and new. Its centerpiece, the original domed Sky Theater inside a 12-sided building, dates from 1929. Wrapped in a C-shape around that edifice is the Sky Pavilion, an angular, glass-walled, two-story Art Moderne addition completed in 1999. The pavilion has seven general exhibit areas; one of the most interesting is a sphere dotted with holes through which you can see the constellations visible in the Chicago area. There are special Sky Theater programs designed for children age 6 or younger; call to plan for one of these if you have small children. If your child gets scared of the dark, consider thoughtfully whether she or he is really ready for a planetarium show. Galileo's restaurant is open from 8:30 A.M. to 3:30 P.M. and serves sandwiches, salads, and snacks. There's also a gift shop with out-of-this-world souvenirs.

MUSEUM OF SCIENCE AND INDUSTRY (all ages)

5700 Lake Shore Drive (at 57th Street), Chicago 60637; (773) 684–1414; for the hearing impaired, TDD (773) 684–3323. Hours are 9:30 A.M. to 5:30 P.M. daily from late May through Labor Day. The rest of the year, hours are 9:30 A.M. to 4 P.M. Monday through Friday and 9:30 A.M. to 5:30 P.M. Saturday and Sunday. General admission costs $7 for anyone age 13 through 64, $6 for adults age 65 or older, and $3.50 for kids age 3 through 12; children age 2 or younger get in free. If you want to include an Omnimax viewing, the rates go up to $13, $11, and $8.50, respectively, with children age 2 or younger free only if they sit on an adult's lap; they pay $3 if they occupy a seat. General admission is **Free** *on Thursday, but there is still a respective charge for Omnimax of $8, $7, $6, and free or $3 if occupying a seat. Rental strollers are available for $2. Wheelchairs are available at no charge. Parking in the museum's underground garage costs $7 per vehicle. CTA bus numbers 6 and 10 stop at the museum. Internet: www.msichicago.org.*

This is a bright, busy place with lots to see and do. Many of the exhibits have hands-on features for youngsters to enjoy. Visitors of all ages can walk through a 16-foot-tall replica of the human heart to better understand its workings (at least in the physical sense). The *Petroleum Planet* permanent exhibit that opened in 2000 puts you in the place of a hydrocarbon molecule, and as such you go through the process of distillation, transformation, pipeline travel, cleaning, "bump-through" chemical reaction (performed on punching bags), and finished fuel for a race car. Other permanent exhibits include the popular coal mine, the U-505 World War II German submarine, the commercial aviation display with a real Boeing 727 airliner, and the Henry Crown Space Center with the actual *Apollo 8* spacecraft. Special changing exhibits vary. The museum also has an Omnimax theater that shows the kind of vivid big-screen films that seem to surround you. Call for the title of the current film.

GRANT PARK (all ages)

Columbus and Jackson Drives, Chicago; (312) 744–3370 for festivals and special events. Park admission is **Free**, *but special-event tickets for the seating area in front of the band shell do cost some money.*

Grant Park is the site of many of Chicago's biggest music festivals, for which admission to the park is free. Bring a chair or blanket and sit on the lawn to enjoy world-class talent performing at the park's Petrillo

Music Shell. General dates are as follows: Chicago Blues Festival, early June; Chicago Gospel Festival, mid-June; Chicago Country Music Festival, late June; Viva! Chicago Latin Music Festival, late August; Chicago Jazz Festival, early September. The park also sponsors an ongoing series of concerts from mid-June through late August; call for details.

Where to Eat

You can't say you've really visited Chicago until you try some of the city's famous deep-dish pizza. Three downtown restaurants in the Michigan Avenue vicinity are widely considered the standard-bearers: Gino's East, Pizzeria Uno, and Pizzeria Due.

Gino's East. *633 North Wells Street; (312) 943–1124.* Hours are 11 A.M. to 11 P.M. Monday through Thursday, 11 A.M. to midnight Friday and Saturday, and noon to 10 P.M. Sunday. Although it moved here in 2000 from its Superior Street location, this is the original Gino's East, which was a downtown institution for years before it sent satellites into the suburbs. You may have to wait for a table and you'll have an additional wait for the pizza, which takes longer to cook than a thin-crust pie, but it's worth it. $

Pizzeria Uno. *29 East Ohio Street; (312) 321–1000.* Hours are 11:30 A.M. to 1 A.M. Monday through Friday, 11:30 A.M. to 2 A.M. Saturday, and 11:30 A.M. to midnight Sunday. This pizzeria is in an inviting three-story brick building at the corner of Wabash and Ohio Streets. It has a cleaner, brighter look than Gino's East and similarly delicious pizza. $

Pizzeria Due. *Wabash and Ontario Streets; (312) 943–2400.* Hours are 11 A.M. to 1 A.M. Sunday through Thursday and 11 A.M. to 2 A.M. Friday and Saturday. This is Uno's younger sibling (In Italian, *uno* means "one" and *due* means "two.") Housed in a three-story Victorian-style building with an outdoor seating area in front, this restaurant was established in 1955, whereas Uno dates from 1934. $

Lou Mitchell's. *565 West Jackson Boulevard; (312) 939–3111.* Open from 5:30 A.M. to 3 P.M. Monday through Saturday and 7 A.M. to 3 P.M. Sunday. As you might guess by its hours, this landmark luncheonette in the Loop specializes in breakfast. Sit in a booth or at the counter and order up freshly squeezed orange juice and a hearty meal of eggs and hash browns or big fluffy pancakes with real maple syrup. $

Where to Stay

Let's be realistic. It's going to be tough to find anything decent for less than $100 in downtown Chicago, especially during summer. Do ask about specials or package deals at every hotel you call, however; you might get lucky.

Best Western River North. *125 West Ohio Street; (312) 467–0800.* This 150-room hotel received a three-diamond rating from AAA. Amenities include indoor pool, suana, and exercise room. $$$$

Chicago Hilton and Towers. *720 South Michigan Avenue; (312) 922–4400 or (800) 445–8667.* This hotel has an indoor pool and health club, and it's close to Grant Park. $$$$

Chicago Marriott. *540 North Michigan Avenue; (312) 836–0100 or (800) 228–9290.* This huge hotel has 1,172 rooms. Amenities include an indoor pool, sauna, and fitness center. $$$$

Drake Hotel. *140 East Walton Place; (312) 787–2200.* At the north end of Michigan Avenue at Lake Shore Drive. It's ritzy, but there are some activities for kids (no swimming pool, though). $$$$

Fairmont Hotel. *200 North Columbus Drive; (312) 565–8000 or (800) 526–2008.* This 692-room hotel is popular with out-of-town visitors; it has an indoor pool, sauna, and fitness center. $$$$

Motel 6. *162 East Ontario Street; (312) 787–3580 or (800) 466–8356.* This budget chain property has 191 rooms. There's an exercise room but no pool. Still, you may be able to stay just below $100 for the night. $$$

Palmer House. *17 East Monroe Street; (312) 726–7500 or (800) 445–8667.* Like the Drake, the gorgeous Palmer House is a Chicago landmark. But unlike the Drake, the Palmer House does have an indoor pool and fitness center. The hotel is now part of the Hilton chain. $$$$

North Side

Chicago's North Side is largely residential. In the town houses and high-rise apartments of the Near North Side, you'll find many yuppies, some of whom moved into the area in the 1980s as singles but remained after they married and had children. Farther north are middle-class neighborhoods with brick bungalows and small apartment buildings. Nearly a quarter of the North Side's population is Hispanic, and less than one-tenth African-American.

GARFIELD PARK AND CONSERVATORY (all ages)

300 North Central Park Avenue, Chicago 60624; (312) 746–5100. Open from 9 A.M. to 5 P.M. daily. Admission and parking are **Free**. *Internet: www.garfield-conservatory.org.*

Garfield Park is a pretty spot for a family visit. Its opulent conservatory was built in 1907 and features a series of connected greenhouses.

The Palm House, where you enter from outside, features a white marble sculpture carved by the famous American sculptor Lorado Taft. The Show House is where you'll find the special floral displays. The Aroid House looks like a jungle, with tropical plants and hanging vines. The Cactus House provides a dry contrast. The sunken Fernery has two Taft sculptures at its entrance and features a waterfall cascading over fern-studded rock walls and down into a pool that empties into a stream. Stepping-stones in the stream allow you to cross. The Children's Garden, opened in 2000, features tropical plants and giant interactive displays.

POLISH MUSEUM OF AMERICA (age 5 and up)

984 North Milwaukee Avenue, Chicago 60622-4101; (773) 384–3352. Open from 11 A.M. to 4 P.M. daily. Admission is by donation; suggested amounts are $3 for adults, $2.00 for students and seniors, and $1 for kids.

Documents, photographs, and folk art trace Polish immigration to the United States and Chicago at the Polish Museum of America. The Polish community in Chicago is so large and influential that children have the day off school on October 11 for Pulaski Day, which celebrates the birth of Casimir Pulaski, a Polish noble and soldier who immigrated to America and served heroically in the Continental Army.

LINCOLN PARK ZOO (all ages)

2200 North Cannon Drive, Chicago 60614; (312) 742–2000. Open daily, year-round. Hours are generally 8 A.M. to 6 P.M. for the grounds and 10 A.M. to 5 P.M. for the buildings; closing times are about an hour earlier in winter and an hour later on summer weekends. Admission is **Free***. Parking in a lot along Cannon Drive costs $7. Internet: www.lpzoo.com.*

Lincoln Park Zoo, near Fullerton Avenue and the lakefront, is a major family attraction on the North Side. This 35-acre zoo contains about 2,000 animals, including big cats, primates, bears, birds, and seals. The Farm-in-the-Zoo section is a treat for city kids who have never set foot near a barnyard. If you come at Christmastime, you could join the group of carolers who sing to the animals. It's hard to say whether the animals really enjoy the serenade, but it always makes the local TV news. At the north end of the zoo is the **Lincoln Park Conservatory,** on the corner of Fullerton Avenue and Stockton Drive. This Victorian-style conservatory contains towering palm and fig trees and exotic plants from around the world. There's a waterfall here, too. Conservatory hours are 9 A.M. to 5 P.M. daily, and admission is **Free**.

WRIGLEY FIELD (all ages)

1060 West Addison Street, Chicago 60613; (773) 404–2827. Chicago Cubs season runs from early April through early October. Tickets cost about $10 to $20. The ticket office is open during baseball season from 9 A.M. to 6 P.M. Monday through Friday and 9 A.M. to 4 P.M. Saturday and Sunday (closed Sunday in May when the Cubs are on the road). You also can buy tickets over the phone through Ticketmaster at (312) 831–2827 or order on-line. Internet: www.cubs.com.

Ah, you can't beat fun at the old ballpark. . . . Your visit to the North Side wouldn't be complete without a trip to Wrigley Field. The Chicago Cubs play professional baseball here and consistently draw good crowds, even though the team hasn't made it to a World Series since 1945 and hasn't won one since 1908 (though the Cubs did take division titles in 1984 and 1989 and won a wild-card slot in 1998). It must be the ballpark itself, then, that holds some of the allure. The ivy-covered brick outfield walls do make the "friendly confines" more attractive, and the fans are usually a cheerful lot, accustomed as they are to being hopeless optimists. Despite the addition of stadium lights in 1988, Wrigley Field hosts most of its home games in the afternoon. Avoid the

Silver Screens on the North Side

There are two unique movie houses on the North Side that are worth mentioning, but don't look for the latest Disney flick at either one.

- **Facets Multimedia.** *1517 West Fullerton Avenue; (773) 281–9075.* This theater in the Lincoln Park area shows many fine foreign films that you won't find anywhere else in the city. Most are subtitled in English, so don't take younger kids who can't read yet. Also check for ratings, and don't hesitate to ask about films that are not rated. (European films generally contain less graphic violence than American films, but you may see more flesh in love scenes.)
- **Music Box Theater.** *3733 North Southport; (773) 871–6604.* Farther north, the Music Box is an older theater with classic decor. It shows more arty films and old movies (such as Buster Keaton silent films with a live organist playing the score), and from time to time it hosts film festivals.

Terrace Reserved section if you want to see the full arc of a fly ball—the skyboxes that were added in the early 1990s partially obstruct the view in those seats, although TV monitors help make up for it.

Note: Although there are some shops and restaurants nearby, Wrigley Field is basically in the middle of a residential neighborhood and has no public parking lot of its own. If you drive, you'll crawl through dense traffic and be at the mercy of the local entrepreneurs who operate little lot-size parking lots. The CTA elevated train station on Addison is a block from Wrigley, and CTA buses stop at the ballpark as well, making mass transit an appealing alternative. For more information, call the CTA at (312) 836–7000; for the hearing impaired, TDD (312) 836–4949.

USA RAINBO ROLLER RINK (age 4 and up)

4836 North Clark Street, Chicago 60640; (773) 271–5668. Generally open Wednesday through Sunday and closed Monday and Tuesday. Call for current session times. Cost ranges from $3 to $5 per person, depending on the session, although Thursday night is just $1. Skate rental for all sessions costs $2.50 for regular skates or $3.50 for Rollerblades.

Rainbo Roller Rink is a huge facility with neon lights, a dozen glitter balls, and a 35,000-watt sound system that pumps out the tunes to keep skaters moving. The Family Skate sessions are on Saturday and Sunday afternoon, and the regular Public Skate sessions are generally in the early evening Wednesday through Friday. Both types of sessions feature "Top 100" music. A Saturday night Teen Skate features danceable rock and rap music. You can bring your own skates (regular or in-line) or rent wheels here. If you get hungry, a concession stand offers soft drinks, nachos, and other snacks at reasonable prices.

WAVELAND BOWL (age 4 and up)

3700 North Western Avenue, Chicago 60618; (773) 472–5900. Open 24 hours a day. Cost for bumper bowling is generally $2 per person per game Monday through Friday before 5 P.M. and $3 after 5 P.M. weekdays and all day Saturday and Sunday. Cosmic Bowling for kids is offered from 3 to 5 P.M. Friday and costs $3. Shoe rental costs $2.50. Internet: www.wavelandbowl.com.

This North Side bowling alley has 40 lanes and will fill the gutters with soft bumpers for families upon request. Automated scoring makes it easy to keep track of the pins knocked down. The alley also has a children's theater, showing Disney movies on a big screen, and concessions.

Where to Eat

Leona's. *3215 North Sheffield; (773) 327–8861. Internet: www.leonas.com.* Open from 11 A.M. to midnight daily. After the ball game at Wrigley Field, walk south down Sheffield Avenue a few blocks for dinner at Leona's. This family-owned Italian restaurant has been around since the 1950s but underwent its most notable expansion during the 1990s. There are two floors of seating areas, plus an outdoor rooftop garden that's open during mild weather. Expect a wait on weekends. The pasta is homemade and can be topped with your choice of red or white sauces that are also prepared from scratch. Dinners are served with a crisp lettuce salad loaded with fresh vegetables. You'll also get a loaf of hot bread accompanied by cups of butter and ricotta-and-chive spread. The thin-crust pizza has a satisfying bite. The restaurant has its own private-label wine, Leona's Graffiti Red, that's made in California but evokes the flavor of a good Italian table wine. There is a children's section on the multipage menu. $$

Ann Sather. *929 West Belmont; (773) 348–2378.* Hours are 7 A.M. to 10 P.M. Sunday through Thursday and 7 A.M. to 11 P.M. Friday and Saturday. Also not far from Wrigley Field, this restaurant bears the name of its Swedish founder and is famous for its exquisitely luscious cinnamon rolls. If you come for breakfast, you can get bacon and eggs to go with them, or you can try the Swedish pancakes with tart lingonberry preserves. Dinner entrees include Swedish meatballs, roast pork, meat loaf, and other hearty dishes. $

Byron's Hot Dogs. *850 West North Avenue; (312) 266–3355.* Hours are 10:30 A.M. to 9 P.M. Monday through Saturday and 10:30 A.M. to 6 P.M. Sunday. This Near North Side establishment is a favorite of kids and adults alike. The turquoise walls are splattered with splotches of red and yellow that look like ketchup and mustard, and there are tomatoes and cucumbers on the ceiling. You almost feel as though you're the hot dog inside a giant bun. Order up a juicy Chicago-style hot dog with a little bag of hot, crispy fries and a cup of Green River lime-flavored soda. You can get whatever toppings you like, from plain ketchup to a mound of freshly chopped garden veggies to chili and cheese. The menu also includes burgers, pasta, chicken, soups, salads, and desserts. $

Where to Stay

Best Western Hawthorne Terrace. *3434 North Broadway Avenue; (773) 244–3434 or (800) 528–1234.* One long block west of Lake Michigan; a short cab ride or perhaps a half-hour walk to Wrigley Field. This 59-room hotel opened in 1998. It has a sauna and whirlpool but no swimming pool. $$$$

Comfort Inn. *601 West Diversey Parkway; (773) 348–2810 or (800) 228–5150.* Near Lincoln Park Zoo. This chain property has 74 rooms but

Hancock Observatory - Free 4↓
Navy Pier - $2 for 2-11
Chicago Childrens Museum - 6 50 1↑
Sears Tower - free 4↓
Buckingham Fountain
Field Museum - $4 3-17
Shedd Aquarium - 11 3-11
Museum of Science + Industry - 8.50 3-12

no pool. The room rate includes continental breakfast, which is a big savings given Chicago prices. $$$

O'Hare Marriott Hotel. *8535 West Higgins Road; (773) 693–4444 or (800) 228–9290.* If you are flying in and out of O'Hare airport for your Chicago visit, you might want to stay here to avoid scrambling too much for your return flight. The hotel allows pets, and for the human guests it has indoor and outdoor pools, sauna, spa, and fitness center. Special rates on weekends and for tourists can lower the cost. $$$$

Flights of Fancy In the northwest corner of Chicago, jutting out like an island surrounded by suburbs, is O'Hare International Airport. Even if you aren't flying, it's an interesting place to visit. United Airlines Terminal One inherited the Field Museum's four-story mounted dinosaur model, *Brachiosaurus,* in 2000 after the museum cleared it out to make room for Sue (see Field Museum entry). The lower level of the two-part United terminal has a groovy display of wavy, multicolored neon patterns suspended above the people mover (moving sidewalk), and the International Terminal is decorated with flags and alive with the sounds of excited travelers chattering in foreign languages. As long as they aren't too sensitive to noise, little kids love watching the planes take off and land. In the late 1990s, the airport even added a kids' play area to keep young passengers occupied until their flight departure. All this activity is Free except for parking—which at about $3 an hour does add up.

West Side

About half the residents of Chicago's West Side are African-American, more than a quarter Hispanic, and slightly less than a quarter whites of European ancestry. The West Side was at one time a prime industrial district. In the latter half of the 1900s, however, many industries downsized or moved to the suburbs, hurting the economy of the area and its people. As a result, there are many decaying neighborhoods in this part of town. The neighborhoods on the Near West Side, however, have benefited since the opening of the United Center in 1994. Real estate investors began to take a closer look, and a massive redevelopment program began to reconnect isolated public housing with the surrounding area. Ugly high-rise buildings in the crime-ridden Henry Horner complex have been torn down and replaced with tidy brown-brick row houses to be split evenly between low-income and working-class families. Statistics in the 1990s reflected some improvement, showing an increase in employment and a decrease in crime.

UNITED CENTER (all ages)

1901 West Madison Street, Chicago 60612; (312) 455–4000 for Bulls, (312) 455–7000 for Blackhawks.

Probably the biggest attraction on the West Side is the United Center. There's a one-ton bronze leaping figure of athlete extraordinaire Michael Jordan out front. This stadium opened in 1994 and is the home court for the Chicago Bulls, the National Basketball Association (NBA) team with which Jordan won six championships—in 1991, 1992, 1993, 1996, 1997, and 1998 (he spent 1994 and most of 1995 away from the Bulls playing baseball). Although MJ has retired, the championship banners remain to remind visitors of the Bulls' glory days. The good news is that tickets are easier to come by as the Bulls rebuild their franchise. The Chicago Blackhawks of the National Hockey League (NHL) also play at the United Center; call for details about "cold steel on ice."

UIC PAVILION (all ages)

525 South Racine Avenue (at Harrison Street), Chicago 60607; (312) 413–5700. Call for current schedule of events.

The Near West Side was revitalized somewhat during the 1960s with the construction of the West Side Medical Center and the University of Illinois at Chicago. Old factories became artists' studios, and new apartments and houses were built in the area. The Pavilion schedules various special events, including tennis tournaments and other sporting matches.

MUSEUM OF HOLOGRAPHY (all ages)

1134 West Washington Street, Chicago 60607; (312) 226–1007. Hours are 12:30 to 5 P.M. Wednesday through Sunday. Admission costs $3 for adults and$2.50 for young people age 6 through 17. Children age 5 or younger get in free.

This facility claims to be the only museum in the United States devoted to holography. It has more than 75 of the three-dimensional, laser-generated images on display.

MEXICAN FINE ARTS CENTER MUSEUM (age 4 and up)

1852 West 19th Street, Chicago 60608; (312) 738–1503. Hours are 10 A.M. to 5 P.M. Tuesday through Sunday. Admission is Free.

The Mexican Fine Arts Center Museum is reportedly the largest museum of its type in the United States. You can see exhibits of contemporary and folk art by Mexican and Mexican-American artists.

Where to Eat

Billy Goat Tavern. *1535 West Madison Street; (312) 733–9132.* Near the United Center. Hours are 6 A.M. to 10 P.M. Monday through Friday, 7 A.M. to 10 P.M. Saturday, and 10 A.M. to 4 P.M. Sunday. Don't let the *tavern* part of its name keep you away from the Billy Goat. This offshoot of the original Lower Michigan Avenue eatery specializes in the "cheezborger, cheezborger" made famous on the classic John Belushi *Saturday Night Live* skit. It's a thin, greasy burger on a chewy Kaiser roll that may make you wonder what all the fuss is about, but it's a Chicago legend. Top it to your liking with ketchup, mustard, onions, or relish. Contrary to the "no fries–chips" part of the skit, you can get french fries with your burger. The menu also includes a grilled chicken sandwich, hot dog, steak, chili, and soup. Photos of sports stars and Hollywood celebrities decorate the walls. $

Leona's Neighborhood Place. *1936 West Augusta; (312) 292–4300. Internet: www.leonas.com.* Hours are 11 A.M. to 11 P.M. Monday through Thursday, 11 A.M. to 1 A.M. Friday, noon to 1 A.M. Saturday, and noon to 10:30 P.M. Sunday. If you can't make it up north to Sheffield Avenue, this Leona's in the Wicker Park neighborhood has the same sort of Italian menu as its Wrigleyville progenitor. It also has a special place for kids: the Jungle Room, which has a tropical rain forest motif and offers such attractions as climbing equipment, a ball pit, games, and finger painting. The Jungle Room is popular for birthday parties, however, so call ahead before coming to make sure it's available. $$

Where to Stay

The attractions listed in this section are not that far from downtown Chicago. It is recommended that you stay overnight there and take public transportation or a cab to the West Side.

South Side

Chicago's South Side has more people than either of the other two sections outside downtown and a greater mix of residential and industrial areas. The population is about 60 percent African-American, with the balance composed of Hispanic, Asian, and white European communities. Although some areas are racially integrated, most are not.

COMISKEY PARK (all ages)

333 West 35th Street, Chicago 60616; (312) 674–1000. Chicago White Sox season runs from early April through early October. Tickets cost about $10 to $22. During baseball season the box office is open from 10 A.M. to 6 P.M. Monday through Friday and 10 A.M. to 4 P.M. Saturday and Sunday. You also can buy tickets over the phone through Ticketmaster at (312) 831–1769 or order on-line. Internet: www.whitesox.com.

Catch a major league baseball game on the South Side at the "new" Comiskey Park. This ballpark opened in 1991 to replace the deteriorated 80-year-old original of the same name that stood a few blocks away, and it is home field for the Chicago White Sox. The new Comiskey promises an unobstructed view from each of its 40,000 seats, and there are family picnic areas below the outfield bleachers. In recent years the Sox also have had much better ball clubs than the Cubs have.

Chinatown The Asian community of Chinatown, at the crossroads of Wentworth and Cermak Avenues, is one of the most active neighborhoods on the South Side. About 10,000 people live within a 10-block radius, and you'll find fabulous restaurants and shops here. There are many special events throughout the year. For detailed information about the area, contact the Chicago Chinatown Chamber of Commerce, 2169B South China Place, Chicago 60616; (312) 326–5320. Internet: www.chicago-chinatown.com. Chinatown is about a five-minute cab ride south of the Loop and is easily accessible by CTA elevated train or bus.

DUSABLE MUSEUM OF AFRICAN-AMERICAN HISTORY (age 4 and up)

740 East 56th Place, Chicago 60637; (773) 947–0600. Hours are 10 A.M. to 5 P.M. Monday through Saturday and noon to 5 P.M. Sunday and holidays; closed Easter, Thanksgiving, and Christmas. Admission costs $3 for anyone age 14 through 64, $2 for students age 15 or older and seniors age 65 or older, and $1 for kids age 6 through 13. Children age 5 or younger get in free. Internet: www.dusablemuseum.org.

The DuSable Museum has cultural and art collections that reflect the work of Africans and Americans of African descent. Of particular note are the collections representing the Works Progress Administration (WPA) era of the 1930s and the civil rights movement of the 1960s.

RIDGE HISTORICAL SOCIETY (all ages)

10621 South Seeley Avenue, Chicago 60643; (773) 881–1675. Open from 2 to 5 P.M. Thursday and Sunday. Admission is **Free***, but donations are appreciated.*

This museum has a number of exhibits for children that make history interesting and hands-on. They can crank the wringer of an old-fashioned washing machine, try on costumes from Granny Ridge's Trunk, use tools to make something in Grandpa Ridge's Workshop, or unearth an object in the archaeological exhibit called *I Dig the Ridge Historical Society.*

Where to Eat

Dixie Kitchen and Bait Shop. *5225 South Harper Avenue; (773) 363–7723.* In the Harper Court mall in the Hyde Park neighborhood. Open from 11 A.M. to 10 P.M. Sunday through Thursday and 11 A.M. to 11 P.M. Friday and Saturday. No, you can't buy fishing bait here, but the atmosphere is designed to evoke a roadside diner along the Mississippi bayou, complete with zydeco music. The food is Southern style, of course. The menu includes gumbo, jambalaya, red beans and rice, fried catfish, blackened chicken breast, bread pudding, and peach cobbler. $

Gladys' Luncheonette. *4527 South Indiana Avenue; (773) 548–4566.* Hours are 7 A.M. to 11:45 P.M. Tuesday through Sunday; closed Monday. A Chicago fixture for more than 50 years, this casual South Side restaurant serves traditional African-American entrees such as barbecued ribs, breaded catfish, ham hocks, and roasted pork, accompanied by side dishes including collard greens, black-eyed peas, and pickled beets. Save room for the sweet potato pie for dessert. $

Where to Stay

Holiday Inn Midway. *7553 South Cicero Avenue; (773) 581–5300 or (800) 465–4329.* This 161-room property near Midway Airport has a fitness center and an outdoor swimming pool. $$$

Hyatt at University Village. *625 South Ashland Avenue; (773) 243–7200 or (473) 473–7373.* There are 113 rooms and an exercise room here, but no pool. Pets are allowed. $$$$

Ramada Inn Lake Shore. *4900 South Lake Shore Drive; (773) 288–5800 or (800) 237–4933.* This 184-room property has an outdoor swimming pool. Pets are allowed. $$$$

Other Things to See and Do in Chicago

January: Chicago Winterbreak Celebration, various locations; (312) 744-3370

February: Chinese New Year Parade, Chinatown; (312) 225-6198

Chicago Auto Show, McCormick Place; (312) 791-7000

March: St. Patrick's Day Parade, Downtown; (312) 744-3370

April: Earth Day Celebration, Shedd Aquarium, Downtown; (312) 939-2438

May: Lakeview Mayfest, North Side; (773) 665-4682

June: Festival of Ethnic Arts, Beverly Art Center, South Side; (773) 445-3838

Grant Park Music Festival Free Concerts Series, Downtown; (312) 744-3370

July: International Children's Fest, Navy Pier, Downtown; (312) 595-7437

August: Chicago Air and Water Show, North Avenue Beach, Downtown; (312) 744-3315

Bud Billiken Parade and Picnic, King Drive, Downtown; (312) 225-2400

September: Celtic Fest Chicago, Downtown; (312) 744-3370

October: Columbus Day Parade, Downtown; (312) 828-0100

Boo Fest, Museum of Science and Industry, Downtown; (773) 684-1414

November: Jingle Elf Parade, Michigan Avenue, Downtown; (312) 935-8747

December: "Christmas Around the World," Museum of Science and Industry, Downtown; (773) 684-1414

Chicagoland

The Chicago metropolitan area extends for many miles beyond the city limits. The adjacent communities can easily be called suburbs, but the farther out you go, the harder it is to determine what's a suburb, an exurb, or simply a smaller town that happens to be within an hour or so's driving distance—and often one blends into the next with little more than a city limits sign to give you a clue that you've crossed a border. Complicating matters further is the fact that while some of these cities and towns are eager to be perceived as linked to Chicago, others shun such connections. Ultimately, no label or boundary will satisfy everyone, so the decision becomes rather arbitrary. For this book Chicagoland will be defined as everything in Lake, DuPage, Will, Kankakee, and Cook Counties outside the city of Chicago. We will move in a roughly counterclockwise sweep from north to west to south.

Lake County is sandwiched between the state line with Wisconsin and the concentrated population of Cook County. As such, it contains both rural areas dotted with parks and urban communities lying along the affluent North Shore of Lake Michigan. For general information about the county, contact the **Lake County, Illinois, Convention & Visitors Bureau,** 401 North Riverside Drive, Suite 5, Gurnee 60031; (847) 662-2700 or (800) 525-3669. Internet: www.lakecounty.org.

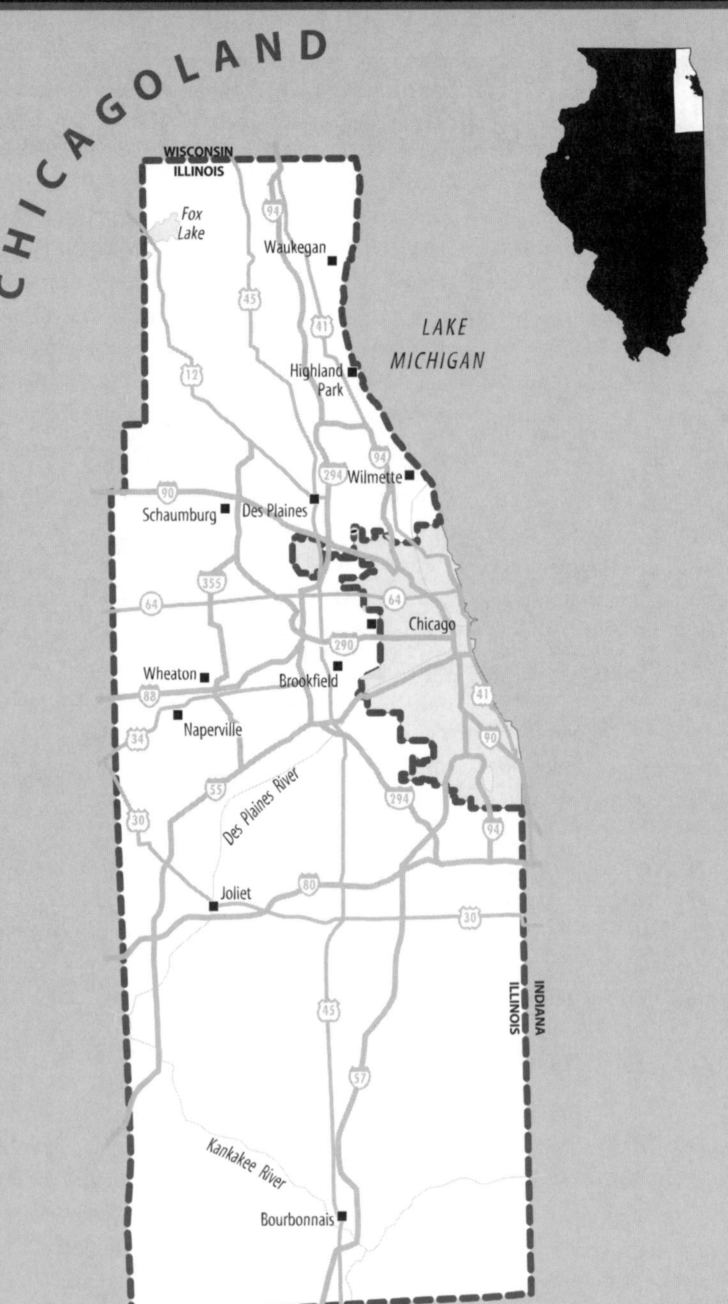
CHICAGOLAND
WISCONSIN
ILLINOIS
Fox Lake
Waukegan
LAKE MICHIGAN
Highland Park
Wilmette
Des Plaines
Schaumburg
Chicago
Wheaton
Brookfield
Naperville
Des Plaines River
Joliet
INDIANA
ILLINOIS
Kankakee River
Bourbonnais
94
45
41
12
294
90
355
64
290
88
34
55
30
80
57

Gurnee

Population: 13,701. This far-northern suburb along Interstate 94 has two of the Chicago metro area's biggest attractions—literally.

SIX FLAGS GREAT AMERICA (all ages)

I–94 at Illinois Highway 132, Gurnee 60031; (847) 249–1776. Opens in late April and closes in mid-September. From mid-June through late August, the park is open from 10 A.M. to 10 P.M daily. Hours at the beginning and end of the season are more limited; call ahead of time and check. Admission costs $42.99 for anyone 48 inches (4 feet) tall or taller and $21.49 for anyone less than 4 feet tall and older than age 2. Children age 2 or younger get in free. The price includes all the rides and shows (but not taxes, arcade games, souvenirs, or food and drink). Ask about special deals and season passes. Parking costs $8. The park is accessible for strollers and wheelchairs.

As you're driving along I–94 near its intersection with Illinois Highway 132 in Gurnee, you can't miss Six Flags Great America—you can see this sprawling amusement park from the road, beckoning you tantalizingly. This isn't one of those let's-stop-in-for-an-hour attractions; there's a lot to see and do here, and you'll pay a pretty penny for it, so plan for an all-day outing to get your money's worth. You might want to start with a 20-minute overview of the park on the Six Flags Great America Scenic Railway; that way you can scope out the rides you most want to try.

The Viper is an elegant wooden roller coaster patterned after the classic Coney Island Cyclone. But don't let the lovely latticework lull you into a false sense of security. After the cars ratchet up a 100-foot incline along a single track, you'll scream your head off as they plunge 80 feet downhill. You get 10 more drops and some whizzing turns in a ride that lasts just under two minutes. The American Eagle double-track wooden coaster, introduced in 1981, remains a popular ride as well. If steel coasters are more your style, loop the loop seven times on the Shock Wave or ride standing up for a 90-foot drop and more loops on the Iron Wolf. Batman fans and big-time thrill seekers will want to try Batman the Ride, billed in all its stomach-churning glory as "the world's first suspended, outside looping thrill ride." If it's a hot day, the Splashwater Falls and Roaring Rapids rides will cool you off. Use good parental judgment in determining whether your kids are ready for these thrill rides.

Especially popular with families are the ornate double-decker Columbia Carousel and the motion simulator Space Shuttle America. The Games Gallery has a wide variety of arcade games. Children who are 54 inches tall or shorter can enter the Bugs Bunny's Yukon Adventure play area. The theme features Looney Tunes characters in a Yukon mining town. Your little varmints can enjoy five kiddie rides, including the Tweety's Bird Cages Ferris wheel, plus activity areas to climb and crawl around in with themed names such as Tweety's Twee House and Wile E. Coyote's Cave. The Warner Brothers area was expanded in 1998 to include even more fun stuff for kids to do.

You can sit down for a while and take in a show. The wee ones will like the "Hip Hop Hare" show, starring adult performers in full-body costumes as Bugs Bunny and other Warner Brothers classic cartoon characters. The Batman Stunt Show will appeal more to adolescents, who will find the explosions and action awesome. Then there are assorted song-and-dance shows, with music ranging from ragtime to country-and-western fare. Concession choices range from hot-dog stands to a sit-down restaurant, and there are plenty of tempting souvenirs to buy.

GURNEE MILLS (all ages)

6170 West Grand Avenue, Gurnee 60031; (800) 937–7467. Open from 10 A.M. to 9 P.M. Monday through Saturday and 11 A.M. to 6 P.M. Sunday. The mall is accessible for strollers and wheelchairs. Internet: www.millscorp.com/gurnee.

Reportedly the world's largest outlet mall, Gurnee Mills has roughly 200 stores along a 2-mile-long, S-shaped strip, plus two food courts, each with about a dozen eateries, including a Rainforest Cafe. Major stores include Saks Fifth Avenue, Spiegel, and JCPenney Outlets. Stock up on your toddler's play clothes at Carter's Childrenswear or the Children's Place. Kay-Bee Toys and World of Science have outlets here, too. Among the other types of stores are shops selling adult and teen apparel, shoes, jewelry, cosmetics, fashion accessories, sporting goods, books, and music and electronics. You can drop off your roll of film—with the Great America pictures you took yesterday—at the Ritz Camera One Hour Photo, and they'll be ready when you're finished shopping. You can even catch a movie at the Marcus 20-Screen Cinema.

SERPENT SAFARI (age 2 and up)

In Gurnee Mills outlet mall, 6170 West Grand Avenue, Gurnee 60031; (847) 855–8800. Open from 10 A.M. to 9 P.M. Monday through Saturday and 11 A.M. to 6 P.M. Sunday. Twenty-minute tours cost $6.95 for anyone age 13 or older and $4.95 for kids age 3 through 12; children age 2 or younger go free.

This store has an exhibit area (accessible only by tour) with about 40 large reptiles, including the world's largest snake, according to the *Guinness Book of World Records*—a Burmese python 27 feet long, weighing 400 pounds.

Where to Eat

Cracker Barrel. *I–94 and Grand Avenue; (847) 244–1512.* Hours are 6 A.M. to 10 P.M. Sunday through Thursday and 6 A.M. to 11 P.M. Friday and Saturday. See Restaurant Appendix for description. $

Pizzeria Uno. *6593 Grand Avenue; (847) 856–0000.* Across from Gurnee Mills. Hours are 11 A.M. to midnight daily. This suburban cousin of the Chicago fixture offers the trademark deep-dish pizza as well as pasta dishes, sandwiches, chicken, and ribs. $

TGIFriday's. *6557 Grand Avenue; (847) 855–0007.* Hours are 11 A.M. to midnight Sunday through Thursday and 11 A.M. to 1 A.M. Friday and Saturday. See Restaurant Appendix for description. $$

Where to Stay

Comfort Inn. *6080 Gurnee Mills Boulevard; (847) 855–8866 or (800) 228–5150.* This economical chain property has 64 rooms and an indoor heated pool. Continental breakfast is included in the room rate. $$$$

Fairfield Inn. *6090 Gurnee Mills Boulevard; (847) 855–8868 or (800) 228–2800.* This inn has 63 rooms. Amenities include indoor pool and whirlpool. Room rate includes continental breakfast. $$$

Hampton Inn. *5550 Grand Avenue; (847) 662–1100 or (800) 426–7866.* Across the street from Great America. There are 134 rooms and an outdoor swimming pool at this inn. Room rate includes continental breakfast. $$$

For More Information

Lake County Convention and Visitors Bureau, *401 North Riverside Drive, Gurnee 60031; (847) 662–2700.*

Long Grove

Population: 4,740. Settled in the 1800s by a group of German farmers, this off-the-beaten-path Lake County town is centered around the historical village at the crossroads of Illinois Highways 53 and 83. Under Long Grove's Historic Landmark Ordinance, all new buildings at that crossroads must conform to the architecture of the early 1800s.

LONG GROVE HISTORICAL VILLAGE (all ages)

307 Old McHenry Road, Long Grove 60047; (847) 634–0888. Open year-round. Regular business hours are 10 A.M. to 5 P.M. Monday through Saturday and noon to 5 P.M. Sunday. Individual shop hours may vary slightly. Some buildings have stairs and are not accessible for wheelchairs or strollers. Internet: www.longgrove.net.

This village is a collection of quaint shops and restaurants, all housed in historic one- and two-story buildings. They line the streets for a block or two along Old McHenry Road and Robert Parker Coffin Road, more commonly known as Illinois Highways 53 and 83. At this junction, however, the roads are only one lane wide in either direction, and the traffic usually isn't too bad. Everything is clustered together closely enough that the walking distances are easy for most people. You can stroll at leisure and browse the windows or go in if the merchandise particularly intrigues you. Among the shops most interesting to families with children age 12 or younger are the following.

- **Bobby's Land of Animals,** (847) 634-6050. Paradise for lovers of Beanie Babies, Gund, Boyd, Steiff, and other stuffed animals, all under a ceiling that features an oval stained-glass panel in lovely hues of blue, green, and yellow.
- **Bobby's Toyland,** (847) 634-6901. Narrow aisles and tall shelves crammed with toys including Lego, Brio, Playmobil, Breyer horses, Barbies, and Effanbee and Madame Alexander dolls.
- **Creative Hands,** (847) 634-0545. Beanie Babies, dough art, Cat's Meow Village, Wee Forest Folk, and miniatures that are sooo cute!
- **The Dog House,** (847) 634-3060. Collars, toys, beds, clothing, treats, and all manner of merchandise for your four-legged friend, who can come into the store with you.
- **Julia's Doll and Gift Shoppe,** (847) 634-1325. Raggedy Ann, Hummels, and those nifty little wooden Russian nesting dolls.

- **Long Grove Confectionery Co.,** (847) 634–0080. An absolute must; handmade chocolates as beautiful as they are succulent.
- **Long Grove Soap & Candle Co.,** (847) 634-9322. Fascinating soap-making demonstrations on weekends using hand-operated equipment (on the second floor, no elevator) and a sampling of the finished product as well as fancy soaps made elsewhere.
- **Nickelby's Rubber Stamp Emporium,** (847) 634-6552. A mind-boggling array of rubber stamps.

Where to Eat

Joan's Country Cupboard. *In the historic village; (847) 634–3493.* Open from 5 A.M. to 9 P.M. daily. This casual cafe on the second floor (accessible only by stairs) serves soups, sandwiches, and desserts. The children's menu is about $3.50 and includes hot dogs and sandwiches. $

Seasons of Long Grove. *In the historic village; (847) 634–9150.* Hours are 11 A.M. to 2 P.M. Monday through Saturday and 10 A.M. to 2 P.M. Sunday. This restaurant is a fairly formal, sit-down place. It isn't your best bet with toddlers but could be a treat for a school-age child who can be patient with the slower service and impressed by the fresh flowers and cloth napkins on the table. The $5.95 children's menu is pretty pricey, however, especially since the selections include fairly ordinary items like a burger, hot dog, pizza, and grilled cheese sandwich. Adults can enjoy the elaborate luncheon buffet for $9.95 or order an entree off the menu. $$

Where to Stay

There are no hotels or motels in Long Grove. Plan to make this community a day trip from wherever you live or are staying in the Chicago metropolitan area.

For More Information

Long Grove Community Development Corporation, *307 Old McHenry Road, Long Grove 60047; (847) 634–0888. Internet: www.longgrove.net.*

Waukegan

Population: 69,392. Right along Lake Michigan but still a ways north of the ritzy North Shore area is the unpretentious town of Waukegan, birthplace of author Ray Bradbury *(Fahrenheit 451, Martian Chronicles)*.

FUN HARBOUR FAMILY ENTERTAINMENT CENTER (all ages)

651 Lakehurst Road, Waukegan 60085; (847) 578–5400. Open year-round; hours are 11 A.M. to 10 P.M. daily. Miniature golf costs $3.50 for adults and $2.50 for kids. Go-karts cost $5. Laser tag costs $4.25 for a 10-minute game. Wristband for the children's play area costs $2. Batting cage takes four tokens; tokens cost $1 for four.

This nautically themed amusement center offers both indoor and outdoor recreation. If the weather's nice, head outdoors for 18 holes of miniature golf. Anyone at least 54 inches tall may rent a go-kart and zip around the track. The flying saucer ride is a favorite for younger children. You can eat outside at the picnic area or inside at the full-service restaurant. Also indoors is an arcade with about 100 games, some for littler kids and others for older ones. Older kids also may want to try the laser tag. Little kids can buy a wristband that allows all-day access to a play area with tubes to crawl through and plastic-ball pits to roll around in.

Good Tidings from Zion North of Waukegan, Illinois Beach State Park is the only Illinois state park on Lake Michigan and also has the state's only sand dunes. Naturally, there are beaches here for swimming, and you can also enjoy fishing, picnicking, hiking, and pedaling along the bike trails. The park is at Sheridan and Wadsworth Roads in Zion; (847) 662–4811. It's open from 8 A.M. to 10 P.M. daily, year-round. Admission is Free.

Where to Eat

Boston Market. *919 North Green Bay Road; (847) 623–7000.* Hours are 11 A.M. to 10 P.M. Monday through Saturday and 11 A.M. to 9 P.M. Sunday. See Restaurant Appendix for description. $

Where to Stay

Best Western of Waukegan. *411 South Green Bay Road; (847) 244–6100 or (800) 528–1234.* This two-story motel has 49 rooms and an indoor swimming pool. Rates include breakfast. $$$

Ramada Inn Waukegan/Gurnee. *200 North Green Bay Road; (847) 244–2400 or (800) 272–6232.* The inn has 185 rooms and an indoor swimming pool. $$$$

For More Information

Lake County Chamber of Commerce, *5221 Grand Avenue, Waukegan 60085; (847) 249–3800.*

A Sweet Little Excursion North Chicago is not directly north of Chicago, it's *way* north of Chicago, just south of Waukegan. But it will be worth your while to find North Chicago, because it is home to the Goelitz Confectionery, maker of Jelly Bellies, those tasty little jelly beans that come in so many wacky flavors. You can take a tour of the factory and see how Jelly Bellies are made—not by Oompah-Loompahs, but in big machines. The Free tour takes an hour, starting with a short video explaining what you're about to see and then moving into the production area. At the end you'll get samples of the finished product and an opportunity to buy more.

Goelitz Confectionery is at 1539 Morrow Avenue; call (847) 689-8950 to make the required reservation and receive directions. Tours operate year-round and start at 8:45, 9:15, 10, 10:30, and 11:15 A.M. and 12:45 and 1:15 P.M. Monday through Friday. (Yes, those hours are going to pose a problem for working parents, and school-age kids most likely will have to wait until summer vacation to take the tour.) Children age 4 or younger must be in strollers or carried.

Highland Park

Population: 30,575. This upper-crust North Shore suburb has several attractions of interest to families.

RAVINIA FESTIVAL (all ages)

1575 Oakwood Avenue, Highland Park 60035; (847) 266–5100. Call for current schedule. The festival runs from late June through early September. Lawn tickets cost $10 for anyone age 11 or older and $5 for kids age 10 or younger. Most pavilion tickets are in the $15 to $35 range. Parking is available on-site, at a cost of $5 for evening pavilion events and free at other times. Internet: www.ravinia.org.

The Ravinia Festival has been a tradition for more than 60 years. Nestled among 36 acres of wooded and landscaped grounds are an outdoor pavilion, an indoor recital hall, and numerous restaurants and high-class food stands (you'll think you've died and gone to heaven when you taste the cappuccino ice cream). The Chicago Symphony Orchestra provides the mainstay classical music that dominates the schedule, but you can also hear jazz and pop concerts, and there's a special series of concerts aimed at kids. Don't limit your family to the kids' concerts, however—jazz and classical music can be exciting even to the youngest listeners, especially when you get to have a picnic at the same time. There's a sprawling lawn section where you can bring in your own basket and spread out your blanket or set up your folding chairs. You see a real cross section of people here: families with baby strollers, groups of high school and college students, couples out for a romantic evening, and parties of well-to-do North Shore–ites whose "picnic" consists of haute cuisine entrees dished up on fine china and served on a low table covered with a linen cloth and set with silver utensils and candlesticks. But everyone pays the same price for a lawn ticket. If you want a better view of the concert, you can buy a seat in the pavilion. The park is just off Green Bay Road (a major north-south artery along the North Shore). From downtown Chicago you can take the Metra Union Pacific North Line train right to Ravinia's main entrance (call 312–836–7000 for schedule and fare information) or ride a chartered bus from selected hotels for about $15 round-trip (call the Ravinia number for details). This is a wonderful evening under the stars.

RIVER'S EDGE ADVENTURE GOLF (age 3 and up)

2205 Skokie Valley Highway, Highland Park 60035; (847) 433–3422. Open from 10 A.M. to 10 P.M. daily during summer. Cost is $5 for anyone age 16 or older and $3.50 for kids age 15 or younger. The respective prices are $6 and $4 after 6 P.M. and on Saturday and Sunday.

You can play 18 holes of miniature golf at this facility operated by the Park District of Highland Park. Nine of the holes are billed as "handicap accessible."

HIDDEN CREEK AQUA PARK (all ages)

1220 Frederickson Place, Highland Park 60035; (847) 433–3170. Open from 9 A.M. to 8 P.M. Monday through Saturday and 10 A.M. to 8 P.M. Sunday during summer. Admission costs $12 for anyone age 4 or older; children age 3 or younger get in free.

This facility has a zero-depth pool and a children's play area with water slides and a big sandbox. There are bigger slides for the bigger kids and adults, and there is a lap pool for those who want exercise as well as recreation. There is a concession area, too.

Where to Eat

Judy's Pizza. *1855H Deerfield Road (in Garrity Square strip mall); (847) 579–8330.* Open from 11 A.M. to 9 P.M. daily; carryout only. Double-decker pizza is the specialty here—sauce and cheese are sandwiched between two thin layers of crust and then covered with more sauce, cheese, and toppings. Take one with you to Ravinia. $

Where to Stay

Courtyard by Marriott. *1505 County Line Road; (847) 831–3338 or (800) 321–2211.* The Courtyard chain is geared more toward business travelers than families, but you can sometimes get a bargain rate over the weekend, when the business people have gone home. This particular property has 149 rooms. Amenities include indoor swimming pool, whirlpool, and fitness center. $$$

For More Information

Highland Park Chamber of Commerce, *610 Central Avenue, Highland Park 60035; (847) 432–0284.*

At this point we cross the boundary from Lake County into northern Cook County. A number of northern and northwestern suburbs share Cook County with the city of Chicago.

Wilmette

Population: 26,690. This posh North Shore suburb, founded in 1872, has a couple of interesting museums to check out.

KOHL CHILDREN'S MUSEUM (ages 1–8)

165 Green Bay Road, Wilmette 60091; (888) 564–5543. Hours are 9 A.M. to 5 P.M. Monday through Saturday and noon to 5 P.M. Sunday; Monday closing time is noon from Labor Day through Memorial Day. Admission costs $5 per person for anyone age 1 or older. Infants less than a year old get in free. Internet: www.kohlchildrensmuseum.org.

Founded in 1985, this children's museum draws more than a quarter million visitors annually. It specializes in learning experiences for children age 1 to 8—the formative years, according to many experts—but does so in such fun ways that it doesn't seem like "education." Some of the exhibits miniaturize real-life experiences, such as riding a Chicago Transit Authority (CTA) train or shopping at a Jewel-Osco grocery store.

A Natural Attraction Commune with nature in the Chicago Botanic Garden, which is actually quite a ways north of the city (but in Cook County) in the North Shore suburb of Glencoe. The entrance is on Lake-Cook Road about half a mile west of Green Bay Road and half a mile east of I–94. The garden is open from 8 A.M. to sunset daily, year-round. Admission is **Free**, but there's a fee of $7 per car for parking. Tram tours of the grounds take 45 minutes and cost $4 for adults, $3 for seniors, and $2 for children. One tram is wheelchair accessible. The spacious grounds are a riot of color in spring and summer, yet there's a pristine beauty to them even in winter, when the snow covers everything. In fall the flowers are goners, so the surrounding trees pick up the slack by trotting out their best red-yellow hues. Three greenhouses on the grounds were built in the 1870s and contain a variety of interesting flora. The main building has a collection of plants that kids are actually supposed to touch, plus another group of useful plants such as cotton, pineapple, coffee, and cacao. There may also be a temporary display of art or craft items, such as prints or quilts. Rest rooms are in this building, too. You can get a bite to eat in the Food for Thought Cafe, open from 8:30 A.M. to 4 P.M. Monday through Friday and 8:30 A.M. to 5:30 P.M. Saturday and Sunday. Souvenirs are available in the Garden Shop, and there's also a library. Call (847) 835–5440 for further information. Internet: www.chicago-botanic.org.

Others are historical in nature, such as the Phoenician sailing ship, while still others are ultramodern, such as the technology center. Especially appealing to the tinier tots are the Duplo Room (where they can play with oversize Lego building blocks called Duplos) and the H_2O water play area (you may want to stuff a change of clothes in your carryall bag if your toddler is especially fond of splashing, pouring, and floating things, because there's a lot to do here). Cozy Corner features activities for children younger than age 2. Orbit the Robot, who looks like a Fisher-Price version of R2D2 from *Star Wars,* is a popular attraction for all the young visitors.

WILMETTE HISTORICAL MUSEUM (age 6 and up)

609 Ridge Road, Wilmette 60091; (847) 853–7666. Hours are 10 A.M. to noon and 1 to 4 P.M. Tuesday and Thursday and 1 to 4 P.M. Wednesday and Sunday. Admission is **Free**. *The building is accessible for wheelchairs. Call for details about current exhibits.*

The building that houses this museum is itself a piece of history. The two-story Victorian structure was built in 1896 to serve as the Gross Point Village Hall. (The town of Gross Point existed from 1874 to 1924.) It was named to the National Register of Historic Places in 1991. Inside are exhibits chronicling the history of the area. The permanent Fire House exhibit includes a hands-on activity area for children.

Where to Eat

Walker Brothers Original Pancake House. *153 Green Bay Road; (847) 251–6000.* Open from 7 A.M. to 10 P.M. daily. There's a special kids' menu, and the silver-dollar pancakes are just the right size. $

Bakers Square. *200 Skokie Boulevard; (847) 256–6080.* Hours are 7 A.M. to midnight Tuesday through Saturday and 7 A.M. to 11 P.M. Sunday and Monday. See Restaurant Appendix for description. $

Where to Stay

There are no hotels or motels in Wilmette. See entry for Highland Park.

For More Information

Wilmette Chamber of Commerce, *1150 Wilmette Avenue, Wilmette 60091; (847) 251–3800.*

Des Plaines

Population: 53,223. The Des Plaines River runs along the eastern edge of this Cook County suburb just north of O'Hare International Airport. Interstate 294 and Interstate 90 skirt the eastern and southern edges of town and Illinois Highway 83 the western edge. Illinois Highway 58 runs through the northern part, and U.S. Highways 14 and 12/45 crisscross in the middle. About a block north of Lee Street (the main drag for the small downtown) on the west side of River Road is a little re-creation of the first McDonald's burger joint, complete with big golden arches. You can peek in the windows at the mannequins posed at the counter, but you can't go inside.

JUNGLE JIM'S PLAYLAND (ages 2–12)

723 West Golf Road (Illinois Highway 58), Des Plaines 60016; (847) 640–5500. In a strip mall on the southeast corner of the intersection with Elmhurst Road (Illinois Highway 83). Hours from late August through early June are 10 A.M. to 8 P.M. Monday through Thursday, 10 A.M. to 9 P.M. Friday and Saturday, and 11 A.M. to 8 P.M. Sunday. In summer the facility opens an hour earlier Monday through Saturday; all other times remain the same. Admission costs $6.99 Monday through Friday and $8.99 Saturday and Sunday for anyone age 17 or younger (but this place definitely isn't made for teenagers); accompanying adults get in free. The price includes unlimited rides and access to the play areas. Arcade games cost extra; you buy tokens to play them.

This indoor carnival's bright colors and lighting give it a cheery ambience. Kid-size rides include a Ferris wheel, animal bumper cars, and several round-and-round ones. There are also "jungle play areas" where children can climb, jump around, and slide. Arcade games are geared toward grade-schoolers and younger children. You can buy some pizza and Pepsi and eat at one of the many picnic tables in the concession area; birthday party groups also congregate here.

MYSTIC WATERS FAMILY AQUATIC PARK (all ages)

2025 Miner Street, Des Plaines 60016; (847) 391–5700. Open from mid-June through late August. Hours are 11 A.M. to 9 P.M. Monday through Friday and noon to 8 P.M. Saturday and Sunday. Admission costs $8 for adults and $7 for anyone age 17 or younger.

This community swimming pool was remodeled in the late 1990s to become a family-friendly water park. The pool now has a zero-depth end where tiny tots can frolic. Kids also like the new sand play area. There are three kinds of slides: twisty water slides, drop slides, and a dolphin slide. If you don't feel like swimming, you can just float along a "river" in an inner tube. Concessions are available, and there is a changing station in the women's rest room.

Where to Eat

ChooChoo Grill. *600 Lee Street; (847) 298–5949.* Hours are 6 A.M. to 7:30 P.M. Monday through Friday and 6 A.M. to 5 P.M. Saturday; closed Sunday. This little diner's claim to fame is the miniature railroad track that runs along the counter. If you sit on a stool at the counter, the choo-choo will deliver your plate of toast. $

Perry's X-press. *1065 East Oakton Street; (847) 823–4428.* Open from 11 A.M. to 11 P.M. Monday through Thursday, 11 A.M. to midnight Friday and Saturday, and noon to 10 P.M. Sunday. This local Italian restaurant occupies a building that was once a bank, and the drive-up teller window has been transformed into a drive-through carryout window. Both pan pizza and "panzarotti" (in which the crust is folded over to encase the toppings, sort of like a big turnover) are popular, and you can order a variety of pasta dishes. $

Where to Stay

Comfort Inn O'Hare. *2175 East Touhy Avenue; (847) 635–1300 or (800) 228–5150.* About 2 miles from O'Hare International Airport; a free courtesy car will take you to and from the airport. The inn has 145 rooms with coffeemakers. There is a health club on the premises but no swimming pool. The room rate includes continental breakfast. $$$$

Travelodge. *3003 Mannheim Road; (847) 296–5541 or (800) 578–7878.* This economy motel has 95 rooms with recliners and coffeemakers, plus an outdoor pool. Pets are allowed. $$$

For More Information

Des Plaines Chamber of Commerce, *1401 East Oakton Street, Des Plaines 60016; (847) 824–4200. Internet: www.dpchamber.com.*

Elk Grove Village

Population: 33,429. This suburb is easily accessible from I-90, I-290, I-355, and Route 53. If you're flying in and out of O'Hare airport or planning to shop till you drop at Woodfield Mall just up the road in Schaumburg, you may get a better motel rate if you stay in Elk Grove Village.

PIRATES' COVE (ages 2–10)

499 Biesterfield Road, Elk Grove Village 60007; (847) 437–9494 or (847) 439–2683. Open only during summer; hours are 10 A.M. to 5 P.M. Monday through Friday and noon to 4 P.M. Saturday and Sunday. Admission costs $5 per child age 10 or younger; accompanying adults or anyone age 11 or older gets in free. Good accessibility for strollers and wheelchairs. Rest rooms have fold-down changing tables. From I–290, I–355, or Route 53, exit at Biesterfield Road and head east, and then turn south onto Leicester Road and follow the signs. From I–90 or Route 72, exit south onto Arlington Heights Road and continue a few miles to Biesterfield Road. Turn right, heading west on Biesterfield, and then south onto Leicester Road. Signs direct you to the entrance building, with its salmon pink Mediterranean-style facade.

This pint-size amusement park is a cute place to take your tiny tots and younger grade-schoolers. Administered by the Elk Grove Park District, the facility has a clean, attractive appearance. Brick walkways wind through the landscaped grounds, with beds of marigolds, geraniums, and other flowers lending a splash of color. Trees are tall enough to afford some shade, and there are benches where the adults can sit to wait for the kids. The admission price, verified by a colorful wristband, covers unlimited use of about a dozen attractions. Children must be able to ride by themselves—parents are not allowed on the rides, and it's easy to see why. Even kids as old as 8 or 9 may feel a bit oversize on some of them. A unique ride is a little train that is powered by the kids themselves. They each get their own private locomotive, and they crank a handle as vigorously as possible to make it go around the track, which passes under a couple short tunnels. A merry-go-round with 20 horses is also popular. There are two water rides, the Bumper Boats and the Jungle Cruise, both of which are very gentle. Cute animal puppets at the end of the cruise make it a memorable ride. Behind a castle wall is a free-form playground with ladders, platforms, nets, tires, and a slide that forms the back of a green dragon that puffs steam out its nostrils. Older kids will enjoy the cable ride or the 20-foot climbing wall. The pirate ship in the center of the park has tables and chairs on the upper level and ice cream and souvenirs on the lower. You can bring your own picnic or buy food from a concession shop that sells pizza, drinks, and other goodies.

RAINBOW FALLS WATERPARK (all ages)

Elk Grove Boulevard and Lions Drive, Elk Grove Village 60007; (847) 437–9494. One block east of Arlington Heights Road. Season runs from mid-June through mid-August. Hours are 10 A.M. to 8 P.M. Monday through Thursday, 10 A.M. to 7 P.M. Friday, and 11 A.M. to 5 P.M. Saturday and Sunday. Admission *costs $9 for adults and $8 for young people age 2 through 17; children age 1 or younger get in free. Accessible for strollers and wheelchairs. From I–290, I–355, or Route 53, exit at Biesterfield Road and turn right onto Biesterfield, heading east a mile or so. Turn left, heading north, onto Arlington Heights Road, following it around a curve, and then turn right onto Elk Grove Boulevard and right again onto Lions Drive. From I–90 or Route 72, exit south onto Arlington Heights Road; turn left onto Elk Grove Boulevard and then right onto Lions Drive.*

This facility, operated by the Elk Grove Park District, has something for everyone. For the tinier tots there's a shallow "adventure pool" with a turtle fountain, a little slide, and squirt guns. For the older family members, the park has a swimming pool, giant water slides, a waterfall, and a 300-foot floating inner-tube ride. If you're really adventurous, try the "cliff" diving off one of two high platforms. A miniature golf course winds among the falls and fountains; no extra charge to play. The three-story family funhouse resembles an amusement park funhouse, only with water stuff. You can exit the funhouse down the "space bowl slide," which is a bit like being flushed down a toilet, albeit a clean, chlorinated one. The park has an on-site concession stand, but you're allowed to bring your own lunch if you choose, as long as you don't pack any glass containers or alcoholic beverages.

Where to Eat

Le Peep. *130 Biesterfield Road; (847) 439–7337.* In a strip mall on the north side of the road. The curb in front could pose a problem for wheelchairs from the parking lot, but the restaurant is on one level and negotiable. Hours are 6:30 A.M. to 2:30 P.M. Monday through Friday and 7 A.M. to 2:30 P.M. Saturday and Sunday. This airy restaurant with crisp white walls, dark green carpeting, and burgundy accents is a comfortable place for a hearty breakfast or lunch. The specialty dish is a *skillet,* a ceramic dish shaped like its namesake and filled with a mixture of diced potatoes, onions, and cheese, topped with two sunny-side-up eggs; you can get it with other ingredients added also. A Schuldt favorite is the crepe stuffed with seafood, mushrooms, and broccoli and lathered in hollandaise sauce. The children's menu items are priced from $1.99 to $3.50, *not* including drink. Kids can choose pancakes, French toast, grilled cheese sandwich, burger, or chicken strips. $

Giordano's. *1800 South Elmhurst Road; (847) 290–8000.* Open from 11 A.M. to 11 P.M. Monday through Thursday, 11 A.M. to midnight Friday and Saturday, and noon to 11 P.M. Sunday. See Restaurant Appendix for description. $

Portillo's. *1500 Busse Highway; (847) 228–6677.* Hours are 10:30 A.M. to 8 P.M. Monday through Friday and 10:30 A.M. to 5 P.M. Saturday; closed Sunday. See Restaurant Appendix for description. $

Where to Stay

Best Western Midway Hotel. *1600 Oakton Street; (847) 981–0010 or (800) 528–1234.* Don't let the "Midway" in the name fool you—it's more in the vicinity of O'Hare airport. This chain property has 165 rooms on three floors, with elevator. Amenities include a domed atrium with indoor pool and steam room. Restaurant on premises. No pets. $$$

Comfort Inn Elk Grove Village. *2550 Landmeier Road; (847) 364–6200.* This chain motel has 100 comfortable rooms but not much in the way of amenities; no pool. Room rate includes continental breakfast. $$$$

Days Inn O'Hare West. *1920 East Higgins Road; (847) 437–1650.* A basic chain property, the motel has 78 rooms with cable TV; no pool. Room rate includes continental breakfast. $$

Holiday Inn Elk Grove. *1000 Busse Road; (847) 437–6010 or (800) 465–4329.* This four-story hotel has 159 rooms and features indoor pool, sauna, and fitness center. Pets allowed. Room rate includes full breakfast. $$$

Schaumburg

Population: 68,586. This suburb's Woodfield Mall has made it a commercial mecca. The village and the mall are accessible off I–290 (a spur off I–90) and Illinois Highways 53, 58, and 72. There's other family fun here, too.

WOODFIELD MALL (all ages)

Golf Road (Illinois Highway 58) and Illinois Highway 53, Schaumburg 60173; (847) 330–0035 or, outside the Chicago metro area, (800) 332–1537. Regular mall hours are 10 A.M. to 9 P.M. Monday through Friday, 10 A.M. to 7 P.M. Saturday, and 11 A.M. to 6 P.M. Sunday. Holiday hours vary, so call ahead to check. The mall is accessible for strollers and wheelchairs. No smoking inside the mall.

Woodfield is the world's largest mall in terms of retail space. (The Mall of America in Minnesota covers more total space but includes a huge indoor amusement park in addition to the retail stores.) Woodfield has 235 stores, anchored by JCPenney, Lord & Taylor, Marshall Field's, Nordstrom, and Sears. This two-and-a-half-story mall is made for serious shoppers, too, without a lot of obstacles to impede foot traffic—the few aesthetic touches here include glass elevators and a fountain in the central courtyard. The lack of numerous kiosks and much decorative greenery makes the walkways more navigable for baby strollers and wheelchairs as well. It's hard to imagine something you couldn't buy at Woodfield; there are so many different kinds of stores—clothing, books, music, electronics, home furnishings, wacky gifts, you name it. The Warner Bros. Studio Store has a mind-boggling collection of clothing, toys, desk accessories, and other memorabilia featuring the classic "Looney Tunes" and newer "Animaniacs" characters. The WTTW store has all sorts of educational and entertaining gadgets. Other stores appealing to kids are Fun and Learn, Nickelodeon, Kay-Bee Toys, and the Disney Store. Unlike many other malls, Woodfield has no food court. Instead, restaurants and snack shops are scattered throughout (McDonald's is in the small middle level sandwiched between the expansive upper and lower levels). The most popular spot to eat is the Rainforest Cafe on the lower level. You'll pay inflated prices for burgers and other casual fare, but the place makes up for it with its vividly entertaining atmosphere. Often there's a line to get in, so don't wait until you're on the brink of starvation to wander over there. The parking areas are fairly well marked, as are the access points along the ring road encircling the mall.

MEDIEVAL TIMES DINNER AND TOURNAMENT (age 5 and up)

2001 Roselle Road, at I–90, Schaumburg 60173; (847) 843–3900. The dinner program starts at 7:30 P.M. Wednesday and Thursday, 8 P.M. Friday and Saturday, and 4 P.M. Sunday; closed Monday and Tuesday. Reservations are required. The price, which includes both the meal and the pageantry, is $38 to $42 per person age 13 or older and $28 per kid age 12 or younger, depending on which night you go. Advertisements in the newspaper frequently have coupons that may allow you to save money off the regular prices, sometimes even admitting a child free. Souvenirs, including the aggressively hawked photographs, cost extra. Tickets for the dreadful Dungeon exhibit cost $2. The Great Hall area (including rest rooms) and the back of the arena area are accessible for wheelchairs. Except for one small nonsmoking section, smoking is allowed everywhere in the hall area. Smoking is not allowed in the arena area. There are no changing tables in the rest rooms, and the paper-towel dispenser is mounted too high on the wall to be easily reached by children or by people in wheelchairs.

Looking for a change of pace? Here's joust the thing. Inside a climate-controlled castle, you'll feast on a hearty dinner while watching colorfully clad "knights," mounted on real horses, put on a two-hour show in the arena below. The moment you enter the castle—well, after you pay the admission and in return receive a table number and a paper crown in one of six colorful designs—you are cheerfully greeted by lavishly costumed actors in the role of king and queen, and a mandatory photograph is taken of each member of your party standing with them. Onward you proceed into the Great Hall, an open, high-ceilinged room with wooden chandelier and a balcony from which royal proclamations are issued. Everyone stays out here until the doors to the arena are opened. In the meantime you can wander around and, the management hopes, spend a lot of money. The souvenir counter has a tantalizing assortment of wooden weapons, golden goblets, and colorful costumes, plus mugs and T-shirts. At the very least you'll want to spend a dollar per kid on a "cheering pennant" to wave during the show. Prices for the individual items are not too bad, but the cost adds up fast if you have more than one child or buy more than one thing. If you're willing to spend $15, your boy or girl can be officially knighted, receiving a photograph of the king touching the sword to the kid's shoulder, plus an inscribed scroll. Even adults sometimes opt for this feature.

You may have purchased tickets at the admission booth for the Dungeon, which is located down a hallway off the Great Hall. Be forewarned that this display is far too disturbing for many children and some adults. (The ticket sellers don't tell you that, and by the time you see the NOT SUITABLE FOR SMALL CHILDREN sign by the door, you've already bought the tickets.) It is a room filled with replicas of medieval instruments of torture, accompanied by written descriptions, some sketches, and a mannequin or two. Although you may think that doesn't sound *so* bad, wait until you find out how some of these things actually were used—slowly tearing muscles, rupturing internal organs, or asphyxiating the victim in an excruciating manner. Often the alleged crime or the punishment involved the sexual organs. Do you really want to get into all that with a child? No thanks. While it could be argued that the Dungeon is only for entertainment and shouldn't be taken so seriously, the truth is that this kind of hideous torture really did happen in human history and is not some make-believe thing that can merely be wished away. In the vernacular: You don't want to go there.

Once the doors to the arena open, the real magic begins. Guests are ushered in, grouped according to the design of their crowns, and seated at long tables in six sections around the perimeter of the oval arena. The table assignments are first come, first served, so the earlier you arrive, the closer you'll sit to the action (but the longer you'll have to wait around in the hall; it's a trade-off). The tables are stair-stepped so that everyone gets a clear view of the arena floor. Plexiglass walls prevent flying dirt from getting into your food. Another photo of the whole family is snapped as soon as you get to your seat, and then the meal is served.

You start with soup and garlic bread, followed by roasted chicken, barbecued ribs, and twice-baked potato, and conclude with a flaky apple pastry. All the food is eaten without silverware, in the style of the Middle Ages, but napkins and, later, wet washcloths are provided to control the mess. For mass-produced food, the fare is surprisingly tasty—hot, flavorful, and fun to eat. Two servings of Pepsi are included in the price of the meal, but additional soft drinks or alcoholic beverages may be ordered at extra charge from the roving "wenches."

The show begins once everyone has their first course, with a parade down the middle of the arena featuring the king and queen, six handsome young men dressed in knightly regalia, and all the members of the "court," including your waiters. Then there's a display of dressage, which means horses performing stately maneuvers. An exciting exhibition of falconry follows, with a live bird of prey swooping high above the arena. There's a bit of a story line, but mainly the spectacle consists of the six knights competing on horseback in various contests of skill and eventually going one-on-one with weapons. The fights are choreographed, but even so, there remains an element of risk that makes them thrilling to watch. Special effects with a wizard are also, shall we say, enchanting? Grade-schoolers will think it's all "really cool," but the action and the dim lighting might make the experience too intense for younger children.

Oh, and about those pictures? Toward the end of the show, your waiter will offer you 8-by-10-inch prints of all of them—for $8 apiece. Let's see, that's one of the group at the table, one each of Mom, Dad, and Junior with the king and queen—ho, we're talking 32 bucks here! That's a pretty steep demand for a family budget. And most people won't buy more than one or two of the photos, if any. (Perhaps if the prices were lowered or fewer photos taken to begin with, there would be less waste and disappointment.)

Clearly, all the expenses beyond the basic admission price make Medieval Times the kind of attraction you probably can't afford very often. But try to save your money and go at least once. The pageantry is worth it.

SCHAUMBURG FLYERS (age 4 and up)

Games are played at Alexian Field, 1999 Springinsguth Road, Schaumburg 60173; (847) 891–2255 or toll-free (877) 691–2255. A phone recording provides good driving directions. Season runs from late May through late August. For the 2000 season, tickets cost $7 for reserved seats, $4 for lawn or bleachers, all ages. Parking is free in an adjacent paved lot. Facility is accessible for wheelchairs and strollers. Internet: www.flyersbaseball.com.

Minor-league baseball of the independent Northern League is what you'll see at this beautiful redbrick ballpark that opened in 1999 with a team managed by former Chicago White Sox outfielder Ron Kittle. Little planes flying overhead toward the nearby Schaumburg regional airport were the inspiration for the team's name and pilot-head logo. The cute mascot, Bearon, is a huge teddy with aviator hood and goggles who charms kids and adults alike. As at other minor-league ballparks, at each game the mascot races a kid around the bases (and of course comes in second). Other gimmicks include skill contests with Wiffle bats, golf clubs, hula hoops, and two couples dancing on the dugout roofs. The wide concrete aisles of the main concourse are easy to navigate. Rest rooms are evenly spaced along the length of the concourse, one of them a "family" rest room that alleviates the father-daughter/ mother-son issue of which one to use. The lawn sections at either end of the first- and third-base sides have a rather steep slope. The reserved seats are surprisingly narrow for a newer ballpark; expect a bit of a squeeze if you're at all overweight. The cup holders are a nice touch, however. Skyboxes are placed above and behind the reserved seats, so no one's view is blocked. Concessions are reasonably priced, although the cups for tips seem inappropriate at this sort of facility. A basic hot dog is a bargain at $1.75. Soft drinks cost about $2, beer $3 to $4. Popcorn, peanuts, pretzels, cotton candy, and Cracker Jack are in the $2 to $3.50 range. Bratwurst, Italian beef, and chicken sandwiches cost $3.25 to $5. For the more health conscious, a fruit or veggie plate or a cold deli sandwich is $3.50. Souvenirs sporting the team's navy and orange colors include caps, shirts, mugs, pens, stuffed toys, soft baseballs, and miniature bats; some of the smaller items can be purchased for less than $5 each.

Where to Eat

Portillo's. *611 East Golf Road; (847) 884–9020.* Hours are 10:30 A.M. to 10:30 P.M. Monday through Saturday and 11 A.M. to 10 P.M. Sunday. See Restaurant Appendix for description. $

Red Lobster. *680 North Mall Drive; (847) 605–1550.* Near Woodfield Mall. Hours are 11 A.M. to 10 P.M. Sunday through Thursday and 11 A.M. to 11 P.M. Friday and Saturday. See Restaurant Appendix for description. $$

TGIFriday's. *1893 Walden Office Square; (847) 397–2437.* Open from 11 A.M. to midnight Sunday through Thursday and 11 A.M. to 1 A.M. Friday and Saturday. See Restaurant Appendix for description. $

Reigning Cats and Dogs The three-story glass-enclosed concourse at Arlington International Racecourse is the spacious venue for the annual Chicagoland Family Pet Show in mid- to late March. The weekend event normally runs from 2 to 9 P.M. Friday, 9 A.M. to 9 P.M. Saturday, and 10 A.M. to 6 P.M. Sunday, so it's easy to work around toddlers' nap times. Cats and dogs are the kings and queens of this show, but you'll find small areas with such exotic pets as rats, ferrets, hedgehogs, snakes, turtles, and assorted smaller reptiles. More than 250 booths with all sorts of pet-related merchandise and services fill one whole huge section of the concourse. It's a wonderful place to spend a few hours. (Concessions are available if you want a snack or a meal, but frankly, the food is overpriced and generally mediocre.)

In the cat section hundreds of gorgeous felines rest in fancy cages or in their owners' arms, awaiting their turn to compete for a blue ribbon. To prevent the spread of germs, touching or petting the animals is prohibited, and the owners of these expensive show cats do not take kindly to people who disregard that rule, so have a talk with your little one beforehand and then stay close enough to make sure the child obeys. Some of the professional breeders who bring cats to the show also bring kittens for sale. You might be able to take one home for a mere $400.

The dogs are not on display like the cats, but you'll still be able to find a few wandering about–on leashes, of course–or resting in one of the booths with its owner. Some owners will let kids pet their animal, and others prefer not to, so always ask before you touch. The dogs are paraded into a show ring for judging, and when there's a lull in the competition, there's usually some form of canine entertainment. You'll see "dancin' doggies," Frisbee-catching pooches, and guard dogs.

Arlington Racecourse is located just off Euclid Avenue, east of Illinois Highway 53, in Arlington Heights. Tickets cost $8 for anyone age 13 or older and $4 for kids age 3 through 12, with tots age 2 or younger admitted free. Area Dominick's grocery stores usually carry discount coupons. Parking costs $5, or you can take the Metra Union Pacific Northwest Line train and get off at the nearby Arlington Park stop and walk over. The concourse is accessible for strollers and wheelchairs, and there are elevators as well as escalators between floors. Smoking is allowed indoors only in one hazy corridor and is absolutely forbidden in the animal areas. For further information contact Tower Show Productions at (630) 469–4611. Internet: www.towershow-productions.com.

Where to Stay

Hampton Inn. *1300 East Higgins Road; (847) 619–1000.* This economy chain motel has 128 comfortable rooms but no swimming pool. The room rate includes continental breakfast. $$$$

Hyatt Regency Woodfield. *1800 East Golf Road; (847) 605–1234 or (800) 233–1234.* Hyatt is a more upscale chain that's typically beyond a family budget, but if you can afford to pamper yourselves a bit, give this one a try. It has 469 rooms and is loaded with amenities, including indoor and outdoor pools, whirlpool, and fitness center. There is a restaurant on the premises. $$$$

La Quinta Motor Inn. *1730 East Higgins Road; (847) 517–8484 or (800) 531–5900.* This budget chain property has 121 rooms and an outdoor swimming pool. Pets are allowed. The room rate includes continental breakfast. $$$

For More Information

Greater Woodfield Convention and Visitors Bureau, *1375 East Woodfield Drive, Suite 100, Schaumburg 60173; (847) 605–1010 or (800) 847–4849.* Thirteen communities in the northwest suburbs form the Greater Woodfield area, which encompasses Woodfield Mall, Medieval Times, more than 60 restaurants, and more than 30 hotels and motels.

Barrington

Population: 9,504. In northwestern Cook County, straddling the line with Lake County, is the town of Barrington.

HEALTH WORLD (age 5 and up)

1301 South Grove Avenue (near the intersection of Barrington and Dundee Roads), Barrington 60010; (847) 842–9100. Open from 10 A.M. to 3 P.M. daily (until 8 P.M. Friday). Admission costs $5 per person age 3 or older; children age 2 or younger get in free. Internet: www.healthworldmuseum.org.

This spacious, two-story facility is geared toward kids from kindergarten through eighth grade and offers them a way to have a lot of fun while learning important information about health and safety. The brightly colored exhibit areas—with catchy names such as Living Gadget, Brain Teaser, and Oak Forest with Pete's Tree House—have entertaining hands-on activities.

Where to Eat

Chessie's. *100 Appleby; (847) 382–5020.* Hours are 11:30 A.M. to 10 P.M. Monday through Thursday, 10:30 A.M. to 11 P.M. Friday and Saturday, and 10 A.M. to 9 P.M. Sunday. Serving lunch, dinner, and Sunday brunch. This downtown restaurant is housed in the old train station, and you can eat inside a real 1927 Pullman railcar. The menu features sandwiches, salads, steaks, seafood, chicken, and pasta. The $4.95 children's menu includes drink and ice cream; among the entree choices are burgers, spaghetti, and grilled cheese. $$

Where to Stay

Days Inn. *405 West Northwest Highway (Route 14); (847) 381–2640 or (800) 329–7466.* This three-story motel has 58 rooms with coffeemakers. Amenities include outdoor swimming pool and indoor whirlpool and exercise room. $$

For More Information

Barrington Chamber of Commerce,
325 North Hough, Barrington 60010;
(847) 381–2525.

Our sweep of Chicagoland now reaches DuPage County in the west. For general information about this region, contact the **DuPage County Convention and Visitors Bureau,** 915 Harger Road, Oak Brook 60523; (630) 575-8070 or (800) 232-0502.

Roselle

Population: 20,819. This suburb has several family-oriented attractions all within a mile or so of one another along or just off Lake Street, also known as U.S. Highway 20. The area is just east of Gary Avenue, a few miles north of Bloomingdale's Stratford Square Mall.

4OUR SEASONS GATEWAY TO THE WEST INDOOR GOLF (age 4 and up)

1350 West Lake Street, Roselle 60172; (630) 980–8882. Open year-round from 10 A.M. to 10 P.M. daily. An 18-hole game costs $4.75 per person age 11 or older and $4.25 per child age 10 or younger. Each subsequent game costs $2 per *person, all ages. The building entrance is accessible for strollers and wheelchairs, but the golf course is not—it has steps and irregular terrain that would make the course very difficult to navigate. No smoking in the golfing area, but it is allowed in the entryway and the rest rooms. Rest rooms do not have changing tables.*

If you didn't already know this miniature golf course was here, you probably wouldn't stumble across it, and then you'd miss something special. The redbrick facade at the end of a strip mall behind a bank and a gas station looks plain and small, but step inside and the place is huge. Beyond the admission-and-concession booth is a room the size of a warehouse. Skylights and a row of windows near the high ceiling make it bright and airy. Murals on the walls depict the American Southwest, and tunes from a country-music radio station contribute to the ambience. With your colored golf ball in hand, you walk through a replica of the St. Louis arch, perhaps 15 feet high, to receive your clubs and start golfing. All the holes are par 3, and while some are a bit tricky, they're generally not too hard for kids (especially when Mom and Dad allow a bit of interpretation in tallying the shots). Your score card labels what landmark each hole represents, the most obvious being Mount Rushmore. That's as "educational" as the experience gets–no fancy plaques with wordy history lessons, so just go out and have fun! You'll get to aim your ball between a giant cowboy's legs, through a Sioux tepee, across a Yellowstone waterfall, up and over the Golden Gate Bridge, around a looping track for Hollywood, into and out of a cannon at the Alamo, and finally into the wheel of a New Orleans paddle wheeler. 4our Seasons has been in business since 1979, and some parts show a bit of wear, but that only enhances the old-fashioned charm of the place. It takes roughly an hour to get through the course. Children of all ages are allowed, but they'll enjoy it much more if they're old enough to use the clubs and have some concept of the game, thus the estimate of 4 as the suggested minimum age. Concession prices are quite reasonable; you can get a Pepsi, chips, candy, a soft pretzel, or an ice-cream bar for under $1, and hot dogs and pizza cost less than $2.

LAKESIDE ENTERTAINMENT CENTER (age 2 and up)

1100 West Lake Street, between Gary Avenue and Bloomingdale Road, Roselle 60172; (630) 351–2100. Open year-round except for miniature golf, which is an outdoor course open only in summer. Main facility hours are noon to midnight Monday through Wednesday, noon to 9 P.M. Thursday, noon to 2 A.M. Friday, 10 A.M. to 2 A.M. Saturday, and 10 A.M. to midnight Sunday. Game tokens are sold *four for $1, with a slight discount for larger quantities. Miniature golf costs $5 before 5 P.M. Monday through Friday and $6 after 5 P.M. Monday through Friday and all day Saturday and Sunday. Call ahead to check current hours for open bowling and Cosmic Bowling. A line of bowling, regular or Cosmic, costs $3.75 per person, all ages, during the school year. Weekday summer prices are 99 cents per line for regular or $1.99 for Cosmic. Shoe rental costs $2.99 per person, all ages; no street shoes allowed on the lanes. Bumpers available at no extra charge. Check for package deals on the Cosmic Bowling. Smoking is allowed, so beware if someone in the family is particularly sensitive.*

This facility has three main parts. The **game room** in front has games for tots and teens alike. The wee ones will have fun using a big padded mallet to clobber things that pop up in the RoboBop and Whak A Mole games, while the teens will find air hockey, pinball, and video games to attract their interest, and everyone can try the Skeeball. Games spit out tickets at the end of a round of play, and those can be redeemed for brightly colored plastic prizes when you leave.

Around to the east side downstairs, with its own entrance, is a 32-lane Brunswick **bowling alley** where you can try the newest wild gimmick, Cosmic Bowling, which will push your senses to the limit. You bowl in black light (ultraviolet), so wear white if you really want to glow. Multicolored lights flash, and three big screens above the lanes carry dance-style music videos by the likes of Madonna, Hammer, Janet Jackson, and Buster Poindexter (remember him, the one-hit wonder with "Hot, Hot, Hot"?). Automated scoring on video screens means you don't have to count pins or remember how to add a spare, and you can request a lane with bumpers that fill the gutters to make it easier for everyone to hit some pins. The lightest ball available weighs 6 pounds, so make sure your youngster is strong enough to heft it—probably about age 4 or 5—to get the most pleasure out of the experience. Basic snacks and drinks are available to keep you fueled; budget a few extra bucks. Cosmic Bowling is aptly named and a lot of fun.

The third section is the outdoor **miniature golf course,** in back and off to the east side but visible from the road. This eye-catching 18-hole course has a castle, a Victorian mansion, and numerous waterfalls and fountains set amid landscaped grounds with colorful flower beds. But think twice before bringing younger children here—the course is much trickier than it looks, and even adults may have trouble making par. The water hazards will cost you an extra dollar if you knock your ball in and can't get it back out, which happens a little too easily.

COACHLITE ROLLER SKATING CENTER (age 5 and up)

1291 Bryn Mawr Avenue, at Lake Street, Roselle 60172; (630) 893–4480. Hours vary; call ahead for current schedule. Admission costs range from $3 to $6 per person, depending on the session; usually there's one session per week in which kids age 12 or younger get in free. Skate rental costs $1.50 for regular skates or $3.50 for in-line or speed skates. You may bring your own (clean) skates.

Inside this plain brick building is a lively spot for some family recreation. Kids of all ages are allowed, but many don't have the necessary strength and balance until about kindergarten—you be the judge of your own child's capabilities so that the experience will be safe as well as fun. Also keep in mind that even if your youngster whizzes around the neighborhood on Rollerblades, he or she will be surprised on the first visit to an indoor rink like this one at how slippery the smooth parquet floor is. But once they get the hang of it, wheeee! During summer the center offers a two-hour session with organ music for old-fashioned fun. Other sessions have a disc jockey playing the tunes and calling for occasional special restrictions, such as girls-only, boys-only, couples, or backward skate. You'll also get a chance to do the hokey-pokey and the chicken dance on wheels. The painted rainbow that runs along the back wall reflects the flashing multicolored lights overhead that pulse to the beat of the music. Skate pickup is at the far end of the rink; you trade your shoes for the skates. There are 50-cent lockers along the wall for stowing other stuff. The concession area has Pepsi, candy, hot dogs, and pizza, with most items under $2. A game room and a gift shop can siphon off a bit more of your money.

Where to Eat

Skippy's Gyros. *1322 Lake Street, at Bryn Mawr; (630) 894–9960.* Open from 10:30 A.M. to 9 P.M. Sunday through Thursday and 10:30 A.M. to 10 P.M. Friday and Saturday. This little eatery is in a strip mall just north of Coachlite Roller Skating Center and just east of 4our Seasons Indoor Golf. It modestly claims to have "The Best Food in Town" and challenges you to "Taste the difference between franchise food and our food!" (That's easy enough to do with a Subway sandwich shop right next door.) A gyro, the signature Greek sandwich, features seasoned roasted lamb or chicken packed in pita bread with onion, tomato, and cucumber sauce, and is a bargain at less than $4. For more conventional tastes the menu contains hamburgers, hot dogs, fried chicken and shrimp, and barbecued ribs. The prices are low enough that a children's menu really isn't necessary. The sole dessert is worth savoring—Greek baklava, layers of flaky pastry with minced almonds and honey. $

Nancy's Pizzeria. *1232 West Lake Street; (630) 924–1040.* Hours are 4 to 10 P.M. Monday through Thursday, 4 to 11 P.M. Friday and Saturday, and 4 to 9 P.M. Sunday. Carryout and delivery only. See Restaurant Appendix for description. $

Where to Stay

There are no hotels or motels in Roselle. The Holiday Inn on Gary Avenue in Carol Stream is about 5 miles south of the attractions listed for Roselle; see entry for Carol Stream.

For More Information

Roselle Chamber of Commerce, *81 East Devon Avenue, Roselle 60172; (630) 894–3010.*

Bloomingdale

Population: 16,614. This town reportedly dates back to the early 1800s. The Old Town section just west of Bloomingdale Road, between Lake Street and Schick Road, is rather like historic Long Grove, only on a smaller scale. But for the most part, Bloomingdale blends into the amalgamation of suburbs sprawling out to the west of Chicago.

STRATFORD SQUARE (all ages)

Corner of Gary Avenue and Army Trail Road, accessible from either, Bloomingdale 60108; (630) 539–1000. Hours are 10 A.M. to 9 P.M. Monday through Saturday and 11 A.M. to 6 P.M. Sunday. Accessible to strollers and wheelchairs; strollers available for rent. No smoking inside the mall or any of its stores. Internet: www.shopstratford.com.

Stratford Square is one of the most pleasant indoor shopping malls in the entire state for families with small children. It offers a storytime for kids during summer, and the Back-to-School train typically runs from late July through mid-August to make the obligatory fall pilgrimage more palatable to the wee ones. The mall is laid out roughly in a T-shape, with upper and lower levels that are connected via escalators and a glass elevator that kids love to ride. Skylights augment and soften the artificial light so that the place usually looks bright and airy. Several ponds with fountains add character and an aura of tranquillity. (All the fountains accept penny-pitched wishes.) There are six anchor department stores to suit a wide range of tastes and budgets, from the economical Sears to the midrange Kohl's, JCPenney, and Carson Pirie Scott to the tonier Marshall Field's. There are also some stores of particular interest to kids of all ages, such as the Disney Store, Zany Brainy, and Natural Wonders. If you set clear budgetary limits beforehand, they can enjoy themselves just looking around. Gymboree and Gap Kids are among a handful of specialty children's clothing stores at the mall. The centralized food court on the first floor features kid-pleasing fare like pizza, burgers, and hot dogs, plus baked potatoes or Chinese food for children with broader tastes. Have a deliciously gooey cinnamon roll for dessert at Cinnabon on the second floor. If you want to make a full day of it, you can take in a movie at the theater complex at one end.

Where to Eat

Red Lobster. *391 West Army Trail Road; (630) 529–0097.* Near the mall. Open from 11 A.M. to 10 P.M. Sunday through Thursday and 11 A.M. to 11 P.M. Friday and Saturday. The smoking section is fairly well separated from the nonsmoking area here, although smoking is allowed in the lobby. See Restaurant Appendix for description. $$

Popeyes Chicken. *405 Army Trail Road; (630) 893–1070.* Near the mall. Open from 10 A.M. to 11 P.M. daily. Smoking allowed in one section. See Restaurant Appendix for description. $

Old Country Buffet. *154 South Gary Avenue; (630) 529–5056.* Near the mall, in an outdoor strip plaza called Stratford Promenade Shopping Center. Hours are 11 A.M. to 8:30 P.M. Monday through Friday, 8 A.M. to 9 P.M. Saturday, and 8 A.M. to 8 P.M. Sunday; breakfast on weekends only, lunch and dinner daily. Smoking section is fairly well separated from the rest of the restaurant. See Restaurant Appendix for description. $

Where to Stay

Indian Lakes Resort. *250 West Schick Road; (630) 529–0200 or (800) 334–3417.* This deluxe facility has 308 rooms and lots of amenities: indoor and outdoor pools, indoor whirlpool and sauna, outdoor miniature golf course, tennis court, volleyball, two 18-hole regular golf courses, and two restaurants. The expansive grounds feature landscaping and ponds. Kids age 11 or younger stay free in the same room with their parents. Book a room here when you want more than just a place to sleep. Special packages can keep the cost down near $100 a night, not bad for a luxury resort. $$$$

For More Information

Bloomingdale Chamber of Commerce, *107 South Third Street, Bloomingdale 60108; (630) 980–9082.*

Carol Stream

Population: 31,716. This suburb is mainly an industrial and residential area, but you can find some educational and fun things to do with the kids here. At the corner of Gary Avenue and Lies Road is a large fountain that marks the lovely Town Center park, completed in 1998.

DUPAGE COUNTY SOLID WASTE EDUCATION CENTER (age 5 and up)

Fullerton Avenue, between Gary Avenue and Schmale Road, Carol Stream 60188; (630) 681–2400. **Free** *tours are available to families during summer, usually on weekday afternoons or evenings, and take about two hours. Call ahead to schedule one. (Tours are restricted to school groups during the school year.) The facility, which looks like a big warehouse, is not easily accessible for strollers or wheelchairs; the center is on the second floor, up a long, narrow flight of stairs.*

Do your kids ever wonder what happens to all the stuff the recycling truck picks up at the curb? They can see for themselves at the DuPage County Solid Waste Education Center in the DuPage County Recycling Center. Visitors can watch the procedure by which glass and plastic bottles and newspapers are sorted and baled by huge machines in the recycling center. In the education center they can try hands-on experiments that demonstrate on a smaller scale how certain processes work: for example, how paper dissolves in water or how a magnet can distinguish between tin and aluminum cans. The education center also displays an array of products made from recycled items.

BRUNSWICK GALA LANES NORTH (age 4 and up)

170 West North Avenue, Carol Stream 60188; (630) 682–0150. Regular hours are 10 A.M. to midnight Sunday through Thursday and 10 A.M. to 2 A.M. Friday and Saturday. Summer Cosmic Bowling hours are noon to 4 P.M. Tuesday and Thursday, noon to 2 P.M. Saturday and Sunday, and 7 P.M. to 2 A.M. Friday and Saturday. A line of regular bowling costs 99 cents per person, all ages, from 10 A.M. to 6 A.M. in summer; after 6 P.M. it costs $3.75 per person, all ages. Cosmic Bowling costs 99 cents Tuesday and Thursday, $3.59 Saturday and Sunday afternoon, and $4.39 Friday and Saturday night. Shoe rental costs $2.79 per person, all ages; no street shoes allowed on the lanes. Bumpers available at no extra charge. Check for package deals on the Cosmic Bowling. Smoking is allowed, so beware if someone in the family is particularly sensitive.

This bowling alley is similar to the one in Roselle but costs slightly less. It, too, has the funky Cosmic Bowling by black light, with big-screen music videos pumping up the volume and multicolored lights splashing color all around. Automated scoring displayed on video screens and bumpers in the gutters take the frustration out of playing. A food court offers snacks to keep you going.

CAROL STREAM ICE RINK (age 5 and up)

540 East Gunderson Drive, Carol Stream 60188; (630) 682–4480. Session times vary; call to check current schedule. Admission costs $4 per person, all ages. Skate rental is $2.

This indoor facility offers public ice-skating year-round. Bring your own skates or rent them there. Vending machines provide the only concessions.

Where to Eat

Pizza Hut. *333 South Schmale Road; (630) 682–4020.* Hours are 11 A.M. to 11 P.M. Sunday through Thursday and 11 A.M. to midnight Friday and Saturday. Dine in or carryout. See Restaurant Appendix for description. $

Sammy's Family Restaurant. *877 East Geneva Road; (630) 871–7636.* Open from 6 A.M. to 9 P.M. daily, serving breakfast, lunch, and dinner. Smoking allowed in one section. This popular place offers standard family favorites like burgers, steaks, and chicken. Children's menu is $3.25 for breakfast, including pancakes, eggs, or French toast, with sausage or bacon and juice or milk, and $3.95 for lunch and dinner, including entree such as grilled cheese sandwich, hot dog, spaghetti, or chicken, with soup and ice cream (but drink not included). $

Where to Stay

Holiday Inn Carol Stream. *150 South Gary Avenue, just south of North Avenue (Illinois Route 64); (630) 665–3000 or (800) 800–6509.* This attractive four-story chain property has 154 rooms with cable TV. Amenities include indoor pool, Jacuzzi, and game room. Restaurant on premises. $$$

For More Information

Carol Stream Chamber of Commerce, *150 South Gary Avenue, Carol Stream 60188; (630) 668–1900.*

Wheaton

Population: 51,464. You would expect this western suburb, home of the Billy Graham Center at Wheaton College, to have plenty of wholesome family activities, and it does. Railroad tracks run along Front Street downtown, and the area has been developed with brick walkways and fountains into a very pleasant place to hang out on a nice day. Wheaton also has numerous well-maintained parks throughout the city.

DUPAGE COUNTY HISTORICAL MUSEUM (age 4 and up)

102 East Wesley Street, Wheaton 60187; (630) 682–7343. Hours are 10 A.M. to 4 P.M. Monday, Wednesday, Friday, and Saturday and 1 to 4 P.M. Sunday; closed Tuesday and Thursday. Admission is **Free***, but donations are appreciated. Call for information on current special exhibits and programs. Internet: www.co.dupage.il.us/museum.*

The first historical thing you'll encounter at this museum is the building it's in. Designed by noted Chicago architect Charles Sumner Frost and constructed in 1891, it has a light brick facade, Gothic windows, a steep roof, and a tower at one end. The museum arrived in 1965. A highlight here is the model railroad, which is part of an exhibit that also includes artifacts and photographs chronicling the history of railroading in DuPage County. Other ongoing exhibits invite visitors' participation. There are enjoyable free programs for adults and children throughout the year, among them demonstrations of games and toys from the 1800s.

KELLY PARK (all ages)

South off Roosevelt Road (Illinois Highway 38) on Main Street, a block west of Naperville Road, Wheaton 60187; (630) 665–4710. Open from dawn to dusk daily. **Free**.

Women have been in the majority on Wheaton's park district board, and it's probably no coincidence that this community has a better-than-average collection of kid-friendly local parks. An easy one to reach is Kelly Park, on Main Street at the intersection with Elm Street in a residential neighborhood. There are separate play areas for tiny tots and for older kids, each with colorful, modern, metal-and-plastic playground equipment. A paved bicycle path surrounds and passes between the playgrounds. Children of all ages like to climb the "spider" of red nylon webbing that reaches a height of about 10 feet. There's a drinking fountain near the picnic tables, and in warmer weather there's usually a portable toilet available.

CANTIGNY (all ages)

15151 Winfield Road, Wheaton 60187; (630) 668–5185. Cantigny is accessible off Roosevelt Road (Illinois Highway 38) from the north or Butterfield Road (Illinois Highway 56) from the south and is well marked by brown signs. Parking costs $5, but everything else is **Free.** *Grounds are open from 9 A.M. to sunset Tuesday through Sunday; closed Monday. Museum hours are 10 A.M. to 4 P.M. Tuesday through Sunday; closed Monday. The museum stays open an hour later in the summer. Grounds and museum are closed in January. Internet: www.rrmtf.org/cantigny.*

One of the more notable landmarks in Wheaton is this 500-acre estate of the late Colonel R. R. McCormick, former editor and publisher of the *Chicago Tribune*. You can stroll through 10 acres of landscaped gardens and have a picnic on the grounds. Sometimes you can catch a musical concert at the gazebo. There are three buildings to visit, too. The Visitors Center has a large map of the grounds embedded in the floor. Here you can also view a 10-minute orientation film. You can get a bite to eat in the Tack Room Cafe, where toddlers can sit in a saddled high chair. There's also a gift shop. Tours of the R. R. McCormick Mansion depart every 15 minutes, the first at 10 A.M. and the last at 4:15 P.M., and take about 45 minutes. The First Division Museum uses life-size dioramas and exhibits to tell the story of the First Infantry Division of the U.S. Army.

WHEATON RICE POOL (all ages)

1777 South Blanchard Road, Wheaton 60187; (630) 690–4880 or (630) 665–4710. East off Naperville Road a mile or 2 north of Butterfield Road (Illinois Highway 56). Hours are 11 A.M. to 8:30 P.M. Monday through Saturday and noon to 8:30 P.M. Sunday. Nonresident admission costs $14 for adults age 22 through 59 and $8 for young people age 3 through 21 and seniors age 60 or older. Children age 2 or younger get in free.

The swimming facility is outdoors behind the Wheaton Park District Community Center, a modern redbrick building. In addition to the main pool, it has a kiddie pool with a waterfall and a sand play area for children. Unlike other pools, Wheaton Rice Pool charges extra to ride the water slides: $2 for a 10-ride wristband. This pool is nice, but it is more expensive than others in the area.

COSLEY ZOO (all ages)

1356 Gary Avenue, Wheaton 60187; (630) 665–5534. Open year-round. Hours are 9 A.M. to 4 P.M. Monday through Thursday and 10 A.M. to 6 P.M. Friday through Sunday. Admission is **Free**, *but much-appreciated donations may be slipped into the unobtrusive box near the train station. Internet: www.wheatonparkdistrict.com/facilities/cosley.html.*

This small museum is a pleasant place to pass a few hours. Bring your own lunch and sit at the picnic tables in a partially shaded area next to a vintage train car that kids can play in. You can wheel the stroller along a paved walkway next to a duck pond and go into a barn filled with horses, cows, sheep, goats, pigs, chickens, and other farm animals. The zoo also displays some native Illinois wildlife, such as foxes, coyotes, deer, owls, and hawks. The re-created train station houses exhibits, a gift shop, and rest rooms.

Where to Eat

Café Wheaton. *133 West Front Street; (630) 668–8866.* Open from 11 A.M. to 11 P.M. Monday through Thursday, 11 A.M. to midnight Friday, 8 A.M. to midnight Saturday, and 8 A.M. to 10 P.M. Sunday. This cozy corner restaurant in downtown Wheaton serves hearty breakfast Saturday and Sunday mornings; the eggs Benedict, served with stuffed tomato and fruit, are delicious. Dinners include steaks, chicken, seafood, pasta, and nightly specials. The children's menu includes burgers, chicken fingers, and the like. $$

Where to Stay

Wheaton Inn. *301 West Roosevelt Road; (630) 690–2600.* This lovely redbrick bed-and-breakfast inn has 16 guest rooms, each with private bathroom. For families, the McCormick Room is recommended. It has a king-size bed and enough floor space to wheel in a rollaway bed that can sleep two. It also has the most economical rate (although it still will be more than $100—a place this nice doesn't come cheap). Some of the more expensive rooms have a fireplace, a Jacuzzi, or both. Cookies and milk are served in the evening, and a hot buffet breakfast in the morning; both are included in the room rate. Reservations should be made well in advance. $$$$

For More Information

Greater Wheaton Chamber of Commerce, *303 West Front Street, Wheaton 60187; (630) 668–2739. Internet: www.wheatonchamber.org.*

Glen Ellyn

Population: 24,944. This west suburban town dates back to the mid-1800s. It has an old-fashioned downtown with specialty stores, boutiques, coffee shops, restaurants, and a movie theater that shows mainly arty and foreign films.

SUNSET POOL (all ages)

483 Fairview Avenue, Glen Ellyn 60137; (630) 858–7655. Open from late May through early September. Regular hours are 12:30 to 9 P.M. Monday through Friday and noon to 8 P.M. Saturday and Sunday. Some days, typically a Tuesday, Thursday, or Saturday, the pool closes at 6 P.M. because of a swim meet, so if you're planning an evening swim, call ahead to check. Nonresident admission costs $13 per adult age 18 through 54 and $8 for young people age 3 through 17 and seniors age 55 or older. Tots age 2 or younger get in free. You'll be admitted at the resident rate, half the price of nonresident admission, if you come with someone who lives in Glen Ellyn. The facility is accessible for wheelchairs.

This community pool's shallow end has a zero-depth edge, spray jets, a kiddie slide, and a waterfall cascading down from what looks like a 10-foot-tall mushroom or umbrella. The deep area has 1-, 3-, and 10-meter diving boards and lap-swimming lanes. There are two snaking water slides, one the usual open style and the other an enclosed tube (yes, it's dark around the first turn). Kids are ejected from the water for

10 to 15 minutes each hour so that adults can have some swimming time alone, the lifeguards can relax a bit, and the kids themselves can rest. Most go over to the giant sandbox and play there until the announcement is given for their return. At the north end of the pool deck are grassy areas where you can spread a towel if the lounge chairs are all taken, which is usually the case on a hot day. A separate lap-swimming pool was added to the west end of the facility in 2000. Often only one or two of the six lanes are roped off, so kids may play in the remaining space. This pool is 3 to 5 feet deep, so make sure your kids know how to swim if they go in. If the parking lot is full, you can park along any of the surrounding residential side streets except Main Street.

Biking the Prairie Path The 45-mile Illinois Prairie Path extends from Maywood to Aurora, but some of the prettiest stretches are through Villa Park, Glen Ellyn, and Wheaton, where the communities have done landscaping or created a parklike setting for the trail. Surfaced with crushed limestone in some parts and paved with asphalt in others, the path is favored by bicyclists, who outnumber walkers and runners about three to one. Motorized vehicles are prohibited on the Prairie Path. Police on bicycles patrol the path in some communities, and the incidence of vandalism or other crime has remained low.

LAKE ELLYN (all ages)

645 Lenox Road, Glen Ellyn 60137; (630) 858–2462. Open from dawn to dusk daily. **Free**. *Internet: www.gepark.org.*

One of the prettiest community parks for families in the suburbs is Lake Ellyn Park, nestled in a wooded area with a small lake behind Glenbard West High School (take Park Boulevard or Main Street north of downtown and turn east onto Hawthorne; you'll see the park on the left as Hawthorne dead-ends behind the high school). The children's playground is of modern design but in shades of green, tan, and brown that blend in with the surrounding trees, which provide merciful shade on hot sunny days. There's a nearby but separate area for littler kids, plus tables where you can have a snack you brought or simply set down the diaper bag. The park's boathouse has rest rooms and an outdoor drinking fountain. You can fish off the deck in summer. In winter you can ice-skate on the frozen lake.

WILLOWBROOK WILDLIFE CENTER (age 3 and up)

525 South Park Boulevard, at 22nd Street, Glen Ellyn 60137; (630) 942–6200; TDD (800) 526–0857. Open year-round from 9 A.M. to 5 P.M. daily; closed Thanksgiving, Christmas Eve, Christmas, and New Year's Day. Admission is by donation; suggested amount is $1 per person, all ages. Internet: www.dupageforest.com/education/willowbrook.html.

The center is a haven for animals that have been permanently disabled and are incapable of living in the wild. A 10-minute video explains how the staff treat and care for injured animals, and there are indoor and outdoor exhibits of critters. The Baby Nursery has, you guessed it, baby animals. The center's hands-on museum for children has animal puppets and a stage for creating their own nature shows. Outdoors there are picnic tables and a nature trail.

HAROLD D. MCANINCH ARTS CENTER AT COLLEGE OF DUPAGE (all ages)

22nd Street between Park Boulevard and Lambert Road, Glen Ellyn 60137; (630) 942–4000. Call for current schedule of events. Internet: www.cod.edu/ArtsCntr.

The Arts Center, which opened in 1986, is home to five resident professional ensembles but attracts big-name concert performers and theatrical productions as well. There are periodic special shows geared toward children, including the popular "Kid Jazz," and a group of College of DuPage thespians puts on cute adaptations of children's stories outdoors in the courtyard during summer.

Where to Eat

Alfie's. *425 Roosevelt Road; (630) 858–2506.* Open from 11 A.M. to 11 P.M. daily. Smoking is allowed in a separate section, but the ventilation is adequate. This local favorite calls itself "The Camelot of Glen Ellyn" and has a suit of armor standing guard in the waiting area. But it's not a fancy place at all; the specialty "Sir Alfie Loinburger," a big, juicy hamburger served with fries and a pickle, costs less than $4. The restaurant also serves chicken, shrimp, barbecued ribs, and large salads. The kids' menu features many of the same items on the regular menu, only in smaller sizes and at lower prices. Children get a helium-filled balloon when they leave. $

Beijing. *404 Roosevelt Road; (630) 469–1535.* Hours are 11:15 A.M. to 9:30 P.M. Sunday through Thursday and 11:15 A.M. to 10:30 P.M. Friday and Saturday. At this charming restaurant owned by Johnny and Bee Chen, family groups are always welcome. The Chinese cuisine here includes Hunan,

Mandarin, and spicy Szechwan styles. Among the more unusual entrees is Mongolian lamb: While similar in preparation to Mongolian beef, the lamb gives this dish a milder, sweeter flavor. Mu-shu pork and cashew chicken are among the tastier nonspicy dishes. If you want to go all-out, call ahead and order a succulent Beijing duck, which will feed a family of four quite generously. You can try some Chinese beer with your meal or order a round of Singapore Slings and Shirley Temples. $$

Where to Stay

Holiday Inn. *1250 Roosevelt Road; (630) 629–6000 or (800) 465–4329.* This recently remodeled four-story hotel has 120 rooms with cable TV. Amenities include fitness center and outdoor pool. Pets are allowed. $$$

For More Information

Glen Ellyn Chamber of Commerce, *444 North Main Street, Glen Ellyn 60137; (630) 469–0907.*

Lombard

Population: 39,408. Like many of the western suburbs, this one traces its roots back into the 1800s. Wear purple if you visit Lombard during a couple special weeks in May—that's Lilac Time. The centerpiece of the action is Lilacia Park downtown, where hundreds of bushes are in bloom. During the festival the village charges a few dollars to walk through the park; at other times admission is free. Stores have special sales, and a portable carnival sets up to offer rides and concessions to visitors. A Sunday parade down Main Street is another Lilac Time highlight. The parade usually features about 150 units, including themed floats, marching bands, and antique cars, and attracts about 10,000 spectators.

Which Main Is Main? A helpful hint for visitors: Wheaton, Glen Ellyn, and Lombard all have a Main Street that runs from north to south, and these three towns run consecutively from west to east, so be sure you're in the right one for the Main Street you want.

ENCHANTED CASTLE (all ages)

1103 South Main Street (at Roosevelt Road/Highway 38), Lombard 60148; (630) 953–7860. Hours are 11 A.M. to 10 P.M. Sunday through Thursday, 11 A.M. to midnight Friday, and 10 A.M. to midnight Saturday. ImaGYMnation Station admission costs $4 per child, 54 inches (4 feet, 6 inches) tall or shorter, with the accompanying adult admitted free. Q-Zar cost is $5 per person Monday through Friday and $6 per person Saturday and Sunday. Miniature golf costs $3 per person, the bumper cars $2, and the Rage ride $3.50. An unlimited play pass is offered for $12 to $15. Billiard tables rent for $12 an hour for up to four people. Dartboards take game tokens. Internet: www.enchanted.com.

This is one of the larger family amusement centers in the area. Everything is indoors, under one roof, and there are recreational activities for all ages. Smaller children can frolic in the ImaGYMnation Station, a playground with tubes, slides, and the like. There are also kiddie rides with miniature cars, trucks, trains, and ponies, plus a pint-size Ferris wheel. Older kids may want to play Q-Zar laser tag or try out one of the simulation rides. For these rides, you sit in a seat similar to an amusement park ride, facing a movie screen. The seat rocks and sways in time with the action shown on the screen. The Rage Theatre offers six different simulated adventures. Enchanted Castle also has bumper cars, a nine-hole miniature golf course, billiard tables, dartboards, and about 280 arcade games. An intriguing attraction here is Bowlingo, which is like bowling but not quite. You use a wooden ball 16 inches in diameter and without holes, and you stand in one place to roll it down the lane rather than taking gliding steps as you release it. The score is kept automatically by the alley computer. Dine on pizza, pasta, and salad in the Enchanted Theatre on-site restaurant; Toby the Birthday Dragon, Wally the Wizard, and their entourage of animated puppets will keep you company. If you're an uninhibited sort, grab the mike and belt out a song during free karaoke time some evenings.

YORKTOWN CENTER (all ages)

Highland Avenue and Butterfield Road, Lombard 60148; (630) 629–7330. Easily accessible off I–88. Hours are 10 A.M. to 9 P.M. Monday through Friday, 10 A.M. to 7 P.M. Saturday, and 11 A.M. to 6 P.M. Sunday. Accessible for wheelchairs and strollers. Internet: www.yorktowncenter.com.

Yorktown is one of the more appealing shopping malls in the western suburbs. This brightly lit, two-level indoor mall has wide walkways and an open central area where youngsters can ride a three-car choo-choo around a circular track. Rides cost 50 cents for three go-rounds. The train ride is enclosed by a white lattice fence, and the area inside the track has a changing seasonal display with mechanized figures—the Christmas one is especially cute. The anchor department stores are Carson Pirie Scott, JCPenney, and Von Maur. Stores of particular appeal to children include Natural Wonders, Kay-Bee Toys, and the Disney Store. Gap Kids and Gymboree sell children's clothes. The food court has a generous seating area surrounded by restaurants that offer Chinese, Japanese, and Italian foods, plus baked potatoes, big soft pretzels, and lusciously gooey cinnamon rolls. Oh, there's a McDonald's, too. Toward the back of the food court and off to one side is a huge arcade filled with video games.

MORAN WATER PARK (all ages)

433 East St. Charles Road, Lombard 60148; (630) 627–6127. Open daily throughout summer. Hours are 11:30 A.M. to 9 P.M. Monday through Thursday and 11:30 A.M. to 8 P.M. Friday through Sunday. Nonresident admission costs $10 for adults age 18 through 64 and $8 for young people age 3 through 17 and seniors age 65 or older. Children age 2 or younger get in free.

This water park is a family-friendly facility. The separate children's area has two pools that are zero-depth for the entire circumference, connected by a rock waterfall structure between them. There's a sand play area for children, too. The larger pool has diving boards at the deeper end and a play area about 4 to 5 feet deep at the other end that appeals especially to older grade-schoolers. Teenagers flock to the sand volleyball court, and everybody likes the two 210-foot winding water slides. A concession area provides snacks and tables.

Where to Eat

Jonathan's. *667 West Roosevelt Road; (630) 627–3300.* Hours are 11 A.M. to 10:30 P.M. Monday through Thursday, 11 A.M. to 11:30 P.M. Friday and Saturday, and 11:30 A.M. to 9 P.M. Sunday. This local favorite serves delicious steaks, seafood, chicken, and pasta. The prime rib and the chicken marsala are particularly good. The children's menu costs $3.99 to $4.99, including fries and beverage; kids can choose a burger, chicken nuggets, fried shrimp, fish sandwich, grilled cheese sandwich, or pasta of the day. $$

Old Country Buffet. *551 East Roosevelt Road; (630) 916–8809.* Open from 11 A.M. to 8:30 P.M. Monday through Thursday, 11 A.M. to 9:30 P.M. Friday, 8:30 A.M. to 9:30 P.M. Saturday, and 8 A.M. to 8:30 P.M. Sunday. See Restaurant Appendix for description. $

Pizzeria Uno. *Roosevelt Road at Main Street; (630) 792–1400.* Hours are 11 A.M. to 11 P.M. Sunday through Thursday, 11 A.M. to 1 A.M. Friday and Saturday, and 11 A.M. to 10 P.M. Sunday. This suburban offshoot of the downtown Chicago establishment features the same deep-dish pizza. You can also get the thin-crust type, plus a variety of pasta dishes, sandwiches, salads, and soups. $

Where to Stay

Hampton Inn. *222 East 22nd Street; (630) 916–9000 or (800) 426–7866.* This inn has 128 rooms. Rates include continental breakfast. No pool. $$$$

For More Information

Lombard Area Chamber of Commerce, *315 West St. Charles Road, Lombard 60148; (630) 627–5040.*

Downers Grove

Population: 46,858. This town, which was settled in the 1800s, makes several historical claims: It was a stop on the route of the first railroad, it was a transfer point on the Underground Railroad, and in 1892 it was the site of the nation's first 18-hole golf course, 9 holes of which are still in use today. But for families, the most interesting spot of historical significance may well be the old-fashioned cinema downtown. In August the city is overrun with wheels for the annual International Criterium In-Line Skating and Cycling Championships. Entertainment and family activities accompany the weekend event. In September 1998, Downers Grove launched a three-year downtown redevelopment program that is expected to make the area even more appealing.

TIVOLI THEATRE (all ages)

5021 Highland Avenue, Downers Grove 60515; (630) 968–0219. Tickets cost $1.75 per person. The theater shows mainly second-run feature films. Call for titles and show times; matinees on Saturday and Sunday, organist plays before shows Friday and Saturday nights. The theater is accessible for wheelchairs in all areas except the rest rooms. No smoking. From the main stretch of Highland Avenue that slices *through downtown, turn east at Warren Street near the railroad station and jog over 1 block. There's a small public parking lot near the theater.*

One look at this place and you'll think you've stepped through a time warp. The three-story brick building has rounded marble arches carved with leafy scrollwork, and the glowing marquee looks just as it did in 1928, when the Tivoli opened on Christmas Day. Four thousand people lined up to buy tickets for this 1,000-seat theater, reportedly the second cinema in the United States designed and built for "talking movies." Buy your tickets, get your popcorn, and then walk across the burgundy-patterned carpeting through the lavishly appointed lobby, with its chandeliers, tall potted palms (fake but realistic looking), wing chairs, and golden-framed wall mirror through one of *five* entry doors to the cavernous auditorium. The interior walls and ceiling are painted in shades of sky blue and burgundy with gilded ornate trim. Lamps in wrought-iron sconces provide gentle lighting, and a red-lit dome draws your eyes upward in the center of the theater. There are 29 long, long rows of seats, and the floor slants downward so that the views are fairly unobstructed (although an adult sitting one row in front of a child probably will block the kid's view). There are a couple of modern touches: plastic cup holders added behind each row of seats and a square clock with illuminated dial placed over the exit sign on one side. Reasonably priced concessions are pretty basic—popcorn, sodas, and candy—and include one free refill. The rest rooms, built in the days before accessibility was the law, each have one step up to get inside, and the women's then has a full flight of stairs down to the stalls. The staff say that there are plans to eventually build a stepless rest room on the main floor and to add a fourplex of new screens in place of the current adjacent parking lot and build a new parking lot underground, but nothing definite has been determined. None of that would alter the main theater, which is protected by its historic landmark status.

TIVOLI LANES BOWL (age 4 and up)

938 Warren Avenue, Downers Grove 60515; (630) 969–0660. Hours vary; call for open bowling hours and rates. Cost is $1.75 per game per person, all ages, and $1.75 for shoes. The bowling alley is around the corner from the Tivoli Theatre, but its basement location down a narrow flight of stairs makes it inaccessible for wheelchairs. Smoking is allowed.

This cozy little alley has just 12 lanes, but automated scoring on video screens has brought the place into the modern era. The small snack bar has cold drinks and munchies.

DOWNERS GROVE ICE ARENA (age 5 and up)

5501 Walnut Avenue, Downers Grove 60515; (630) 971–3780. Open year-round; public skating hours vary. Admission costs $4 per person, all ages. Skate rental costs $2 per person. Internet: downersgroveicearena.com.

If you're looking for something different to do to escape summer heat, how about ice-skating? This indoor facility is open year-round, and while there may be a line out the door during winter, you and the kids may have the rink nearly to yourselves in summer. Just make sure you bring long pants, a sweatshirt, and maybe even gloves, because the temperature stays pretty cool to keep the ice frozen. Glide along to easy-listening music and imagine your favorite Olympic ice dancer.

Where to Eat

Downers Grove has tons of restaurants and fast-food franchises. Here are but a select few; for more, contact the Visitors Bureau (see For More Information) or check the local yellow pages.

Joe's Crab Shack. *1461 Butterfield Road; (630) 960–2033.* Hours are 11 A.M. to 10 P.M. Sunday through Thursday and 11 A.M. to 11 P.M. Friday and Saturday. Smoking is allowed, including—unfortunately—cigars. Opened in 1996, Joe is giving nearby Red Lobster a run for the money. This funky restaurant has a casual atmosphere. The young waitstaff wear bright tie-dyed T-shirts, and strings of multicolored lights brighten the kitschy interior. But the real draw for families is the outdoor porch area with its adjacent sand playground. Come in summer and sit out here, where Mom and Dad will have a chance to linger over coffee and adult conversation while the kids have a blast playing. The menu features crab, of course, and other standard seafood dishes plus chicken and steaks. Entrees on the kids' menu cost about $3, including a drink and a dish of ice cream, and feature both seafood and nonseafood items, such as tasty fried chicken "fingers." The breading for all the fried dishes is a bit on the spicy side, so you may need extra ice water. Adults may enjoy the wide selection of beers to accompany their meal. $$

KC Masterpiece. *1400 Butterfield Road; (630) 889–1999.* Hours are 11 A.M. to 10 P.M. Monday through Thursday, 11 A.M. to 11 P.M. Friday and Saturday, and 11 A.M. to 9:30 P.M. Sunday. Maybe you've seen the sauce in a bottle on the supermarket shelf, but it won't quite duplicate the flavor of the ribs served at its namesake restaurant—unless you have a big smoker at home to cook them the same way. While pork ribs are the specialty, you can also get the tasty sauce on chicken or beef or in a shredded pork sandwich. $

Red Lobster. *3001 Finley Road, at Butterfield Road; (630) 515–0565.* Open from 11 A.M. to 10 P.M. Sunday through Thursday and 11 A.M. to 11 P.M. Friday and Saturday. See Restaurant Appendix for description. $$

Old Country Buffet. *1410 75th Street; (630) 810–0154.* Hours are 11 A.M. to 8:30 P.M. Monday through Thursday, 11 A.M. to 9:30 P.M. Friday, 8 A.M. to 9:30 P.M. Saturday, and 8 A.M. to 8:30 P.M. Sunday. See Restaurant Appendix for description. $

Olive Garden. *1211 Butterfield Road; (630) 852–4224.* Hours are 11 A.M. to 10 P.M. Sunday through Thursday and 11 A.M. to 11 P.M. Friday and Saturday. See Restaurant Appendix for description. $

Portillo's. *1500 Butterfield Road; (630) 495–9033.* Hours are 10:30 A.M. to 10:30 P.M. Monday through Thursday, 10:30 A.M. to 11 P.M. Friday and Saturday, and 10:30 A.M. to 9:30 P.M. Sunday. See Restaurant Appendix for description. $

Where to Stay

Comfort Inn of Downers Grove. *3010 Finley Road, off Butterfield Road; (630) 515–1500 or (800) 228–5150.* This property has 121 rooms with cable TV. Amenities include an outdoor heated pool, an indoor whirlpool, and a sundeck. Restaurants nearby. Room rates include continental breakfast buffet. No pets. $$$

Doubletree Suites. *2111 Butterfield Road; (630) 971–2000.* This is an all-suite hotel with 251 rooms. Amenities include indoor heated pool, whirlpool, sauna, and fitness center. The room rate includes full American breakfast. $$$$

Holiday Inn Express. *3031 Finley Road; (630) 810–0059 or (800) 465–4329.* This three-story property has 123 rooms with cable TV and free in-room movies. No pool. The room rate includes continental breakfast buffet. $$$

Red Roof Inn. *1113 Butterfield Road; (630) 963–4205 or (800) 843–7663.* Rooms have cable TV and free in-room movies. No pool. Pets allowed. Restaurants nearby. $$

For More Information

Downers Grove Visitors Bureau, *5202 Washington Street, Suite 2, Downers Grove 60515-4776; (630) 434–5921 or (800) 934–0615. Internet: www.vil.downers-grove.il.us.*

Lisle

Population: 19,512. If you visit Lisle during late June and early July, look up—it's the Eyes to the Skies Festival of hot air balloons. The four-day event at Lisle Community Park features a balloon launch at six o'clock each morning, with the rest of the festival events starting at noon. If you're not an early riser, you can catch a second launch at six o'clock in the evening on three of the four days. Games and contests, arts and crafts, carnival rides, food booths, and musical performances are all part of the festival. Admission costs $7 a day for anyone age 13 or older; a four-day pass costs $14. Young people age 12 or younger get in **Free**. Parking also is free, with free shuttle buses providing transportation from the more remote lots. For the current year's schedule of events, call (800) 733-9811.

MORTON ARBORETUM (all ages)

4100 Route 53, Lisle 60532; (630) 719–2400. Off Illinois Highway 53 near I–88. Grounds are open year-round from 7 A.M. to dusk daily. Admission costs $7 per car ($3 on Wednesday). Internet: www.mortonarb.org.

Here is a lovely place to commune with nature. It's been around since 1922, plenty of time for some of the trees to get nice and big. The trees and other woody plants—more than 3,000 kinds in all—cover the 1,500-acre tract, and 25 miles of hiking trails wind throughout. Some specially maintained areas, such as a field of daffodils, will have you waxing poetic. Not everything here is natural, however—the arboretum has a visitor center with rest rooms, a restaurant, and a gift shop. During summer you can ride an open-air tram for a tour of the arboretum. Buy your $3-per-person tickets at the visitor center and pick up the tram in the main parking lot. It departs at 10:45 A.M., noon, and 1:15 and 2:30 P.M. daily. The ride takes 50 to 60 minutes and covers about 8 miles.

LISLE DEPOT MUSEUM (all ages)

919 Burlington Avenue, Lisle 60532; (630) 968–0499. Two blocks south of Ogden Avenue and 2 blocks east of Main Street. Hours are 1 to 4 P.M. Tuesday through Thursday and Sunday. Admission is **Free**.

This 1874 train station was built in the Federal style of architecture. It was a working station for 104 years, but now it houses a museum with ticket office, waiting room, station master's living quarters, and exhibits on Lisle's history. Just west of the depot is the Netzley-Yender farmhouse, which has been restored to show what rural life in 1850 was like.

SEA LION AQUATIC CENTER (all ages)

1825 Short Street, Lisle 60532; (630) 964–3410. Open from noon to 5:30 P.M. and 6:30 to 9 P.M. Monday through Thursday and noon to 5:30 P.M. and 6:30 to 10 P.M. Friday through Sunday. Nonresident admission costs $13 during the day or $9 at night for anyone age 4 or older. Children age 3 or younger always get in free.

The Sea Lion Aquatic Center has four drop slides, which launch swimmers into the air before they splash into the water. The pool here has zero-depth entry, and there's a separate tot pool with kiddie slide. The sand volleyball court appeals to teens, and an adult deck with hot tubs soothes weary parents. There is a concession area, too.

LISLE LANES (age 4 and up)

4920 Lincoln Avenue, Lisle 60532; (630) 968–1300. On Illinois Highway 53 just south of Ogden Avenue. Hours are noon to 11 P.M. Sunday through Thursday and noon to midnight Friday and Saturday. Bumper bowling costs $14 an hour for the lane. The price for regular bowling is $2.85 a line, but Lisle Lanes runs a lot of discounted specials, such as the summer special of $1.75 Sunday through Thursday and $2.25 Friday and Saturday. Cost for shoes is $2.25 at all times.

Kids can enjoy bumper bowling (with long inner tubes placed in the gutter so that the ball stays in the lane) at Lisle Lanes, and the charge is for the lane, not per person, so it's a good value for a family group or maybe a couple of moms with their kids. You should call ahead so they can get the bumpers set up for your arrival. The alley has 32 lanes. Concessions are available.

Where to Eat

Country House. *6460 College Road; (630) 983–0545.* Open from 11 A.M. to 10 P.M. Monday through Thursday, 11 A.M. to 11 P.M. Friday and Saturday, and noon to 10 P.M. Sunday. Serving lunch and dinner. The adult menu features steaks, pork chops, burgers, barbecue beef sandwiches, soups, and salads. Children's menu entrees are in the $2.50 to $3.75 range and include burgers, chicken nuggets, spaghetti, and fish and chips. $

Nancy's Pizzeria. *Ogden Avenue, between Naper Boulevard and Yackley Road; (630) 428–9900.* Open from 4 to 10 P.M. Monday through Thursday, 4 to 11 P.M. Friday and Saturday, and 4 to 9 P.M. Sunday. Carryout and delivery only. See Restaurant Appendix for description. $

Where to Stay

Lisle isn't the place to look for a cheap motel. All four of its major hotels are at the deluxe end of the lodging spectrum, so give up and indulge yourselves if you want to stay overnight in this town.

Radisson Hotel. *3000 Warrenville Road; (630) 505–1000 or (800) 333–3333.* This luxury hotel has 242 rooms. The huge spa and fitness center includes an indoor pool, whirlpool, and racquetball court. The on-site restaurant is in a seven-story atrium. $$$$

For More Information

Lisle Convention & Visitors Bureau,
4756 Main Street, Lisle 60532; (800) 733–9811.

Naperville

Population: 85,351. Naperville is a fairly convenient and hospitable place to stay overnight. It is easily accessible off Interstate 88, which links up farther east with north-south thoroughfares such as Interstate 355 and Interstate 294, eventually merging into Interstate 290, heading east into Chicago. The year 2000 was a busy one in Naperville. On July 4, the city dedicated its new Millennium Carillon at the base of Rotary Hill by the Riverwalk. The tower stands 155 feet high and houses 72 bells. Also in 2000, the DuPage County Children's Museum broke ground for a new Naperville facility. Construction is expected to be completed in 2001.

NAPER SETTLEMENT MUSEUM VILLAGE (all ages)

523 South Webster Street, Naperville 60540; (630) 420–6010. Museum village is open from April through October. Hours are 10 A.M. to 4 P.M. Tuesday through Saturday and 1 to 4 P.M. Sunday. Admission costs $6.50 for adults age 18 through 61, $5.50 for seniors age 62 or older, and $4 for kids ages 4 through 17. Children age 3 or younger get in free. Internet: www.napersettlement.org.

Enjoy a bit of living history at the Naper Settlement Museum Village. This 12-acre site contains 25 historic homes, businesses, and public buildings, all peopled by costumed interpreters portraying life during the period from 1831 to 1900. Children may be able to get a hands-on feel for the ways things used to be done by writing with a quill pen, churning butter, or carrying buckets of water with a yoke. Special events include Civil War Days in May and Christmas Memories in December.

GREAT ODYSSEY FAMILY FUN CENTER (age 2 and up)

1515 West Aurora Avenue, Naperville 60540; (630) 355–7622. Hours are 10 A.M. to midnight Sunday through Thursday and 10 A.M. to 2 A.M. Friday and Saturday. Pay $1 to $1.50 per ride or buy an all-day pass for unlimited rides at a cost of $7.95 Monday through Friday or $8.95 Saturday and Sunday. Regular bowling costs $3 for anyone age 18 or older and $2.25 for young people age 17 or younger; Cosmic Bowling costs $4.49 per person, all ages. Shoe rental costs $2.79. Fun Playhouse costs $3.

Billed as the largest indoor amusement center in Illinois, this spacious complex features a full-size classic carousel and four other rides. Younger kids also can frolic in the Fun Playhouse, with its tubes, slides, and ball pits. There's an arcade with more than 200 video games, most just a quarter. The center has 40 lanes of bowling, and you can try the Cosmic Bowling here at selected times. That's when you bowl by black light and the balls and pins glow, while lively music and flashing lights jazz up the atmosphere.

A Cool Pool The Bolingbrook Aquatic Center actually has two pools to offer year-round swimming. The indoor pool has a zero-depth end with spraying fountains and a section of lap lanes. The larger outdoor pool has a zero-depth end, two twisting water slides (one for inner tubes), and a kids' Sprayground with waterfall. The center is at 200 South Lindsey Lane, near Naperville Road. Hours are noon to 8 P.M. Monday through Saturday and noon to 6 P.M. Sunday. Nonresident admission costs $7 per person age 3 or older; children age 2 or younger get in free. Concessions are available.

ALL SEASONS ICE ARENA (age 5 and up)

31W330 North Aurora Road, Naperville 60563; (630) 851–0755. Family skate is from 3:30 to 5 P.M. Sunday. Public skate sessions are from 11:30 A.M. to 1 P.M. Monday through Thursday, 9 to 10:30 P.M. Friday, and 3:30 to 5 P.M. and 8:30 to 10 P.M. Saturday. Admission costs $4.50 for anyone age 13 or older and $3.50 for kids age 12 or younger. Skate rental costs $2.50.

This indoor facility is open year-round. Two ice-skating rinks offer public or family skating sessions every day. Even if it's a hot summer day, you'll want to bring along a sweatshirt to ward off the chill of the ice.

Where to Eat

Connie's Pizza. *1170 Iroquois Drive; (630) 357–8807.* Hours are 11 A.M. to 10 P.M. Monday through Thursday, 11 A.M. to 11 P.M. Friday and Saturday, and noon to 10 P.M. Sunday. Some people swear that this chewy, cheesy pizza is the best in Chicagoland. $

Lou Malnati's Pizzeria. *131 West Jefferson, downtown; (630) 717–0700.* Hours are 11 A.M. to 11 P.M. Monday through Thursday, 11 A.M. to midnight Friday and Saturday, and noon to 10 P.M. Sunday. Another local favorite. $

Bacino's. *1504 Naperville Road (at Ogden Avenue); (630) 505–0600.* Hours are 11 A.M. to 10 P.M. Monday through Thursday, 11 A.M. to midnight Friday, noon to midnight Saturday, and 3 to 10 P.M.

Sunday. Here you can get four kinds of pizza: flat-crust, deep-dish, stuffed, and wood-fired oven "gourmet." $

Olive Garden. *620 Route 59; (630) 355–2818.* Hours are 11 A.M. to 10 P.M. Sunday through Thursday and 11 A.M. to 11 P.M. Friday and Saturday. See Restaurant Appendix for description. $$

Skating Away at Seven Bridges The suburb of Woodridge has one of the largest ice-skating facilities in the United States, with three rinks: one Olympic, one collegiate, and one conforming to National Hockey League (NHL) standards. Seven Bridges Ice Arena prides itself on its computerized control system that keeps the air fresh (of course, smoking is not allowed) and the ice the right temperature for the best possible skating experience. To keep yourself in good shape off the ice as well, there's a fitness center staffed with professional trainers who can help you work out. There's also a glass-enclosed children's playroom. Open skating times vary. Public sessions cost $6.00 for anyone age 12 or older and $5.00 for kids age 11 or younger. Skate rental costs $2 per person, all ages. Call (630) 271–4423 for the current open-ice times. The arena is on Double Eagle Drive, north off Hobson Road west of Highway 53. Internet: www.sevenbridgesicearena.com.

Where to Stay

Courtyard by Marriott. *1155 East Diehl Road; (630) 505–0550 or (800) 321–2211.* The two-story inn has 147 spacious rooms with cable TV. Amenities include indoor swimming pool, whirlpool, and minigym with exercise equipment. This chain actually is geared toward business travelers, but you often can get a good rate for a Friday or Saturday night when most of them have gone home for the weekend. $$$

Holiday Inn Select. *1801 Naper Boulevard; (630) 505–4900 or (800) 465–4329.* This seven-story hotel has 295 rooms with coffeemaker, hair dryer, and iron and ironing board. Amenities include indoor swimming pool, fitness center, and game room. $$$$

Sleep Inn. *1831 West Diehl Road; (630) 778–5900 or (800) 753–3746.* This basic chain property has 69 comfortable rooms but few amenities; no swimming pool. The room rate does include continental breakfast. $$

For More Information

Naperville Area Chamber of Commerce, *9 West Jackson Street, Naperville 60566; (630) 355–4141.*

Megamovie Mania In the late 1990s there was an explosion of megamovie complexes in the Chicago suburbs. These huge theaters encompass more than a dozen screens—over two dozen, in some cases—and feature a new concept in comfort: *stadium seating.* What that means is that the floor is stair-stepped so that each row of seats is several feet higher than the one in front of it, allowing clear sight lines looking down and across at the large screen. Cup holders in the armrests prevent spillage of soda pop kicked over on the floor. Some theaters also have *love seats,* which are sofalike seats wide enough for two people to sit together with no armrest between them. Less obvious at first glance are the technical improvements in the sound and projection systems, but you'll notice those once the film starts. Most chain theaters in the Chicago metro area are now hooked into a telephone system using the local area code and the number 444–FILM, or 444–3456. By punching in a code for the theater you want, you can hear a recorded listing of current show titles and times and can even buy the tickets over the phone with a credit card. Theater locations and show times also are published in area newspapers.

General Cinema. *Chain includes Yorktown 18, Randhurst 16, Northbrook Court 14, and City North 14. Internet: www.generalcinema.com.* The crème de la crème of the Chicago area's megamovie complexes is the Yorktown Cinema in Lombard. Opened in March 1998, it has a cool blue-green exterior with eye-pleasing geometric designs. The indoor front lobby has nine ticket windows, including one that's low enough for people in wheelchairs to approach comfortably, so the lines never get too awful and you don't have to stand outside in the elements to wait. Yorktown shows first-run films, but all moviegoers get the discounted child ticket price of $5.75 before 6 P.M. After 6 P.M. adults pay $8.75. Inside, the theaters branch off down two rectangular corridors from the central concession area. The complex has a total of 18 screens, all with stadium seating plus several rows of regular theater seats on a gently sloping floor in front. There are spaces for moviegoers in wheelchairs. The staff here are all friendly, from those who tear tickets and direct you to your cinema to those who serve up your treats. Concession prices are $2.50 to $3.50 for Pepsi, $2.75 to $5.25 for popcorn (which you yourself squirt "buttery topping" on to suit your own taste), and $2 to $4.25 for pretzels, nachos, candy, ice cream, hot dogs, or Uno pizza. A gourmet shop off to one side also offers Starbucks coffees and pastries. There are ample rest rooms on either side, so an emergency potty run won't take long. There are changing tables in the women's rest room. If you arrive early, you can while away the wait in the balcony arcade in the central concession area. It has a variety of video games and even a pinball machine. Yorktown also has one deluxe theater that's designed more for impressing a date than accommodating a family. It shows a first-run film, usually a PG-13 or R-rated one, in a fancy room with pairs of tan leather seats that have little tables next to them; a restaurant adjoining serves gourmet food and alcoholic beverages that you can bring in to enjoy while the film rolls. Valet parking is included in the $15 ticket price.

AMC. *The Cantera 30 and Barrington 30 represent this chain. Internet: www.amctheatres.com.* These two are by far the biggest megaplexes in Chicagoland. Both opened in March 1998 and each can seat more than 6,000 people at one time. Once you make the long trek across the expansive parking lot, the building looks like a mall—and that's kind of what it is, a movie mall. As at Yorktown, the box offices are indoors. Each AMC complex has two banks of nine-window ticket booths. Ticket prices are $5.50 for anyone age 13 or older before 6 P.M. (or $4.50 for specially designated late-afternoon "twilight" shows) and $8.50 after 6 P.M. Children age 12 or younger pay $4.50 at all times. All 30 theaters have stadium seating and love seats. Larger theaters are clustered around a central concession area decorated in funky futuristic neon lighting. The other theaters are located along two long hallways extending in either direction, each with its own concession counter at the end. The fare includes soft drinks, popcorn, candy, nachos, ice cream, and hot dogs, all in the $2 to $3 range, with a few candies under a dollar. You butter your own popcorn here, too. Arcade games are sprinkled along these aisles as well. Rest rooms are adequate in both placement and stall capacity, and there is a changing table in the wheelchair-accessible stall.

Cinemark Theatres. *Tinseltown USA in North Aurora and Cinemark Theatres in Melrose Park and Woodridge represent this chain. Internet: www.cinemark.com.* This chain jumped into the Chicagoland megaplex market in September 1998. Tinseltown USA is just off I–88 at Illinois Highway 31 to the south; from the highway, the building is somewhat hidden behind a giant hardware store. The complex is set back from the street, with a massive parking lot in front. The decor is supposed to be art deco, but the exterior looks more like a funky factory in hues of red, purple, and lime green, with three tall "smokestacks" behind the marquee. The complex is accessible for wheelchairs. Inside the front doors is a lobby with three ticket booths, each with several windows. All tickets cost $4.50 before 6 P.M.., except the first show of the day Monday through Friday, which is only $3.50; after 6 P.M. the adult price rises to $6.75. All 17 of Tinseltown's theaters have stadium seating with high-back rocking chairs and cup holders in the armrests, plus several regular rows of seats in front. Although one entrance to each theater comes in at the bottom of the stadium seating section, which is the standard design, Tinseltown adds a back stairway that emerges at the top of the section so that patrons can walk down from behind instead of across and up, passing in front of others already seated. The theaters branch off down two corridors from a central area with a long concession counter; smaller concession counters are at the end of either corridor. TV monitors above the concession counters play movie previews, which are interesting but a bit too loud, making it hard for the servers and the customers to hear one another. Fare includes popcorn, candy, soft drinks, and hot dogs, all generally in the $2 to $4 range. Rest rooms are ample and clean, although they lack changing tables. Outside the rest rooms, drinking fountains on the wall are placed at three different heights to accommodate adults, children, and people in wheelchairs. The art deco motif is played out much more successfully inside the building. Each theater has a portrait of a legendary Hollywood movie star at its entrance, and other framed pictures decorate the central area.

Marcus Cinemas. *This chain includes multiplexes in Addison, Gurnee, Orland Park, and Western Heights. Internet: www. showtimes.hollywood.com.* All theaters in these complexes have stadium seating, and although the ticket and concession stations are not as large as some others, these are still generally nice theaters. The one in Addison has an art deco lobby in soothing shades of salmon, light green, and purple, and the walls are adorned with "stuffed" cloth murals of scenes from *Raiders of the Lost Ark, Star Wars,* and *Superman.* It also has an IMAX theater. The bargain matinee price of $5.50 is offered for all shows before 5:30 P.M. After 5:30 P.M. adults pay $8. IMAX costs more.

Regal Cinema. *The Lincolnshire 20 represents this chain.* This theater opened in 1998. It includes an IMAX theater on one side and a 20-screen regular movie theater complex on the other; enter both through the doors in front. The IMAX theater has a giant curved screen that surrounds viewers and makes them feel a part of the action; recent films have featured mountain climbing, deep-sea diving, and the basketball heroics of Michael Jordan. The regular theaters all have stadium seating in comfortable seats with cup holders. Concessions are available in the main lobby and at the far end. Rest rooms are adequate in both location and capacity. Tickets cost $4.75 for all shows before 6 P.M. Adults pay $8.50 after 6 P.M.

Across the DuPage County borderline in the west are the Cook County communities of Melrose Park and Brookfield, both of which have key family attractions—a longtime children's amusement park and the state's biggest zoo.

Melrose Park

Population: 20,859. Illinois Highway 64, also known as North Avenue, slices right through Melrose Park. The town's major family attraction is along this thoroughfare.

KIDDIELAND (ages 2–10)

8400 West North Avenue, Melrose Park 60160; (708) 343–8000. At the corner of North and First Avenues. Opens in mid-April and closes at the end of October. Peak summer hours are 10:30 A.M. to 10 P.M. daily. Hours are more restricted earlier and later in the season; call ahead to check for the day you want to visit. Admission before 6 P.M. costs $17.50 for anyone age 6 through 60; after 6 P.M. the rate drops to $14.50. For kids age 3 through 5, the respective rates are $14.50 and $11.50. Adults age 61 or older pay $10.50 anytime. Children age 2 or younger are admitted free. Stroller rental is available for $5. Internet: www.kiddieland.com.

This old-fashioned amusement park has been around for years and remains a favorite for many Chicago-area children. The park is situated at the corner of a busy intersection, and heavy traffic whizzes by beyond the gates, but no one notices that inside. The small scale makes Kiddieland especially inviting for little kids in the 3-to-6 age range, and most kiddie rides are reserved for children who are no taller than 4 feet, 6 inches. Aside from the choo-choo train, most of the kiddie rides are the vehicular kind that go round and round. The little boats even float atop a few inches of real water. There are rides with cars, helicopters, airplanes, and flying saucers. The Mushroom is a tame, pint-size Scrambler, and the tiny Ferris wheel has six cages, so there's no chance of falling out. The Lava Run is a child-size go-kart track, and the Volcano play area next to it has a rope to climb and a slide to slip down. The roller coaster is the traditional variety—it runs on a double-rail track in a white wooden framework—just up and down, no loop-de-loops. The most charming of the children's rides, however, is the German carousel. Scenes from Grimm's fairy tales are painted along the top outer panels, and painted figurines of musicians stand in the center. Kids sit on motorcycles or in little cars, a bus, or a fire truck. One area of the park has rides for bigger people, such as a full-size carousel, a regular Ferris wheel, bumper cars, a Tilt-A-Whirl, a Scrambler, and a Galleon. An arcade features Skeeball, pinball, video games, and skill games. Another section has two water rides. The Log Jammer flume ride floats you gently along, but watch out when you come to the bridge. Someone standing on the bridge can put a token into a machine and trigger water jets that squirt the riders below. The Pipeline is billed as "a high speed water coaster full of quick turns and drops, in the dark," and that pretty well describes it. While it resembles the sort of twisting water slide you see at many suburban swimming pools, it is totally enclosed and indeed very dark. Pairs of riders zip through on a yellow inflated raft, sliding along a long, open flume at the end. You do get rather wet on this ride, so save it for last if you don't want to walk around the rest of the park soaked. The surface at Kiddieland is all asphalt, so rolling along in a stroller or wheelchair is easy. A centrally located brick building contains rest rooms, a first aid station, and concessions. Both the women's and men's rest rooms have a diaper-changing table. Concessions include soft drinks and an assortment of snacks—the cotton candy is especially flavorful—plus hot dogs and pizza. Prices are better than at most amusement centers. Compared to Six Flags Great America or to carnivals where you pay by the ride, Kiddieland offers good value for the money. If you come around Halloween, you'll find a fairly mild haunted house and a place for hayrides in a horse-drawn wagon, plus seasonal food like brats, corn on the cob, and caramel apples.

Where to Eat

Chuck E. Cheese's. *1314 North Avenue; (708) 343–1224.* Hours are 10 A.M. to 10 P.M. Sunday through Thursday and 10 A.M. to 11 P.M. Friday and Saturday. See Restaurant Appendix for description. $

Where to Stay

Days Inn. *1900 North Mannheim Road; (708) 681–3100 or (800) 325–2525.* This no-frills budget property has 119 rooms with cable TV but not much else; no swimming pool. Room rate includes breakfast. $$

For More Information

Melrose Park Chamber of Commerce, *1718 West Lake Street, Melrose Park 60160; (708) 338–1007.*

Goin' to the Zoo, Zoo, Zoo Brookfield Zoo is the largest zoo in Illinois and a premier Chicago-area attraction where you can easily pass an entire day. You'll find it at First Avenue and Thirty-first Street in the western suburb of Brookfield; (708) 485–0263. Internet: www.brookfield-zoo.mus.il.us. The closest major thoroughfare is U.S. Highway 34 (Ogden Avenue), but the zoo is accessible from Illinois Highway 38 (Roosevelt Road), Illinois Highway 43 (Harlem Avenue), U.S. Highway 45 (Mannheim Road), and I–55 and I–290. Open year-round, the zoo has both indoor and outdoor animal exhibit areas. Hours are 9:30 A.M. to 6 P.M. daily from Memorial Day weekend through Labor Day and 10:00 A.M. to 5 P.M. daily the rest of the year. Closing time is extended to 9 P.M. Saturday and Sunday from mid-June through July. Adult admission costs $7 for anyone age 12 through 64, and the price is $3.50 for kids age 3 through 11 and senior citizens age 65 or older. Admission is Free on Tuesday and Thursday from October through March. Children age 2 or younger always get in free. The $4-per-car parking fee is the same every day. There are additional costs for certain optional amenities inside the zoo, so pay heed to the next few paragraphs and compute your own family tally.

Wide, paved avenues throughout the zoo accommodate both foot and wheeled traffic. If your kids are small enough to fit in a stroller, bring it along—even peppy young grade-schoolers may wear out from the amount of walking needed to cover the expansive but beautiful grounds (flower beds and a central fountain are among the touches that add aesthetic appeal). You can rent a stroller for $5, plus a refundable $5 deposit. A little red wagon (holds two or three small children) or an adult pushchair rents for $6, plus a refundable $4 deposit. You can also relieve your feet by hopping aboard the Motor Safari open-air tram; a ride costs $2.50 for adults and $1.50 for kids and seniors.

The wee ones will want to visit the children's zoo, where they can mingle with the goats, pet an exotic animal held by a zoo handler, or watch a cow or goat being milked. Small mammals, birds, and farm animals are the dominant creatures here. Admission to the children's zoo costs $1 for adults and 50 cents for kids and seniors.

Another premium attraction is the entertaining dolphin show, which costs $2.50 for adults and $2 for kids and seniors. Hour-long shows are scheduled from late morning through midafternoon; check for exact times. Outdoor pools nearby contain seals, sea lions, and walruses.

Concession and souvenir stands are scattered throughout the zoo grounds. The former provide anything from an ice-cream treat to a complete meal, while the latter range from cheap kitsch to finely crafted artworks with animal motifs.

Finally, you'd better budget a few extra dollars for the irresistible Mold-O-Rama figurines. The machines that press these animal figures out of hot plastic are located throughout the zoo (the dolphin one is by the Dolphin House, the koala by the Australia House, and so on) and cost $1 each. Let each child pick one favorite animal and mold it.

So what is free here? About 2,500 animals in settings designed to resemble their natural habitats. Outdoor exhibit areas for elephants, bears, apes, and big cats are family favorites. In the Fragile Desert building near the big cats, a glass exhibit wall extends all the way to the floor to afford a full view of the playful meerkats, chasing one another around or piling into a heap as if in a scrum. There are plenty of creepy-crawlies in the Reptile House, and you'll have a g'day waltzing through the Australia House. The Habitat Africa! area has a watering hole for giraffes, zebras, and antelope of the savanna. The huge Tropic World building contains three spacious rooms, each representing a tropical rain forest of South America, Asia, and Africa and containing native plants and animals. Spanish moss hangs from the ceiling in the building housing The Swamp, home of some river otters that are a favorite of families. For the Swamp's "boat tour," you sit in a real boat facing a screen that plays a three-minute video of the American cypress swamp of the southern United States. Photographs and music enhance the atmosphere. The Living Coast has some really nifty things to see. The moon jellies are fascinating; these gelatinous white globules float suspended in water like blobs in a lava lamp. Humboldt penguins and brown pelicans play in their habitat area. And then there's "the wave." In "Quest to Save the Earth," visitors walk along a life-size game board and have to choose between the easier "throwaway society" approach or the more responsible environmental awareness in actions that will preserve the planet for all its life forms. The newest exhibit area, Salt Creek Wilderness, is a marshland environment.

Brookfield Zoo also has a free children's playground area with swings, slides, and climbing equipment in case your kids get tired of watching the animals have all the fun. There are picnic tables here, too, where you can eat your own home-packed lunch (a good way to economize). Rest rooms are scattered throughout the zoo, so you shouldn't have to run too far if your toddler announces, "I have to go potty!"

Southern communities in Will and suburban Cook Counties are represented by the **Chicago Southland Convention & Visitors Bureau,** 2304 173rd Street, Lansing 60438; (708) 895-8200 or (888) 895-8233. Internet: www.Lincolnnet.net/Chicago-Southland-CVB.

Another source of regional information is the **Heritage Corridor Visitors Bureau,** 8695 Archer Avenue, Willow Springs 60480; (708) 839-1322.

Alsip

Population: 18,227. Interstate 294 runs through this southern suburb that borders the South Side of Chicago.

FUN TIME SQUARE (age 4 and up)

11901 South Cicero Avenue, Alsip 60658; (708) 388–3500. Opens in April and closes in September. Summer hours are 10 A.M. to midnight Sunday through Thursday and 10 A.M. to 1 A.M. Friday and Saturday. A round of miniature golf costs $3 for anyone age 11 or older and $2.50 for kids age 10 or younger. Go-karts and bumper boats each cost $3.50 for a four-minute ride. Water tag and laser tag each cost $2.50 for four minutes of play. Batting cages give 15 pitches for 75 cents, and video games take both quarters and tokens.

This outdoor facility has plenty of things to keep a family busy for a few hours. Play a round or two on the 18-hole miniature golf course, and then take a ride on the bumper boats or go-karts, whee! If your kids play baseball or softball, they can get in some batting practice. Water tag is offered during the day and laser tag at night.

Where to Eat

Bakers Square. *4839 West 111th Street; (708) 636–0212.* Hours are 7 A.M. to 11 P.M. Sunday through Thursday and 7 A.M. to midnight Friday and Saturday. See Restaurant Appendix for description. $

Where to Stay

Baymont Inn. *12801 South Cicero; (708) 597–3900.* This hotel has 102 comfortable rooms but no swimming pool. Pets are allowed. Room rate includes breakfast. $$

For More Information

Alsip Chamber of Commerce,
12159 Pulaski Road, Alsip 60658;
(708) 597–2668.

Bronzeville Children's Museum is dedicated to teaching kids ages 3 through 11 about the heritage and contributions of African-Americans. Exhibits change periodically. One that opened in 2000, *Amazing Dinosaurs and Africa's First Humans,* included a brief talk by a staffer, a hands-on puppet-making activity, and a short film. The museum is in the lower level of Evergreen Plaza shopping center, at 95th Street and Western Avenue in Evergreen Park. Hours are 10 A.M. to 5 P.M. Tuesday through Saturday; closed Sunday and Monday. Admission costs $3 for adults and $2 for anyone age 17 or younger. Call (708) 636–9504 for further information.

Crestwood

Population: 10,823. This southern Cook County suburb lies to the southwest of Alsip. There are two popular family attractions here.

HOLLYWOOD PARK (all ages)

51 Cal Sag Road, Crestwood 60445; (708) 389–7275. At 131st Street, behind Target. Open year-round. Summer hours are 10 A.M. to midnight daily. During the school year the hours are 11:30 A.M. to 10 P.M. Monday through Thursday, 11:30 A.M. to midnight Friday, 10 A.M. to midnight Saturday, and 10 A.M. to 10 P.M. Sunday. Prices for miniature golf are $4 for anyone age 11 or older and $3 for kids age 5 through 10; children age 4 or younger play free. Playland admission costs $3 for kids age 12 or younger, with accompanying parents free. Laser tag costs $3 for five minutes. The FX Simulator costs $2 per ride. Arcade tokens are four for $1.

Indoor and outdoor recreational activities are available at Hollywood Park. Kids age 10 or younger enjoy Playland. This indoor playroom has tunnels, ball pits, and slides. Kids must wear socks, and the park will sell you some if they come without. Also indoors are a large game room and the Hollywood Cafe & Pizzeria, where you'll find a robotic talking tree. The FX Simulator ride surrounds you with projected pictures that create the illusion of motion. Grade-schoolers and teens love it, but it may be a bit too intense for tiny tots. Outdoors you can enjoy laser tag or play miniature golf on one of two 18-hole courses. This place hosts a lot of birthday parties, so don't expect to have it all to yourself.

COOK COUNTY CHEETAHS (all ages)

Games are played at Hawkinson Ford Field, 14100 South Kenton, Crestwood 60445; (708) 489–2255. Season runs from June through August. Most games are in the early evening. Ticket prices are $7 for lower deck and $6 for upper deck. Regular box office hours are 9 A.M. to 5:30 P.M. Monday through Friday, with Saturday hours from 10 A.M. to 2 P.M. added during baseball season. Smoking is not allowed in the stands but seems pervasive anyway. Internet: www.gocheetahs.com.

The Cook County Cheetahs play minor-league baseball in the independent Frontier League. Their slogan is "Baseball the Way It Used to Be," which seems to mean low-frills. The field is located in an industrial area, and tall electrical towers stand watch beyond the ballpark along the first- and third-base lines. The stadium is a utilitarian tan-and-clay brick building with dark green seats, and the outfield scoreboard offers simply a line score of the game. Hawkinson Ford Field does have one neat thing many small parks lack, however—an upper deck. Red-shirted Cheetah mascot Lucky Chucky schmoozes with the crowd on both levels. Concessions are located at either end of the concourse, and there is a large area with long tables near the one on the first-base side. "Picnic parties" are offered that include unlimited soft drinks and beer for 90 minutes before the game. Unfortunately, this deal encourages some people to drink too much of the latter, making the overall atmosphere less family-friendly that at some other minor-league ballparks around the state. The entertainment between innings is also weak compared to other parks. Call ahead of time to see if guest announcer "Take Me Out Harry" will be featured, and if he is, pick another date. His attempt to impersonate Hall of Fame broadcaster Harry Caray will insult anyone who was his fan; he displays none of the real Harry's warmth, humor, or understanding of the game of baseball. His commentary can spoil an otherwise pleasant outing.

Where to Eat

IHOP. *Cal Sag Road and Cicero Avenue; (708) 824–1886.* Open 24 hours a day. See Restaurant Appendix for description. $

Portillo's. *Route 83 and Cicero Avenue; (708) 385–6400.* In the Rivercrest Center shopping plaza. Hours are 11 A.M. to 10:30 P.M. Sunday through Thursday and 11 A.M. to 11 P.M. Friday and Saturday. See Restaurant Appendix for description. $

Where to Stay

Hampton Inn. *13330 South Cicero Avenue; (708) 597–3330 or (800) 426–7866.* This 123-room property has a fitness center and an outdoor pool. Free shuttle transportation to and from Midway Airport is available. Pets are allowed. Room rate includes continental breakfast. $$$

For More Information

Village of Crestwood, *13840 Cicero Avenue, Crestwood 60445; (708) 371–4800.*

Tinley Park

Population: 37,121. Tinley Park is a southern suburb in Cook County, just north of the border with Will County. Illinois Highway 43 runs through the town, and U.S. Highways 6 and 45 skirt it to the north and west, respectively.

ODYSSEY FUN WORLD (all ages)

191st Street and Oak Park Avenue, Tinley Park 60477; (708) 429–3800. Hours are 10 A.M. to midnight daily, with the outdoor area opening an hour later and closing an hour earlier than the indoor. Exploration Adventure admission costs $5.95 for kids age 12 or younger, with accompanying parent admitted free. Laser tag costs $6. Go-karts, bumper boats, and miniature golf cost $6 per person each. Batting cage tokens cost $1 for 16 pitches. A $6.99 wristband covers unlimited kiddie rides in Kids' Adventure Park. Other wristband deals offer various combinations of attractions that allow unlimited use for a fixed price, ranging from $9.99 to $18.99.

Odyssey Fun World offers both indoor and outdoor family recreation. The huge indoor area covers more than an acre, with arcade games you can play to earn prize tickets for accumulation and redemption. Older kids may opt to play laser tag. Younger kids will want to check out the Exploration Adventure, a four-level "soft playland" with equipment to climb, jump in, go through, slide down—you name it. The children must wear socks to play here. The dining room features singing and dancing robotic characters and serves Connie's Pizza, a Chicagoland favorite. The outdoor recreation area covers more than a dozen acres. Choose from among bumper boats, go-karts, batting cages, and two 18-hole miniature golf courses, one of them ominously titled Whitewater Doom. There's a special Kids' Adventure Park section with rides for youngsters age 8 or younger.

TINLEY PARK ROLLER RINK (age 5 and up)

17658 Oak Park Avenue, Tinley Park 60477; (708) 532–4021. Hours and rates are as follows: Wednesday from noon to 3 P.M., $4 admission plus $2 skate rental; Saturday Family Night from 8 to 11 P.M., $6 with or without skate rental; Saturday and Sunday from noon to 4 P.M., $4 plus $2 skate rental. Schedule and prices are subject to change; call ahead to check.

Another place for family fun in this suburb is the Tinley Park Roller Rink. You can bring your own skates or Rollerblades or rent them there.

CENTENNIAL LANES (age 4 and up)

159th Street and South Harlem Avenue, Tinley Park 60477; (708) 633–0500. Hours are 9 A.M. to midnight Tuesday through Thursday, noon to midnight Monday and Friday, and 6 P.M. to midnight Saturday; closed Sunday. Bumper bowling costs $1.25 per person, all ages, before 5 P.M. After 5 P.M. it's $2.35 for adults and $1.85 for kids. Shoes cost $2 per person, all ages.

This bowling alley has 32 lanes, all with automatic scorekeeping. You can get the soft bumpers to fill the gutters so that littler kids (and parents) won't throw any gutter balls. There is a concession area for drinks and snacks to keep you going.

Where to Eat

Old Country Buffet. *16060 South Harlem Avenue, in the Park Center Plaza; (708) 614–0202.* Regular hours are 11 A.M. to 8:30 P.M. Monday through Thursday, 11 A.M. to 9 P.M. Friday, 8 A.M. to 9 P.M. Saturday, and 8 A.M. to 8:30 P.M. Sunday. See description in Restaurant Appendix. $

Where to Stay

Baymont Inn & Suites. *7255 West 183rd Street; (708) 633–1200 or (800) 301–0200.* This four-story economy hotel has 101 rooms with coffeemakers. Amenities include indoor pool and whirlpool. Small pets are allowed. The room rate includes continental breakfast delivered to your door. $$

For More Information

Tinley Park Chamber of Commerce, *16250 South Oak Park Avenue, Tinley Park 60477; (708) 532–5700.*

Lansing

Population: 28,086. This southern suburb lies in Cook County at the Indiana border. Interstate 80/94 slices through the northern part of town, and U.S. Highway 6/Illinois Highway 83 runs along its western edge.

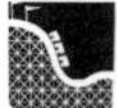

HOLLYWOOD PARK (age 4 and up)

2635 Bernice Road, Lansing 60438; (708) 474–8989. Hours are 10 A.M. to midnight daily. Miniature golf costs $4 for anyone age 11 or older, $3 for kids age 5 through 10, and $2 for children age 4 or younger. Go-karts cost $3.50 for a three-minute ride, and batting cages cost 50 cents. Arcade tokens cost 25 cents each.

This indoor-outdoor recreation facility is a sister to the park in Crestwood. This one has more than a hundred arcade games, the Hollywood Dine-In Theatre, and a 1950s-style restaurant indoors. Outdoors you'll find two 18-hole miniature golf courses, go-karts, and batting cages.

Where to Eat

IHOP. *16851 Torrence Avenue; (708) 474–2240.* Across from Home Depot, north of I-80. Open from 6 A.M. to midnight daily. See Restaurant Appendix for description. $

Where to Stay

Best Western Chicago Southeast. *2505 Bernice Road; (708) 895–7810 or (800) 528–1234.* This property has 101 rooms with cable TV including free HBO. It also has an outdoor pool. Continental breakfast is included in the room rate. $$

For More Information

Lansing Chamber of Commerce, *3404 Lake Street, Lansing 60438; (708) 474–4170.*

Joliet

Population: 76,836. Joliet is the largest community in Will County. I–80 skirts the southern edge of town, and numerous other roadways crisscross through, among them U.S. Highways 6, 30, and 52 and Illinois Highways 7, 53, and 171.

ROUND BARN FARM MUSEUM (all ages)

Briggs Street; (815) 478–3215. Four miles south of I–80. (Mailing address: 24115 South U.S. Highway 52, Manhattan 60442.) Open from 9:30 A.M. to 6:30 P.M. Tuesday through Sunday; closed Monday. Admission costs $4 for anyone age 2 or older; children age 1 or younger get in free. Pony rides cost $2 extra.

Technically, the barn is 20-sided, but that's close enough to round. Its six levels are filled with antique farm equipment and home appliances. Outside are areas for picnicking, swimming, fishing, and boating, plus a petting zoo. For an extra fee, the kids can get a pony ride.

HAUNTED TRAILS FAMILY AMUSEMENT PARK (all ages)

1423 North Broadway Street, Joliet 60435; (815) 722–7800. Open year-round, but outdoor attractions are closed during winter and inclement weather. Hours are 10 A.M. to 11 P.M. Sunday through Thursday and 10 A.M. to midnight Friday and Saturday. Miniature golf costs $4 for anyone age 13 or older and $3 for kids age 12 or younger. Go-kart rides cost $3.75, the Junior Speedway $3.25. Kids' bumper boats and Junior Pirate ship cost $1.25 each. Batting cages cost 50 cents.

Haunted Trails Family Amusement Park provides active family recreation. Visitors of all ages can play miniature golf on an 18-hole course. Older and bigger kids can ride the regular go-karts, but there is also a Junior Speedway exclusively for children who are 41 through 54 inches tall—that's 3 feet, 5 inches through 4 feet, 6 inches. Kids who weigh less than 100 pounds may ride the special bumper boats made just for them. The Junior Pirate Ship also is designed for younger children. Little Leaguers can get some extra practice in the batting cages. Video and skill games in the arcade take 25-cent tokens and dispense reward tickets that can be collected and later redeemed for prizes. There is a restaurant on the premises, serving meals and snacks.

PILCHER PARK NATURE CENTER (all ages)

227 North Gougar Road, near U.S. Highway 30, Joliet 60432; (815) 741–7277. Open year-round. Hours are 9 A.M. to 4:30 P.M. daily. Admission is **Free**. *The building is accessible for wheelchairs and strollers.*

This indoor-outdoor facility allows visitors to connect with nature. The building has observation windows that will please bird-watchers, and there are large aquariums and indoor turtle ponds that will delight toddlers. Display rooms feature hands-on exhibits. Outdoors the grounds have picnic areas, playgrounds, and hiking trails.

Where to Eat

Chuck E. Cheese's. *1965 West Jefferson Street; (815) 725–2044.* Hours are 10 A.M. to 10 P.M. Sunday through Thursday and 10 A.M. to 11 P.M. Friday and Saturday. See Restaurant Appendix for description. $

Old Country Buffet. *2811 Plainfield Road; (815) 254–0045.* Hours are 11 A.M. to 8 P.M. Monday through Thursday, 11 A.M. to 9 P.M. Friday, 8 A.M. to 9 P.M. Saturday, and 8 A.M. to 8:30 P.M. Sunday. See Restaurant Appendix for description.$

Where to Stay

Comfort Inn North. *3235 Norman Avenue; (815) 436–5141 or (800) 228–5150.* This economy chain property has 64 comfortable rooms and an indoor pool. Continental breakfast is included in the room rate. $$

Fireside Resort. *4200 West Jefferson Street (I–55 and U.S. Highway 52); (815) 725–0111.* The resort has 108 comfortable rooms. Amenities include indoor pool, sauna, and fitness center. $$$

For More Information

Heritage Corridor Convention and Visitors Bureau, *81 North Chicago Street, Joliet 60432; (815) 727–2323 or (800) 926–2262.*

The far southern part of Chicagoland is Kankakee County. For general information about the area, contact the **Kankakee County Convention & Visitors Bureau,** 1711 Route 50 North, Suite 1, Bourbonnais 60914; (815) 935-7390 or (800) 747-4837. Internet: www.visitkankakeecounty.com.

Bourbonnais

Population: 13,934. This town just north of the Kankakee River is easily accessible off Interstate 57, U.S. Highway 45, or Illinois Highway 102. Here you'll find some pleasant family activities.

KANKAKEE RIVER STATE PARK (all ages)

Highway 102 and DeSelm Road, P.O. Box 37, Bourbonnais 60914; (815) 933–1383. Hours are 6 A.M. to 10 P.M. daily, year-round. Admission is **Free**. *No alcoholic beverages allowed.*

This is a lovely park with big, shady trees. Picnic tables, some with shelters, and playground equipment are scattered throughout. The smooth black asphalt bike trail is inviting; bring your own bicycles or rent them at the park. You can also rent a canoe if you want to try paddling along Rock Creek. A bridge over the creek affords a scenic view of the shallow water below, with anglers fishing from the banks. The park also has a designated Handicap Fishing Pier, a wooden platform slightly overhanging the water that could be used by someone in a wheelchair. (There's no place for swimming here, however.) For comfort and convenience, there's a spot with rest rooms, a pay phone, and a Pepsi machine. Outhouses are placed in other locations for those whose needs are too urgent to wait for a trek to the rest room that has plumbing. You can get burgers, pop, ice cream, and candy at a small concession building adjacent to the one for bike and canoe rentals.

KANKAKEE RIVER STATE PARK RIDING STABLES (age 6 and up)

In Kankakee River State Park, off DeSelm Road, Bourbonnais 60914; (815) 939–0309. Open year-round, weather permitting; horses will not be taken out in extreme heat or cold or if it's raining. Hours are 10 A.M. to 6 P.M. daily. Anyone age 6 or older and 43 inches (3 feet, 7 inches) tall or taller is allowed to ride the horses on the guided trail rides. The rate on Friday, Saturday, and Sunday is $8 per person for half an hour or $15 per person for a full hour. The rates drop to $7 and $13, respectively, for rides taken Monday through Thursday. Reservations *strongly recommended. For $5, a child age 5 or younger may ride a pony around the arena next to the stable, but a parent—not a stable employee—must walk along and lead the pony. This facility is not well equipped to serve persons with disabilities.*

Here is a good place to introduce your grade-schooler to the pleasures of horseback riding. Headed by a feisty mother hen named Mary, the friendly and knowledgeable staff at this stable will help novices learn how to mount one of the gentle horses for a short ride through the woods. Mary and her staff try to match riders' size and ability to the temperament of the horses, so trust them and take whichever one you're given. Each outing is led by a guide on horseback, and you'll be glad for that as you wind through dense forest along unmarked dirt trails. Although the foliage is trimmed back regularly, you'll avoid poison ivy and scratches and generally be more comfortable if you wear long pants. The horses are familiar with the trails and don't need much reining in, so even a first-time rider is likely to settle in and enjoy the slow-paced ride. In summertime the sound of insects and birds will lull you along. Or try an outing in fall when the trees are a palette of yellows, reds, and browns, or perhaps a winter trek through a quiet blanket of snow. There are just two caveats. First, be aware that the horses *walk* the trail–this is not the place for people with visions of some wild gallop like one they've seen in a movie, nor is it the place for skilled equestrians to show off their English riding skills; it's just a simple horsie ride. Second, the stable area has very little in the way of amenities: picnic tables, an outhouse, and a can of pop you can buy at the office. Go to the main area of the park if you want more.

EXPLORATION STATION . . . A CHILDREN'S MUSEUM (ages 2 to 10)

396 North Kennedy Drive (U.S. Highway 45), in Perry Farm Park, Bourbonnais 60914; (815) 935–5665. Summer hours are 10 A.M. to 5 P.M. Monday through Thursday and Saturday, noon to 8 P.M. Friday, and 1 to 5 P.M. Sunday. During the school year the museum is closed Mondays. Admission costs $4 for anyone age 19 months or older; tots age 18 months or younger get in free. Residents of Bourbonnais, Bradley, and St. George pay just $2. No smoking. Ramps and wide doors help make the facility easily accessible for strollers and wheelchairs.

This is one of the most visually appealing children's museums in the state. Its vivid colors and varied shapes start on the outside–a yellow converted grain silo in front of an angular barnlike building painted with bright red and white stripes and slate-blue accents–and continue throughout the interior rooms. The masterpiece of the museum is a multilevel medieval castle with towers, a dungeon, and a fabric drawbridge that can be raised (rolled up, actually) using a hand-operated chain pulley. There are dress-up clothes inside that enable kids to become kings, queens, princesses, and knights. Nearby are some funhouse-style mirrors that will evoke a few giggles. Another large display is a wooden ship with red trim. Some kids could spend half an hour or more in the little post office, whipping dummy letters and postcards through a hand-cranked canceling machine and then sticking them into the space of their choice in a wall full of mail slots. An airplane display features a "cockpit" with computer simulator and real airline seats for "passengers," who can watch a video of a flight on a TV monitor. The medical room has a real ambulance that kids can sit inside and play in, plus real equipment such as crutches, an intravenous fluid bag, a gurney, and a light board with X ray. A computer here is equipped with role-playing

I Canoe—Can You? Sure you can! In the Bourbonnais-Bradley area, you can go paddling down the Kankakee River, courtesy of **Reed's Canoe Trips** at 907 North Indiana Avenue in Kankakee; (815) 932–2663. Internet: www.reedscanoetrips.com. Look for the corrugated metal building off Illinois Highway 50; there will probably be several of the company's yellow trucks in the big parking lot. This outfit will take you to the river and pick you up at the end of your journey. Six different trips are offered, ranging from a couple of hours to a couple of days. The shortest one, about two to three hours, covers 6 miles and costs $29 for two adults, with an additional cost per person of $8 for anyone age 13 or older. Children age 3 through 12 ride free. Tots age 2 or younger are not allowed in the boat. A $10 deposit is required. Each canoe seats a maximum of two adults and two small kids. Such tours depart at 11:30 A.M. and 12:30 and 1:30 P.M. daily in season. Reservations are not required but are a good idea, especially on Saturday. Reed's is open from 8 A.M. to 5 P.M. daily from mid-April through mid-October.

One final note about safety: If you want to try one of these trips, make sure that you and the kids are *good* swimmers (capable at least of doing several pool laps of the crawl stroke in water over your head) before you attempt it. You'll have life jackets on, of course, but you shouldn't depend on those alone to save you if you tip over. River currents can be tricky, and you don't want anyone to panic. The more confident you are in the water, the more relaxed you'll be and the more fun you'll have. Also be sure to wear comfortable clothing and rubber-soled shoes.

software that enables a would-be doctor to diagnose a patient. The Wet Room is filled with water and PVC pipes to play with and lives up to its name—bring an extra set of clothes if you want to let your kids go in there. Glass display cases show off collections of fossils, model airplanes, and dolls dressed in foreign costumes. Near the entryway is the Make It and Take It room, the name of which pretty much says it all. A low, round table is stocked with markers, glue, scissors, and bits of paper, yarn, cloth, and Styrofoam for kids to create their own souvenir. There is also a small gift shop off to one side with toys, books, and costumes that tie in with the exhibits. The rest rooms here are exceptionally well equipped for families. Not only is there a changing table for babies, but there are also tiny toilets and a low sink and paper-towel dispenser that preschoolers can reach. A box of tissues on the counter also is much appreciated. Most families can spend at least an hour here, some perhaps a whole afternoon.

Where to Eat

Aurelio's Pizza. *12 Heritage Plaza, just off U.S. Highway 45 on John Casey Road; (815) 935–1212.* Hours are 11 A.M. to 10 P.M. Sunday through Friday and 11 A.M. to 11 P.M. Saturday. This place claims the distinction of being voted "#1 pizza in the Chicago Southland five years in a row!!" You be the judge. $

Bakers Square. *1315 Armour Road; (815) 933–2042.* Open from 6 A.M. to 11 P.M. Sunday through Thursday and 6 A.M. to midnight Friday and Saturday. See Restaurant Appendix for description. $

Hardee's. 430 South Main Street; (815) *932–7265.* Hours are 5:30 A.M. to 10 P.M. Sunday through Thursday and 5:30 A.M. to 11 P.M. Friday and Saturday. Forget Arby's—Hardee's has the best roast beef sandwich, and it's hard to find farther north in Illinois. Treat yourself here. $

Where to Stay

Motel 6. *1311 Route 50 North; (815) 933–2300.* This basic motel has 96 rooms and outdoor pool. $

Fairfield Inn. *1550 Illinois Highway 50 North; (815) 935–1334.* The inn has 57 rooms and indoor pool. Room rates include breakfast. $$

Hampton Inn. *60 Ken Hayes Drive; (815) 932–8369.* This motel has 59 rooms and indoor pool. Room rates include continental breakfast. $$

Holiday Inn Express and Suites. *62 Ken Hayes Drive; (815) 932–4411 or (800) 465–4329.* This three-story property has 74 rooms and 18 suites. Rooms have coffeemaker and iron and ironing board. Suites also have microwave and refrigerator, and there is a door separating the living room and bedroom areas—a real plus for families with young children. Rates for both include continental breakfast. Amenities include indoor pool, whirlpool, and fitness center. $$$ (room), $$$$ (suite)

Bradley

Population: 10,792. This town is a next-door neighbor to the south of Bourbonnais. It has another commercial attraction of interest to families.

HIDDEN COVE FAMILY FUN PARK (age 3 and up)

70 Ken Hayes Drive (Illinois Route 50), behind JCPenney store of Northfield Square Mall, Bradley 60915; (815) 933–9150. General park hours during the summer are 11 A.M. to 10 P.M. Sunday through Thursday and 11 A.M. to 11 P.M. Friday and Saturday. Hours are shorter during the school year; call to check. For activities, pay at the register; the receipt becomes your ticket. Miniature golf costs $4 per person, go-karts and Fun Jungle $3.50, and skating $1 to $4, depending on the session. Skate rental costs $1 to $2. For the driving range, $1 rents a driver and a coin-fed machine outside dispenses the balls for your bucket. Arcade games take Arcade Tokens, which are four for $1 or a little less per token if you buy $10 or $20 worth at a time. Parts of the facility are not easily accessible for strollers and wheelchairs. Smoking is allowed outdoors and in some areas indoors.

This indoor-outdoor family amusement center has a variety of activities for family fun. Indoors you'll find an arcade on the upper floor with games for younger children such as Bozo Buckets and Hungry Hungry Hippos, plus a giant Play Jungle of tubes, nets, slides, and a plastic ball pit. Downstairs are video games for adolescents, pool tables, and air hockey. The major attraction down here, however, is a huge sky-blue roller rink. Colored lights and glitter balls hang from the high ceiling and swing into action during a skating session. Observation windows upstairs allow parents to watch older kids down on the rink while the littler ones play upstairs. Next to the roller rink is a small room with a half dozen bumper cars. Both indoor levels have concession areas with tables where you can enjoy pizza or munchie snacks and sodas. The indoor area is open year-round. The outdoor area, which is open all summer and at other times as weather permits, has five activities: an elliptical go-kart track, batting cages (baseball and softball at varying speeds), a golf driving range, two 18-hole miniature golf courses, and paddleboats (moored in a little lagoon off the six-acre artificial lake). The centerpiece of the miniature golf is a wooden twin-masted pirate ship. The two courses wind through landscaped grounds dotted with flowers, fountains, rocks, and evergreens. One course is designed for amateurs, the other for players with more experience.

Where to Eat

Monical's Pizza. *Village Square Shopping Center; (815) 939–3245.* Open from 11 A.M. to 10:30 P.M. Sunday through Thursday and 11 A.M. to midnight Friday and Saturday. Tasty thin-crust pizza is the specialty of this central Illinois-based franchise. $

Old Country Buffet. *1690 North Illinois Highway 50; (815) 932–9777.* Open from 11 A.M. to 8:30 P.M. Monday through Thursday, 11 A.M. to 9 P.M. Friday, 8 A.M. to 9 P.M. Saturday, and 8 A.M. to 8 P.M. Sunday. See Restaurant Appendix for description. $

Where to Stay

Bradley Inn. *800 North Kinzie Avenue; (815) 939–3501.* This 160-room property was formerly a Ramada Inn. It has an indoor pool and hot tub, plus game room, laundry facility, and on-site restaurant. Continental breakfast is included in the room rate. Parking for trucks and RVs is available. $$

For More Information

Bourbonnais-Bradley Chamber of Commerce, *1690 Newton Drive, Bradley 60915; (815) 932–2222.*

Other Things to See and Do in Chicagoland

January: Festival of Lights, Lansing; (708) 474-6160

February: Home Show, Bradley; (815) 937-4241

March: Kids Day on the Farm, Kankakee County Fairgrounds; (815) 932-6714

April: Home and Trade Show, Zion; (847) 746-5500

May: Geneva on the River; (630) 232-6060

June: Elmfest, Elmhurst; (630) 834-6060

Kankakee Valley Strawberry Festival, Kankakee; (800) 747-4837

Oswego Prairiefest; (630) 554-1010

July: Wauconda Championship Rodeo; (847) 526-5580

Joliet Waterway Daze; (815) 740-2216

West Chicago Railroad Days; (630) 231-3003

Most communities have a Fourth of July celebration, and many county fairs are in July and August.

August: Grayslake Summer Days Festival; (847) 223-6888

Momence Gladiolus Festival; (815) 472-6730 or (800) 747-4837

Westmont Summerfest; (630) 963-5252

September: Arts and Crafts Faire, Antioch; (847) 395-2233

Thomson Melon Days; (815) 259-5705

Winfield Good Old Days; (630) 682-3712

October: Boo! at the Zoo, Brookfield; (708) 485-0263

Will County Pioneer Crafts Festival, Lockport; (815) 838-5080

November: Turkey Trot, Palos Park; (708) 361-1535

Countryside Christmas, Long Grove; (847) 634-0888

December: Gallery of Trees, Kankakee; (800) 747-4837

Lunch with Santa, Park Forest; (708) 748-1112

Northern Illinois

Perhaps the most varied of the state's six regions, 14-county Northern Illinois stretches across the top, from the fringe of the Chicago suburbs westward to the Mississippi River boundary with Iowa. In between you'll find state parks, historic towns, and—surrounded by an ocean of farmland—the largest city in Illinois beyond Chicagoland: Rockford.

Our exploration will follow a path from east to west, using a number of major arteries: (1) U.S. Highway 14, (2) Interstate 90 and U.S. Highway 20, (3) Illinois Highway 64, (4) Interstate 88, and (5) Interstate 80.

Crystal Lake

Population: 24,512. U.S. Highway 14 cuts straight through this rapidly growing town. Crystal Lake has two indoor spots that are popular with families.

CRYSTAL WHEELS (age 5 and up)

691 Virginia Road, Crystal Lake 60014; (815) 356–8705. Family skating hours and admission prices during the school year are 4:30 to 6:30 P.M. Tuesday, $3 per person; 6:30 to 9 P.M. Wednesday, $2; and overlapping sessions of 1 to 4 P.M. and 2:30 to 5:30 P.M. Saturday and Sunday, $4.50 for one session or $6 for both. Summer hours and prices are 1 to 3:30 P.M. Tuesday and Thursday, $4.50; 6:30 to 9 P.M. Wednesday, $2; and 1 to 4 P.M. Saturday, $4.50. Also in the summer, if it's raining, the rink is open from 1 to 3:30 P.M. Monday, Wednesday, and Friday; $4.50. Old-fashioned sessions with organ music are held occasionally; call for times. Skate rentals at all times are $1.50 for regular skates, $4.50 for in-line skates. You may bring your own skates.

This rink opened in a brand-new building in the late 1990s. It has a large, natural maple wood floor and cheery decor in yellow, green, and

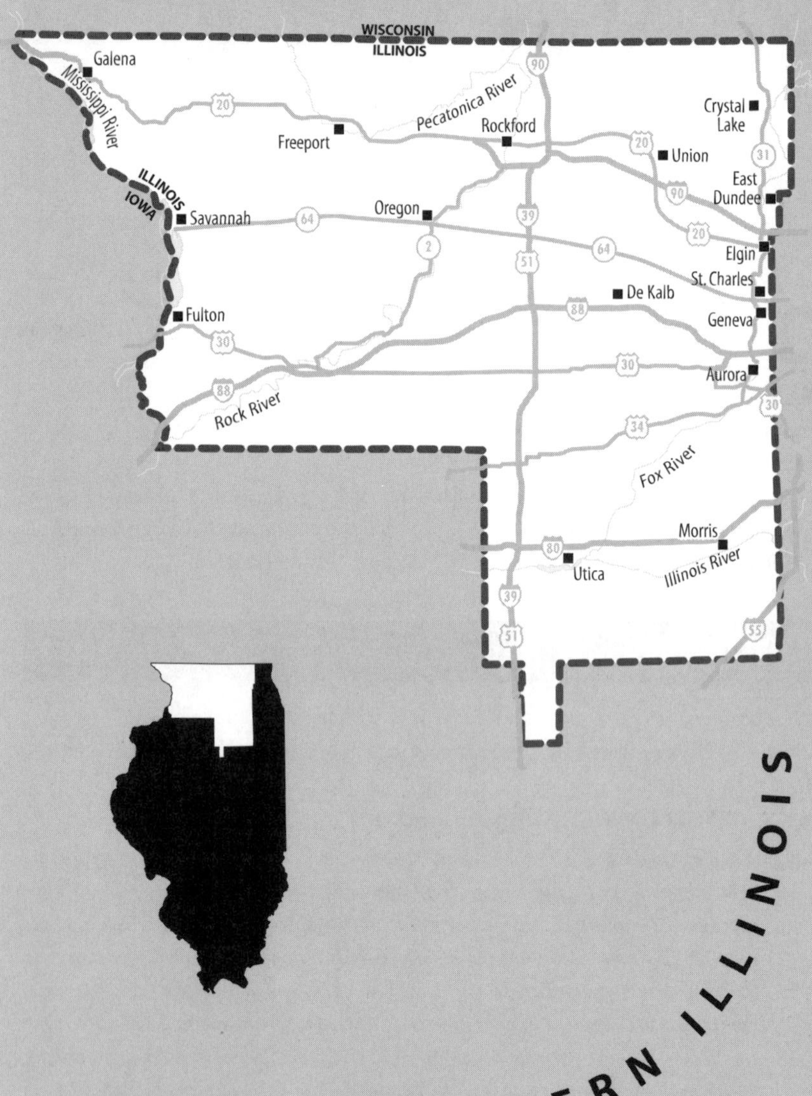

NORTHERN ILLINOIS

white. Matinee sessions feature top pop tunes and include special skates in the dark with flashing multicolored lights. Arcade games and concessions are available.

LEAPIN' LIZARDS (ages 2–10)

19 East Berkshire Drive, Crystal Lake 60014; (815) 356–5656. Hours are 10 A.M. to 8 P.M. Monday through Saturday and noon to 8 P.M. Sunday. Admission is $4.95 for children age 10 or younger and free for anyone age 11 or older.

This indoor playground is geared toward the younger crowd. Although you'll find a handful of video games, the space is predominantly devoted to the padded climbing area, with all sorts of interesting obstacles to maneuver around. There are two ball pits. There's also a separate toddler play area on a smaller scale. Concessions include pizza, hot dogs, and soft drinks.

Where to Eat

Bakers Square. *5689 Northwest Highway (U.S. 14); (815) 477–9480.* Open from 7 A.M. to 11 P.M. Sunday through Thursday and 7 A.M. to midnight Friday and Saturday. See Restaurant Appendix for description. $

Old Country Buffet. *6322 Northwest Highway (U.S. 14); (815) 356–0355.* Hours are 11 A.M. to 8:30 P.M. Monday through Friday and 8 A.M. to 8:30 P.M. Saturday and Sunday. See Restaurant Appendix for description. $

IHOP. *6606 Northwest Highway (U.S. 14); (815) 356–3965.* Open from 6 A.M. to 10 P.M. Sunday through Thursday and 6 A.M. to midnight Friday and Saturday. See Restaurant Appendix for description. $

Where to Stay

Holiday Inn Crystal Lake. *800 South Route 31 (Illinois 31 at U.S. 14); (815) 477–7000 or (800) 465–4329.* This six-story, 196-room property has an indoor swimming pool, whirlpool, and fitness center. There is a restaurant on the premises. $$$

Super 8. *577 Crystal Point Drive (off U.S. 14 about 1 mile west of Illinois 31); (815) 455–2388 or (800) 800–8000.* This budget motel has 59 rooms with cable TV. Pets are allowed. No pool. $$

For More Information

Greater Crystal Lake Area Chamber of Commerce, *427 Virginia Street, Crystal Lake 60014; (815) 459–1300.*

Now let's return to the eastern edge of Northern Illinois and head west along Interstate 90 and U.S. Highway 20. These two thoroughfares run sort of parallel, although Highway 20 starts out south of I-90 but then intersects it and continues north of it along a similar northwesterly course into Rockford. At Rockford, I-90 veers straight north toward Wisconsin, and we'll continue west on Highway 20 alone to the Illinois border at Galena. Our first stop on this route is East Dundee, north off I-90 at Illinois Highway 25.

East Dundee

Population: 2,721. The two towns of East and West Dundee share a name, but most of the family attractions are in East Dundee. Chief among these are Santa's Village and the Racing Rapids Action Park, two separate but related facilities at the corner of Illinois Highways 25 and 72.

SANTA'S VILLAGE (all ages)

Routes 25 and 72, East Dundee 60118; (847) 426–6751 or (847) 426–6753. Open daily between the beginning of June and Labor Day. Some weekend hours, 11 A.M. to 6 or 7 P.M., are also offered in May and September. Summer hours are 10 A.M. to 6 P.M. Monday through Friday and 11 A.M. to 7 or 8 P.M. Saturday and Sunday, with the earlier closing time applying early and late in the season. Admission costs $15.95 Monday and Tuesday and $18.95 Wednesday through Sunday for anyone age 3 or older; children age 2 or younger get in free. A "combo pass" with Racing Rapids Action Park costs $22.95 Monday and Tuesday and $25.95 Wednesday through Sunday. Inside Santa's Village and run by the same company is the Polar Dome Ice Arena, which is not open in summer; call for current schedule and prices. Internet: www.santasvillageil.com.

Santa's Village is one of the best amusement parks in the Chicago area for families with young children. Although the admission price may sound a bit steep, it's a good deal compared to places that charge a couple bucks a ride, where the cost mounts fast. Santa's Village is easy to recognize—a giant Santa Claus and snowman stand out front. The ticket booth and front offices are housed in A-frame buildings in bright shades of red, yellow, orange, and lime green. The park offers rides, shows, and concessions. It has been here for more than 40 years—well before the rise of many of today's megaparks. Its full name, the Three Worlds of Santa's Village, reflects the park's tripartite nature. The Santa's World section has the original Snowball Ride, plus midway and kiddie rides such as a miniature roller coaster with a dragon head at the front, a carousel, teacups, fire trucks, planes, a miniature 18-wheeler truck convoy, and balloons that go round and round high up in the air. The Frog Hopper is a kiddie thrill ride. Rides are fairly short, which is enough time for fun but not enough to be scary, and that keeps the lines moving, too. There are numerous benches in this area for waiting parents to sit on, many in the cooling shade of evergreens and big oak trees. Near the kiddie rides are two arcades, one with Skeeball and the other with pinball machines and video games.

The second section, Coney Island, has more appeal for older kids and teens, although there are kiddie rides here, too, such as the L'il Stingers and Space Ships. The Galleon Pirate Ship gives an ordinary pendulum ride a nautical twist: The row of seats is decorated like a galleon, and you walk up an inclined wood-and-rope "dock" to reach the ride platform. The Galleon reaches a height of 40 feet off the ground as it swings back and forth. Other favorites include the Tilt-A-Whirl, Himalaya, YoYo, and Wipeout. The Skyliner aerial tram ride passes over part of this section. Get on near the roller coaster, but be cautious about bringing squirmy youngsters on this ride because it is not well enclosed. You sit in a seat like the kind on a traditional Ferris wheel, and the safety bar in front latches but doesn't lock. As the seat lurches along on its cable, an adult's feet can touch the treetops below. In some ways it's scarier than the thrill rides because you feel as though you could fall out any second. And speaking of thrill rides, the pièce de résistance of the park is the Typhoon roller coaster. "It will blow you away!" is the slogan, and that seems accurate. The typhoon climbs 63 feet in the air; it dips, it turns, and it loops the loop, all at dizzying speed. It's not for the faint of heart, so of course teens love it. A couple of other family-friendly rides that board near the Typhoon are the cute choo-choo that's painted to resemble an Amtrak train and some little two-seater old-fashioned cars that go around a track and through a tunnel. Attendants for all the rides tend to be young and cheerful.

Old McDonald's Farm is the park's third section, a glorified petting zoo that also offers pony rides and sleigh rides. Entertainment features peppy, wholesome young people singing and dancing, or sometimes it's a magic show. There's a picnic area with tables where you can bring your own food, or you can partake of the reasonably priced concessions, including burgers, hot dogs, "junior" pizzas, chips, french fries, pickles, pretzels, cotton candy, and snow cones. As a treat for Mom or Dad, a beer and a bratwurst won't set you back much. Soft drinks and bottled water are also available. There are few drinking fountains, so bring extra money for drinks (or extra sippy cups!) to make sure that everyone stays adequately hydrated on a hot day. The park has reasonably ample rest rooms, with a changing table in the women's. You can exit the park in one of two ways: (1) into the Racing Rapids Action Park, if you bought a combo pass, or (2) through the gift shop. The latter makes it tough not to take home a souvenir. Most of the stuff here is cheap, both in price and in quality, but it's fun.

RACING RAPIDS ACTION PARK (all ages)

Routes 25 and 72, East Dundee 60118; (847) 426–5525 or (847) 426–6753. Open daily between the beginning of June and Labor Day. Hours are 11 A.M. to 6 or 7 P.M. Monday through Thursday and 11 A.M. to 7 or 8 P.M. Friday through Sunday, with the earlier closing times applying early and late in the season. Admission costs $12.95 for the day for anyone age 3 or older; children age 2 or younger get in free. A "combo pass" with Santa's Village costs $22.95 Monday and Tuesday and $25.95 Wednesday through Sunday.

Racing Rapids Action Park, adjacent to Santa's Village, has all sorts of water rides for all ages. There are two big water slides, each of which you zoom down on a flexible foam mat. The Little Ducks is for kids as young as 3 or 4, while the 50-foot Slidewinder caters to older, bigger kids and adults. Then there's the Lazy River Tube Ride, in which you sit in an inner tube and float down a "river" of chlorinated water. It's not so lazy on a really hot day when the place gets crowded. The tube ride winds around several nice kiddie wading pools and fountains, where the toddlers can play with Mom or Dad while their older siblings ride the tubes. The Auto Kid's Wash is a cute idea. It's modeled after a drive-through car wash, and the kids walk, crawl, or run the gauntlet of squirting jets and flopping fabric flaps. The park also has bumper boats and go-karts. Valuables can be stored in 50-cent lockers in the main area. The locker rooms have showers and toilets. The concession stand carries most of the same items you'll find in Santa's Village, sans beer and brats, and there is a tent canopy shading the nearby picnic tables where you consume your food and drink. On a hot day, the lines for concessions get very long. Also, the park's asphalt surface heats up to an uncomfortable temperature, and it's slippery when wet. If you choose to take the combo ticket and come here after Santa's Village, keep a close eye on your kids so that they don't get too exhausted—that's when many accidents happen.

Where to Eat

Milk Pail Village and Restaurant. *14N630 Route 25; (847) 742–5040.* On Highway 25, north of I–90. Hours are 8 A.M. to 8 P.M. Sunday through Thursday and 8 A.M. to 10 P.M. Friday and Saturday. This restaurant serves breakfast, lunch, and dinner daily. You'll eat in antiques-filled dining rooms set in McGraw's Wildlife Preserve. Dinner entrees include pheasant and trout as well as more standard fare such as prime rib, turkey, and chicken. The facility also features a collection of specialty shops. $$$

See also listings for West Dundee.

Where to Stay

There are no hotels or motels in East Dundee. See subsequent entries for West Dundee and Elgin.

For More Information

Dundee Township Visitor Center, *319 North River Street, East Dundee 60118; (847) 426–2255.*

West Dundee

Population: 3,728. There are more restaurants in this town than in its sister city to the east, and of course there's the mall.

SPRING HILL MALL (all ages)

Illinois Highways 31 and 72, West Dundee 60118; (847) 428–2200. Hours are 10 A.M. to 9 P.M. Monday through Friday, 10 A.M. to 7 P.M. Saturday, and 11 A.M. to 6 P.M. Sunday. Accessible for strollers and wheelchairs.

This one-story indoor shopping mall has about 150 stores, anchored by Marshall Field's, Carson Pirie Scott, JCPenney, Kohl's, and Sears department stores. You'll have lots of company if you bring a stroller; this is a popular mall for families. Kids will be particularly interested in the pet store, the Disney Store, and Kay-Bee Toys. You can buy children's clothes at the Gymboree and Gap Kids specialty stores. There is a food court with about 10 eateries to choose from.

Where to Eat

Gino's East. *98 West Main Street; (847) 426–0500.* Hours are 10 A.M. to 10 P.M. Monday through Thursday, 11 A.M. to 11 P.M. Friday and Saturday, and 10 A.M. to 9 P.M. Sunday. This pizza place specializes in the same deep-dish kind that you can get at its parent restaurant in downtown Chicago, but you can get the thin-crust type, too. $

Old Country Buffet. *1438 Spring Hill Mall; (847) 836–9611.* Open from 11 A.M. to 9 P.M. Monday through Friday, 8 A.M. to 9 P.M. Saturday, and 8 A.M. to 8 P.M. Sunday. See Restaurant Appendix for description. $

Red Lobster. *701 Spring Hill Ring Road (Highway 31); (847) 428–0820.* Hours are 11 A.M. to 10 P.M. Sunday through Thursday and 11 A.M. to 11 P.M. Friday and Saturday. See Restaurant Appendix for description. $

Where to Stay

Courtyard by Marriott. *2175 Marriott Drive (off I-90 at U.S. 30 exit); (847) 429–0300.* This 126-room motel opened in 2000. Courtyard properties are geared more toward business travelers, but families often can get a good deal on weekends. At this motel, rooms come equipped with hair dryer, ironing board, desk, two phones, and dataports with high-speed Internet access. Amenities include indoor pool, whirlpool, and mini-workout facility. Full buffet breakfast is available on-site at extra cost. $$

Elgin

Population: 77,010. South of the Dundees off I-90 or U.S. Highway 20 is Elgin. This community has a lot of downtown redevelopment projects going on, so the city continues to improve as an Illinois tourism destination. You can stop by the Visitors Information Center in the Grand Victoria Pavilion (250 South Grove Avenue; 847-608-9976) to get the latest scoop. You can get a map of the city's historic districts, too. Elgin also has numerous festivals throughout the year. If you're a bicycling enthusiast, the visitor center can provide you with a map of the Fox River Trail, which goes along Riverside Drive through the downtown district. Elgin is about the halfway point for this bike trail, which runs north to south for 35 miles from Crystal Lake to Aurora.

Clang, Clang, Clang Went the Trolley A detour off Highway 20 down Highway 31 takes you to South Elgin and the Fox River Trolley Museum (3 blocks south of the State Street traffic light); (847) 697–4676. Internet: www.foxtrolley.org. Here you can ride an electric trolley car on a scenic 3-mile round-trip along the west bank of the Fox River. The line traces its history back to 1896. The trolley runs from 11 A.M. to 5 P.M. on weekends only: Saturday between late June and the end of August and Sunday from Mother's Day through early November. One ride costs $2.50 for anyone age 12 through 60, $2 for adults age 65 or older, and $1.50 for children age 3 through 11. For two rides the rate is $3, $2.50, or $2 per person, respectively. Children age 2 or younger always ride free. The museum also houses more than two dozen pieces of railway equipment from the early 1900s. There are all sorts of special events throughout the year, too, such as the Trolleyfest in August and the Haunted Trolley around Halloween.

LORDS PARK ZOO (all ages)

In Lords Park, east off Illinois Highway 25, Elgin 60120; (847) 931–6120. Open from 10 A.M. to 5 P.M. daily during summer. **Free** *admission.*

This cute little zoo has half a dozen buffalo, plus deer, elk, pigs, cows, goats, and chickens. There's a petting area where kids can have some hands-on time with the goats. Lords Park also has picnic areas and playgrounds scattered around its three lagoons.

HEMMENS CULTURAL CENTER (all ages)

150 Dexter Court, downtown Elgin 60120; (847) 931–5900. Call for performance schedule and ticket prices.

The Children's Theatre of Elgin and the Fox Valley Youth Theatre Company stage regular plays here. *Jungle Book, Black Beauty, Charlotte's Web, Peter Pan,* and *Alice in Wonderland* are among the recent productions.

ELGIN AREA HISTORICAL MUSEUM (age 4 and up)

360 Park Street, Elgin 60120; (847) 742–4248. Hours are noon to 4 P.M. Thursday through Saturday and 1 to 4 P.M. Sunday from June through August and noon to 4 P.M. Wednesday through Saturday from September through May. Admission is $2 for adults and $1 for students and children. Accessible for wheelchairs. Internet: elghome.northstarnet.org/eahs.

The Elgin Area Historical Museum, more commonly known as Old Main, is housed in a historic three-story building with a white cupola.

Here you'll find old tools, articles from the Elgin National Watch Company, and memorabilia from the Elgin National Road Race.

Where to Eat

Cracker Barrel. *415 Airport Road; (847) 742–2500.* Hours are 6 A.M. to 10 P.M. Sunday through Thursday and 6 A.M. to 11 P.M. Friday and Saturday. See Restaurant Appendix for description. $

IHOP. *Lake Street and Randall Road; (847) 289–4801.* Open from 6 A.M. to 10 P.M. Monday through Thursday and then from 6 A.M. Friday until 10 P.M. Sunday. See Restaurant Appendix for description. $

Steak 'n Shake. *290 South Randall Road; (847) 741–0679.* Open 24 hours a day. See Restaurant Appendix for description. $

Where to Stay

Baymont Inn. *500 Toll Gate Road; (847) 931–4800 or (800) 301–0200.* Off Illinois Highway 31. This economy chain property has 80 rooms with cable TV and coffeemaker. No pool. Pets are allowed. The room rate includes continental breakfast delivered to your room. $$

Days Inn Elgin. *1585 Dundee Avenue; (847) 695–2100 or (800) 654–2000.* This 96-room budget chain property has an indoor swimming pool. Continental breakfast is included in the room rate. $$

Hampton Inn. *405 Airport Road; (847) 931–1940 or (800) 426–7866.* Each of the 109 rooms here has cable TV, coffeemaker, and iron and ironing board. Amenities include indoor pool with whirlpool. Continental breakfast is included in the room rate. $$$

Holiday Inn Crowne Plaza. *495 Airport Road (off Illinois 31 north of I–90); (847) 488–9800 or (800) 227–6963.* This eight-story, 243-room hotel opened in 1999. It features an indoor heated pool, whirlpool, game room, and exercise room. Room rate includes continental breakfast. $$$

Ramada Inn. *345 West River Road; (847) 695–5000 or (800) 272–6232.* This 203-room property has indoor pool, whirlpool, sauna, exercise room, and video games. No meals are included in the room rate. $$$

For More Information

Elgin Area Convention and Visitors Bureau, *77 Riverside Drive, Elgin 60120; (847) 695–7540 or (800) 217–5362.*

Huntley

Population: 2,453. Moving westward on Highway 20, a jog north up Highway 47 takes you to Huntley. This town is seeing some growth in its tourist business as a result of the outlet mall built in the mid-1990s.

PRIME OUTLETS AT HUNTLEY (all ages)

11800 Factory Shops Boulevard, Huntley 60142; (847) 669–9100. Off Illinois Highway 47 just north of I–90. Hours are 10 A.M. to 9 P.M. Monday through Saturday and 11 A.M. to 6 P.M. Sunday.

This outdoor factory outlet mall is very visible from I–90. Light gray stone buildings have awnings in green and white stripes with yellow accents. The green-domed food court stands in the center and offers such fast-food fare as pizza, tacos, baked potatoes, and even Chinese dishes. Stores feature clothing, housewares, and such special items as books, music, and chocolates. The Carter's store is great for babies' and children's clothes. Gap Outlet and OshKosh B'Gosh have good bargains, too.

TOM'S FARM (all ages)

10214 Algonquin Road, Huntley 60142; (847) 669–3421. East off Highway 47 north of the outlet mall. Hours are 9 A.M. to 7 P.M. Monday through Friday, 9 A.M. to 6 P.M. Saturday, and 9 A.M. to 5 P.M. Sunday.

A giant strawberry takes the place of the letter O in the word *Tom's* on the barn roof, and you can pick your own strawberries in June on 21 acres. The farm has an annual yield of about 160,000 pounds of strawberries, about half of which are picked by visitors and the other half sold to fine restaurants and selected stores. Throughout summer you'll find a variety of fresh fruits and vegetables. Tom's also is a fun place to visit in fall, as many school groups do. You can go out in a field and pick your own Halloween pumpkin or some decorative gourds, and a farm stand offers fresh apples and other produce for sale. Kids have fun wandering through a giant maze made out of bales of straw—stacked round bales in front sport colorful flags, giving the entrance the appearance of a castle.

Where to Eat

Parkside Restaurant. *11721 East Main Street; (847) 669–8496.* Restaurant hours are 11 A.M. to 9 P.M. Sunday through Thursday and 11 A.M. to 10 P.M. Friday and Saturday; closed between 3 and 5 P.M. Friday. This local favorite offers outdoor seating in the milder seasons. Enjoy a juicy burger or order from the extensive menu of sandwiches. Friday and Saturday nights also feature a "fish boil," and Saturday you can get barbecued ribs. $

Where to Stay

Huntley has no hotels or motels (*yet*, emphasizes the Chamber of Commerce); see entries for Elgin or Rockford.

For More Information

Huntley Chamber of Commerce, *10436 Route 47, Huntley 60142. (847) 669–0166.*

Union

Population: 542. There's not much to see in this tiny McHenry County town just off U.S. Highway 20; however, two outlying attractions that bear its name as an address are major draws for family fun in Northern Illinois during spring, summer, and fall.

ILLINOIS RAILWAY MUSEUM (all ages)

Off Olson Road, Union 60180; (815) 923–4000 or (800) 244–7245. Open from 10 A.M. to 4 P.M. Monday through Friday from Memorial Day through Labor Day, 10:30 A.M. to 5 P.M. Saturday from May through October, and 10:30 A.M. to 5 P.M. Sunday from April through October. Closed from November through March. The Monday-through-Friday admission rate is $6 for anyone age 12 through 61 and $4 for kids age 5 through 11 and seniors age 62 or older. The regular weekend rates are $7 and $5, respectively. The rates jump to $8 and $6 on days when steam or diesel trains operate and to $9 and $7 on days with special events going on. All rates include unlimited rides on all equipment running that day. Admission is always free for children age 4 or younger. Call to hear a recording detailing which trains will run on which days. Most parts of the facility are accessible for strollers and wheelchairs. From I–90, take the exit for U.S. 20/Marengo. Off the exit turn left, heading west, and continue about 4½ miles. Turn right, heading north, onto South Union Road. Keep going until South Union Road dead-ends at West Union Road and then turn right, heading east. (There are signs to *help guide you.) Continue east through downtown Union (don't blink or you'll miss it) and then soon afterward turn right, heading south, onto Olson Road. Once you've crossed the railroad tracks, look to the left for the gravel road heading into the grassy parking lot. Ironically, there are no trains that run from Chicago or the suburbs to Union. For a brochure with complete directions, schedules, and prices, contact Illinois Railway Museum, P.O. Box 427, Union 60180. Internet: www. irm.org.*

This museum, a nonprofit organization founded in 1953 and moved to Union in 1964, is a marvelous work in progress. There are things you can do and see today, but there will be new things the next time you visit as the collection constantly expands and equipment is restored. The station near the entrance has display cases of memorabilia, and it's also where you'll find the rest rooms (the women's has a changing table). Parked near the station are two railway cars containing a gift shop and a bookstore with some really nifty souvenirs. Beyond them you can wander the grounds and walk through about half a dozen large "barns"—more like huge metal airplane hangars, really—to get a closer look at various types of engines, railway cars, and streetcars. Other locomotives stand outside. Signs tell you where you may or may not climb or enter. Some trains have ramps, and visitors in wheelchairs can maneuver inside, but others are accessible only by climbing narrow metal stairs. The grounds are manageable to walk for able-bodied adults and older children, but little kids' feet will likely tire if they don't get a break. You can bring a stroller and have no trouble on the paved sidewalks; just watch out for the trolley tracks. In summer you'll find several spots where you can stand under a nozzle that emits a fine spray of cool mist, aaaah. Concessions are pretty limited—soft drinks, hot dogs and brats, potato chips, and ice-cream bars—but are reasonably priced and enough to keep you going. Alternately, you can bring your own picnic (no grilling and no alcoholic beverages) and eat at one of several sites furnished with picnic tables.

The people who operate the working trains are all volunteers, and their love of railroading is evident in the wealth of information they are able to share. The most charming of the museum's vintage vehicles is the trolley, an electric streetcar that travels in a loop around the perimeter of the grounds. It makes stops at several of the barns, where you can get off and look around, and then reboard the trolley on its next pass. It's so much fun just to ride the trolley that you won't want to get off. Car number 1374, for example, is made of polished mahogany and cherry, most of it dating back to 1905, when the streetcar was built. Woven cane seat covers were imported from India to replace the original material, which had deteriorated beyond repair. The seats had been removed when the trolley was taken out of service in 1936, and it was used for a time as a salt car (like today's salt trucks) during the winter before it arrived at the museum for restoration. Chicago reportedly once had the largest streetcar system in the United States, with more than 1,100 miles of track, before the trolleys stopped running in the late 1950s. You can also take a short ride on an electric trolley bus that was built in 1951 and used on the streets of Chicago until the Chicago Transit Authority abandoned the system in 1973—right about the time of a major oil crisis, go figure.

On the railroad's main line, you can board an electric, steam, or diesel train (the type available varies) for a 9-mile round-trip through Northern Illinois farmland filled with corn and soybean fields, wild plants, prairie grasses, and trees. (A special wheelchair lift is available on the platform to help board passengers who have disabilities.) In this pastoral setting, the relaxing chug-a-chug-a of the wheels could lull you to sleep. The mournful wail of a 1916 steam engine's whistle evokes a sense of a bygone era; it sounds quite different from the sharp, whiny blast of a modern Chicago commuter train. Inside the passenger cars are many original fixtures, including lamps, rotary fans, and advertising billboards, mostly for cleaning supplies and medical products.

The barns house a variety of interesting equipment. Barn 7, for example, has the oldest artifact, a cute little horse-drawn streetcar (sans horse, of course), along with a three-wheeled red velocipede from 1890 and a yellow lever-powered handcar like the kind you see in funny old black-and-white movies or "Roadrunner" cartoons. Barn 9 has some of the biggest trains. The gleaming silver *Nebraska Zephyr* of 1940 would have looked like a speeding bullet flying down the rails. In 1995 the museum acquired its largest piece, *No. 2903,* a 1943 mammoth black steam locomotive of the Atchison, Topeka & Santa Fe Railway that had previously been on display for more than 30 years at the Museum of Science and Industry in Chicago. (Yes, you'd better believe it was tricky to transport this 340-ton, 121-foot-long nonworking behemoth from downtown Chicago out to Union.) You'll marvel at its sheer size. Its largest wheels, about 6 feet in diameter, are probably taller than you—stand next to one and compare. Barn 3 has the most elegant artifact, an 1889 Pullman passenger car with dark wood interior and furnished with a brass bed, a manual typewriter on a writing desk, and a dining table set with fine china, crystal, and linens. Only the wealthiest travelers could afford such finery, of course, but we can always dream.

DONLEY'S WILD WEST TOWN (ages 2–12)

8512 South Union Road, just north of U.S. Highway 20, Union 60180; (815) 923–9000. Hours are 10 A.M. to 6 P.M. daily from Memorial Day through Labor Day and 10 A.M. to 6 P.M. Saturday and Sunday only during the months of April, May, September, and October. Closed from November through March. Admission costs $10 per person age 3 or older; children age 2 or younger get in free. Most parts of the facility are accessible for strollers and wheelchairs. From I–90, take the exit for U.S. 20/Marengo. Off the exit turn left, heading west, and continue about 4½ miles. Turn right, heading north, onto South Union Road. Look to the right for the four bronze cowboys on horseback. Internet: www.wildwesttown.com.

Hey, pardners, this here's a right fine place to bring your young'uns for a safe taste of the Old West. And if they don't behave, you can get the sheriff to throw them in jail. (Don't worry—he won't lock up anyone who's truly unwilling, and they can usually make bail by singing the "Barney" song or some other kiddie ditty.) Three features of this theme park, all of which are included in the admission price, are not to be missed: pony rides, panning for gold, and the gunfight. The pony rides are especially good for kids ages 3 through 6; those age 10 or older probably would feel a bit silly sitting on such a small mount, and for those in the 7-to-9 range, it depends on the kid. The ponies walk a roughly elliptical path around a fenced-in corral, led by youthful cowboys and cowgirls. Panning for gold takes place at the Sweet Phyllis Mine. There's no underground section to this mine, just a series of wooden troughs filled with water and pebbles. Would-be miners pick up a black plastic pan shaped like a pie tin, dip it into the cloudy but chlorinated water, and pull up a load of stones. Careful sifting will net you a few tiny nuggets of pyrite, a glittery but inexpensive mineral that looks enough like gold to please the kids. Parents enjoy this activity, too. Piped-in fiddle and banjo music helps set the mood. For the gunfight, spectators are ushered into an arena and seated on bleachers. A split-rail fence separates them from the staging area, which has open space in front and a movielike facade of a Wild West town in back. A young actor in cowboy costume comes out to address the audience before the show, explaining how it's all pretend and that although the guns used are real, they shoot something called *blanks,* which have gunpowder that makes a bang but no metal tip to penetrate a victim. A demonstration with an aluminum can gives the audience a chance to hear the bang before the show and also see that even a blank fired at close range can dent the can—so don't try any of this at home. This warning at the beginning is not only a responsible thing to do in a society in which children armed with guns are increasingly making headlines, but it also helps reassure the wee tots that this live performance is make-believe. The show itself is quite funny, involving a lot of jokes and pratfalls as well as some entertaining stunts with bad guys getting shot off the rooftops.

You won't forget that this facility is a commercial enterprise, however. To enter the museum or the grounds, you have to pass through a well-stocked gift shop, and most of the other shops in the town carry a price tag as well: toy shop, ice-cream parlor, rock shop, Native American "trading post," saloon (where you can get root beer or real beer, including Lone Star from Texas), and photography studio with Old West costumes and props (about $20 for an 8-by-10-inch portrait). Unless you're a real fiduciary hard-liner, you'd better bring along extra money.

Finally, do be sure to spend some time in the indoor museum portion, either before or after going outside into the town. This is where the Larry Donley family started their enterprise in 1975, and the real stuff on display here is definitely worth a look. Along one wall is a wonderful collection of vintage phonographs, circa 1900, and related equipment. If Grandma and Grandpa are along for the visit, they may have some recollections of their own grandparents' homes that will personalize the exhibit. Other glass cases contain western memorabilia including guns, housewares, American Indian clothing, and the death masks and ball-and-chain shackles of criminals.

Where to Eat

Donley's Old West Steakhouse and Buffet. *8512 South Union Road; (815) 923–8000.* Just north of U.S. Highway 20, adjacent to Donley's Wild West Town. The restaurant's five all-you-can-eat buffet bars feature meat dishes, pasta, Mexican food, salads, and desserts—even the pickiest eater should be satisfied. The dinner buffet costs $6.95 per child age 3 through 11 and $14.95 per person for anyone age 12 or older. Soft drinks are included in these prices, but alcoholic beverages cost extra. You can order off the menu if you want a steak or one of the day's specialty entrees. $$

Where to Stay

There are no hotels or motels in Union (see entries for Elgin or Rockford if that's what you want), but if you don't mind roughing it a bit, try this:

KOA Kampground. *8404 South Union Road; (815) 923–4206 or (800) 562–2827. Internet: www.koakampgrounds.com.* Just north of U.S. Highway 20, adjacent to Donley's Wild West Town. Open from April 15 through October 15. Bring an RV, a trailer, or a tent to camp here. The facility has an outdoor pool, a game room, basketball, vc ball, and bicycles. Rates are $25 for the first two people if you want water or electrical hookup or both, $22 without any hookups. Either way, add $2.50 per person age 3 through 17 to calculate your total family rate. $

Cherry Valley

Population: 1,615. This little suburb just east of Rockford along U.S. Highway 20 has several of the area's major attractions.

MAGIC WATERS WATERPARK (all ages)

7820 North Cherry Vale Boulevard/Bell School Road, Cherry Valley 61016; (815) 332–3260 or (800) 373–1679. Magic Waters is open from Memorial Day through Labor Day. Hours are 10 A.M. to 6 P.M. daily. Admission costs $16 for anyone 4 feet tall or taller and $13 for anyone shorter than 4 feet and age 3 or older. Children age 2 or younger pay $1. Tube rentals cost $4 per day for a single or $6 for a double. Internet: www.magicwaterswaterpark.com.

Along Bypass 20, near the junction with I-39, is Magic Waters. Even from the highway you can see the water slides looming like giant intestines at this 35-acre water park. There are three of them, each about five stories tall, boasting the ability to propel a human body at speeds up to 30 miles per hour. The wave pool here is reportedly the largest in Illinois, with churning waves that reach up to 5 feet in height—definitely do not take your tiny tots in here, or even your grade-schoolers unless they're very good swimmers. The Little Lagoon is the place for the younger set. Decorated with figurines of aquatic creatures, it has fountains and slides. Nearly everyone can enjoy floating in an inner tube along the 1,200-foot-long Splashmagic River Ride. But the centerpiece of this water park is Splashmagic Island, which rises to a height of 50 feet with its fountains, slides, and giant water pail that tips over to dump a thousand gallons of H_2O down the slide and onto the people in the pool below. If you need a break from the watery stuff, there are concessions, a video arcade, and a gift shop on the grounds.

CHERRYVALE MALL (all ages)

Harrison Avenue and Perryville Road, Cherry Valley 61016; (815) 332–2440. Hours are 10 A.M. to 9 P.M. Monday through Saturday and 11 A.M. to 6 P.M. Sunday. Accessible for strollers and wheelchairs. Internet: www.shopyourmall.com.

This is the biggest and best indoor shopping mall in the greater Rockford area. Its 110 stores are anchored by Marshall Field's, Bergner's, and Sears department stores. The mall has a food court.

CHERRY VALLEY GOLF AND GAME (age 3 and up)

7282 CherryVale Mall Drive, Cherry Valley 61016; (815) 332–3399. Open from March 15 through October 31. Hours are 10 A.M. to 10 P.M. Monday through Thursday, 10 A.M. to 11 P.M. Friday and Saturday, and noon to 9:30 P.M. Sunday. Miniature golf costs $4 before 6 P.M. and $5 after 6 P.M. for all ages. Bumper boats cost $3.50 for the driver and $1.50 for a passenger. The facility is accessible for strollers and wheelchairs.

Near the mall, this outdoor entertainment center has an 18-hole miniature golf course with a castle and a stream. You'll also find bumper boats, batting cages, an arcade, and a concession stand.

Where to Eat

Bakers Square. *7105 CherryVale North Boulevard; (815) 332–9557.* Hours are 7 A.M. to 11 P.M. Sunday through Thursday and 7 A.M. to midnight Friday and Saturday. See Restaurant Appendix for description. $

TGIFridays. *2408 South Perryville Road; (815) 332–5355.* Open from 11 A.M. to 10 P.M. Sunday through Thursday and 11 A.M. to midnight Friday and Saturday. See Restaurant Appendix for description. $

Where to Stay

Exel Inn. *220 South Lyford Road; (815) 332–4915 or (800) 356–8013.* Near CherryVale Mall and Magic Waters. This two-story property in the Midwestern regional chain has 101 rooms, each equipped with coffeemaker, hair dryer, and iron and ironing board. No pool. Cribs available free on request. Room rate includes continental breakfast. $$

See also entry for Rockford.

For More Information

Village of Cherry Valley, *202 East State Street, Cherry Valley 61016; (815) 332–3441. Internet: www.cherryvalley.org.*

Rockford

Population: 139,426. Highway 20 splits as it enters Rockford from the east. If you want to go into the heart of the city, look for the BUSINESS 20 sign. If you want to skirt the edge of town (maybe you're on the way to somewhere else and don't want to stop this time), you'll need Bypass 20. This distinction will be clearer if you get a Rockford map ahead of time.

DISCOVERY CENTER MUSEUM (ages 1–12)

711 North Main Street, Rockford 61103; (815) 963–6769. During the school year the museum is open from 11 A.M. to 5 P.M. Tuesday through Saturday and noon to 5 P.M. Sunday, plus Monday school holidays. Summer hours are 10 A.M. to 5 P.M. Monday through Saturday and noon to 5 P.M. Sunday. Admission costs $4 for adults and $3 for young people age 2 through 18. Children age 1 or younger get in free. Accessible for wheelchairs. No smoking.

Science is the emphasis at the family-oriented Discovery Center Museum in Riverfront Museum Park. Among the things you can do: make your hair stand on end with an electrostatic generator, walk through an "infinity tunnel," or manipulate an assortment of levers, pulleys, and gears. A planetarium will let you explore the stars, and the Body Shop has displays and demonstrations on the workings of the human body. Children age 5 or younger can play in the Tot Spot, which has a variety of sturdy plastic toys and a water area. A unique feature of the Discovery Center Museum is the outdoor science park, a two-story wooden maze that looks like a playground but sneaks in entertainingly educational exhibits about weather, water, sound, and caves.

ROCKFORD ART MUSEUM (age 5 and up)

711 North Main Street, Rockford 61103; (815) 968–2787. Hours are 11 A.M. to 5 P.M. Tuesday through Saturday and noon to 5 P.M. Sunday. Admission is **Free**. *The building is accessible for wheelchairs. Internet: www.rockfordartmuseum.com.*

You'd expect the second largest city in Illinois to have an art museum, and this is a respectable one. As an established Regional Arts Institution, it carries many pieces by artists from around the Midwest. The annual *Stateline Vicinity Exhibition* includes paintings, photographs, and sculptures by regional artists. Contemporary art is also a specialty. For example, the museum's permanent collection includes Alexander Calder's 1973 lithograph *Balloons*. Another ongoing exhibition features brilliant glass pieces. A particularly interesting section of the museum contains works by self-taught African-American artists. About a dozen different exhibitions are displayed at the Rockford Art Museum each year, and since 1938 the museum has hosted an annual art fair in downtown Rockford in late September.

FOREST CITY QUEEN AND TRACK TROLLEY CAR 36 (all ages)

324 North Madison Street, Rockford 61103; (815) 987–8894. Forest City Queen *sails at 1, 2, and 3 P.M. Tuesday through Sunday; an extra sailing is added at noon Wednesday and at 4 P.M. Saturday. The trolley departs at 11 A.M., noon, and 1, 2, and 3 P.M. Tuesday and Thursday and at noon, 1, 2, 3, and 4 P.M. Saturday and Sunday. Fare for either one is $3.50 for adults, $3 for young people age 5 through 17, and free for children age 4 or younger. Accommodations are made for passengers with disabilities.*

Cruise the Rock River on the *Forest City Queen* sight-seeing boat or take a trip on a reproduction open-air trolley along the historic riverfront through Sinnissippi Gardens.

MIDWAY VILLAGE AND ROCKFORD MUSEUM CENTER (age 3 and up)

6799 Guilford Road, Rockford 61107; (815) 397–9112. The village and museum are open from April through October. Hours are noon to 4 P.M. Thursday through Sunday. Admission costs $5 for adults and $3 for young people age 3 through 16. Kids age 2 or younger get in free. Thursday is Donation Day, when you pay an amount of your choice. Visitors are requested to call ahead to verify hours and fees before coming. The facility is accessible for wheelchairs.

Midway Village is a re-creation of a typical town from the late 1800s and early 1900s. The buildings contain authentic furnishings, and interpreters in period costumes help visitors understand what life was like during that time. There are some hands-on activities available, such as churning butter. The Rockford Museum Center contains galleries chronicling Rockford's history. Among the contemporary displays is one about the rock band Cheap Trick, which started out in Rockford. You won't want to miss the full-size airplane in the aviation exhibit.

RIVERVIEW ICE HOUSE (age 4 and up)

324 North Madison Avenue, Rockford 61103; (815) 963–7408. Open daily, but public skating hours vary; call for current times. Cost is $4.25 per person. Skate rental costs $2, or bring your own.

There are two ice-skating rinks at this indoor facility. It offers public skating sessions year-round, an unusual way to beat summer heat.

ROCKFORD LIGHTNING (age 3 and up)

Lightning home games are played at the MetroCentre, 300 Elm Street, Rockford 61101; (815) 968–5222 or (815) 968–5600. Season runs November through March. Call for current schedule and ticket prices. Internet: www.metrocentre.com.

You can see minor-league sports action on the basketball court with the Rockford Lightning. This team belongs to the Continental Basketball Association, the official developmental league of the National Basketball Association (NBA).

KLEHM ARBORETUM AND BOTANIC GARDEN (all ages)

2701 Clifton Avenue, Rockford 61102-3537; (815) 965–8146. Open year-round, from 9 A.M. to 4 P.M. daily. Admission is **Free**. *The site is accessible for strollers and wheelchairs. Internet: www.klehm.org.*

Paved pathways wind for a mile through a lovely array of flowers, bushes, and trees. You can strike off on your own or make a reservation ahead of time to take a guided tour. The 155-acre site is a joint development project of the Northern Illinois Botanical Society and the Winnebago County Forest Preserve, so expect it to look better each visit.

TINKER SWISS COTTAGE MUSEUM (age 5 and up)

411 Kent Street, Rockford 61102; (815) 964–2424. Tours are given at 1, 2, and 3 P.M. Tuesday through Sunday and last 45 minutes. Cost is $4 for adults, $3.50 for seniors age 65 or older, and $1 for young people age 17 or younger. The building is accessible for wheelchairs. Internet: www.tinkercottage.com.

Atop a limestone bluff, this 20-room cottage was built in 1865 in the style of a Swiss chalet. Painted murals adorn the walls and ceilings, and the home is filled with fancy furniture, porcelain, and artworks. The museum may be visited by tour only; you can't just go in and wander around. Due to the length of the tour and the number of delicate objects that must not be touched, this attraction is not recommended for children age 4 or younger.

Where to Eat

Bing's Drive-In. *3613 South Main; (815) 968–8663.* Open from 11 A.M. to 8 P.M. daily from late spring through the first week of September. This is an old-fashioned place with carhops who deliver your order. You can eat in your car or at picnic tables set up along with a little playground on the restaurant grounds. Sandwiches include barbecued beef, breaded pork, hamburgers, and hot dogs, with french fries or onion rings if you choose. But the biggest treat is the soft-serve ice cream, which you can order in cones, sundaes, or shakes. The latter come in some yummy flavors, such as lemon and black raspberry. The orange shake tastes just like a Dreamsicle. $

Giordano's. *333 Executive Parkway, off Mulford Road; (815) 398–5700.* Open from 11 A.M. to midnight Sunday through Thursday and 11 A.M. to 1 A.M. Friday and Saturday. See Restaurant Appendix for description. $

HomeTown Buffet. *525 South Perryville Road, at State Street; (815) 227–1770.* Hours are 10:30 A.M. to 8:30 P.M. Monday through Friday and 8 A.M. to 9:30 P.M. Saturday and Sunday. See Restaurant Appendix for description. $

Old Country Buffet. *6403 East State Street, at Mulford Road; (815) 394–1702.* Hours are 10:30 A.M. to 9 P.M. Monday through Thursday, 10:30 A.M. to 9:30 P.M. Friday, 8 A.M. to 9:30 P.M. Saturday, and 8 A.M. to 9 P.M. Sunday. See Restaurant Appendix for description. $

Where to Stay

Best Western Clock Tower Resort and Conference Center. *7801 East State Street (I–90 and Business 20); (815) 398–6000 or (800) 358–7666.* This resort offers 252 rooms of lodging in a facility with indoor and outdoor pools, sauna, whirlpools, volleyball and basketball courts, indoor tennis, planned kids' activities, and an adults-only fitness center. There are four restaurants and lounges on the premises. No pets allowed. The resort offers a variety of accommodation packages that include golf at the adjacent 18-hole course or a dinner-theater performance. $$$$

Comfort Inn. *7392 Argus Drive (along Business 20); (815) 398–7061 or (800) 228–5150.* This economical chain property has 64 rooms. Amenities include indoor heated pool and whirlpool. Continental breakfast is included in the room rate. $$$

Hampton Inn. *615 Clark Drive (along Business 20); (815) 229–0404 or (800) 426–7866.* There are 122 rooms in the inn. Amenities include indoor pool and whirlpool and Nordic Track room. The room rate includes continental breakfast. $$$

Holiday Inn. *7550 East State Street (I–90 and Business 20); (815) 398–2200 or (800) 383–7829.* This seven-story hotel has 202 rooms and lots of amenities, including heated indoor pool and Jacuzzi, fitness center, putting green, and table tennis. The on-site Hoffman House restaurant specializes in prime rib. The hotel also has a gift shop, a beauty salon, and a Hertz car rental office. $$$

Howard Johnson Lodge. *3909 Eleventh Street; (along Illinois Highway 251 South); (815) 397–9000 or (800) 446–4656.* This property has 148 rooms, each with a coffeemaker, and 12 apartments. Amenities include an indoor pool, whirlpool, sauna, exercise room, and game room. $$

For More Information

Rockford Area Convention and Visitors Bureau, *211 North Main Street, Rockford 61101; (815) 963–8111 or (800) 521–0849. Internet: www.gorockford.com.*

Loves Park

Population: 15,462. This suburb to the north of Rockford has several attractions of interest to action-oriented families.

SKI BRONCS WATER SKI SHOW (all ages)

In Shorewood Park, 5000 Forest Grove, at Evelyn Avenue, Loves Park 61111; (815) 654–1155. Shows are at 7 P.M. Wednesday and Friday from mid-May through Labor Day. **Free**.

Just show up at the park and find a spot near the water to enjoy this waterskiing spectacle. The Ski Broncs have been ranked third in the nation for their performances, which combine athletics with theatrics. Bring along a picnic, or partake of on-site concessions.

CARLSON ARCTIC ICE ARENA AND PLAYWORLD (age 1 and up)

4150 North Perryville Road, Loves Park 61111; (815) 969–4069. Call for current public skating times. Cost is $4.25 per person age 5 or older. Children age 4 or younger get in free. Bring your own skates, or rent them for $2 per person, all ages. Playworld hours are 11 A.M. to 8 P.M. Monday through Friday, 10 A.M. to 6 P.M. Saturday, and 11 A.M. to 6 P.M. Sunday. Admission costs $3.50 for kids age 3 through 12, $2.25 for 2-year-olds, and $1.50 for 1-year-olds.

This family recreation complex is open year-round. Public skating sessions are offered at the ice rink. Maybe one parent can take the grade-schoolers there while the other parent monitors the younger kids' activity in the Playworld, a three-story apparatus with tubes, slides, nets, and ball pits. You can come to the Playworld even when the ice rink is closed or off-limits to the public while lessons are going on. The facility has a video arcade and concessions as well.

ROCKFORD RAPTORS AND ROCKFORD DACTYLS (age 3 and up)

Games are played at Wedgebury Soccer Complex, 8800 East Riverside Boulevard, Loves Park 61111; (800) 521–0849. Season runs from April through early Sep-

tember. Tickets cost about $3 to $5. Call for current schedule. Internet: www.indoorsportscenter.com.

The Raptors are a men's "professional" soccer team and the Dactyls a women's "amateur" soccer team; the main difference in the designations is that the men get paid to play and the women do not. The teams belong to the United States Intercontinental Soccer League (USISL) and the U.S. Intercontinental Women's Soccer League (USIWSL), respectively. So you don't have to wait for World Cup to come around once every four years before you can watch live soccer action and shout "Gooooooooal!"

Where to Eat and Stay

See entries for Rockford.

Freeport

Population: 25,840. Continuing west from Rockford on U.S. Highway 20 brings you to Freeport. At Douglas and State Streets stands a statue of Abraham Lincoln that marks the site of the second debate between Lincoln and Stephen Douglas in 1858.

SILVER CREEK AND STEPHENSON RAILROAD (all ages)

Corner of Lamm and Walnut Roads, Freeport 61032; (800) 369–2955. Excursions run on selected weekends from May through October; call for exact schedule. Tickets cost $4 for anyone age 12 or older and $2 for kids age 11 or younger. Accommodations are made for passengers with disabilities.

Take a 4-mile ride on a 1912 Heisler steam locomotive with three antique cabooses and a covered passenger flatcar. You'll cross a bridge 30 feet above Yellow Creek on this short but scenic journey. The railroad is staffed by enthusiastic volunteers.

KRAPE PARK (all ages)

Park Boulevard at Empire Street, Freeport 61032; (815) 235–6114. The park is open year-round, from dawn to 10:30 P.M. daily, and park admission is **Free**. *Miniature golf hours are noon to 10 P.M. daily during summer, and the cost is $2.50 for adults age 21 or older, $2 for young people age 13 through 20, and $1.50 for kids age 12 or younger.*

Krape Park has lots of family activities. You'll find a playground, a picnic area, a duck pond, a waterfall, tennis courts, and some hiking trails. For just a quarter you can ride on an old-fashioned carousel. The park also has an outdoor miniature golf course. Paddleboat and canoe rentals are available if you want to go up a creek *with* a paddle. In winter you can go ice-skating on Yellow Creek or sledding down Bandshell Hill.

PECATONIA PRAIRIE PATH (all ages)

Hillcrest and East River Road, Freeport 61032; (815) 233–0814 or (800) 369–2955. Open from sunrise to sunset. **Free**.

This scenic 20-mile nature trail goes between Freeport and Rockford. Its surface is a hard-packed dirt called "railroad ballast." The path is used by hikers, mountain bikers, horseback riders, and, in winter, cross-country skiers. It goes across the Pecatonia River on a 250-foot double-span trestle bridge. You can stop en route in Pecatonia for a picnic in Sumner Park, where there's a playground if you're carrying young passengers who need a chance to stretch their legs.

Where to Eat

Cannova's. *1101 West Empire Street; (815) 233–0032.* Hours are 5 to 10 P.M. Sunday through Thursday and 5 to 11 P.M. Friday and Saturday. No smoking in the restaurant, but it is allowed in the adjoining lounge. This Italian restaurant has been a Freeport tradition since 1921. In addition to pasta and pizza, you can get chicken or fish entrees. $

Golden Corral. *1404 West Galena Avenue; (815) 235–7036.* Open from 11 A.M. to 10 P.M. daily. Smoking allowed in a designated section. Children's menu available. Order a steak, chicken, or seafood entree and then pick your own side dishes at the all-you-can-eat buffet. $

Pizza Hut. *1428 West Galena Avenue; (815) 235–3733.* Open from 10:30 A.M. to 11 P.M. Sunday through Thursday and 10:30 A.M. to 1 A.M. Friday and Saturday. See Restaurant Appendix for description. $

Where to Stay

Best Western Stephenson Hotel. *109 South Galena Avenue; (815) 233–0300 or (800) 383–0300.* This eight-story brick hotel has 73 rooms, each with cable TV and coffeemaker. It has an outdoor swimming pool and an indoor exercise room. $$$

Freeport Ramada. *1300 East South Street; (815) 235–3121 or (800) 272–6232.* This 85-room property features indoor pool, whirlpool, game room, and exercise facilities. Pets are allowed. $$$

For More Information

Stephenson County Convention and Visitors Bureau, *2047 AYP Road, Freeport 61032; (815) 233–1357 or (800) 369–2955. Internet: www.freeportillinois.com.*

Smile and Say "Cheese"! While in Lena, not far beyond Freeport to the west of U.S. Highway 20, remember that you are only about a dozen miles south of the Wisconsin border. Then it won't seem unusual to find two specialty cheese shops in a community of fewer than 3,000 people.

- **Kolb-Lena Cheese Company** is off U.S. Highway 20 at 3990 North Sunnyside Road; (815) 369–4577. This outlet store offers daily specials and samples; the Delico cheese is a specialty. Hours are 10 A.M. to 6 P.M. daily; closed Sunday in January and February.
- **Torkelson Cheese Company** is off Illinois Highway 73 at 9453 Louisa Road; (815) 369–4265. Specialties here are Muenster and brick cheeses and heavy cream (bring your own jar). Hours are 8 A.M. to 4 P.M. Monday through Friday and 9 A.M. to 3 P.M. Saturday; closed Sunday.

Galena

Population: 3,647. The picturesque town of Galena, near the Mississippi River, does an exceptionally high volume of tourist business here, given its size; about a million visitors come through town each year, mostly from June through October. Galena reportedly started out as a boomtown during the nation's first mineral rush. Ulysses S. Grant was born here in 1822 and spent most of his life here, when he wasn't fighting the Civil War or serving as president. By 1900 lead production was declining and so was the town. Galena began its resurgence in the 1950s, cashing in on its historical appeal. The Illinois Department of Resources is hoping to build a bike path between Galena and Savanna, to the south, which would be a key link in the planned Grand Illinois Trail to circle the northern part of the state in a 500-mile network of trails for biking, hiking, and horseback riding.

If you intend to visit the downtown area, stop first at the Visitor Information Center 2 blocks north of Highway 20 on the east bank of the Galena

River, which runs through the center of town. Housed in an old train depot, the center is stocked with maps and brochures and staffed with helpful people to answer your questions. It's open from 9 A.M. to 5 P.M. Monday through Thursday, 9 A.M. to 7 P.M. Friday and Saturday, and 10 A.M. to 5 P.M. Sunday. The center also has a big parking lot across the railroad tracks, and it would be a good place to leave your car if you plan to wander around downtown for more than a couple hours; parking along the narrow streets there is hard to come by and has a two-hour limit.

Main Street is more than just a name in Galena. Here you'll find the concentration of shops for which the town has become famous. There's a multitude of antiques shops, the biggest claim to fame, but you'll have better luck saving the antiques browsing for a time when the kids are staying at Grandma and Grandpa's. Instead look for spots that may be of particular interest to youngsters, such as the shops that sell dolls, teddy bears, toy soldiers, and sweets.

Here Comes the Fudge Fudge lovers will travel for miles to find a mouthwatering morsel of the creamy confection. Here are a couple area shops that have been favorably compared to those of the renowned mecca of Mackinac Island, Michigan.

- **Galena's Kandy Kitchen.** *100 North Main Street, Galena 61036; (815) 777–0241.* Reportedly owned and operated by the son of the guy who invented Chuckles gumdrop-style candy, Kandy Kitchen offers pick-your-own candies and jelly beans, along with numerous chocolate creations, including five kinds of fudge, all made with a 40 percent butterfat cream. You can watch some of the candy making in progress (the fudge maker hides in back, sorry). Hours are 10 A.M. to 9 P.M. daily from May through October and 10 A.M. to 5 P.M. daily from November through April.
- **Rocky Mountain Chocolate Factory.** *207 South Main Street, Galena 61036; (815) 777–3200 or (800) 235–8160. Internet: www.rmcfusa.com.* Choose from among hand-dipped chocolates, truffles, chocolate chip cookies, frozen chocolate-covered bananas, and brownies, along with the fudge that is made out front. Try the specialty Oreo or black walnut fudge. Hours are 9:30 A.M. to 5:30 P.M. Sunday through Thursday and 9 A.M. to 9 P.M. Friday and Saturday.

ULYSSES S. GRANT HOME STATE HISTORIC SITE (age 7 and up)

500 Bouthillier Street, Galena 61036; (815) 777–0248 or (815) 777–3310. Hours are 9 A.M. to 4:45 P.M. daily, contingent upon continued state funding. In times of budget cuts, the site is closed Tuesday and Wednesday, so call ahead to be sure it's open when you want to visit. Admission is **Free***, but donations are encouraged. The suggested amount is $3 for adults and $1 for young people age 18 or younger. The site is accessible for wheelchairs.*

The Ulysses S. Grant Home State Historic Site is one of the most famous places to visit in Galena. The Italianate house was built in 1860 and presented to General Grant when he returned from the Civil War in 1865. Today it is owned and operated by the Illinois Historic Preservation Agency, which has taken pains to maintain the home as it appeared in Grant's time. It has many original furnishings.

GALENA POST OFFICE (all ages)

110 Green Street, Galena 61036; (815) 777–0225. Hours are 8:30 A.M. to 4:30 P.M. Monday through Friday and 9 A.M. to noon Saturday. The building is closed Sunday. **Free**.

Mail a postcard to a friend and see another bit of history at the same time when you stop in at the Galena Post Office. The Renaissance Revival building was constructed from 1857 to 1859 under the supervision of Ely Samuel Parker, a Seneca Iroquois Indian who was General Grant's military secretary during the Civil War (1861-1865). Parker would go on to become a brigadier general in 1867, and then be appointed U.S. commissioner of Indian affairs in 1869 by President Grant. The Galena Post Office is one of the oldest continuously operating post offices in the United States.

VINEGAR HILL LEAD MINE AND MUSEUM (age 4 and up)

8885 North Three Pines Road, Galena 61036; (815) 777–0855. About 6 miles north of U.S. Highway 20 off Illinois Highway 84. Open from 9 A.M. to 5 P.M. daily from June through August and from 9 A.M. to 5 P.M. Saturday and Sunday only in May, September, and October; closed November through April. Admission, which includes the tour, costs $5 for adults and $2.50 for students age 5 or older. Children age 4 or younger get in free.

Founded in the early 1800s by John Furlong, an Irish soldier, and passed down through subsequent generations, the underground mine is maintained as a tourist attraction by Mark Furlong, John's great-great-

great-grandson. You can take a half-hour tour that starts in the museum with an explanation of the tools and methods used, then don a hard hat and descend into the mine.

ALICE T. VIRTUE MEMORIAL POOL AND WATER PARK (all ages)

North of town, on Stagecoach Trail, in Recreation Park, Galena 61036; (815) 777–1050. Open daily during summer from 12:30 to 4:30 P.M. and 5:30 to 8 P.M. Admission to the water park costs $3.75 for adults age 19 or older, $2.75 for young people age 6 through 18, and $1.25 for children age 5 or younger.

The water park has a pool with zero-depth shallow end plus a separate wading pool and a 131-foot water slide. Recreation Park itself has picnic areas with grills and shelters, a playground, a horseshoe pit, a sand volleyball court, diamonds for baseball and softball, and a concession stand. Admission to Recreation Park alone is **Free**.

SHENANDOAH RIDING CENTER (age 8 and up)

200 North Brodrecht Road, Galena 61036, about 8 miles east of town, in the Galena Territory; (815) 777–2373. Open from 8:30 A.M. to 4:30 P.M. daily. A one-hour trail ride costs $23 per person age 8 or older. Children age 7 or younger are not allowed on the trail. Reservations are required. Internet: www.shenandoahridingcenter.com.

Here you can take a one-hour trail ride. The path includes wooded areas and open fields, even meandering along a creek for a while. The center also can offer you a hayride, or—in winter—a sleigh ride.

Where to Eat

Log Cabin. *201 North Main Street; (815) 777–0393.* Reportedly Galena's oldest restaurant, the Log Cabin serves lunch and dinner. Choose from a menu of soups, salads, sandwiches, steaks, and seafood—plus Greek specialties. Try some saganaki, the flaming cheese appetizer. *Opah!* $$

Happy Joe's Pizza and Ice Cream Parlor. *9919 Highway 20 East; (815) 777–1830.* Open from 7 A.M. to 10 P.M. Sunday through Thursday and 7 A.M. to midnight Friday and Saturday. Here is a good place for a family meal. The kids can watch the model train travel its course while waiting for their pizza. At lunchtime there's a smorgasbord with salad bar. Just be sure to save room for dessert—ice cream, of course, prepared in a variety of tasty ways. $

Skiing in the Galena Area If you're visiting the area in winter and your kids are old enough, consider going skiing. Both downhill and cross-country are offered here.

- **Chestnut Mountain Resort.** *8700 West Chestnut Road, Galena 61036; (815) 777–1320 or (800) 397–1320. Internet: www.chestnutmtn.com.* Illinois doesn't have a lot of downhill skiing, but you'll find some here. The resort has 17 runs, the longest of which is 3,500 feet. The biggest vertical drop is 475 feet. Chairlifts (including a quad lift), rope tows, equipment rental, and lessons are available. The lodge is on top of a bluff overlooking the Mississippi River, offering spectacular views. The facility is open from Thanksgiving Day through St. Patrick's Day. Rates for lift tickets and ski rental vary with time of day, day of the week, and number of days you plan to ski. Call for an exact quote.
- **Eagle Ridge Resort.** *Route 20 East, Galena 61036; (815) 777–2500.* Here you can go cross-country skiing along 34 miles of trails through the woods and around the lake.

Where to Stay

Forget about finding a cheap motel around here. Plan to stay overnight when you can splurge on a luxury resort, stay in the historic downtown hotel, or perhaps try a quaint bed-and-breakfast.

Eagle Ridge Inn and Resort. *Route 20 East; (815) 777–2444 or (800) 892–2269. Internet: www.eagleridge.com.* You can't get anywhere near Galena without seeing signs for the Eagle Ridge Inn and Resort, off U.S. Highway 20 about 8 miles east of town. In summer you'll see golfers aplenty on the four championship 18-hole courses. From November through March the resort's winter activities are open to the public, including sleigh rides, ice-skating, sledding, snowshoeing, and cross-country skiing. There is a trail fee, and there are other charges for renting equipment. Lodging at the resort comprises 80 inn rooms and more than 300 other accommodation units, including houses, town houses, condos, and golf villas. Guests may enjoy the indoor pool, whirlpool, sauna, fitness center, game room, indoor golf center, and children's playroom. There are lots of package deals offered. $$$$

Chestnut Mountain Resort. *8700 West Chestnut Road; (815) 777–1320 or (800) 397–1320. Internet: www.chestnutmtn.com.* This resort sits atop a high bluff overlooking the Mississippi River, 8 miles southeast of town. Guests may enjoy the indoor pool, whirlpool, and sauna, along with numerous other amenities that are also open to the public. For example, play miniature golf or, for a real adventure, try the Alpine Slide, where you ride a wheeled sled down a 2,500-foot-long, toboggan-like track—whee! The resort has a restaurant on the premises that serves breakfast, lunch, and dinner daily, with a special Sunday brunch offered from May through October. The specialties are fresh catfish and barbecued ribs. $$$$

Amber Creek's Territory Lodging can help you find a place to stay. This outfit manages such vacation rentals as furnished cottages, town houses, and houses, some of which can accommodate as many as 12 people—a boon for larger families. Rental prices vary greatly depending on when and where you stay; they range from $75 to $400 a night. Call (815) 777-9320 for details.

DeSoto House Hotel. *230 South Main Street; (815) 777–0090. Internet: www.desotohouse.com.* This three-story brick building dates back to 1855 and is listed on the National Register of Historic Places. But don't let the period decor fool you: The 55 rooms have central air and cable TV. There's no swimming pool, though. If you stay during the week or in the less temperate off-season time, you'll get a lower rate. The hotel also offers a variety of package deals that include meals, downhill skiing, or entertainment with the room. $$$$

Best Western Quiet House Suites. *U.S. Highway 20 East; (815) 777–2577 or (800) 528–1234.* Rated three diamonds by AAA. This lovely two-story motel has 42 rooms. Those that face outdoors have little balconies. Amenities include indoor and outdoor swimming pools, whirlpool, and fitness center. Pets are allowed for $15 but must be attended. $$$$

B&Bs. Many bed-and-breakfast places don't cater to families and thus are generally not listed among lodging choices in this book. However, the Galena area is an exception. Jo Daviess County has become known as the "B&B capital of the Midwest" for its abundance of bed-and-breakfast houses and inns. Not all of the 50-plus B&Bs in the area accept children (some do so only with age restrictions such as "over 10" or "over 12"), but some do advertise themselves with "children welcome." Ask for a list of B&Bs (see For More Information section that follows).

For More Information

Galena/Jo Daviess County Convention & Visitors Bureau, *101 Bouthieller Street, Galena 61036; (815) 777–0203 or (800) 747–9377. Internet: www.galena.org.*

Let's return to the eastern border of Northern Illinois and head west along Illinois Highway 64. We'll start in St. Charles, right along the Fox River.

St. Charles

Population: 22,501. When the city of St. Charles paved its Main Street (Illinois Highway 64) in 1928, it created a direct route west from Lake Street in Chicago. The city hosts a number of events throughout the year. The Pride of the Fox RiverFest takes place in June. Come to St. Charles in mid-October to catch the annual Scarecrow Festival. You'll see handcrafted scarecrows and can even try making your own. Costumed characters, including a scarecrow on stilts, liven up this family-oriented event. There are kiddie rides, puppet shows, a petting zoo, and a special haunted house just for kids. Live bands, concessions, and an arts-and-crafts show round out the offerings. Another special event is the 16-day international St. Charles Art and Music Festival, held in July every other year, in odd-numbered years. Call the festival office at (630) 584–3378 for details.

ST. CHARLES BELLE AND *FOX RIVER QUEEN* (age 3 and up)

Cruises depart from Pottawatomie Park, on the east bank of the Fox River about 1½ miles north of Illinois Highway 64, St. Charles 60174; (630) 584–2334. Season runs from May through mid-October. Sailing times for June through August are 3:30 P.M. Monday through Friday; 2, 3, and 4 P.M. Saturday; and 2, 3, 4, and 5 P.M. Sunday. In May, September, and October, departures are at 2, 3, and 4 P.M. Saturday and Sunday only. Tickets cost $5 for anyone age 16 or older and $3.50 for kids age 2 through 15. Children age 1 or younger ride free.

You can catch a ride up the Fox River on one of two double-decker paddle wheelers, the *St. Charles Belle* and the *Fox River Queen.* Weekday cruises last one hour, weekend cruises 50 minutes.

RIVER VIEW MINIATURE GOLF (age 3 and up)

In Pottawatomie Park, on the east bank of the Fox River about 1½ miles north of Illinois Highway 64, St. Charles 60174; (630) 584–1028. Open daily from Memorial Day through Labor Day and weekends only in May, September, and October. Hours are 11 A.M. to 10 P.M. Sunday through Friday and 11 A.M. to 11 P.M. Saturday. Cost is $5 for anyone age 16 or older, $4 for young people age 6 through 15, and $1 for children age 5 or younger with a paid adult.

This 18-hole outdoor miniature golf course has a waterfall, ponds, and gardens. You should be aware that there's a $5-per-car entrance fee to get into Pottawatomie Park. The fee is waived if you're coming in for the riverboat ride, and you can do other things in the park afterward.

TEKAWITHA WOODS NATURE CENTER (all ages)

35 W 076 Villa Marie Road, St. Charles 60174; (847) 741–8350. Hours are 9 A.M. to 4 P.M. Monday through Thursday and noon to 4 P.M. Saturday and Sunday; closed Friday. **Free***, but donations are appreciated. The center is accessible for strollers and wheelchairs.*

The namesake woods are at the big bend of the Fox River, making a scenic setting for this hands-on nature center. The "discovery corner" is especially for children, and there is a wildlife observation room. Exhibits and nature programs vary.

PHEASANT RUN RESORT AND CONVENTION CENTER (all ages)

4051 East Main Street, St. Charles 60174; (630) 584–6300 or (800) 999–3319. Call for current rates; be sure to ask about package deals. Internet: www.pheasantrun.com.

About 500 people work here to keep this sprawling complex operating and the guests happy. The accommodation section has 473 rooms. Amenities include indoor pool and game room. Kids Klub offers supervised activities for children. On the weekends entertainment at the resort is provided by a magician, a clown, and a caricature artist. Ask about the Splash Bash Family Get-Away package.

The resort has a beauty salon, a golf shop, and several other shops full of gifts and souvenirs. The conference center, modestly named the Mega ExpoCenter, covers 39,000 square feet. Add in the 42 meeting rooms and the total space jumps to about 100,000 square feet.

The Pheasant Run Resort Dinner Theatre has a special family series of productions called "The Adventures of Rat Dog and Princess Toad," which modernize traditional fairy tales. After the show comes a kids' brunch during which they can meet the actors.

CHARLESTOWNE MALL (all ages)

3800 East Main Street, St. Charles 60174; (630) 513–1120. At Illinois Highway 64 and Kirk Road. Hours are 10 A.M. to 9 P.M. Monday through Saturday and 11 A.M. to 6 P.M. Sunday. Free wheelchair and stroller rental are available in the office beside the arcade. Internet: www.charlestownemall.com.

This attractive, two-story indoor shopping mall has about 120 stores, anchored by department stores Carson Pirie Scott, JCPenney, Kohl's, and Sears. The mall has an open, airy feel. Pastel green steel beams frame the glass-paneled ceiling above the corridors and a central atrium with a glass elevator and central fountain. Floor tile is in light earth tones: tan, heather green, soft burgundy. The aisles are wide and unobstructed, so much so that two strollers can comfortably wheel along side by side without totally blocking everyone behind. Stores of interest to kids include the Disney Store and a handful of gift shops that carry Beanie Babies and Pokémon merchandise. There are upscale clothing stores and shops full of art prints for more adult tastes.

The highlight of Charlestowne is its double-level carousel, which was custom-made in Italy for the mall's 1991 opening and is showcased in a glass-walled, skylit atrium facing the back of the mall. Painted scenes on the ceiling and around the top outer edge depict Venice, each framed in ornate, creamy gold. White lights outline the exterior. A few of the gilded horses pump up and down in the traditional manner, but most rock gently forward and back. There are teacups and bench seats for riders who want a flatter surface to sit upon. Tickets for the carousel cost $1. Children age 5 or younger must be accompanied by an adult age 18 or older. In this case, the adult does not have to pay; only the child needs a ticket.

Rest rooms and a food court are located near the carousel, as is the Time Out arcade. It has games for all ages, from Spider Stomp and Bozo's Grand Prize Game for younger children to bloody, violent video games that appeal to teens. Most games take one or two tokens, which cost 25 cents apiece. The machines spit out tickets that can be exchanged for plastic prizes or candy.

NORRIS THEATRE (age 3 and up)

1040 Dunham Road, St. Charles 60174; (630) 584–7200. North off Illinois Highway 64. Call for current schedule and prices.

This modern, brick arts center complex offers a variety of family-oriented dramatic and musical performances. Shows in 2000 included the original musical *The Careful Critters* and singer-guitarist Dave Rudolf.

THE MARKET (age 5 and up)

12 North Third Street, St. Charles 60174; (630) 584–3899. Hours are 10 A.M. to 5:30 P.M. Monday through Friday (sometimes open until 8 P.M. Thursday), 10 A.M. to 5 P.M. Saturday, and 11 A.M. to 5 P.M. Sunday.

This enclosed minimall has about two dozen shops—stalls, actually—under one roof. There are antiques, but kids may be more interested in Beanie Babies, Gund bears, rubber stamps, beads, American Girl books and dolls, and whimsical ceramic mugs with cats and characters from Disney and *Star Wars.* There are too many tempting things for toddlers to grab at, and the narrow aisles are not very handy for strollers, so please don't bring children younger than grade-school age.

ARCADA THEATRE (age 3 and up)

105 East Main Street, St. Charles 60174; (630) 584–0755. Showing first-run feature films; call for current show titles and times. Tickets cost $4.50 for children, students, and seniors at all times and for adults before 6 P.M., $6.75 for adults after 6 P.M.

Built in 1926 in an ornate style called Venetian Spanish, this theater was designed by architect Elmer F. Behrns, the same guy who did the Chicago Theatre and the Tivoli in Downers Grove. Today the original decor, balcony, and stage are intact. Outside is a big, blazing marquee. Inside, the auditorium has light peach-colored stucco walls and a wrap-around balcony with a black wrought-iron railing. Arches and columns below the balcony frame the back of the theater. Hanging lamps with matching wrought iron lend soft illumination to the cavernous interior, which is capped by a domed ceiling painted with blue sky and puffy clouds. Dark wooden crossbeams in the ceiling are adorned with fancy designs in deep reds and greens. There is a curtained, columned balcony on either side of the stage. The proscenium arch frames a gigantic screen, and speakers all around pump out state-of-the-art sound that is an acceptable modification of the original system. The red plush seats also are acceptably modern, with cup holders. Some spaces are left open for theatergoers in wheelchairs. There is also a special accessible rest room with changing table. The balcony is open on Tuesday night only. On Friday and Saturday before the first evening show, the huge pipe organ rises up from the orchestra pit, and an organist plays a little concert.

Where to Eat

Colonial Juice Cafe. *110 North Third Street; (630) 584–9878.* Open from 10 A.M. to 10 P.M. daily. Near the Market minimall; look for the giant pink ice-cream cone out front. This is one of three St. Charles locations for the family-owned dairy and ice-cream business that's been around since 1905. The rich ice cream comes in a variety of flavors; order one of the generous scoops in a plain or sugar cone. At this location another specialty is the smoothie, a blend of whole fruit and fruit juices punched up with protein, vitamins, and minerals. But despite all that healthy stuff, it tastes like liquid sherbet—yum. At no extra charge you can add "boosters" like wheat germ, ginseng, or even bee pollen. A variety of sandwiches, salads, and munchies rounds out the menu. $

Kane County Rookies Sports Grille and Pizza. *1545 West Main Street; (630) 513–0681.* Hours are 11 A.M. to 1 A.M. Sunday through Thursday and 11 A.M. to 2 A.M. Friday and Saturday. The large family-oriented dining area in front offers good views of the TVs posted all around, tuned to sports, of course. One of Michael Jordan's jerseys hangs in a frame on the wall, along with autographed photos and other memorabilia. The horseshoe-shaped bar is in back. Cheesy thin-crust pizza is the house specialty, but you can also order barbecued ribs, a huge burger, or other sandwiches. $

Gino's East. *1590 East Main Street; (630) 513–1311.* Hours are 11 A.M. to 10 P.M. Sunday through Thursday and 11 A.M. to 11 P.M. Friday and Saturday. This pizza place specializes in the same deep-dish kind that you can get at its parent restaurant in downtown Chicago, but you can get the thin-crust type, too. $

Bakers Square. *1510 East Main Street; (630) 584–2737.* Hours are 7 A.M. to 11 P.M. Sunday through Thursday and 7 A.M. to midnight Friday and Saturday. See Restaurant Appendix for description. $

Where to Stay

Best Western Inn. *1635 East Main Street; (630) 584–4550 or (800) 528–1234.* There are 54 rooms at this two-story brick motel between Charlestowne Mall and downtown. Amenities include heated outdoor pool, indoor whirlpool, and fitness room. The room rate includes continental breakfast. Note: All rooms at this property are nonsmoking and have cable TV. $$$

Days Inn. *100 Tyler Road; (630) 513–6500 or (800) 329–7466.* This three-story, tan-and-brick property was remodeled in 1998. It has 82 rooms, including one-room and two-room suites, plus an indoor pool. Continental breakfast is included in the room rate. $$

Holiday Inn Express. *1600 East Main Street; (630) 584–5300 or (800) 465–4329.* This two-story property opened in 1997. It has 122 rooms. Amenities include outdoor pool, fitness center, and laundry room. The room rate includes continental breakfast. $$

Super 8. *1520 East Main Street; (630) 377–8388 or (800) 800–8000.* This three-story Tudor-style budget motel has 68 rooms, but that's about all. No pool. $$

For More Information

St. Charles Convention and Visitors Bureau, *311 North Second Street, St. Charles 60174; (630) 377–6161 or (800) 777–4373.*

Geneva

Population: 12,617. Just south of St. Charles is Geneva, sort of a sister city to St. Charles (extensive development over the past decade makes a boundary between the two cities nearly indistinguishable). Illinois Highways 25 and 31 and a number of local north-south streets link Geneva and St. Charles. The easiest entry into Geneva from east or west is Illinois Highway 38 (Roosevelt Road). North-west Illinois Highways 25 and 31 also link up with Highway 38. Off Interstate 88, exit north at the Farnsworth-Kirk exit and proceed north to Highway 38. Geneva is the end of the line for the Union Pacific Metra West Line commuter service from downtown Chicago.

In the downtown area Geneva has lots of historic homes dating back to the mid-1800s. Many of them have been converted to specialty shops featuring apparel, art prints, pottery, jewelry, woodworking, wine, cheese, crafts, toys and games, and restaurants. For a Free brochure containing a map and a complete list of shops with their addresses and phone numbers, write to the Third Street Merchants Association, P.O. Box 95, Geneva 60134.

GRAHAM'S FINE CHOCOLATES AND ICE CREAM (all ages)

227 South Third Street, Geneva 60134; (630) 232–6655. Hours are 10 A.M. to 9 P.M. Monday through Thursday, 10 A.M. to 10 P.M. Friday and Saturday, and noon to 5 P.M. Sunday.

This downtown shop deserves special mention. You can watch candy making and chocolate dipping in action here, and then buy some handmade chocolates and gourmet ice cream.

KANE COUNTY COUGARS (all ages)

Games are played at Philip B. Elfstrom Stadium off Illinois Highway 38 (you can see it from the highway) at 34W002 Cherry Lane, Geneva 60134; (630) 232–8811. Season runs from April through early September. Most weekend games are in the afternoon, most weekday games in the early evening. Ticket prices in 2000 ranged from $5 for lawn sections to $8 for box seats. There's no discount for kids or seniors, but sometimes there are special promotions that reduce the price. Children age 2 or younger get in free. Free parking in gravel lot. Call for the current schedule and prices. During the season the box office is open from 9 A.M. to 5 P.M. Monday through Friday and 10 A.M. to 1 P.M. Saturday; hours are shorter the rest of the year. On game days the box office stays open through the end of the game. Internet: www.KCCOUGARS.com.

Having celebrated their tenth anniversary of existence in 2000, the Kane County Cougars remain one of the state's most popular minor-league baseball clubs. The Cougars are the A-level affiliate of the Florida Marlins. A 1998 renovation expanded the stadium's capacity to about 9,200 seats, including some red box seats with cup holders and a row of spaces for wheelchairs behind the last row of stands. Some of the additional seating space was taken from the lawn sections along the outfield foul lines. There's still plenty of room in those sections if you want to bring a blanket and sit there; just be aware that there's a fairly steep slope to the turf. There are no awnings or overhangs, so use plenty of sunscreen for day games. A big outfield video screen displays player stats, crowd shots, and advertisements. The concourse behind the seating areas is wide and navigable for wheelchairs and strollers. Rest rooms, including one for families, are adequate and well spaced. Concessions are abundant and varied, including fruit-flavored ices and grilled sandwiches as well as the usual ballpark fare. In the souvenir shops you'll find numerous items in Cougar green as well as Marlin turquoise. Cougars games include entertaining stunts and promotions such as the human bowling ball. A volunteer from the crowd is secured inside a metal-framed ball, which is then rolled down a ramp toward a set of giant plastic bowling pins. In the Mascot Dash, a child volunteer races Ozzie the Cougar around the bases (somehow Ozzie always comes in second).

FOX RIVER TRAIL (all ages)

Along the Fox River, Geneva; (630) 232–6060. Open from sunrise to sunset daily. **Free**.

This paved, 32-mile trail for hiking and biking passes through scenic parks with picnic areas and playgrounds.

Where to Eat and Stay

See entries for St. Charles.

For More Information

Geneva Chamber of Commerce, *8 South Third Street, Geneva 60134; (630) 232–6060. Internet: www.GenevaChamber.com or www.geneva.il.us.*

Oregon

Population: 3,891. This town along Illinois Highway 64 has a number of attractions that will help you enjoy the natural beauty that surrounds you.

LOWDEN-MILLER STATE FOREST (all ages)

River Road, Oregon 61061; (815) 732–7329. Open year-round from dawn to dusk daily. Free.

Heading north off Highway 64 on River Road leads you to Lowden State Park, a 207-acre tract situated on a bluff across the Rock River from Oregon. Towering above the park is a 48-foot-tall statue completed in 1911 by the famous sculptor Lorado Taft, who named the piece *Eternal Indian,* but everyone calls it Black Hawk, after the Sauk Indian leader. Picnicking, hiking, fishing, and boating are among the activities you can enjoy here.

PRIDE OF OREGON (age 3 and up)

1469 Route 2 North, Oregon 61061; (815) 732–6761 or (800) 468–4222. Lunch and dinner cruises offered Monday through Saturday. Champagne brunch buffet cruise departs at 11 A.M. and 2:30 P.M. Sunday. Prices are $20 for lunch, $30 for dinner, $24 for champagne brunch, and $12 for sight-seeing only on any cruise.

Another river attraction is the *Pride of Oregon.* This elegant paddle wheeler is 102 feet long, with the upper deck open for sight-seeing and the lower deck enclosed by glass windows and reserved for dining. Board at the Maxson Manor dock, off Illinois Highway 2 north of Illinois Highway 64 for a two-hour cruise, with or without a meal.

CASTLE ROCK STATE PARK (all ages)

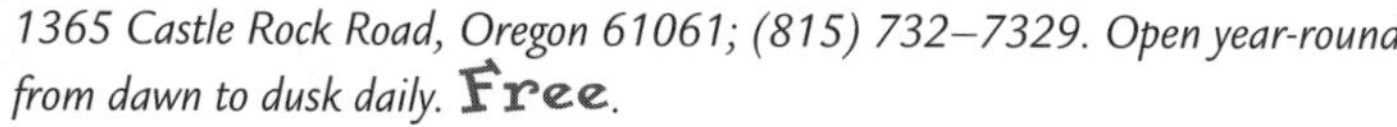

1365 Castle Rock Road, Oregon 61061; (815) 732–7329. Open year-round from dawn to dusk daily. Free.

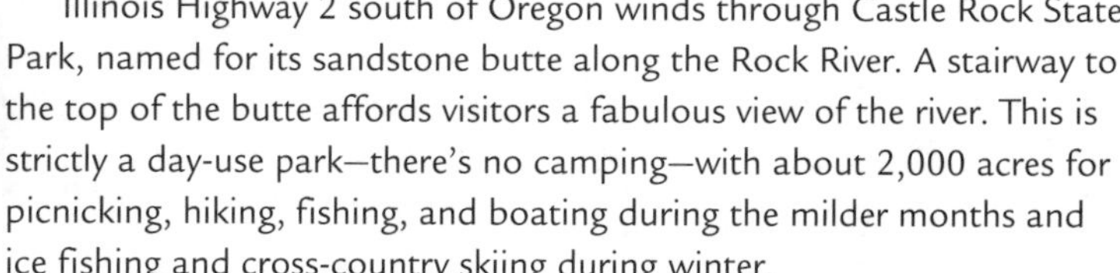

Illinois Highway 2 south of Oregon winds through Castle Rock State Park, named for its sandstone butte along the Rock River. A stairway to the top of the butte affords visitors a fabulous view of the river. This is strictly a day-use park—there's no camping—with about 2,000 acres for picnicking, hiking, fishing, and boating during the milder months and ice fishing and cross-country skiing during winter.

SUMMER FUN RECREATION

6030 West Pines Road, Oregon 61061; (815) 732–7004. Open in summer from 1 A.M. to 9 P.M. Tuesday through Friday, 10 A.M. to 10 P.M. Saturday, and 10 A.M. to 8 P.M. Sunday; closed Monday. A go-kart ride at either track costs $4 per person. Miniature golf costs $3 per person.

Continuing west on Highway 64 from Oregon, you can pick up the pace a bit at Summer Fun. The larger "maxi" track is a quarter mile long and restricted to people who are at least 9 years old and 4 feet, 6 inches tall. There's a separate "mini" track for younger, smaller kids. Players of all ages can putt on the 18-hole miniature golf course, which has lots of moving obstacles to maneuver around.

Where to Eat

Red Apple. *400 Route 64; (815) 284–4549.* Hours are 6 A.M. to 9 P.M. Tuesday through Saturday and 6 A.M. to 4 P.M. Sunday; closed Monday. Serving breakfast, lunch, and dinner. Steaks and chicken are the chief dinner entrees. Children's menu features chicken, fish, and hot dogs. $

Pizza Hut. *Illinois Highway 64; (815) 732–4444.* Hours are 11 A.M. to 10 P.M. Sunday through Thursday and 11 A.M. to 11 P.M. Friday and Saturday. See Restaurant Appendix for description. $

Where to Stay

Hansen's Hideaway Ranch. *Rural Route 2; (815) 732–6489.* Drive 5 miles west of Oregon on Pines Road, and then turn south onto Harmony Road and continue about 1 mile. This family campground has a ranch atmosphere. Campsites have water and electrical hookups, and there's a shower building that also has flush toilets. Amenities include outdoor swimming pool, playground, game room, snack bar, and firewood. $

Lake LaDonna Family Campground. *1302 South Harmony Road; (815) 732–6804.* Drive 5 miles west of Oregon on Pines Road, and then turn south onto Harmony Road. This facility has three rental cabins with kitchen and bath, plus campsites with water and electrical hookups and showers. The spring-fed Lake LaDonna has two docks, one with a slide and the other with a rope swing. Other amenities include basketball court, volleyball courts, and horseshoe pits. $$

For More Information

Oregon Chamber of Commerce,
Third and Franklin Streets, Oregon 61061; (815) 732–2100.

Mount Morris

Population: 2,919. Eight miles west of Oregon along Illinois Highway 64 is Mount Morris. Many places here have "White Pines" in their name. So guess what kind of trees you'll see a lot of? You got it—white pines.

WHITE PINES FOREST STATE PARK (all ages)

6712 White Pines Road, Mount Morris 61054; (815) 946–3717. Open year-round from 8 A.M. to sundown daily. Free.

You can turn off Illinois Highway 64 to the south for White Pines Forest State Park. Here you'll find what is reportedly the southernmost stand of virgin white pine in the United States. Seven well-maintained hiking trails wind through the trees so you can get a good look. You also can have a picnic or fish here. The Chicago-Iowa trail that borders the south side of this 385-acre park once was a main east-west road through Illinois.

WHITE PINES SKATING CENTER (age 5 and up)

6929 West Pines Road, Mount Morris 61054; (815) 946–9988. Open year-round from 7 to 10 P.M. Friday and Saturday and 1 to 4 P.M. Saturday. Cost is $4.50 per person for evening sessions, $3 for afternoon. Skate rental is $1. You may bring your own in-line skates.

This local rink offers a change of pace from the great outdoors. The facility has a game arcade and snack bar.

Where to Eat

White Pines Inn. *6712 West Pines Road; (815) 946–3817.* Open daily from March through December. The lodge dining room is open to the public for dinner and Sunday Cornhusker Buffet. Fresh fish, baked chicken, and barbecued ribs are among the featured entrees, all served with freshly baked bread. Save room for homemade red raspberry pie, peach cobbler, or a chocolate dessert. Or combine food with entertainment in the White Pines Dinner Theatre. $$

Where to Stay

White Pines Inn. *6712 West Pines Road; (815) 946–3817.* Open from March through December. Here you'll find 25 one-room log cabins that were built in the 1930s by the Civilian Conservation Corps. Each cabin sleeps up to four people. Package plans are available. The lodge restaurant, which maintains the knotty pine decor, is open for breakfast, lunch, and dinner. $$

For More Information

Mount Morris Village Hall, *105 West Lincoln, Mount Morris 61054; (815) 734–6425.*

Savanna

Population: 3,819. If you continue west on Highway 64 all the way to the Mississippi River, you'll reach the town of Savanna. The Grand River Trail for biking goes between Savanna and Moline, roughly along the Great River Road (Illinois Highway 84) route.

MISSISSIPPI PALISADES STATE PARK (all ages)

4577 Highway 84 North, Savanna 61074; (815) 273–2731. Open year-round from 9 A.M. to sunset daily. Admission is **Free**.

Illinois Highway 84 runs through Savanna. If you head north, you'll come to Mississippi Palisades State Park. This park has some fascinating rock formations that were carved by erosion. You can have a picnic or go fishing or hiking during summer or go cross-country skiing in winter. There's also a camping area with electric hookup if you want to stay overnight.

PALISADES AND PREHISTORIC INDIAN ARTIFACTS (age 5 and up)

Illinois Highway 84 North, Savanna 61074; (815) 273–2741. Two miles north of Savanna. Open daily from 10 A.M. to 5 P.M. Museum admission costs $3.50 for anyone age 11 or older and $1.50 for children age 10 or younger.

This little museum has artifacts from the region dating back to prehistoric times. The items are enclosed in glass cases. Souvenirs are available from the friendly fellow in the adjacent store.

Where to Eat

Davey's Riverside Inn. *16416 Highway 84 North; (815) 273–5014.* Hours are 5 to 9 P.M. Wednesday and Thursday, 5 to 10 P.M. Friday and Saturday, and 10 A.M. to 8 P.M. Sunday; closed Monday and Tuesday. Serving dinner daily plus brunch on Sunday. Reservations are recommended on weekends. This is the area's biggest restaurant, and one of the most popular. The adult menu features steak and seafood entrees, while the children's menu ($3.95 to $4.95, including drink and applesauce) includes burgers, chicken strips, ham, and corn dogs. $$

Pizza Hut. *701 North Main Street; (815) 273–2233.* Hours are 11 A.M. to 10 P.M. Sunday through Thursday and 11 A.M. to 11 P.M. Friday and Saturday. See Restaurant Appendix for description. $

Where to Stay

Lake Wood Resort and Gardens. *6577 Mill Hollow Road; (815) 273–2898.* One mile north of Mississippi Palisades Park. The campground here has water and electrical hookups and showers. There's also a primitive camping area "among the wildflowers." Stroll among the annuals and perennials in the gardens or hike in the woods. Guide service is available for the best fishing spots. Hunting is allowed in designated parts of the 140-acre grounds in season with a guide. $

For More Information

Savanna Chamber of Commerce, *51 South Main Street, Savanna 61074; (815) 273–2722.*

Fulton

Population: 3,698. Illinois Highway 64 goes into Savanna, where it picks up Illinois Highway 84, also known as the Great River Road. To reach Fulton from Savanna, travel south on Highway 84 to about where it intersects with U.S. Highway 30.

GREAT RIVER BIKE TRAIL (all ages)

Throughout the town of Fulton; (815) 589–4545. Open daily from sunrise to sunset. Free.

This 11-mile paved section includes a 6-mile loop in and around Fulton. Although it's called a bike trail, you can hike or jog the pathway as well.

HERITAGE CANYON (all ages)

515 North Fourth Street, Fulton 61252; (815) 589–2838. A little over a mile west of Illinois Highway 84. Open from April through mid-December. Hours are 9 A.M. to 5 P.M. daily. Admission is **Free**, *with suggested donation of $1 per person.*

This 12-acre wooded area in the heart of a former rock quarry is the site of a re-created 1860s town, complete with house, log cabins, school, church, doctor's office, and blacksmith shop.

U.S. LOCK AND DAM 13 (all ages)

4999 Lock Road, at the river off Illinois Highway 64, Fulton 61252; (815) 589–3313. Open daily for viewing at any time. Guided tours are given at 1 P.M. Sunday between Memorial Day and Labor Day. Viewing and tours are both **Free**.

You never know what you'll see in the lock when you visit here, but chances are there will be a huge barge in the vicinity. Tours help visitors understand how the system works.

Where to Eat

Fulton Family Restaurant. *1318 17th Street; (815) 589–4499.* Hours are 6 A.M. to 9 P.M. Sunday through Thursday and 6 A.M. to 10 P.M. Friday and Saturday. Serving breakfast, lunch, and dinner. This casual restaurant offers a big selection of sandwiches, plus dinner entrees including steak, pork chops, chicken, and fish. The children's menu includes burgers, hot dog, grilled cheese sandwich, fish sandwich, and spaghetti, each including french fries and drink, at prices ranging from $2.50 to $3.05. $

Where to Stay

Pine Motel. *19020 13th Street; (815) 589–4847.* This cozy local property has nine rooms in the main building and one cottage. All are equipped with air-conditioning, telephone, cable TV, and kitchenette with refrigerator and microwave. No pool. $

For More Information

Fulton Chamber of Commerce,
1021 Fourth Street, Fulton 61252;
(815) 589–4545.

We'll return one more time to the eastern border of Northern Illinois and make a sojourn west along Interstate 88.

Batavia

Population: 17,076. Batavia lies along Illinois Highway 31 between Highway 64 and Interstate 88, so we'll make a quick stop here first. The Windmill City Festival in early June features a parade, a carnival, family activities, and food.

FERMILAB (age 5 and up)

Kirk Road and Pine Street, Batavia 60510; (630) 840–3351. Buildings are open from 8:30 A.M. to 5 P.M. daily, grounds from 6 A.M. to 8 P.M. daily. **Free** *admission. The buildings are accessible for wheelchairs. Internet: www.fnal.gov.*

Perhaps the biggest claim to fame in Batavia is the Fermi National Accelerator Laboratory, more commonly called Fermilab, the physics research facility that has the Tevatron, the highest-energy particle accelerator in the world. You may be surprised to discover that you can take a free tour of this facility. Stop first at the front desk of Wilson Hall, a 16-story, A-shaped high-rise you can't miss, and pick up a brochure directing you through a self-guided tour that includes videos and hands-on activities and ends up in the smaller brick Science Center. If you'd rather have a guide who can answer your questions take you through, call (630) 840–5588 in advance to arrange this type of free tour. The expansive grounds also encompass a hiking trail through restored tallgrass prairie and a pasture populated by about 75 buffalo. You can even go fishing in Casey's Pond—watch out for mallard ducklings in the water.

BATAVIA DEPOT MUSEUM (age 4 and up)

155 Houston Street, Batavia 60510; (630) 406–5274. Open from March through November; closed December through February. Hours are 2 to 4 P.M. Monday, Wednesday, and Friday through Sunday; closed Tuesday and Thursday. Admission is **Free**.

You'll find a variety of railroad and local history exhibits in the Batavia Depot Museum. The bed and dresser used by Mary Todd Lincoln during her stay at Bellview Sanitarium also are on display in this 1854 building. Near the museum is the Batavia Riverwalk park and boardwalk, where you can take a leisurely stroll through a wildflower garden.

FUNWAY ENTERTAINMENT CENTER (age 2 and up)

1335 South River Street (Route 25), Batavia 60510; (630) 879–8717. Open from mid-June through late September. Outback Park and Arcade hours are 11 A.M. to 10 P.M. Sunday through Thursday, 11 A.M. to 11:30 P.M. Friday, and 10 A.M. to 11:30 P.M. Saturday. Miniature golf costs $4.50 per person for anyone age 13 or older and $3.50 for kids age 12 or younger. Regular go-karts cost $3.75 and bumper boats cost $3.25 per person. Kiddie go-karts, bumper boats, and Jumpshot Basketball cost $2.50 each. Adrenaline Rush, Kiddie Bounce, and Kiddie Train cost $2 each. Water Wars costs $1. Package deals can reduce individual costs. Kids Towne, designed for children age 2 through 8, is open from 10 A.M. to 2 P.M. Saturday only; admission costs $4 per child. Roller rink sessions include matinee skates from noon to 3 P.M. Wednesday and Friday and 12:30 to 3:30 P.M. Saturday and Sunday; admission costs $4 per person, and skate rental is $1.50 for regular skates or $3 for in-lines. Tuesday Family Night skate session runs from 6:30 to 9:30 P.M. and costs $4 per person, with standard skate rental free or in-lines $1.50. Internet: www.funwaybatavia.com.

Funway Entertainment Center has a plethora of indoor and outdoor activities for families. Indoors you'll find a roller rink with a cool, sky-blue floor and a video arcade with bumper cars, for which kids must be at least 52 inches tall to ride. Numerous other activities are outdoors. For the regular go-kart track, you have to be 52 inches tall to ride alone. Special kiddie go-karts are available for youngsters age 6 through 9. These karts use the same track but not at the same time as the bigger ones. The 12 bumper boats (one- or two-seater; height restriction to ride alone is 45 inches) splash around in a pool that also has a jet-stream fountain. The 18-hole Western Trails miniature golf course has a fairly simple layout decorated with flowers, shrubs, rocks, waterfalls, and a cute trail wagon. Batting cages, Jumpshot Basketball, and two huge inflated enclosures—Kiddie Bounce for jumping and Adrenaline Rush for crawling and sliding—are other attractions outdoors. The outdoor activities shut down in rainy weather and over winter. Pizza, hot dogs, and snacks are available in the Outback Cafe outdoors and in the roller rink indoors.

Also at the Funway Entertainment Center, but with its own entrance, is **Kids Towne,** a complete little village geared toward children age 2 through 8. The various areas are furnished with props, and the kids supply the imagination. They can sit at a desk or write on the chalkboard in the schoolroom; shop in the grocery store, placing the items on a belt and ringing them up at the register; count play money at a teller window in the bank; mail a letter in the post office; or put on a performance in the theater. There's also a mural wall the kids can write on, and they can play with toys such as sponge puzzles and giant Lego blocks. Although the regular hours are on Saturday only, you can reserve a time Sunday through Friday if you have at least 10 kids; this option is exercised by a number of parent-tot play groups, but it could work for a family reunion as well.

RED OAK NATURE CENTER (all ages)

Route 25, 1 mile north of Route 56, Batavia 60510; (630) 897–1808. Open from 9 A.M. to 4:30 P.M. Monday through Friday and 10 A.M. to 3 P.M. Saturday and Sunday. Admission is **Free**.

Learn more about the Fox River Valley at this nature center filled with native plants. Naturalists in the facility's interpretive center can explain about the plants, insects, and birds in the area. There are trails for hiking and biking, the shortest being a quarter mile and the longest a mile and a half.

HAROLD HALL QUARRY BEACH (all ages)

Union and Water Streets, Batavia 60510; (630) 406–5275. Open from late May through late August. Hours are 12:40 to 8 P.M. Sunday through Friday and 10 A.M. to 6 P.M. Saturday. Nonresident admission costs $8 for adults age 18 through 64, $6 for young people age 3 through 17, and $4 for seniors age 65 or older. Children age 2 or younger get in free. Resident rates are a bit lower.

Here is a fun summer spot for families. This former rock quarry has a sandy beach, a swimming area with a straight tunnel drop slide (plus a smaller slide for the little kiddies), sand volleyball courts, and a picnic area where you can bring your own basket (no glass containers or alcoholic beverages allowed) or eat what you buy from the concession stand on the premises.

Where to Eat

Al's Cafe and Creamery. *Illinois Highway 25 at Wilson Street; (630) 406–8855.* Open from 11 A.M. to 3 P.M. Monday, 11 A.M. to 8 P.M. Tuesday and Wednesday, 11 A.M. to 9 P.M. Thursday, 7 A.M. to 9 P.M. Friday and Saturday, and 7 A.M.

to 7 P.M. Sunday. As you might guess from the name, ice cream and related concoctions like malts and shakes are the specialty. But before dessert, try one of the deli-style sandwiches, fresh soup of the day, or a grilled chicken salad. There are burgers and hot dogs on the menu, too. $

Where to Stay

There are no hotels or motels in Batavia. See subsequent entry for Aurora.

For More Information

Batavia Chamber of Commerce,
100 North Island Avenue, Batavia 60510; (630) 879–7134. Internet: www. bataviachamber.com.

Aurora

Population: 99,581. Just south of Interstate 88, between Illinois Highways 59 on the east and 47 on the west, is the city of Aurora. There are lots of things for families to see and do here all year long, covering interests from sports to arts to science to history.

MICHAEL JORDAN GOLF CENTER (age 4 and up)

4523 Michael Jordan Drive, Aurora 60504; (630) 851–0023 or (800) 746–5365. Turn west off Illinois Highway 59 onto Liberty Street; the center is a mile or so down the road on the north side. The miniature golf course is open from spring through fall, depending on weather conditions. Hours are 8 A.M. to 11 P.M. daily. Cost is $6 for anyone age 13 or older, $5 for kids age 12 or younger.

Everybody knows that when Michael Jordan wasn't performing miracles on the basketball court for the Chicago Bulls, he was out on the links playing golf. He wanted to share his love of golf with others, so he created the Michael Jordan Golf Company and had this place built in the late 1990s to offer lessons and clinics for both kids and adults. But you and your family can have an hour or two of fun just playing 18 holes on the *miniature* golf course, where the player with the lowest score at the end is named MVP—most valuable putter. The astroturf greens have sandstone borders, and decorative touches include cascading water in several spots. There are few obstacles, so the course looks deceptively simple. Some tricky curves make it challenging, however, although not so difficult that children playing will become frustrated; it is possible to get a hole in one. What makes the course appealing is its link to Jordan. His Airness left his footprints in concrete, so you can literally follow in his footsteps from one hole to the next. At each hole you'll find a placard with an MJ trivia question, the answer to which appears at the following hole. For example, did you know that the 6 foot, 6 inch Jordan scored 40 points against every team in the NBA? Or how about this question on the more personal side: How often does Michael shave his head? You'll find the answer on the course. The holes that do have obstacles carry out the basketball theme—for example, one with a basketball you must maneuver around, another with a backboard, and a funny one where you shoot the ball through the bull's nostrils. The trees around the course are still fairly small, so there isn't much to stop the wind that sweeps across from the fields beyond on a blustery day, but they'll grow. Have a snack at the indoor MJ Grill when you're through playing. There are souvenirs for sale, all fairly nice quality but on the expensive side as a result. You can also buy golf shirts and equipment. The small rest rooms are well maintained and accessible for wheelchairs, but there's no changing table. The women's has a cute framed photo on the wall of Michael wearing plaid boxers—that alone makes it worth a trip to the potty.

FOX VALLEY CENTER (all ages)

Off Illinois Highway 59 at New York Street, Aurora 60504; (630) 851–7200. Hours are 10 A.M. to 9 P.M. Monday through Saturday and 11 A.M. to 6 P.M. Sunday. No smoking inside the mall. Internet: www.foxvalleycenter.com.

This two-story indoor shopping mall has about 180 stores, anchored by Marshall Field's, Carson Pirie Scott, JCPenney, and Sears department stores. The mall was renovated in 1998, and skylights that were added give the place a brighter, more cheerful atmosphere. Gently sloping ramps with wooden handrails offer easy access from one level to another for visitors in strollers or wheelchairs. Square clay bricks surface the floors. Kids may gravitate toward the Disney Store, Gamers Paradise, Natural Wonders, Waldenkids, Noodle Kidoodle, or Kay-Bee Toys. Yet despite the presence of these stores, the overall impression is that this mall doesn't cater as strongly to families with younger kids as some other malls do. It feels a little more teen oriented, judging by the clientele and by the abundance of stores carrying clothes, shoes, CDs, videos, and novelties. There is a centralized food court on the lower level, but there are also restaurants all along the ring road that encircles the mall. Signs around entrance and exit points off that road are pretty good at helping you find the street you want.

PHILLIPS PARK FAMILY AQUATIC CENTER (all ages)

828 Montgomery Road, Aurora 60504; (630) 851–8686. Open from June through the first week of September. Hours are noon to 8 P.M. Sunday through Friday and 10:30 A.M. to 6 P.M. Saturday. Nonresident admission costs $10 Monday through Friday and $11 Saturday and Sunday for anyone age 4 or older. Children age 3 or younger get in free.

This is the place for outdoor summer action. It has five pools, four water slides, beaches, and even hot tubs. You can zip down a body slide or a tube slide. Teens may head for the sand volleyball court while their younger siblings enjoy a separate sand play area. The pool has a kids' play area with a waterfall and a kiddie slide. The center has a concession area, so you can spend the better part of a day here if you bring enough sunscreen.

PARKSIDE LANES (age 2 and up)

34W185 Montgomery Road, Aurora 60504; (630) 898–5678. Hours vary; call ahead to check for open bowling times. Cost ranges from $2 to $3.50 per game, depending on day and time. In summer there's usually a special rate of $1.25 per game on Monday. Thursday Family Night specials feature Glow Ball and cost $12 per lane per hour for up to six people. Shoe rental is $1.25 for children in size 1 or smaller, $2 for everyone else.

With 54 lanes, this is one of the largest bowling alleys in the state. It's a popular venue for families, because it carries small shoe sizes, lighter balls, and bumpers to fill up the gutters to make it easier and more enjoyable for younger children to play. Computerized scoring makes it easier for Mom and Dad to relax and have fun, too. On occasion, usually a weekend evening, the facility offers "Glow Ball" bowling in which the overhead lighting is by black light and the lanes, pins, and balls become luminescent. Rock music plays and laser lights flash. It's funk-a-delic! There is a snack bar as well as the Tiffany's Pizza place to satisfy your hunger.

AURORA REGIONAL FIRE MUSEUM (all ages)

53 North Broadway, downtown, Aurora 60506; (630) 892–1572. Corner of New York and Broadway. Open year-round. Hours are 10 A.M. to 4 P.M. Tuesday through Saturday; closed Sunday and Monday. Admission costs $3.50 for adults age 19 through 49, $2.50 for high-school students and adults age 50 or older, and $1.50 for kids age 4 to high school. Children age 3 or younger get in free.

This museum is housed in the old Central Fire Station that was built in 1894. Items on display include uniforms, pieces of fire-fighting equipment, an old-fashioned hand pumper, and several fire engines.

PARAMOUNT ARTS CENTRE (age 3 and up)

23 East Galena Boulevard, Aurora 60506; (630) 896–6666. Call for current schedule. The center is accessible for wheelchairs. Internet: www.paramountarts.com.

This 1930s movie house was restored in 1978 and now hosts a variety of musical and dramatic productions, many of them appropriate for families. Shows in 2000 included *Cinderella, The Lion King of Mali,* and *Lyle, Lyle Crocodile.*

SCITECH (all ages)

18 West Benton Street, downtown Aurora 60506; (630) 859–3434. Hours are noon to 5 P.M. Wednesday, Friday, and Sunday, noon to 8 P.M. Thursday, and 10 A.M. to 5 P.M. Saturday; closed Monday and Tuesday. Admission costs $5 for anyone age 2 through 64 and $4 for seniors age 65 or older; tots age 1 or younger get in free. There's also a family admission that can be used in lieu of the individual rates: $15 admits up to six people, including children, their parents, and their grandparents. Internet: scitech.mus.il.us.

SciTech brings principles such as light, motion, magnetism, and chemistry to life with more than 200 exhibits and hands-on activities. Encase yourself in a giant soap bubble. Walk through a tornado. Launch a balloon to the ceiling. Look for sunspots through the solar telescope. Speak into a microphone and watch the needle jump on the connected volume meter. Make a shadow on the wall that stays behind after you move. These are the sorts of interactive activities you'll find in this high-ceilinged downtown building that years ago was a post office.

FOX RIVER BICYCLE TRAIL (all ages)

Along the Fox River; (630) 857–0516 for information or (800) 477–4369 for a map. Open from dawn to dusk daily. **Free**. *Accessible for strollers and wheelchairs.*

This paved, 42-mile bike trail starts in Aurora and heads north along the Fox River to Crystal Lake. It can also be used for walking.

SCHINGOETHE CENTER FOR NATIVE AMERICAN CULTURES (age 5 and up)

347 South Gladstone, Aurora 60506; (630) 844–5512. Open 10 A.M. to 4 P.M. Tuesday through Friday. Saturday and Sunday hours are added during spring and summer. Closed Monday. Also closed all university holidays and the entire month of January. Call ahead for current schedule. Admission is **Free**, *but donations are appreciated. Internet: www.aurora.edu.*

While white settlers moved into the area in the mid-1800s, indigenous Indians were driven out. These peoples today are gone from their homeland but not forgotten when you visit the Schingoethe Center for Native American Cultures, situated in the lower level of Dunham Hall on the northwest corner of the Aurora University campus (Randall Road dead-ends in front of Dunham Hall). In the center's three exhibit rooms, you'll find a permanent collection of more than 3,000 Native American artifacts from numerous North American tribes, donated by local philanthropists Herbert and Martha Schingoethe. There are arrowheads from the area, plus kachina dolls made by the Hopi, wool blankets woven by the Navajo, and items created by the Inuit. Some hands-on activities for families, such as grinding corn or weaving, are available in summer.

BLACKBERRY FARM–PIONEER VILLAGE (all ages)

100 South Barnes Road, Aurora 60506; (630) 892–1550. Open daily from May through Labor Day and Friday through Sunday only from the day after Labor Day until mid-October. Hours are 10 A.M. to 4:30 P.M. Admission costs $7.50 for anyone age 13 through 64 and $6.50 for kids age 2 through 12 and seniors age 65 or older. (Residents of Aurora get in for half those prices, but you must show a photo ID proving residency.) Children age 1 or younger get in free. The park reopens for special events around Halloween and Christmas; call for details. Snacks and souvenirs available. Internet: www.foxvalleyparkdistrict.org/facilities/familyfun/blkFRS.html.

The city's Fox Valley Park District operates the Blackberry Farm–Pioneer Village at West Galena Boulevard (U.S. Highway 30) and Barnes Road. Set on 54 acres of pastoral countryside, this place offers a glimpse of pioneer life of the 1840s. There's a working farm, and on certain weekends you can also see people in period costumes shearing sheep, working in the blacksmith shop, or making craft items. Visit the redbrick schoolhouse to hear a storyteller impart a folktale of the time. Kids can pet farm animals in the Discovery Barn. If your youngsters crave a bit more action, they can whirl around on a beautifully decorated old-fashioned carousel, ride a real pony in the little corral, traverse the grounds in a horse-drawn open wagon, or board the miniature train.

SPLASH COUNTRY AQUATIC CENTER (all ages)

Adjacent to Blackberry Farm–Pioneer Village, west of Barnes Road and north of Prairie Street, Aurora 60506; (630) 906–7981. Open during summer from noon to 8 P.M. Sunday through Friday and 10 A.M. to 6 P.M. Saturday. Admission costs $10 Monday through Friday and $11 Saturday and Sunday. (Residents of Aurora pay half price.)

This water park has a swimming pool with zero-depth end. The deeper part has lap lanes. You can ride inner tubes down one of the water slides or along the 1,100-foot "lazy river" course.

Where to Eat

Papa Bear Family Restaurant. *2340 North Farnsworth Avenue; (630) 851–1055.* Open from 5 A.M. to 11 P.M. daily. Serving breakfast, lunch, and dinner. Entrees include beef, pork, chicken, and pasta dishes, including some Greek food. Children's menu items include burgers, hot beef sandwich, spaghetti, chicken, hot dog, and grilled cheese sandwich, all in the $3 to $4 range, not including drink. $$

Pizzeria Uno. *986 North Route 59; (630) 585–8075.* Hours are 11 A.M. to 11 P.M. Monday through Thursday, 11 A.M. to 1 A.M. Friday and Saturday, and 11 A.M. to 10 P.M. Sunday. This suburban cousin of the Chicago pizzeria features deep-dish and thin-crust pizza, pasta, salads, sandwiches, and assorted beef and chicken entrees. $

Fuddruckers. *4250 Fox Valley Center Drive; (630) 851–9450.* Open from 11 A.M. to 10 P.M. Monday through Saturday and 11 A.M. to 9 P.M. Sunday. This casual eatery serves juicy, gigantic, made-to-order burgers. $

Red Lobster. *4435 Fox Valley Center Drive; (630) 851–9370.* Open from 11 A.M. to 10 P.M. Sunday through Thursday and 11 A.M. to 11 P.M. Friday and Saturday. See Restaurant Appendix for description. $$

Where to Stay

Best Western Fox Valley Inn. *2450 North Farnsworth Avenue; (630) 851–2000 or (800) 528–1234.* This two-story motel has 107 rooms. Amenities include fitness center and outdoor pool. Cribs are available for an extra $5, roll-away beds for $10. $$

Comfort Suites City Center. *111 North Broadway; (630) 896–2800 or (800) 228–5150.* Near Aurora Regional Fire Museum. This three-story hotel has 83 suites, each with coffeemaker, refrigerator, and microwave. There is no door separating the living and sleeping areas. Cribs are available upon request. Amenities include indoor swimming pool, hot tub, and kiddie play center. Continental breakfast is included in the room rate. $$$$

Motel 6. *2380 North Farnsworth Avenue; (630) 851–3600.* This budget motel has 119 rooms. Unlike many properties in this chain, it does have an indoor swimming pool. $$

For More Information

Aurora Area Convention and Tourism Council, *44 West Downer Place, Aurora 60506; (630) 897–5581 or (800) 477–4369. Internet: www.enjoyaurora.com.*

DeKalb

Population: 34,925. DeKalb is the home of Northern Illinois University, and there are some interesting activities connected with the school. Probably the biggest annual event in town is the DeKalb Cornfest, which rolls around in August and features entertainment as well as enormous quantities of freshly picked sweet corn.

HUSKIES BASKETBALL (age 2 and up)

Games are played at Evans Field House, just off Annie Glidden Road on the NIU campus, DeKalb 60115; (815) 753–8040 or (800) 332–4695. Season runs from early November through mid-February. Tickets cost $6 to $8, with half-price tickets for children at selected games around the Christmas break. Call for a current schedule. Internet: www.niu.edu/athletics.

If you want to root for the team in black and red but can't afford Bulls tickets, the Northern Illinois University Huskies are the team for you. Actually, there are two basketball teams, a men's and a women's, both of which play in the Midwestern Collegiate Conference. Their quality of play tends to be fairly high; the Huskies have made some NCAA tournament appearances in recent years. It's especially exciting for sports-minded girls to be able to see women players in action, and they often make better three-point shots than the men do. For the Schuldts an ideal outing is when the two teams play on the same day. We catch the women's afternoon game, go eat supper at Pizza Villa, and then return for the men's evening game. In addition to the basketball, there is entertainment at halftime, be it a guest appearance by the Frisbee-catching Whitney the Wonder Dog or a spirited dance routine by the cheerleaders, accompanied by the NIU band. At games that cater particularly to families by offering half-price kids' tickets, there is usually a halftime slam-dunk contest for children in which they show off their stuff, jamming a junior-size basketball into a Little Tikes hoop. The winner is determined by audience applause as well as judges' opinions. The Huskie mascot roams the stands throughout the games, and children flock to him for a hug or a photo opportunity. Free stringy balloons are passed out in the end zone for Huskie fans to wave as the opposing team shoots free throws, just as they do in the big leagues. The university does a good job of making the atmosphere fun for fans of all ages.

HOPKINS PARK POOL (all ages)

1403 Sycamore Road, DeKalb 60115; (815) 758–8853. Enter the pool through the park building at the west end. Open from 10 A.M. to 8 P.M. Sunday through Friday and 10 A.M. to 6 P.M. Saturday. Nonresident admission costs $8 for anyone age 5 or older and $3 for children age 4 or younger; residents pay $1 less per person.

This local swimming facility has been around for many years but was upgraded in the 1990s. The original pool is a big, extra-wide rectangular one that can accommodate a lot of bodies without feeling overcrowded. A long, twisty water slide was added in the center, where the water below is 4 to 5 feet deep, and a shorter, straighter water slide was placed at the shallower end, where it's about 3 to 4 feet deep. There is a separate deepwater diving pool nearby. The new kiddie pool area is off to one side and enclosed by a fence. It's about 1 foot deep at the edge and 2 feet deep in the middle. Fountain jets spray water inward from the edges, and a little water slide lets the toddlers have their own splashdown. There is a fenced-in concession area with tables if you want to go get a snack.

EGYPTIAN THEATRE (age 3 and up)

135 North Second Street, DeKalb 60115; (815) 758–1215. Call for current schedule of events.

This historic old theater was renovated in 1980 to recapture its past glory. The tall, light-brick facade has figures of pharaohs gazing out from the corners and a sphinx head above the main entrance. Inside, the stage accommodates live theatrical performances, concerts, and movies.

ELLWOOD HOUSE (age 6 and up)

509 North First Street, at Augusta Avenue, DeKalb 60115; (815) 756–4609. Open from March through early December. Guided tours are given at 1 and 3 P.M. Tuesday through Friday and 1, 2, and 3 P.M. Saturday and Sunday. Cost is $4 for anyone age 15 or older and $1 for kids age 6 through 14. Not recommended for children age 5 or younger. Only the first floor is accessible for wheelchairs. Internet: www.dekalbparkdistrict.com/ellwood.htm.

This Victorian mansion was once the home of Isaac Ellwood, who made a fortune with his revolutionary fencing material, barbed wire. You must take a guided tour to see the place; you can't just drop in and wander around. The elegant furnishings reflect the period from the 1870s through the 1920s. The grounds have gardens, a carriage museum, and an 1890s playhouse. The eight-acre site has been declared a National Historic Site. Sometimes there are special events, such as an arts and crafts fair or an ice cream social, on the grounds.

Where to Eat

Pizza Villa. *824 West Lincoln Highway; (815) 758–8116. Internet: www.clickweb.com/pizzavilla.* Hours are 4 to 10 P.M. daily. This family-owned restaurant, which has been around since 1956, is a favorite with college students and families alike. The thin-crust pizza is cheesy and to die for. You can also get pasta dinners, sandwiches, and tasty "broasted" chicken. The decor here is rustic, and kids will like the arcade on the lower level. Bring a quarter for the silly machine that dispenses multicolored plastic eggs filled with trinkets; it has a chipped plaster Fred Flintstone perched above the eggs, and the machine shouts "Yabba-Dabba-Doooo!" when the egg rolls down the chute. (Don't ask what the correlation between Fred Flintstone and colored eggs is—it sure attracts the kids.) One caveat: The owner has the audacity to take a week or two off for vacation in summer and simply close the place, so call ahead before driving out there, to avoid the heartbreak of disappointing your taste buds. $

Red Lobster. *2470 Sycamore Road; (815) 758–1998.* Hours are 11 A.M. to 9 P.M. Sunday through Thursday and 11 A.M. to 10 P.M. Friday and Saturday. See Restaurant Appendix for description. $$

Where to Stay

Travelodge. *1116 West Lincoln Highway; (815) 756–3398.* This budget chain motel has 111 rooms and an outdoor pool. Continental breakfast is included in the room rate. $

Apple Orchards in the DeKalb Area Here are a couple of apple orchards in the vicinity of DeKalb for a few hours of family fun that will last even longer in the form of applesauce, pies, and so on.

- **Pine-Apple Orchard.** *01N145 Watson Road, Maple Park 60151; (815) 827–3317.* East of DeKalb off Illinois Highway 38, turn south onto Watson Road, a dirt road, and proceed 1 or 2 miles until you see the sign and the apple trees. This unpretentious, family-owned orchard is open from Labor Day weekend through mid-December. Hours are 10 A.M. to 5:30 P.M. Tuesday through Friday and 10 A.M. to 5 P.M. Saturday and Sunday; closed Monday. Call ahead to find out which apples are available; usually at least two types are. What's really fun here is that you can pick your own apples—they hand you a plastic bushel bag and send you into a designated section of rows, where you may fill your bag and your stomach at the same time. Kids think it is so cool to be able to pluck the fruit right off the trees, and to sample produce this fresh is to taste a bite of sunshine. When you're finished in the fields, you take the bag into the little building at the top of a gently sloping hill (there are wheelbarrows around to use if you don't want to carry it) and pay for it. The cost is about $13. You can also buy prepicked apples in smaller quantities, freshly pressed cider, and deliciously moist cake doughnuts made with that cider. Shelves lined with homemade apple butter, jellies, jams, and honey will tempt visitors as well. Starting in late September there are pumpkins and gourds available. By late November you can get an evergreen tree for Christmas (there's the *Pine* in Pine-Apple). Finally, beyond the gravel parking lot, there's a small pen of goats for kids to pet and watch.
- **Honey Hill Orchard.** *11747 Waterman Road, Waterman 60556; (815) 264–3337.* From DeKalb head south on Illinois Highway 23 about 15 miles. Turn west onto U.S. Highway 30, and Waterman is about a mile farther. Honey Hill Orchard also is open during early September through October 31. Hours are 9 A.M. to 5:30 P.M. daily. You can pick your own apples here, too, plus raspberries and pumpkins in season. Be sure to take home some of the namesake honey. Apple products for sale include fresh cider, pie, and doughnuts. There is a farm petting zoo here, and sometimes hayrides are offered.

Super 8. *800 West Fairview Drive; (815) 748–4688 or (800) 800–8000.* This 44-room property, unlike most in the chain, has an indoor pool. Continental breakfast is included in the room rate. $$

For More Information

DeKalb Chamber of Commerce, *122 North First Street, DeKalb 60115; (815) 756–6306. Internet: www.dekalb.org.*

Returning to the eastern edge of Northern Illinois one last time, we'll make our final foray westward along Interstate 80.

Morris

Population: 10,270. Dropping south on Illinois Highway 47 from I–80, the first town we come to is Morris. Two state parks are in this area.

GEBHARD WOODS STATE PARK (all ages)

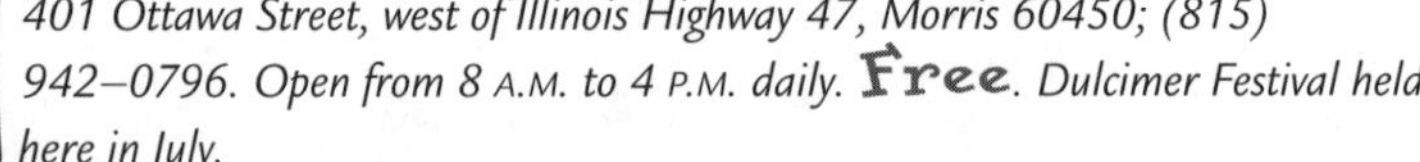

401 Ottawa Street, west of Illinois Highway 47, Morris 60450; (815) 942–0796. Open from 8 A.M. to 4 P.M. daily. **Free**. *Dulcimer Festival held here in July.*

This 30-acre state park extends along the historic Illinois & Michigan (I & M) Canal and is one of the state's more popular parks. You can have a picnic beneath the shade of a maple, sycamore, or eastern cottonwood tree or go hiking or canoeing. There is a park interpreter on-site. Camping is available for a fee.

GOOSE LAKE PRAIRIE STATE NATURAL AREA (all ages)

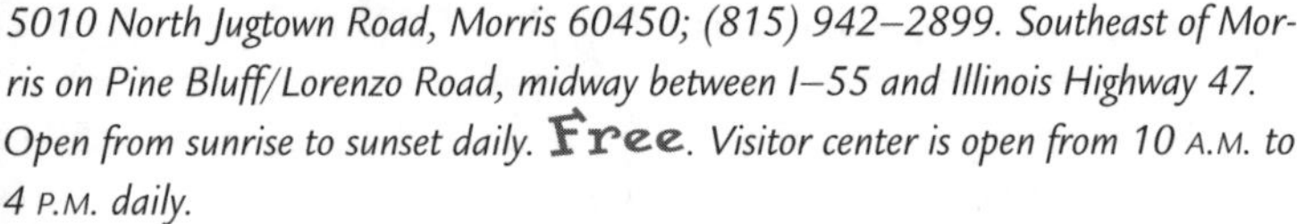

5010 North Jugtown Road, Morris 60450; (815) 942–2899. Southeast of Morris on Pine Bluff/Lorenzo Road, midway between I–55 and Illinois Highway 47. Open from sunrise to sunset daily. **Free**. *Visitor center is open from 10 A.M. to 4 P.M. daily.*

This site covers 2,600 acres, much of it prairie as it was in the mid-1800s. It's reportedly the biggest chunk of prairie left in the state. If you're into identifying plants, look for big bluestem, Indian grass, switchgrass, and forbs. Have a picnic or take a hike. You can fish in Heidecke Lake. There is a park interpreter on-site. The visitor center has exhibits of fossils and a display explaining the prairie ecosystem.

Where to Eat

Maria's Ristorante. *1591 Division Street; (815) 942–3351.* Hours are 11 A.M. to 10:30 P.M. Sunday through Thursday and 11 A.M. to 11:45 P.M. Friday and Saturday. Serving lunch and dinner. Pizza and Italian dishes are a specialty here, but you can also get steak, chicken, seafood, and sandwiches, plus salad bar. The children's menu features pasta, fried shrimp, fried cod, pork chop, hot dog, and grilled cheese, at prices in the $3 to $5 range, not including drink. $$

Where to Stay

Comfort Inn. *70 West Gore Road; (815) 942–1433.* Near the intersection of I-80 and Highway 47. This 50-room inn has an indoor heated swimming pool. Pets are allowed. Continental breakfast is included in the room rate. $$$

Holiday Inn. *I–80 and Route 47; (815) 942–6600 or (800) 465–4329.* This two-story motel has 120 rooms with cable TV and coffeemaker. Amenities include indoor pool with whirlpool. $$$

For More Information

Grundy County Chamber of Commerce and Industry, *112 East Washington Street, Morris 60450; (815) 942–0113. Internet: grundychamber.cbcast.com/index1.html.*

Utica

Population: 848. Utica is south of I-80 along Illinois Highway 178. South of this tiny town, Highway 178 intersects with Illinois Highway 71. Head east on Highway 71 from that point to reach the town's major attractions, Starved Rock and Mathiessen State Parks.

ILLINOIS WATERWAY VISITOR CENTER (all ages)

At Starved Rock Dam, 2 miles east of Utica on Dee Bennett Road; (815) 667–4054. Open year-round from 9 A.M. to 5 P.M. daily; hours extended to 8 P.M. from Memorial Day through Labor Day. **Free**. *The visitor center is accessible for wheelchairs.*

This visitor center overlooks the lock and dam, where you can see towboats push huge barges into the 110-foot-wide lock. The visitor center has a number of exhibits. Kids especially enjoy going inside the pilot house from the Illinois Waterway towboat *John M. Warner,* which sank in a 1982 flood. They can see the boat's original steering console, radio, radar antenna, and spotlight. There is a display of pottery, arrowheads, and other tools and artifacts from the Native Americans who lived in the Illinois River Valley as long as 7,000 years ago. Another exhibit chronicles the history of the Illinois & Michigan (I & M) Canal, a 96-mile-long canal that linked Chicago with LaSalle and was completed in 1848.

STARVED ROCK STATE PARK (all ages)

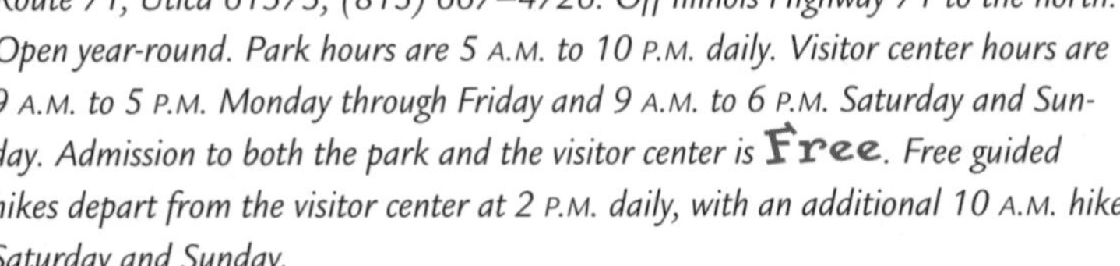

Route 71, Utica 61373; (815) 667–4726. Off Illinois Highway 71 to the north. Open year-round. Park hours are 5 A.M. to 10 P.M. daily. Visitor center hours are 9 A.M. to 5 P.M. Monday through Friday and 9 A.M. to 6 P.M. Saturday and Sunday. Admission to both the park and the visitor center is **Free***. Free guided hikes depart from the visitor center at 2 P.M. daily, with an additional 10 A.M. hike Saturday and Sunday.*

Highway 71 winds through wooded countryside south of Utica to Starved Rock State Park on the south side of the Illinois River. The park's name comes from a story of conflict between Native American tribes in the 1760s. An Illiniwek killed an Ottawa chief, provoking retaliatory attacks against his tribe by both the Ottawa and their allies, the Potawatomi. A group of Illiniwek retreated to a 125-foot sandstone butte, which was promptly surrounded by their enemies. The Illiniwek eventually starved to death up on the rock. Today you can hike to the top of that same butte or along 15 miles of trails. The park also boasts 18 stream-fed canyons and a variety of trees, flowers, and birds. It's a lovely place for a picnic lunch. If you don't want to bring your own food, there's an unobtrusive concession stand in rustic decor where you can buy sandwiches and soft drinks. The park has hiking and equestrian trails, and you can go fishing or boating in the Rock River. Pets must remain on a leash at all times, and their owners are expected to clean up after them.

MATHIESSEN STATE PARK (all ages)

Route 71, Utica 61373; (815) 667–4868. Off Illinois Highway 71 to the south, across the road from Starved Rock State Park. Open year-round from 8 A.M. to 10 P.M. daily. **Free** *admission.*

This park has some interesting canyons and rock formations formed by waterfalls and erosion. A 5-mile trail accommodates hikers in temperate weather and cross-country skiers during winter. There is an equestrian trail, too. Bring a picnic basket and enjoy the natural beauty all around you. Swimming is not allowed in this park, however. Pets must stay on a leash at all times, and their owners must clean up after them. There is a vending machine area, but for any other food or information, you'll have to go over to Starved Rock Park.

STARVED ROCK STABLES (age 10 and up)

Along Highway 71, west of Starved Rock State Park, Utica 61373; (815) 667–3026. Look for two brown buildings and horse pastures. Open from May through October. Trail rides depart at 10 A.M., noon, and 2 and 4 P.M. daily. A one-hour guided tour costs $20 per person, age 10 or older. Kids younger than 10 are not allowed on the trails.

This stable near the parks offers a leisurely ride along its own private trails, which wind through wooded areas and go up and down hills. No trotting is allowed, just gentle walking. It's a pleasant way to pass an hour, indeed.

FAMILY LAND (age 3 and up)

Along U.S. Highway 6 between Utica and LaSalle; (815) 224–4130. Hours are 10 A.M. to 10 P.M. daily from late spring through early fall. Miniature golf costs $2.50 per round for anyone age 11 through 59 and $1.50 for kids age 10 or younger and seniors age 60 or older. Go-karts cost $4.50 per ride. The water slide is open from 11 A.M. to 7 P.M. daily. You get unlimited rides on it for $6.75 per person Friday through Sunday or $3.50 per person Monday through Thursday.

If the kids are tired of nature and restless for a bit more action, head to Family Land. You can play miniature golf on an 18-hole course or take a five-minute ride on the go-karts, although you must be at least 12 years old to ride. There's also a water slide, which is probably the best value because the price covers unlimited trips down the slide.

Where to Eat

Starved Rock Lodge. *In Starved Rock State Park; (815) 667–4211.* Open from 8 A.M. to 9 P.M. daily. Serving breakfast, lunch, and dinner. Reservations strongly recommended for dinner, especially on weekends. You don't have to be an overnight guest to dine in the lodge restaurant. Dinner items include steak, chicken, and pasta dishes. $$

Country Cupboard Ice Cream, Sandwich and Pizza Shoppe. *402 Clark Street; (815) 667–5155.* Hours are 11 A.M. to 9 P.M. Sunday through Thursday and 11 A.M. to 10 P.M. Friday and Saturday. In addition to the ice cream, you can have a light meal of burgers, sandwiches, or soup. $

Other Helpful Regional Sources of Information

- **Blackhawk Waterways Convention and Visitors Bureau,** *201 North Franklin Avenue, Polo 61064; (815) 946–2108.*
- **Lee County Tourism Council,** *112 South Galena Avenue, Dixon 61021; (815) 288–1840 or call toll-free (877) 533–8687. Internet: www.leecountytourism.com.*

Where to Stay

Starved Rock Lodge. *In Starved Rock State Park; (815) 667–4211 or (800) 868–7625. Internet: www.starvedrocklodge.com.* The lodge is a good choice for convenience. The area around here is quite rural, and there aren't a lot of other options nearby. This stone-and-log lodge, which was built in the 1930s by the Civilian Conservation Corps, sits on a bluff southwest of the namesake rock and has 72 luxury hotel rooms, plus a great hall with stone fireplace. There are also 18 cabin rooms. Kids age 11 or younger stay free with their parents. $$$

Starved Rock Family Campground. *In Starved Rock State Park; (815) 667–4726.* Tent camping is available at 133 sites with electrical hookup. The facility has showers and toilets. Fires are allowed in grill pits only. Pets must be kept on leashes at all times, and owners are expected to clean up after them. Alcoholic beverages are prohibited. $

For More Information

Heritage Corridor Visitors Bureau, *723 South Clark Street, Utica 61373; (800) 746–0550. Internet: www.heritagecorridorcvb.com.*

If you keep driving west on Interstate 80, you'll arrive at the Mississippi River and drop southward into Western Illinois, which is the subject of the next chapter.

Other Things to See and Do in Northern Illinois

January: Winterfest, Elgin; (847) 931-6625

Illinois Snow Sculpting Competition, Rockford; (815) 987-8800

February: Rockford Boat, Vacation, and Outdoor Show; (815) 968-5600; Internet: www.metrocentre.com

March: Maple Syrup Festival, Pecatonia; (815) 877-6100

Farm Toy Show, Sublette; (815) 849-5242

April: Antique Toy and Doll World Show, St. Charles; (847) 526-1645

May: North Aurora Pet Parade; (630) 896-6664

Young at Heart Festival, Rockford; (815) 633-3999

June: Harvard Milk Days, Harvard; (815) 943-4614

Sand Festival, South Beloit; (815) 389-3023

July: Old Settlers Days, Rockton; (815) 624-7600

Petunia Festival, Dixon; (815) 284-3361

Sugar Grove Corn Boil; (630) 466-4507, ext. 87

Illinois Storytelling Festival, Spring Grove; (815) 344-0181

August: Marseilles Fun Days; (815) 795-2323

Mendota Sweet Corn Festival; (815) 539-6507

September: Amboy Depot Days; (815) 857-3814

Watermelon Days, Thomson; (815) 259-8278

October: Harvest Time Festival, Waterman; (815) 264-3652

Sycamore Pumpkinfest; (815) 895-5161

November: Christmas in the Country, Sandwich; (630) 466-4546

Holiday Craft Show, Byron; (815) 234-8535

December: Seasonal Sights and Sounds Parade, Sterling; (815) 625-2400

Christmas of Yesteryear, Richmond; (815) 678-7742

Western Illinois

Rivers are the claim to fame for the 20 counties of Western Illinois. The mighty Mississippi forms the western boundary of the region (and the state), and the smaller but lovely Illinois defines its eastern edge. Severe floods in 1993 and 1995 and a more average flood in 1997 made life along the waterways especially tough, but most of the people who live in the river towns sandbagged their way through the hard times and are still around to affirm the area's peaceful beauty.

In the upper west corner of Western Illinois, along the Mississippi River, lie the cities of Moline and Rock Island. Together with the Iowa cities of Davenport and Bettendorf on the other side of the river, they make up the Quad Cities. If you live in the Chicago area, the Quad Cities are only a two- to three-hour drive from home, easily accessible from Interstate 88 or 80. The route is less direct from the south, but you'll have an interesting drive up on U.S. Highways 67 or 51, the latter of which joins up with Interstate 74 around Bloomington and heads in via Peoria and Galesburg.

Special events in the Quad Cities include the Moline Riverfest in late June, the Mississippi Valley Blues Festival in late June or early July, the Rock Island Summer fest in mid-July, the Rock Island County Fair in mid- to late July (both Moline and Rock Island are in Rock Island County), and the Bix Beiderbecke Weekend (Dixieland jazz) in late July; this last event actually takes place across the river in Iowa but may make hotel space tight on the Illinois side as well. For details about special events or for a useful visitor's guide or other information, write the **Quad Cities Convention and Visitors Bureau,** 2021 River Drive, Moline 61265, or call (309) 788-7800 or (800) 747-7800. Fax (309) 788-7898. E-mail: cvb@quadcities.com. Internet: www.quadcities.com/cvb.

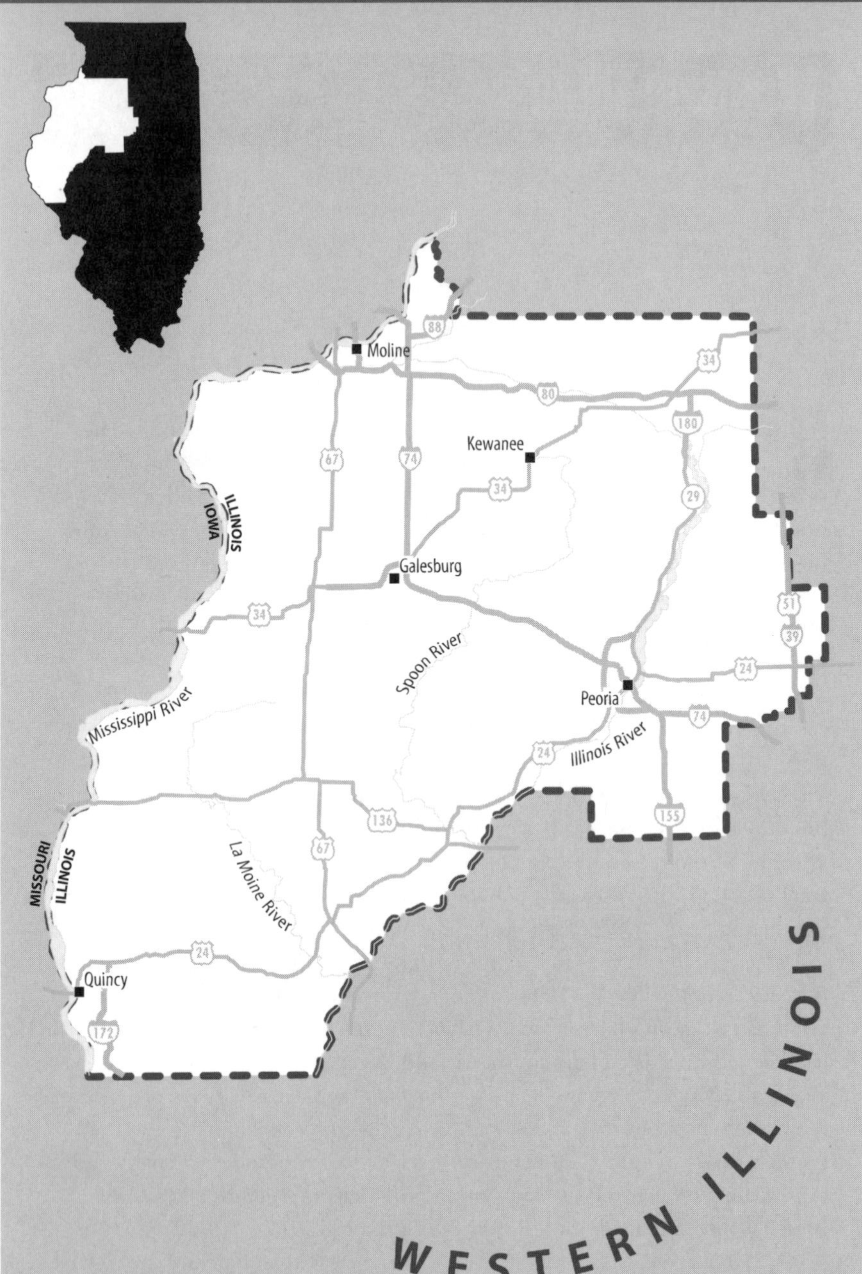

Moline
88
34
80
180
Kewanee
67
74
34
29
ILLINOIS
IOWA
Galesburg
34
51
39
Spoon River
24
Peoria
Mississippi River
74
24
Illinois River
136
155
MISSOURI
ILLINOIS
67
La Moine River
24
Quincy
172
WESTERN ILLINOIS

Moline

Population: 43,202. Let's start our Quad Cities visit in Moline. Most of the city lies between the Mississippi and the Rock Rivers, and I–74 cuts straight through.

DEERE & CO. ADMINISTRATIVE CENTER (all ages)

On John Deere Road (Illinois Highway 5), Moline 61265; (309) 765–4235. Open from 9 A.M. to 5:30 P.M. daily. Admission is **Free**.

You'll be surprised at how much fun you'll have at the Deere & Co. Administrative Center. The facility was designed by the late Eero Saarinen, an acclaimed architect. You'll drive along a smoothly paved road through a wooded area (there's even a pond with swans and ducks) to reach the 20,000-square-foot product display building that is the center's family attraction. The two-story, glass-walled, rectangular building contains a collection of big, new, shiny green farm machines and yellow construction equipment that visitors can climb up into. Some of these rigs have tires that are about 6 feet in diameter, and the view from the cab of the mammoth combine conjures up visions of Stephen King run amok in a cornfield. Kids of all ages love it. Those with a historical bent will enjoy the long, glass-encased wall of memorabilia from the 1800s that includes advertising posters, folk art, and small farm implements and kitchen utensils. (Anyone who watches Roadrunner or Animaniacs cartoons will get a kick out of seeing a real anvil.) Because the center is the world headquarters for John Deere, you'll find plenty of brochures to pick up and helpful staff on the upper floor to answer questions. A small video station nestled under one staircase allows you to sit and watch the latest models of tractors and harvesters in action.

SOUTHPARK MALL (all ages)

I–74 and John Deere Road, Moline 61265; (309) 797–9070. Open from 10 A.M. to 9 P.M. Monday through Saturday and noon to 5 P.M. Sunday. The mall is accessible for strollers and wheelchairs.

If you're in the mood to shop, Moline has this indoor mall. JCPenney, Sears, Von Maur, and Younkers are the anchor department stores, with a wide array of specialty shops making up the balance. A 500-seat food court offers a place for respite. If you've never eaten a Maid-Rite, be sure to get one of these hamburger buns filled with loose, seasoned ground beef (plus cheese, if you like). The eatery also offers fries, shakes, and soft drinks to round out the meal. Yum! (If you don't want to visit the mall, Maid-Rite has shops all over the Quad Cities; check the local phone book for the nearest one.) Stores of particular interest to families with young children include Gymboree, Kay-Bee Toys, and Sam Sandbox Toys and Gifts.

QUAD CITY THUNDER (age 3 and up)

Games are played at the MARK of the Quad Cities, a 12,000-seat arena downtown at 1201 River Drive, Moline 61265; (309) 788–2255. Fax (309) 787–4538. Call for current schedule and ticket information, or you can write Quad City Thunder, 7800 14th Street West, Rock Island 61201. Season runs from mid-November through the end of March, with postseason play completed by the end of April. Tickets cost $6 to $15. The facility is accessible for wheelchairs. No smoking inside the building. Internet: www.qcthunder.com.

The Quad City Thunder were the 2000 conference champions and had the best season record in the Continental Basketball Association (CBA), sort of a minor league for the National Basketball Association. Thunder games combine professional basketball with entertainment and promotions to provide a lively outing for families. Thor, the Viking mascot, strolls courtside and sometimes even into the stands. This burly guy with horned helmet and long black wig and beard carries a huge mallet-like hammer (probably made of rubber) and can really get the fans cheering. The cheerleaders help, too, and they put on an athletic dance routine at halftime. At some games kids can bounce in the inflated Star Castle at no extra charge. The MARK arena opened in 1993. This spacious facility is clean and well lit. Elevators on both sides allow easy access to the upper level for people who have difficulty climbing stairs. Rest rooms are conveniently located, and the women's rooms have changing tables. Concession locations are adequate, and the fare includes popcorn, soft pretzels, nachos, hot dogs, burgers, pizza, chicken strips, Philly cheese steak or pork chop sandwiches, and ice cream, all washed down with Pepsi or beer. Prices are about $2 to $4 for the snacks, hot dogs, and pizza, $4 to $5 for chicken and sandwiches, and $2 to $4 for drinks.

QUAD CITY MALLARDS (age 6 and up)

Games are played at the MARK of the Quad Cities, 1201 River Drive, Moline 61265; (309) 788–7855. Call or surf the Web for current schedule and ticket prices. Internet: www.qcmallards.com.

During hockey season the Thunder basketball court at the MARK gives way to an ice rink for the Mallards, who compete in the United Hockey League.

JOHN DEERE PAVILION (all ages)

River Drive and 15th Street, Moline 61265; (309) 765–1000. Hours are 9 A.M. to 6 P.M. Monday through Friday, 10 A.M. to 5 P.M. Saturday, and noon to 4 P.M. Sunday. Admission is **Free**. *No smoking inside the building.*

This 15,000-square-foot exhibition hall with a glass front is across the street from the MARK of the Quad Cities in downtown Moline. Built in the late 1990s, it is literally a big part of the city's riverfront renovation project. Inside are antique tractors and exhibits related to agriculture. Although it also has some huge farm machines, this facility is more formal than the administrative center described earlier in this section; you can't run around and climb on everything here. The John Deere Store souvenir shop has some quality merchandise, including sturdy toy tractors and Ertl toys. The Planted Earth Cafe has food.

CELEBRATION BELLE (age 4 and up)

2501 River Drive, Moline 61265; (309) 764–1952 or (800) 297–0034. Operates from spring through fall, weather permitting. Standard sight-seeing cruises board at 2:30 P.M. Thursday through Sunday and cost $9 for anyone age 13 or older and $6 for kids age 4 through 12; no reservations are necessary. Tuesday evening family dinner cruise boards at 6:30 and costs $29.95 for anyone age 13 or older and $19.95 for kids age 4 through 12; reservations recommended. Cruises are not recommended for children age 3 or younger.

Amid all the casino boats plying the rivers these days, here's a vessel without gambling that you can take for a family excursion along the scenic waterfront. Operated by Celebration River Cruises, the basic sight-seeing cruise on the *Celebration Belle* lasts one and a half hours. If you can afford it, spring for the Tuesday Family Fun Night dinner cruise, which features a banjo player and a professional magician.

BEN BUTTERWORTH PARKWAY (all ages)

Along River Drive from 26th to 55th Streets, Moline 61265; (309) 797–0785. Open from 6 A.M. to 11 P.M. daily. Admission is **Free**.

This 2.2-mile paved bike bath winds through a scenic park along the Mississippi River. There are three playgrounds and two picnic shelters in the park as well.

RIVER VALLEY GOLF (age 3 and up)

5000 38th Avenue, Moline 61265; (309) 762–7160. Open from spring through fall, weather permitting. Hours are 11 A.M. to 10 P.M. Sunday through Thursday and 11 A.M. to 11 P.M. Friday and Saturday. Cost is $4 per person before 6 P.M.

Monday through Friday only and $4.50 all other times for anyone age 6 or older and $2.75 per person at all times for children age 5 or younger.

This 18-hole outdoor miniature golf course features rock gardens and waterfalls. There are no moving parts, but some tricky angles make the course a challenge.

Where to Eat

TGIFriday's. *1425 River Drive; (309) 764–6400.* Along the riverfront, next to the MARK of the Quad Cities. Hours are 11 A.M. to 11 P.M. Monday through Thursday, 11 A.M. to midnight Friday and Saturday, and 11 A.M. to 10 P.M. Sunday. See Restaurant Appendix for description. $

Miss Mamie's Catfish House. *3925 16th Street (corner of 16th Street and Blackhawk Road); (309) 762–8336.* Near SouthPark Mall. Open from 11 A.M. to 9:45 P.M. Monday through Thursday, 11 A.M. to 10:15 P.M. Friday and Saturday, and 11 A.M. to 9 P.M. Sunday. A lunch basket costs about $6, with dinners in the $7 to $12 range. Items on the kids' menu—such as catfish sticks, chicken sticks, and grilled cheese sandwich—cost about $3.25, including fries but not beverage. $

Rudy's Tacos. *2414 16th Street; (309) 762–3293.* Hours are 11 A.M. to 10 P.M. Sunday through Thursday and 11 A.M. to 11 P.M. Friday and Saturday. Some Quad City natives swear by Rudy's Tacos, the namesakes of which are generously loaded with spicy meat and trimmings. These casual eateries also offer "Mexican burgers," hot dogs, salads, and—unlike Taco Bell—beer, wine, and full bar service in addition to soft drinks. $

Lagomarcino's. *1422 5th Avenue; (309) 764–9548.* Hours are 9:30 A.M. to 5 P.M. Monday through Saturday; closed Sunday. Billed as a "turn-of-the-century ice-cream parlor and confectionery," Lagomarcino's offers ice-cream treats and homemade hand-dipped chocolates, plus sandwiches on homemade bread and salads if you want something besides dessert. $

Old Country Buffet. *3901 41st Avenue; (309) 797–8591.* Hours are 10:30 A.M. to 8:30 P.M. Monday through Thursday, 10:30 A.M. to 9 P.M. Friday, 8 A.M. to 9 P.M. Saturday, and 8 A.M. to 8:30 P.M. Sunday. See Restaurant Appendix for description. $

Where to Stay

Radisson on John Deere Commons. *1415 River Drive; (309) 764–1000 or (800) 333–3333.* Next to the MARK of the Quad Cities. This six-story hotel has 163 rooms. Amenities include an indoor pool and hot tub on the ground floor in front. Dine in the adjoining TGIFriday's restaurant. Continental breakfast can be included in the room rate. $$$

Comfort Inn Moline. *2600 52nd Avenue; (309) 762–7000 or (800) 228–5150.* This motel has 62 rooms. Amenities include a small indoor pool and whirlpool. The room rate includes continental breakfast. $$$

Best Western Airport Inn. *2550 52nd Avenue; (309) 762–9191 or (800) 528–1234.* This tan, three-story motel received a three-diamond rating from AAA. It has 50 rooms with cable TV and hair dryers. Amenities include an indoor swimming pool. Continental breakfast is included in the room rate. $$$

Fairfield Inn. *2705 48th Avenue; (309) 762–9083 or (800) 228–2800.* This 63-room property has an indoor pool and whirlpool. The room rate includes continental breakfast. $$

For More Information

Moline/Quad Cities Welcome Center, *2021 River Drive, Moline 61265; (309) 788–7800, ext. 310.*

East Moline

Population: 20,147. This suburb east of Moline has a couple of fun attractions for active families.

EMPIRE PLAYGROUND (all ages)

In Mississippi Park on Route 84, East Moline 61244; (309) 752–1573. Near the East Moline–Hampton border. Open year-round from 7 A.M. to 10 P.M. daily. Admission is **Free**.

The name of this huge outdoor wooden playground, EMPIRE, is an acronym for East Moline Playground Innovation Recreation Efforts. That's a fancy way of conveying that this was a community effort, built by hundreds of volunteers and financed entirely by donations. It's really something to be proud of–14,000 square feet of towers, tunnels, bridges, rope ladders, and slides. The official count is "48 play stations." The park where you'll find this playground is right on the banks of the Mississippi River. There are picnic tables and two pavilions with electricity, so you can bring lunch or supper to the park–if you can get the kids to stop playing long enough to eat. There's also a bike path.

PUTTIN' AROUND (age 3 and up)

Route 84, East Moline 61244, at the East Moline–Hampton border; (309) 755–1212. Open daily from June through August and Saturday and Sunday only in May and September. Hours are noon to 10 P.M. Monday through Friday, 11 A.M. to 10 P.M. Saturday, and 11 A.M. to 6 P.M. Sunday. Cost for miniature golf is $3 per game for anyone age 13 or older and $2 for kids age 12 or younger. An alternate family rate of $10 covers two parents and up to three school-age kids. Bumper cars cost $3 ($2 Tuesday), Bankshot $3, and Water Wars $2 per bucket. Repeat play of any game costs $2.

The 18-hole miniature golf course is just part of the fun at this outdoor amusement center. You also can ride bumper cars or play two more unusual games. The first, Bankshot, is sort of a cross between basketball, billiards, and miniature golf. You go around a course with 18 stations. At each one you shoot a basketball into a hoop—but the backboards are different sizes and shapes, and sometimes the only way to make the shot is to somehow carom the ball off the backboard. The second unusual game is Water Wars. For this one, two wooden cages or booths stand facing each other some distance apart. Each cage has an opening high up in the wall near the slatted roof. The person inside slings a water balloon out the opening toward the opposing cage. When the balloon splats against the cage, water drips through the roof and sides to dampen the opponent. If you have a really good aim, you might even douse him or her with a direct hit. You get a bucket of eight water balloons per game, and you can have up to three players inside each cage, so you can make it a family feud if you like. There is a concession stand for munchies to keep you going.

Where to Eat

Godfather's. *1347 42nd Avenue; (309) 792–3706.* Hours are 11 A.M. to 11 P.M. Sunday through Thursday and 11 A.M. to midnight Friday and Saturday. The medium-thick, chewy-crust pizza here is loaded with cheese and your favorite ingredients. Round out the meal at the salad bar. $

Where to Stay

Super 8. *2201 John Deere Road; (309) 796–1999 or (800) 800–8000.* This budget chain property has 63 rooms. Amenities include hot tub and exercise room but no swimming pool. Room rate includes continental breakfast. $$

Coal Valley

Population: 2,683. Just south of Moline is Coal Valley, which has one of the area's prime family attractions—the Niabi Zoo.

NIABI ZOO (all ages)

Niabi Road, Coal Valley 61240; (309) 799–5107. The zoo is open from mid-April through Labor Day from 9:30 A.M. to 5 P.M. daily; after Labor Day through mid-October, hours are from 9:30 A.M. to 5 P.M. Saturday and Sunday only. The zoo is closed from mid-October through mid-April. Admission is $4.25 for anyone age 12 or older, $3 for kids age 3 through 11, and free for tots age 2 or younger. The train departs the station every 15 minutes, and a ride costs $1.50 per person for anyone age 1 or older. No smoking throughout zoo grounds.

Driving along U.S. Highway 6 south of the Rock River, turn south onto East 11th Street, which runs into Niabi Road. The entrance area has a small parking lot and a low, one-story building housing the ticket sales area, main concession stand, and gift shop. The zoo grounds rest on 30 acres of Rock Island County Forest Preserve land. *Niabi* is reportedly an Oswego Indian word meaning "young deer spared from the hunter's arrow." Deer and other hooved animals are prominent among the approximately 150 species on display. You're also likely to see lions, camels, bobcats, wolves, wallabies, bears, and Asian elephants. Niabi Zoo is of a traditional style, with iron bars and fencing surrounding the animals' pens or pits. While this style looks rather like a prison, it nonetheless allows closer access to the animals than the more modern, open-spaces zoos do. Primates and birds have both indoor and outdoor display areas. The reptile house is interesting but very stuffy. Wide, paved pathways are easy to navigate with strollers or wheelchairs. The well-maintained grounds feature wildflowers and prairie grasses, and there are picnic tables and playgrounds when you're ready for a break. If the kids' feet get tired, you can take them for a ride around the zoo on the Mel McKay Express, a shuttle-size replica of an old steam engine.

Where to Eat and Stay

See entries for Moline and Rock Island.

Rock Island

Population: 40,552. The most prominent feature of Rock Island is Arsenal Island, which floats in the middle of the Mississippi River but has bridges connecting it to both the Illinois and the Iowa sides. The arsenal is an active U.S. Army factory, so you'll probably see some military personnel as you drive along. The Mississippi River Visitors Center at the west end of the island overlooks Lock and Dam 15 and has displays explaining how the process of "locking through" works so that you'll know what's going on when you see a barge down below. On the mainland the Rock Island Arts and Entertainment District, just called "the District" around town, handles special events and festivals; call (309) 788-6311 for details.

ROCK ISLAND ARSENAL MUSEUM (all ages)

Building 60, Rock Island Arsenal, Rock Island 61204; (309) 782–5021. Open from 10 A.M. to 4 P.M. daily except on Thanksgiving, Christmas Eve, Christmas Day, New Year's Eve, and New Year's Day. Admission is **Free**.

The Rock Island Arsenal Museum houses an extensive collection of vintage firearms among its historical displays. Its Children's Discovery Room has uniforms and helmets that kids (and parents) can try on.

ROCK ISLAND ARSENAL BIKE TRAIL (all ages)

On Arsenal Island; (309) 794–5338. Open from dawn to dusk daily. **Free**.

This paved bike trail around the island is about 4 miles long, passing all the various sites. Helmets are required for all riders on the island.

LANDMARK LINK TROLLEY TOURS (all ages)

2929 Fifth Avenue, Rock Island 61204; (309) 788–3360. Runs from mid-June through late September. Call for current schedule. Fare is $8 per person, all ages.

Ride on this cute red trolley around the Quad Cities. Tours (about one-and-a-half hours) are narrated by a guide who explains the sights and the area's history. Round-trips depart from Rock Island Arsenal, Rock Island, or Moline.

CIRCA '21 DINNER PLAYHOUSE (age 3 and up)

1828 Third Avenue, Rock Island 61204; (309) 786–7733. Call for current schedule and ticket prices. Internet: www.circa21.com.

This dinner theater puts on some children's and family-friendly productions in addition to the usual shows geared toward adults.

QUAD CITY BOTANICAL CENTER (all ages)

2525 Fourth Avenue, downtown Rock Island 61204; (309) 794–0991. Hours are 10 A.M. to 5 P.M. Monday through Saturday and 1 to 5 P.M. Sunday. Admission costs $3.50 for anyone age 13 through 59, $1 for kids age 6 through 12, and $3 for adults age 60 or older. Children age 5 or younger get in free. Internet: www.qcbotanicalgardens.org.

Three square arches frame the walls and roof of glass in this spacious facility opened in 1998. It houses colorful tropical plants and garden greenery.

HAUBERG INDIAN MUSEUM (age 5 and up)

1510 46th Avenue, Rock Island 61204; (309) 788–9536. Open daily from 9 A.M. to noon and 1 to 5 P.M. from March through October; closing time is 4 P.M. from November through February. Admission is **Free**, *although there is a suggested donation of $2 per adult and $1 per child.*

On a wooded hill above Blackhawk Road in Rock Island stands the Hauberg Indian Museum. Nestled in a corner of a stone lodge built by the Civilian Conservation Corps in 1939, this museum is small but interesting if you're willing to take the time to examine it carefully and talk with the guide; kids below grade-school age would probably get bored quickly. Life-size dioramas show day-to-day life among the Sauk and Fox Indians throughout the four seasons during the period of 1750 to 1830. The dioramas contain authentic artifacts, and the summer and winter houses were constructed by residents of the contemporary Mesquakie Reservation. A bronze bust of the famous Sauk chief Black Hawk was made from an original plaster cast of his face.

BLACK HAWK STATE HISTORIC SITE (all ages)

1510 46th Avenue, Rock Island 61204; (309) 788–0177. Open from sunrise to sunset daily. Admission is **Free**.

The Hauberg Indian Museum takes up only a fraction of the 208 acres composing the Black Hawk State Historic Site, which was first occupied by Native Americans as long as 12,000 years ago. The area was home to the powerful Sauk Nation from about 1730 to the late 1820s, when white European settlers began moving in following the questionably legal cessation of the Indian lands to the U.S. government two decades earlier. It is easy to see why anyone would want to live in this forested area along the Rock River, and the Illinois Historic Preservation agency that manages the site has taken care to maintain the indigenous wildflowers, trees, and birds. Please take care to leave them undisturbed when hiking along the site's 4 miles of marked trails.

Where to Eat

Huckleberry's. *223 18th Street; (309) 786–1122.* Hours are 11 A.M. to 9 P.M. Monday through Thursday, 11 A.M. to 11 P.M. Friday and Saturday, and 5 to 9 P.M. Sunday. This local pizzeria offers both hand-tossed and deep-dish varieties. $

Poor Boy's Pizza. *4500 Blackhawk Road; (309) 786–2400.* Open from 10:30 A.M. to midnight Sunday through Thursday and 10:30 A.M. to 1 A.M. Friday and Saturday. The tasty pizza here is another local treat. $

Rudy's Tacos. *2716 18th Avenue; (309) 794–1678.* Hours are 11 A.M. to 10 P.M. Sunday through Thursday and 11 A.M. to 11 P.M. Friday and Saturday. This one's a brother to the Rudy's in Moline. $

Where to Stay

Four Points Sheraton. *Third Avenue and 17th Street; (309) 794–1212.* This eight-story hotel has 175 rooms. Amenities include indoor swimming pool, whirlpool, and exercise room. There is a restaurant on-site. No meals are included in the room rate. $$

For More Information

Mississippi River Visitors Center, *West End of Arsenal Island, Rock Island 61204; (309) 794–5338.*

Kewanee

Population: 12,969. U.S. Highway 34 and Illinois Highways 78 and 81 converge in this Western Illinois town. It's easy to reach from Interstate 80, too—just head south about 10 miles on Highway 78.

WOODLAND PALACE (all ages)

In Francis Park, off Highway 34, Kewanee 61443; (309) 852–0511. Open from mid-April through mid-October. Hours are 1 to 5 P.M. daily. Admission is $1.50 for anyone age 12 or older, $1 for kids age 6 through 11, and free for children age 5 or younger.

Frederick Francis, a 35-year-old inventor who had become wealthy from his patented watch springs, built this unusual house for himself and his wife in 1890. He kept adding handmade features and furniture to it until his death from a hernia at age 70 in 1925. A combination of wood, bricks, and stone, the house has no electricity, yet Francis was able to design an air-cooling system to keep the house comfortable in summer and install radiant-heat deflectors in the fireplace chimney to warm the home in winter. Pocket doors that slide into the wall seem to "disappear." Similarly, screens that retract into the walls above and below the window frames create a now-you-see-it, now-you-don't effect. Although you can wander around by yourselves, you'll enjoy your visit more if you let one of the enthusiastic guides take you through. These guys will point out some of the interesting things you might otherwise miss. Although the posted hours for the home are in the afternoon, guides may be on the premises as early as 8 A.M. or as late as 6 P.M. Tours take roughly an hour but can be abbreviated for families with restless youngsters.

A Bit of Sweden in Western Illinois Leaving the Quad Cities and heading south along I–74, you'll find two communities with a strong Swedish heritage. A few miles east off I–74 on Illinois Highway 81 is the town of **Andover.** On Andover's original colony square lies the 10-acre Andover Lake Park, accessible off Highway 81. The park has playground areas for children, picnic shelters, and sporting facilities for baseball, volleyball, tennis, horseshoes, and fishing. It's open daily from 7 A.M. to 10 P.M.

Less accessible but perhaps more interesting is the historic village of **Bishop Hill** (look for signs along Illinois Highway 82 that direct you down the county roads leading to it). Religious dissidents from Sweden formed a communal society here in the mid-1800s, and many of the original buildings have been preserved. Local artisans make traditional crafts such as pottery, jewelry, woven baskets, and wooden wares. Special events throughout the year include the notable *Jordbruksdagarna,* or Agricultural Days, in late September. For further information contact the Bishop Hill Arts Council, P.O. Box 47, Bishop Hill 61419; (309) 927–3345.

JOHNSON-SAUK TRAIL STATE PARK (all ages)

27500 North 1200 Avenue, Kewanee 61443; (309) 853–5589. Open from 6 A.M. to 10 P.M. daily. Admission is **Free**.

This 1,361-acre state park is just off Illinois Highway 78 about 5 miles north of town. Fifteen miles of trails through the woods are used for hiking in spring, summer, and fall and for cross-country skiing in winter. The park has a 58-acre artificially created lake in which anglers can fish for bass and muskie. Paddleboat rentals are available from the park's concession stand, which is open from May through September. You can get pop and snacks, fishing bait, and camping supplies there, too. The park has 10 picnic areas with tables and grills, two of the areas with shelters as well. You'll also notice a huge round barn in the park. Standing over 80 feet tall and with a diameter of about 85 feet, it was built in 1910 and today contains antique farm equipment and historical displays. The barn is open for tours occasionally; call the park number to find out if there's one coming up around the time you wish to visit. The park was named after Frank Johnson, the Illinois senator who worked to get it established, and the Sauk Indians, whose trail from Lake Michigan to the Mississippi River passed through this area.

Where to Eat

Waunee Farm. *South Tenney Street; (309) 852–2481.* About a mile south of Super 8. Hours are 5 to 10 P.M. Monday through Thursday and 5 P.M. to midnight Friday and Saturday; closed Sunday. Monday night dinner specials are offered, and Tuesday through Saturday you can either order from the menu or opt for the smorgasbord. $

Where to Stay

Johnson-Sauk Trail State Park Campground. *In the park; (309) 853–5589.* There are 68 campsites here. Electrical hookups are available for RVs. Tent campsites are nestled among the pine trees. There is a building with showers. $

Super 8. *901 South Tenney Street; (309) 853–8800.* This two-story motel has 41 rooms with cable TV. Reserve a rollaway bed or crib for $5. The room rate includes a continental breakfast of coffee with toast, English muffin, or bagel. $$

For More Information

Kewanee Chamber of Commerce, *113 East Second Street, Kewanee 61443; (309) 852–2175. Internet: www.kewanee-il.com.*

Galesburg

Population: 33,530. About midway between the Quad Cities and Peoria off Interstate 74 is historic Galesburg. U.S. Highways 34 and 150 and Illinois Highways 41 and 164 all feed into the city as well. Galesburg was founded in 1837, and many stately homes from the late 1800s and early 1900s remain. If you care about architecture, get out your list and check off Federal, Georgian, Gothic Revival, Italianate, Neoclassical, Prairie, and Romanesque as you find them—they're all here. The Seminary Street Historic Commercial District along 2 blocks of South Seminary Street in Galesburg is notable both for its restored buildings and for the specialty shops they contain. You'll find jewelry, pottery, stained glass, wall coverings, crafts, cosmetics, educational toys, chocolates, crepes, and bakery goodies among the items offered here.

CARL SANDBURG STATE HISTORIC SITE (age 10 and up)

331 East Third Street, Galesburg 61401; (309) 343–2361. Open daily from 9 A.M. to 5 P.M. Admission is **Free***, but donations are welcome.*

American poet and historian Carl Sandburg was born in Galesburg on January 6, 1878, in a three-room cottage that is now the Carl Sandburg State Historic Site. A visitor center stands next to the birthplace-museum, and Sandburg's ashes lie beneath Remembrance Rock (so named after his 1948 historical novel with that title) in a little wooded park behind the cottage. Sandburg grew up in Galesburg, dropping out of school at the age of 13 and doing odd jobs around town. At 18 he left to travel and, in 1898, served briefly in the U.S. Army during the Spanish-American War. He returned to Galesburg to attend Lombard College, although he never graduated. The lack of a degree didn't keep him from becoming first a newspaper writer, then a poet and biographer. Sandburg became a member of the "Chicago School" of influential writers who lived in Chicago from about 1912 to the late 1920s. He won the 1940 Pulitzer Prize for history for his comprehensive, six-volume biography of Abraham Lincoln and the 1951 Pulitzer Prize for poetry—not bad for a boy from Galesburg. Sandburg died in 1967.

ILLINOIS CITIZEN SOLDIER MUSEUM (age 5 and up)

1001 Michigan Avenue, Galesburg 61401; (309) 342–1181. Hours are 9 A.M. to 2 P.M. Monday through Friday and 9 A.M. to 4 P.M. Saturday. Admission is **Free**.

The Illinois Citizen Soldier Museum contains military artifacts from many wars, starting with the War of 1812 and continuing up through the Persian Gulf War. The museum is open on Memorial Day and Veterans Day, two especially fitting occasions for a visit.

"OLD MAIN" (age 7 and up)

Cherry and South Streets, Galesburg 61401; (309) 343–0112. Open from September through May. Hours are 8 A.M. to 4:30 P.M. Monday through Friday; closed major holidays. Admission is **Free**.

Galesburg is the home of Knox College, and the college's main administration building, "Old Main," is a National Historic Landmark—it is reportedly the only remaining original structure of the 1858 Lincoln-Douglas debate sites. Two bronze plaques bearing the faces of Abraham Lincoln and Stephen Douglas are mounted on the east wall, the site of the debate. The Gothic Revival building is still in use, so it's typically open whenever school is in session.

GALESBURG RAILROAD MUSEUM (age 4 and up)

423 Mulberry Street, Galesburg 61401; (309) 342–9400. Open from Memorial Day through Labor Day. Hours are noon to 5 P.M. Tuesday through Sunday; closed Monday. Admission is **Free**, *but suggested donation is $1 per adult.*

This museum has a collection of stationary railroad cars and equipment from the early to mid-1900s. A passenger engine built in 1930 is open for tours; it has a caboose, too. Memorabilia are exhibited inside a 1923 Pullman parlor car. There are also two inspection cars from the 1950s that are outfitted with track maintenance tools.

DISCOVERY DEPOT CHILDREN'S MUSEUM (all ages)

128 South Chambers Street, Galesburg 61401; (309) 344–8876. Hours are 4 to 7 P.M. Thursday, 10 A.M. to 3 P.M. Friday and Saturday, and 1 to 4 P.M. Sunday. Admission costs $2.50 for anyone age 8 months or older; babies younger than 8 months get in free.

This facility near the Galesburg Railroad Museum has loads of fun things to do for children of all ages—there's even a special area for "crawlers." Children can serve their parents plastic food in the mock-up cafe, sit in the cab of a corn combine with DVD player that simulates a ride through a cornfield, or play doctor in the medical-dental area. Be sure to check out the jumping area.

Where to Eat

Maid-Rite. *2250 Grand Avenue; (309) 342–2426.* Hours are 10:30 A.M. to 6:30 P.M. Monday through Friday and 10:30 A.M. to 2 P.M. Saturday; closed Sunday. Order one of the namesake loose-meat ground beef sandwiches for a tasty lunch. $

Don's Family Restaurant. *1081 East Main Street; (309) 342–5933.* This restaurant is open 24 hours a day, serving a variety of foods for breakfast, lunch, and dinner. Children's menu items cost $2 to $4 and include burger, grilled cheese, or pork chop. $

Where to Stay

Jumer's Continental Inn. *I–74 at East Main Street; (309) 343–7151 or (800) 285–8637.* This two-story inn opened in 1982 and is part of the Midwestern hotel empire founded in 1960 by D. James Jumer. There are 147 luxuriously appointed rooms here. Amenities include indoor swimming pool, saunas, and whirlpool. This is not the place to bring little children, but older kids will be wowed at the sophistication, especially if you dine in the elegant candlelit restaurant. $$$

Fairfield Inn. *901 West Carl Sandburg Drive; (309) 344–1911 or (800) 228–2800.* This economy chain property in the Marriott family has 56 rooms. Amenities include heated indoor pool and whirlpool. Continental breakfast is included in the room rate. $$

Econo Inn. *1475 North Henderson Street; (309) 344–2401.* This budget motel has 75 rooms and an indoor swimming pool. $

For More Information

Galesburg Area Convention and Visitors Bureau, *2163 East Main Street, Galesburg 61401; (309) 343–2485. Internet: www.galesburg.org/chamber/tourism.*

Peoria

Population: 113,504. I–74 takes an eastward turn beyond Galesburg and heads toward (and through) Peoria. You can reach Peoria from the south via I–155. A scenic route from the north runs along the Illinois River, down Illinois Highway 26 on the east side or Illinois Highway 29 on the west. Both feature lush green foliage in summer and spectacular color in fall. From the north-northeast you can zip down I–55 or I–39, both of which connect with I–74 a bit south of the Peoria area around Bloomington-Normal; each also earlier intersects U.S. Highway 24, which provides a straight shot in from the east.

Peoria often has been the butt of comedians' jokes, but the joke's on you if you don't come and see all the family attractions this area has to offer—there are more than you'd expect. Try to visit during the milder seasons, when you can partake of the many outdoor activities. A good street to use as a focal point is War Memorial Drive: Coming from the east, U.S. Highway 24 turns into War Memorial Drive after you cross the steel-girder bridge over the Illinois River, and the street curves through the middle of town (but a ways north of downtown) until it becomes U.S. Highway 150 as you leave to the west. Most of the way it's two lanes wide in each direction.

LAKEVIEW MUSEUM OF ARTS AND SCIENCES (all ages)

1125 West Lake Avenue, Peoria 61614; (309) 686–7000. Hours are 11 A.M. to 5 P.M. Tuesday, Thursday, and Friday, 11 A.M. to 8 P.M. Wednesday, 10 A.M. to 5 P.M. Saturday, and noon to 5 P.M. Sunday; closed Monday. Admission costs $5 for adults and $4 for young people age 5 through 17 and seniors. Prices jump to $6 and $4, respectively, if you add a planetarium show. Children age 4 or younger get in free, but the planetarium show is not recommended for this age. Call for descriptions of current special exhibits and planetarium shows. The planetarium is closed in September and October.

The Lakeview Museum of Arts and Sciences displays a variety of special exhibits. Permanent features at the museum include the Children's Discovery Center, the Natural Sciences Gallery, the Illinois Folk Art Gallery, and the West African Art Gallery. Children may be especially interested in the dinosaur display. The museum also has a planetarium.

OWENS RECREATION CENTER (age 5 and up)

1019 West Lake Avenue, Peoria 61614; (309) 686–3369. One block north of War Memorial Drive between University Street and Sheridan Road. Open year-round. Public skating hours are 1 to 2:50 P.M. Monday through Friday, 7:30 to 9:30 P.M. Friday and Saturday, and 3 to 5 P.M. Sunday. Cost per session is $3.75 for anyone age 13 or older and $2.75 for kids age 12 or younger. Skate rental costs $1.50 per person.

This facility has two full-size ice rinks. Public skating is offered here even in summer, which is a different way to cool off if you're tired of swimming. The center has concessions.

NORTHWOODS MALL (all ages)

4501 War Memorial Drive, Peoria 61613; (309) 688–0443. Hours are 10 A.M. to 9 P.M. Monday through Saturday and noon to 5 P.M. Sunday.

This indoor shopping mall is the largest in the Peoria area, with more than 100 stores. JCPenney, Sears, and Famous-Barr are the anchor department stores. Kids may want to look around in the Disney Store or Kay-Bee Toys or play arcade games in Aladdin's Castle. Snack on Karmelkorn or cookies. For heartier food there's a pizza place and an A&W.

MT. HAWLEY BOWL (age 4 and up)

8200 North Hale Avenue, Peoria 61603; (309) 692–7555. Open from 10 A.M. to 11 P.M. daily. Cost is $1.95 per person per game before 6 P.M., $2.25 after 6 P.M. Shoes cost $1.50. Family Cosmic Bowling from 2:30 to 5 P.M. Saturday costs $2.75 per person. Ask about a possible family rate.

This alley has 24 lanes, all with computerized scoring. You can bowl the regular way, in full light and with bumpers filling up the gutters for the children, or come during the Cosmic Bowling session, when bowling is by black light and the pins and balls glow.

MT. HAWLEY CASTLE GOLF (age 4 and up)

8200 North Hale Avenue, Peoria 61603; (309) 692–7555. Hours are 10 A.M. to 11 P.M. daily. Cost is $4.75 per person age 9 or older and $4.25 for kids age 4 through 8. Children age 3 or younger play free.

This outdoor facility next to the bowling alley has a 30-foot-tall castle. The attractive course features waterfalls and sand traps that make the play perhaps a bit too challenging for the youngest children.

GLEN OAK ZOO (all ages)

2218 North Prospect Road, Peoria 61603; (309) 686–3365. Open daily from 10 A.M. to 5 P.M. Admission costs $3.75 for anyone age 13 or older and $2 for kids age 4 through 12; tots age 3 or younger get in **Free***.*

South off War Memorial Drive on Prospect Road is the tiny Glen Oak Zoo—watch carefully, because the small wooden signs blend in a bit too well with the park surroundings. You could easily see everything at a leisurely pace within an hour. The zoo layout cleverly forces visitors to pass through an indoor curving walkway lined with glass-walled cases containing reptiles, birds, and small mammals—displays you might otherwise skip—in order to reach the outdoor areas. The meerkats are especially cute, even if you haven't seen *The Lion King*, and it's worthwhile to be able to show your kids the real thing upon which the Disney movie character Timon was based. Reasonable-size monkey cages are at the end of the walkway just inside the doors leading outside; both the primates and the cages are clean and well maintained. There is a larger monkey pen outdoors, too.

Perhaps the nicest outdoor exhibit at the zoo is the lion enclosure, which has tall prairie grass resembling that of the African veld. Vines trail along the high fence, softening the effect of confinement. A glass wall along one section of the enclosure allows visitors to safely observe the felines close-up; on a hot day you may even find a lion lying right up against the cool glass. There is a "Contact Area," a barnlike structure with goats and assorted other critters, but the animals are behind fences, and kids can pet them through the wooden slats but are not allowed in with them. For $1 a zoo attendant will put your youngster on a pony that is led around a small circular path—it's a pretty short ride for a buck, but preschoolers would probably be satisfied. Kids of all ages enjoy the timber playground area; as they run and climb, they bear an eerie resemblance to the monkeys. The outdoor Safari Cafe has a limited but reasonably priced menu, including Pepsi, popcorn, ice cream, hot dogs, and chicken sandwiches. There is a changing table in the women's rest room, which is located inside near a few educational displays.

GEORGE H. LUTHY MEMORIAL BOTANICAL GARDEN (all ages)

2218 North Prospect Road, Peoria 61603; (309) 686–3362. Open year-round. Hours between Memorial Day and Labor Day are 10 A.M. to 5 P.M. daily. Hours during the rest of the year are 10 A.M. to 5 P.M. Monday through Saturday and noon to 5 P.M. Sunday. Admission is **Free***; there is an unobtrusive donations box.*

Adjacent to the zoo is the George H. Luthy Memorial Botanical Garden. It's worth a stroll, especially in peak blooming season, when you'll see an explosion of color. The specialty flower is the rose, and you'll find row after row of the aromatic blooms. The paved aisles are wide enough for baby strollers or wheelchairs. A fountain in the center of this four-acre herb and perennial garden provides pleasant ambient noise as well as visual appeal, and along the perimeter there are plenty of benches where you can rest your feet and still feast your eyes.

PEORIA CHIEFS (age 4 and up)

Home games are played at Pete Vonachen Stadium, 1524 West Nebraska Avenue, Peoria 61604; (309) 688–1622. Season runs from early May through late August. Tickets cost $6 for the field box section, $5 for the reserved section, and $4 for general admission seats on the fringes (there are no outfield bleachers); the best seats are worth the extra $2. Parking on the grass lot adjacent to the field is free. Internet: www.chiefsnet.com.

Baseball fans or not, your family will probably enjoy the Peoria Chiefs, the Class A Midwestern League affiliate of the St. Louis Cardinals. Like other minor-league clubs, the Chiefs offer a variety of gimmicks along with the game: During the National Anthem the words appear on the scoreboard screen and a firework shoots up on "the rockets' red glare"; mascot Rally Redbird races a child volunteer around the bases (of course, the kid always wins); the owner of the dirtiest car in the parking lot wins a free car wash and the embarrassment of having the vehicle's license plate number and description broadcast. And what could compare to the spectacle of seeing Jerry Lewis impersonator Myron Noodleman (one in a series of special guests) doing the chicken dance? The stadium is nicely laid out, with most (if not all) seats affording an unobstructed view of the field. The main concession area is on the lower level. Food prices are average; you can get Pepsi, beer, popcorn, peanuts, ice cream, hot dogs, pizza, and steak and chicken sandwiches. The rest rooms are adequate for a medium-crowded day; women would have to wait in line if the stadium were filled to capacity. The women's rest room has a shelf for changing babies' diapers.

KARTVILLE (age 3 and up)

919 Swords Avenue, just off Farmington Road, Peoria 61603; (309) 676–3628. Open from spring through about October. Hours are 10 A.M. to 10 P.M. daily. Each ride or round of golf costs $2 per person, all ages.

If you crave action, head over to Kartville. As the name suggests, go-karts are among the offerings here. Kids must be at least 9 years old to ride, and the price covers three laps. Dune buggies bounce along dirt trails beyond the kart track. There is no official age limit for the dune buggies, but common sense dictates that you wouldn't send a grade-schooler out on one alone. The bumper boats are a bit tamer, and you could probably let your kindergartner pilot one as long as the other riders weren't all rowdy teenagers. The ride lasts about five minutes. The miniature golf course is sparingly decorated and not too tricky, so little kids can play without getting totally frustrated. Prices are calculated per person per attraction, and the cost can mount quickly if you aren't careful. Ask about the occasional specials in which you get unlimited play for one price. In addition to the aforementioned attractions, Kartville has batting cages, for which you plunk in two quarters. Concessions are a good deal—it's not often that you can buy a little bag of popcorn for just a quarter. A fairly generous Pepsi, ice-cream bars, miniature tacos, and other goodies are mostly in the $1 to $2 range. Families with young children probably would have more fun earlier in the day when it's not as busy; the crowd can get a little rougher later at night, too.

AFRICAN-AMERICAN MUSEUM HALL OF FAME (age 5 and up)

309 DuSable Street, Peoria 61605; (309) 673–2206. Call ahead to check hours, which generally are 10 A.M. to 2 P.M. Wednesday and Friday. Admission is **Free***, but donations are gladly accepted.*

Permanent exhibits here are from the collection of Dr. Romeo Garrett, the first black professor at Bradley University, who died in 2000 at the age of 90. Special exhibits vary; a recent one featured black inventors and their inventions.

SPIRIT OF PEORIA (age 3 and up)

Downtown Peoria Riverfront; (309) 636–6169. Summer sight-seeing cruises depart at 2 P.M. Wednesday and Sunday and last about an hour and a quarter. Tickets cost $10 for anyone age 13 or older, $5 for kids age 12 or younger, and $8 for senior citizens. Buy them at the Gazebo Gift Shop, and be at the boat at least 15 minutes before departure time. Internet: www.spiritofpeoria.com.

For a view of Peoria from the Illinois River, go to the foot of Main Street and board the *Spirit of Peoria,* a working replica of a century-old stern-wheeler that was built in 1988 and can hold up to 350 passengers. This boat is huge, with three levels of ornately decorated decks. The trim and the paddle wheel are both red, making an eye-catching contrast to the white boat and the blue-gray river. You'll see a number of historic and modern sights.

Where to Eat

Fairview Farms Restaurant. *5911 Heurmann Road; (309) 697–4111.* Hours are 5 P.M. to 8 P.M. Tuesday through Saturday and noon to 5 P.M. Sunday; closed Monday. At this restaurant in a converted farmhouse, you can buy a regular dinner or opt for the family-style menu, which entitles you to a choice of two out of the five meat entrees on the menu plus side dishes served in big bowls that you pass around the table. Reservations are recommended on weekends. $

Bob Evans Restaurant. *4915 North Big Hollow Road; (309) 692–3600.* Hours are 6 A.M. to 10 P.M. daily. See Restaurant Appendix for description. $

Godfather's Pizza. *618 West Glen Street; (309) 688–5007.* Hours are 11 A.M. to 10 P.M. Sunday through Thursday and 11 A.M. to midnight Friday and Saturday. The medium-thick, chewy-crust pizza here is loaded with cheese and your favorite ingredients. Round out the meal at the salad bar. $

Olive Garden. *6828 North War Memorial Drive; (309) 691–5975.* Hours are 11 A.M. to 10 P.M. Sunday through Thursday and 11 A.M. to 11 P.M. Friday and Saturday. See Restaurant Appendix for description. $$

Perkins Family Restaurant. *4019 North War Memorial Drive; (309) 682–8616.* Open 24 hours a day. This chain carries a wide array of breakfast, lunch, and dinner foods, including freshly baked cinnamon rolls and muffins. Expect a hearty meal in a clean, wholesome atmosphere. There is a children's menu with the usual assortment of choices. $

Where to Stay

Jumer's Castle Lodge. *117 North Western Avenue, at Moss; (309) 673–8040 or (800) 285–8637.* Kids will like the exterior castle motif, but the opulent Old World European furnishings inside give this place a sophistication that is beyond the appreciation of young children. Wait until the kids are at least 7 or 8 to treat them to the Jumer's experience. This property's 180 guest rooms match the elegant decor of the lobby and restaurant. Modern amenities include an indoor pool and a game room. $$$$

Days Inn. *2726 West Lake Avenue; (309) 688–7000 or (800) 325–2525.* This budget chain property has 120 rooms and an outdoor swimming pool. Room rate includes continental breakfast. $$

Fairfield Inn. *4203 North War Memorial Drive; (309) 686–7600 or (800) 228–2800.* Get off War Memorial at the "exit" for Scenic Drive and drive around the perimeter of the Northwoods Mall onto Teamster Drive to reach the inn, a three-story tan building with royal blue roof. It has 135 rooms and a heated outdoor swimming pool. Continental breakfast is included in the room rate. $$

Holiday Inn Brandywine. *4400 North Brandywine Drive; (309) 686–8000 or (800) 465–4329.* This four-story chain property has 251 rooms with cable TV. Amenities include Holidome with game room, fitness center, indoor pool, and whirlpool. Pets are allowed. $$$

For More Information

Peoria Convention and Visitors Bureau, *403 Northeast Jefferson Street, Peoria 61603; (309) 676–0303 or (800) 747–0302. Internet: www.peoria.org or www.peoriariverfront.com.*

Dunlap

Population: 851. This little town north of Peoria has a fun family attraction you won't want to miss.

WHEELS O' TIME MUSEUM (all ages)

11923 North Knoxville Avenue, Dunlap 61525; (309) 243–9020. Open from May through October from noon to 5 P.M. Wednesday through Sunday. Admission is $4 for anyone age 12 or older, $1.50 for children age 3 through 11, and free for toddlers age 2 or younger. The buildings are accessible for wheelchairs except for the upstairs balcony in the main building.

The Wheels O' Time Museum is a treat to visit. The museum is 8 miles north of downtown Peoria on Illinois Highway 40 (formerly Highway 88). A gas station almost obscures the sign for the entrance on the left, but you can see the Rock Island Locomotive No. 886 parked on a piece of track in front of the peach-colored, two-story building that looks like a windowless warehouse or an airplane hangar. A German-style clock, with dwarves who strike a bell on the hour, breaks the monotony of the facade and gives a hint of the treasures inside. After you enter and pay the admission fee, you are immediately greeted by a cacophony of music from a player piano and from a miniature circus parade inside a glass-walled wagon. Nearby is a roomful of ticking clocks, from delicate miniatures to massive grandfathers.

The most eye-catching aspect of this first-floor showroom is the collection of vintage cars, all lined up and quietly gleaming an invitation to look. A 1916 Glide was manufactured by Peoria's own Bartholomew Company; it originally sold for $1,095—a bargain by today's standards but a sizable investment when you consider that the federal minimum wage didn't go into effect until 1938 and was 25 cents an hour, so a working-class mope in 1916 probably was lucky to make even $5 a week. Parents and grandparents of all ages are likely to find at least one model that brushes against their own past: a 1925 Star Model F, a 1933 Packard and Pierce Arrow, a 1941 Lincoln-Zephyr, a 1956 Bentley, a

1957 Nash Metropolitan, a 1967 Lincoln Continental convertible, a 1972 Datsun 240Z, a 1981 Delorean (anyone who's seen the movie *Back to the Future* will recognize this one). In a back corner there's a kid-size antique car that girls and boys can sit in—no, it doesn't move, but imagination is the best fuel, anyway. There are antique bikes, too, such as the F. E. Ide bicycle manufactured in Peoria in 1894.

Along the periphery of the first floor and in a series of rooms along the balcony upstairs you'll find a marvelous collection of vintage gadgets. The really great thing about them is that they all work. Plunk a nickel into an old jukebox to watch the arm pull out a 45 rpm record (ignore the kids' queries of "What's a record?") and play a tune by Tommy Dorsey, Duke Ellington, or Artie Shaw (for the wee ones, choose Patti Page's "How Much Is That Doggie in the Window?"). Try to tap out a message in Morse code on a telegraph, or tune in to the airwaves on a homemade crystal radio set from the 1920s. Press a button to activate a display of sturdy old electric trains (no cheap plastic on these models). Take the multiple-choice quiz to see how well you can identify kitchen utensils from great-grandma's day. You'll really show your age if, like this writer, you enjoy the resounding clatter of the Royal and Underwood manual typewriters more than the quiet click of a computer keyboard. Then there are numerous displays, including cameras—some accordion-like box models, some more "modern" ones with flash cubes (remember those?)—and dolls, from antiques to the Nancy Ann Storybook Dolls of the 1950s to original *Star Wars* figurines from the late 1970s and early 1980s, long before the first three movies were rereleased in 1997 and a whole new set of toys came on the market.

Head out the back door and down a flower-lined path to reach three more buildings. The first of these houses tractors and farm machinery, plus a nifty collection of old washing machines dating from 1800 through 1940. Push a button to start them gyrating. If Grandma's along, she might be able to explain from firsthand experience how the clothes were fished from the tub below and squeezed through the wringer rolls above. An item that kids will love but some parents will cringe at is the row of steam whistles you can toot with the pull of a chain. One sounds like a calliope; another would signal quitting time for factory workers (or Fred Flintstone). Be warned, however: They are *loud.* The second building contains more vintage cars, plus gas pumps and a horse-drawn doctor's buggy from the late 1800s. The third building is the Firehouse, with fire engines and equipment. You can also climb up inside the engine of that locomotive you saw outside. You can pass a lot of time at Wheels O' Time.

Where to Eat and Stay

See entries for Peoria.

Hanna City

Population: 1,205. To the west of Peoria you'll find the small community of Hanna City and its Wildlife Prairie Park, a wonderful place for families.

WILDLIFE PRAIRIE PARK (all ages)

3826 North Taylor Road, Hanna City 61536; (309) 676–0998. Off I–74 take exit 82 and head south about $2\frac{1}{2}$ miles (or half a mile south off Illinois Highway 8). There are numerous signs, so you shouldn't miss it. Hours between May and September are 9 A.M. to 6:30 P.M. daily; from mid-March through April and from October through mid-December, hours are 9 A.M. to 4:30 P.M. daily. Admission rates are $5 for anyone age 13 or older, $3 for kids age 4 through 12, and free for children age 3 or younger. Call ahead to confirm the hours and rates before you drive all the way out there. You can get an overview of the place for an extra $1 per person to ride the miniature steam train. Internet: www.wildlifepark.org.

This facility brings nature all together—animals, plants, fresh air. Come here when you have plenty of leisure time to enjoy it. The park has numerous well-marked trails for walking. Some of them pass over unobtrusively fenced areas containing such wildlife as cougars, wolves, foxes, otters, birds of prey, and bears. Heed the warnings and stay on the trails. Bison and elk have their own pasture, which you can see from an overlook terrace with tables and chairs. The Pioneer Farmstead area has a working water pump (but don't drink the rusty stuff) and various antique farm implements, plus a covered wagon (minus its canvas). Little kids will like the petting area, with its goats, horses, and other farm animals. The timbered Visitor Center looks rustic from the outside, but inside it's all modern and air-conditioned. The souvenir shop has pretty stained-glass window hangings and other finely crafted items. Open-air buildings near the Visitor Center feature hands-on and interactive displays that help kids learn about the habitat and its occupants. You can get a bite to eat at the Prairie View Snack Shop.

For a real adventure you can spend the night in the Wildlife Prairie Park in one of four refurbished red cabooses. Each caboose contains a trundle bed, a bunk bed, and two futons to sleep up to six people. Other amenities include a small fold-down table with four chairs, a minifridge, a hot pot, a toaster oven, and a tiny bathroom with sink, toilet, and shower. Baseboard heaters and an overhead air-conditioning unit will make the interior comfortable in any weather. Light switches are well labeled; one of the lights is a replica lamp. There's also a specially marked dial you can turn to activate a motor under the caboose that simulates the sound and feel of train movement—major cool. Outside there are several picnic tables and barbecue grills. You'll want to do your own cooking, because you're out in the middle of nowhere—besides, it's fun! Just remember to bring plates, flatware, and a can opener, because the caboose furnishes absolutely zero utensils. With no TV or telephone in the caboose, your family will have to resort to such old-fashioned pastimes as reading, playing games, and even talking to one another. There is a pond close by where you might try your luck at fishing, although the lines and bobbers tangled in the trees offshore will give you a clue that others before you have not always been successful. If you're a city dweller, you may be surprised at the night sounds you hear: frogs, waterbirds, wailing peacocks, maybe even a far-off cougar growl.

Down the road a bit from the cabooses are newer lodgings built in the late 1990s. A converted stable contains five two-room suites, and a cluster of converted grain silos stands nearby. While they lack the seclusion and old-fashioned charm of the cabooses, they are cute in their own way and contain similar amenities. A log cabin sits atop a hill.

Caboose lodging costs $60 (Monday through Thursday) or $70 (Friday through Sunday) per night for two people. The corresponding rates for the stable units are $70 and $80, those for the silo cottages are $80 and $90, and those for the cottage on the hill are $90 and $100. For all four lodgings, tack on another $10 for each additional person. Depending on how large your family is, the rate compares favorably to that at a midrange motel, and it's a more memorable experience. Call (309) 676–0998 to make a reservation. Be prepared to guarantee it with a credit card, although you can pay cash instead once you get there. If you prefer to pay by check in advance, write to Wildlife Prairie Park, Rural Route 2, 3826 North Taylor Road, Hanna City 61536. Either way, you'll get a written confirmation of your reservation, and you should bring that letter along when you check in between 2 and 4 P.M. Check-out time is 11 A.M.

Where to Eat

Bring your own food if you're staying overnight in the Prairie Park. Otherwise, see entry for Peoria.

Where to Stay

If you don't want to try the Wildlife Prairie Park lodging (awww!), see entry for Peoria.

Pekin

Population: 32,254. Illinois Highway 29 goes straight into this town, situated southeast of Peoria. You can also reach Pekin off Interstate 474.

B & N DELSHIRE STABLES (age 8 and up)

211 McNaughton Park Road, Pekin 61554; (309) 382–9117. Open year-round. A one-hour trail ride costs $18 per person and departs at 9:30 and 11 A.M. and 12:30, 2, 3:30, 5, and 6:30 P.M. Monday and Wednesday through Sunday. The two-hour trail ride costs $36 per person and departs at 9:30 and 11 A.M. and 12:30, 2, 3:30, and 5 P.M. Monday and Wednesday through Sunday. Riders must be at least 8 years old for the one-hour ride and 12 years old for the two-hour ride. The facility is closed Tuesday and when the weather's bad. Call ahead.

Introduce your older children to the pleasure of horseback riding. This stable offers a gentle 2½-mile trail ride that passes through grasslands and forest, sometimes even through a cornfield or across a creek—the route varies.

DRAGONLAND WATER PARK (all ages)

1701 Court Street, in Mineral Springs Park, Pekin 61554; (309) 347–4000. Open from Memorial Day through Labor Day. Hours are 11:30 A.M. to 6 P.M. daily. Admission costs $3.50 per person for nonresidents age 4 or older; children age 3 or younger get in free.

For a family with young children, Dragonland Water Park is the ideal place to cool off on a hot summer day. From Peoria take Highway 29 and turn east onto Margaret Street, which merges with Court Street. You'll know you're getting close when you pass Mineral Springs Park pond with a fountain and paddleboats to the left and the "World's

A Trip Back in Time About an hour's drive south of Peoria is the Dickson Mounds State Museum near Lewistown. The *mounds* part of the museum's name refers to the 800-year-old burial sites of the Mississippian American Indian people. The *Dickson* part is in honor of Dr. Don F. Dickson, who began excavating at his family farm in 1927. Archaeologists from the University of Chicago came to the area in the 1930s, and Dickson Mounds became first a state park in 1945, then a part of the Illinois State Museum in 1965. Today it concentrates on the plentiful archaeological artifacts that provide clues about the prehistory of the Illinois River Valley. The museum was renovated in 1994 to provide state-of-the-art exhibits and multimedia presentations. There are numerous hands-on activities in which visitors can touch objects, turn pages, or look through a microscope, for example. The museum's Discovery Center is geared toward kids. They'll especially enjoy the Discovery Drawers, a set of 32 drawers underneath a counter, each labeled with a picture and title. Kids can take out what's in the drawer and do something with it, such as "excavating" a fossil from dirt or dressing up in a costume of the past. Special programs are offered throughout the year, so call to find out what's coming up; you could participate in a hide-tanning workshop or enjoy folk music at a coffeehouse. A picnic area is on the 162-acre grounds, as are the remains of three early Mississippian buildings that you can look at. Museum shops offer snacks and souvenirs.

The address for Dickson Mounds is Rural Route 1, 10956 North Dickson Mounds Road, Lewistown 61542; (309) 547–3721. Heading southwest on U.S. Highway 24, turn south (before you reach the town) onto Illinois Highway 78/97 and proceed a few miles; signs will guide you to the museum. Coming from the south up Highways 78 or 97 or from the east on Illinois Highway 136, cross the bridge over the Illinois River at Havana, and then proceed north on the joined Highway 78/97, where you'll find signs to direct you in. Dickson Mounds is open from 8:30 A.M. to 5 P.M. daily except New Year's Day, Easter, Thanksgiving, and Christmas. Admission is **Free**. Internet: www.museum.state.il.us/ismsites/dickson.

Greatest Sundial" to the right. Look for the sign for Memorial Arena, and turn left onto Mineral West Shore Drive. Being there at opening time is a good idea if you want to snag a chaise lounge; otherwise, there's a nice lawn area that even has a few trees to protect burn-prone people who don't worship the sun. There are no lockers in the locker room; they are located instead outside along a wall facing the pool area.

The pool has a zero-depth area so that even the tiniest tots can tiptoe in the water. For toddlers and young grade-schoolers, the shallow end features Dude the Dragonslide, a green fiberglass guy perhaps 10 feet tall; the children climb a vertical ladder up his back and whiz down the straight, water-slicked slide in front. The deep end of the pool is only 5 feet, making the swimming area less appealing for teens, but they may like the two giant water slides. The narrower red slide is for people alone, while the wider blue one allows sliders to ride huge plastic inner tubes, colored mustard yellow for a single passenger and hot pink for a pair. Little kids can ride with bigger people, but the kids must wear life jackets (available there; no extra charge for life jackets or tubes). The prices in the concession area are quite reasonable, ranging from 50 cents to $3, with many items $1 or less. The menu includes Pepsi, ice-cream bars, candy, popcorn, hot dogs, and hot snacky items such as "pizza sticks." Smokers will be delighted to discover that there is a place within the pool grounds where they can light up, a lawn section between the concession area and the big slides. If you're concerned about rules, there's a typed, 30-item list tacked to a bulletin board near the concession and first aid areas, but most of them are common sense.

PEKIN MALL (all ages)

3500 Court Street, Pekin 61554; (309) 347–7004. Hours are 10 A.M. to 9 P.M. Monday through Saturday and noon to 5 P.M. Sunday.

This one-story indoor shopping mall is anchored by JCPenney and Bergner's department stores. Shops offer an assortment of clothing and gifts. Hobby Lobby has craft kits and supplies. The only real food here is the Lum's restaurant.

Where to Eat

Lum's. *3500 Court Street, in Pekin Mall; (309) 347–4847.* Hours are 8 A.M. to 8 P.M. Monday through Thursday, 8 A.M. to 9 P.M. Friday and Saturday, and 8 A.M. to 5 P.M. Sunday. This restaurant offers burgers, chicken, pot roast, pasta, and assorted other dishes. The $3 to $4 children's menu includes fries and drink; entree choices include burgers, roasted chicken, or a hot dog. $

Where to Stay

Ramada Pekin Inn. *2801 Court Street; (309) 347–5533 or (800) 272–6232.* This property received a three-diamond rating from AAA. The four-story hotel has 124 rooms with cable TV. Amenities include a game room and an outdoor pool. $$

Comfort Inn. *3240 Vandever Avenue; (309) 353–4047 or (800) 228–5150.* The inn has 48 rooms and an indoor swimming pool. Pets are allowed. Continental breakfast is included in the room rate. $$$

For More Information

Pekin Chamber of Commerce,
402 Court Street, Pekin 61554;
(309) 346–2106.

Quincy

Population: 39,681. Quincy overlooks the Mississippi River. From the south or east, you can zip in on I–172 from I–72. From Peoria your best bet is to meander down U.S. Highway 24. The site was originally home to Native Americans from the Sauk, Fox, and Kickapoo tribes. They were displaced in the early 1800s by settlers from New England and immigrants from Germany. Quincy was the largest of the seven cities in which Abraham Lincoln and Stephen Douglas conducted their famous debates in 1858. Mark Twain, whose hometown of Hannibal, Missouri, is not far from Quincy to the south, visited Quincy in the late 1800s. During the 1900s the city built a reputation as an architectural center. Uptown Quincy, the central business district, offers a variety of shopping, dining, and entertainment; call (217) 228-8696 for details.

Take the Plunge If you're in Quincy in early August, don't miss the spectacle of 2,000 skydivers plummeting earthward during the World FreeFall Convention at Baldwin Field Airport off Illinois Highway 104. The annual event is open to the public, and it costs $3 per car to get in. Food and drink booths and a carnival supplement the action. Call (800) 978-4748 for the current year's dates and other information.

VILLA KATHRINE (age 5 and up)

532 Gardner Expressway, Quincy 62301; (217) 224–3688. Open from 9 A.M. to 5 P.M. Monday through Saturday and 1 to 5 P.M. Sunday. Admission costs $2 for anyone age 12 or older and $1 for kids age 7 through 11; children age 6 or *younger get in free. You must take a guided tour; you can't just go in and wander around. Call ahead to make sure a guide will be available.*

One of the most unusual buildings in Quincy is Villa Kathrine, which claims to be the only example of Mediterranean architecture in the Midwest. It was made out of local materials in 1900 by George Metz, a world-traveling Quincian who modeled the residence on Islamic structures he had seen. Its courtyard surrounds a reflecting pool. Restoration is ongoing. Volunteer guides take visitors through the home.

ALL WARS MUSEUM (age 5 and up)

1707 North 12th Street, Quincy 62301; (217) 222–8641. Hours vary; call for current schedule. Admission is **Free**, *but donations are welcome.*

Military buffs will want to check out the All Wars Museum. It is located on the grounds of the Illinois Veterans Home, one of the largest and oldest veterans' homes in the United States. Exhibits in the museum span the American Revolution through the Persian Gulf War.

QUINCY COMMUNITY THEATRE (age 4 and up)

300 Civic Center Plaza, Quincy 62301; (217) 222–3209. Office hours are 10 A.M. to 5 P.M. Monday through Friday; call for current shows and ticket prices. Internet: www.lqct.org.

The QCT organization dates back to 1923, and it moved into its current state-of-the-art facility in 1995. Many of the shows are appropriate for families. For example, the 2000 season featured productions of *Pippi Longstocking, Diary of Anne Frank,* and *Winnie the Pooh.*

WAVERING AQUATIC CENTER (all ages)

In Wavering Park on North 36th Street, Quincy 62301; (217) 228–9220. Open Memorial Day weekend through Labor Day. Hours are noon to 5:30 P.M. daily. Admission costs $3 for adults, $2.75 for teenagers, and $2.50 for kids age 4 through 12. Children age 3 or younger get in free. Family swim nights from 6:30 to 9 P.M. Monday and Wednesday cost $1.50 per person or $5 per family.

This facility features a 230-foot water slide, a diving well, and a sand volleyball court. There is a concession area as well.

BATTING CAGE AND MINIATURE GOLF COMPLEX (age 3 and up)

In Upper Moorman Park on North 36th Street, Quincy 62301; (217) 228–1261. Open from early April through Labor Day. Hours are 10 A.M. to 9 P.M. Monday through Saturday and noon to 9 P.M. Sunday. A round of minigolf costs

$3.25 for anyone age 13 or older and $2.75 for kids age 12 or younger. Tokens for batting cages are offered at four for $1, 16 for $3, or 20 for $5.

Like the two city pools, this complex also is run under the auspices of the Quincy Park District. It boasts Quincy's only 18-hole miniature golf course. The batting cages include two baseball and two slow-pitch softball pitching machines. Feed tokens into the machine to play; two tokens give you ten pitches. Concessions are available.

QUINCY MALL (all ages)

On Broadway between 30th and 36th Streets, Quincy 62301; (217) 223–8713. Hours are 10 A.M. to 9 P.M. Monday through Saturday and noon to 5 P.M. Sunday.

This one-story indoor shopping mall features 70 stores, including Kay-Bee Toys, and five restaurants. JCPenney, Sears, and Bergner's are the anchor department stores.

Where to Eat

Chef's Inn. *129 North Side Street; (217) 228–2723.* Hours are 7 A.M. to 2 P.M. Sunday through Tuesday and 7 A.M. to 8 P.M. Wednesday through Saturday. Hearty homemade breakfasts, such as biscuits and gravy, are popular here. The kids may be thrilled to find liver and onions on the dinner menu (or maybe not). $

Elder's Family Restaurant. *1800 State Street; (217) 223–7790.* Hours are 11 A.M. to midnight Tuesday through Sunday; closed Monday. This is a meat-and-potatoes sort of place that serves steaks, burgers, and what it asserts is the "best fried chicken in town." $

Tower of Pizza. *1221 Broadway; (217) 224–6030.* Open from 4 P.M. to midnight Sunday through Thursday and 4 P.M. to 12:45 A.M. Friday and Saturday. This eatery's claim to fame is that it "serves Quincy's original thick crust pizza," with the dough and sauce made from scratch, along with sandwiches and drinks. Don't let the name fool you into looking for a tower—the restaurant is in a two-story brick building with a cozy brick interior and lots of memorabilia on the walls. There's a drive-up window, or you can order carryout, or they'll deliver to your hotel—they're definitely flexible. $

Where to Stay

Comfort Inn. *4122 Broadway; (217) 228–2700 or (800) 228–5150.* This comfortable chain property has 58 rooms. Amenities include indoor pool and game room. The room rate includes continental breakfast. $$

Holiday Inn. *201 South Third Street; (217) 222–2666 or (800) 465–4329.* This four-story hotel has 155 rooms. Amenities include an indoor pool in the atrium, an exercise room, and a game room, but no free breakfast. $$

For More Information

Quincy Convention & Visitors Bureau, *300 Civic Center Plaza, Quincy 62301; (217) 223–1000 or (800) 978–4748.*

Other Things to See and Do in Western Illinois

January: Bald Eagle Days, Rock Island; (309) 788–5912

World's Toughest Rodeo, Peoria; (305) 673–8900

February: Central Illinois Boat and Water Recreation Show, Peoria; (309) 693–9667

March: Bistate St. Patrick's Day Parade, Rock Island; (309) 788–2341

April: Annual Swap Meet, Rock Island; (309) 788–5912

May: Hornucopia, Rock Island; (800) 747–7800

June: Rhubarb Festival, Aledo; (800) 747–7800

Railroad Days, Galesburg; (309) 343–1194

July: Championship Outboard Boat Races, DePue; (815) 447–2893

Rock Island Summerfest; (309) 788–6311

Most communities have a Fourth of July celebration, and many county fairs are in July and August.

August: Great River Tug Fest, Port Byron; (309) 523–3312

New Windsor Fair and Rodeo; (309) 667–2112

Viola Family Fun Fest; (309) 596–2624 or (309) 596–2561

September: Macomb Balloon Rally; (309) 833–1315

Morton Pumpkin Festival; (309) 263–2491

October: Milan Improvement Project Arts and Crafts Fair; (309) 786–7430

Laser Light Fright Nights, Rock Island; (309) 788–6311

November: Santa Claus Parade, Peoria; (800) 747–0302

December: East Peoria Festival of Lights; (309) 698–4711 or (800) 365–3743

Julmarknad Christmas Market, Bishop Hill; (309) 927–3345

Central Illinois

To drive into Central Illinois from the northeast is to plunge into the heart of the heartland. The sprawl of the suburbs and exurbs thins out until you're surrounded by nearly uninterrupted stretches of prairie—snow-covered, barren, and windswept in the dead of winter but verdantly carpeted with cornfields, wildflowers, and waving grasses during the warmer months. It was into this pastoral setting that Abraham Lincoln moved at the age of 21 and embarked on the long career path that would eventually lead him to the White House. Lincoln lore and historical sites abound in the 28 counties of Central Illinois. For general information about the region, contact the **Central Illinois Tourism Development Office,** 700 East Adams Street, Springfield 62701; (217) 525-7980.

Springfield

Population: 105,227. From Quincy, where we ended the previous chapter, a drive east on Highway 36 takes you to the Illinois state capital, Springfield. I-55 is the major north-south artery into the city, while I-72 comes in from the east. Smaller highways, such as 125, 97, 29, 124, 54, and 4, also feed into the area. Amtrak (800-872-7245) and Greyhound (800-231-2222) serve Springfield as well.

Springfield has tons of historic sites, and you'll want to make a judicious selection so as not to overload your kids (and yourself). Teenagers especially will complain if they think the trip is getting too "educational," so be sure to sprinkle in some purely fun activities amid all those museum visits.

CENTRAL ILLINOIS

ILLINOIS STATE CAPITOL (age 7 and up)

Second and Capitol Streets, Springfield 62701; (217) 782–2099. The capitol is open from 8 A.M. to 5 P.M. Monday through Friday and 9 A.M. to 3 P.M. Saturday and Sunday; closed major holidays. Admission is **Free**. *Tours are given on the hour and half hour. The building is accessible for strollers and wheelchairs. No smoking allowed in the building. If the legislature is not in session, you may be able to park within a block of the building at a metered space along the street; otherwise, the Visitors Center 1 block west of the capitol has a parking lot.*

Let's start downtown with a must-see for adults and school-age children, the Illinois State Capitol. This ornate, silver-domed building is gorgeous, both inside and out. The old adage is true: "They just don't make 'em like that anymore." This one took 20 years to complete—it was finished in 1888—but it was worth the wait. A 1986 restoration of the interior succeeded in bringing out the grandeur of old. Marble floors and columns shine, giant painted tableaux look clean and crisp, and the stained glass in the dome sparkles. No matter what your political persuasion, you can't help but feel as though something really important and special must happen here. State house and senate visitor galleries on the fourth floor (accessible by original stone staircases trimmed with wrought iron or by more modern, utilitarian elevators) flank the chambers at each end of the building, so you can watch the action below. The legislators get to sit in oversize leather armchairs at polished desks of dark wood, with heavy draperies and crystal chandeliers adorning the windows and ceiling. If only the level of discourse were as noble as the surroundings. . . .

ILLINOIS STATE MUSEUM (age 2 and up)

Spring and Edwards Streets, Springfield 62701; (217) 782–7387. Open from 8:30 A.M. to 5 P.M. Monday through Saturday and noon to 5 P.M. Sunday; closed major holidays. A Place for Discovery is open from about 9:30 A.M. to 4 P.M. Monday through Saturday and noon to 5 P.M. Sunday. Admission is **Free**. *The building is accessible for strollers and wheelchairs. No smoking. Internet: www.museum.state.il.us:80/ismsites/main.*

In stark contrast to the lustrous capitol is the Illinois State Museum, a plain, squarish, flat-surfaced edifice a block away. Of the building's three stories, probably the most interesting for families is the lower level, where you'll find A Place for Discovery, a hands-on room geared most strongly toward grade-schoolers. They can grind corn with stones as the Indians did, listen to native birdcalls through headphones, or pull out drawers filled with fossils and bones to examine the contents. The main floor's natural history exhibits are composed of taxidermy and dioramas, which seem rather dated and hokey these days. Except for extinct species, you're better off skipping this floor and looking at live animals in the zoo instead. The top floor features an art gallery and an exhibit worth seeing called *At Home in the Heartland*. This display uses a combination of artifacts (including diaries, letters, and ledgers) and video screens to tell the stories of real Illinois people who lived over the course of the past century or so. The catch is that after conveying some initial information about a given person's life, the narrative stops at a point of decision and asks the viewer to choose from among several options what course of action the person should take (for example, which house or farm equipment to buy or whether to look for work in another city). The viewer's choice is then compared to what the person actually decided and how the alternative options might have turned out. Older kids as well as adults would enjoy this exhibit.

LINCOLN HOME NATIONAL HISTORIC SITE (age 7 and up)

Eighth and Jackson, Springfield 62701; (217) 492–4150. Open from April through October from 8 A.M. to 6 P.M. daily. Admission is **Free**, *but you must pick up a ticket at the Lincoln Home Visitors Center a block away at 426 South Seventh Street. Your ticket will be stamped with the starting time of your 20-minute tour (yes, you have to take the tour—you can't just walk in and browse around). Tours start every 5 to 15 minutes. Stop by early in the day, because the tickets for that day are usually gone by 3 P.M. Stairs leading to the front door and to the upper floor make touring the home difficult for visitors who have trouble walking. The Visitor Center has ways of making accommodations if you call in advance. The Visitor Center also is open from 8:30 A.M. to 5 P.M. from November through March, when the site is closed. No smoking at the Visitor Center or the site. Internet: www.nps.gov/liho.*

One of the places visitors to Springfield tend to remember the longest is the Lincoln Home National Historic Site. It was the only home Abraham Lincoln ever owned, and he and his family lived there for 17 years before he was elected president and moved to Washington, D.C. The two-story tan frame house is furnished as it looked in 1860. Downstairs are the living room, the kitchen, and the family room. Upstairs are the bedrooms for the Lincolns, their children, and their live-in maid. No bathrooms–the outhouse is out back. About 50 items in the house are original Lincoln pieces, most notably the banister and the shaving mirror in his bedroom, and the rest are period pieces. (Lincoln sold all his furniture when he moved to the White House, so it was tough finding any of the original pieces.) Wallpaper in the Lincoln bedroom suite is an exact reproduction copied from a scrap of the original paper that was found during restoration. Guides give a good description of how the Lincolns lived, enlivening the basic facts with anecdotes, such as the time Papa Lincoln had to chase his naked youngest son down the street after the boy escaped from a bath in the kitchen. The Lincoln site includes not only this house, but also neighboring homes in a 4-block area. Wooden-plank sidewalks like the kind that existed in 1860 have been installed, and ongoing restoration work makes the area continue to more closely resemble the period. The Visitor Center, by the way, has an especially nice gift shop with no tacky souvenirs. You'll find postcards, slides, books, coins, and interesting wooden games of the period.

OLIVER PARKS TELEPHONE MUSEUM (age 3 and up)

529 South Seventh Street, Springfield 62701; (217) 789–5303. Hours are 9 A.M. to 4:30 P.M. Monday through Friday; admission is **Free**. *Accessible for strollers and wheelchairs. No smoking.*

If you're already downtown, drop in at the Oliver Parks Telephone Museum, right off the street near the lobby of the big brick Ameritech building. This museum is tiny (one room) and sort of hands-on—you can turn a dial or pick up a receiver, but nothing is hooked up. The phones on display are from the personal collection of namesake Parks (1904–1983), a Decatur native who worked for the phone company his whole life and started amassing the phones in 1949. Most are original, though some are replicas. They date from the late 1800s to the present, so just about every parent will be able to find one that looks like what she or he had as a kid. Were you around in 1954, when the first colored phones came out (they were all black before then), or 1959, when the Princess phone was introduced? How about 1962, for the first touch-tone phones? There are even a couple of those phone-with-TV models that were floated in the 1970s and received a thoroughly tepid public response. Your visit here won't take long, but it will be interesting.

OLD STATE CAPITOL (age 7 and up)

Fifth Street between Adams and Washington Streets, Springfield 62701; (217) 785–7960. Open from 9 A.M. to 5 P.M. daily from March through October and 9 A.M. to 4 P.M. daily from November through February. Admission is **Free**, *although there is a box for suggested donations of $2 per adult and $1 per child. The building is accessible for wheelchairs. No smoking. Internet: www.state.il.us/hpa/sites/OldStateCapitolFrame.htm or www.netins.net/showcase/creative/lincoln/sites/capitol.htm.*

Fun at the Illinois State Fair If you visit Springfield in mid-August, you can take in the Illinois State Fair at the fairgrounds at Sangamon Avenue and Peoria Road. The fair has been going on annually for more than 140 years, and the stately grounds with their big brick buildings reflect that traditional charm. General admission costs $3 for anyone age 13 through 59 and $2 for adults age 60 or older. Kids age 12 or younger get in Free. Parking costs $5. Once you are inside, you'll find a lot of free activities and displays; it's great fun just to wander around and see what you stumble across—maybe harness racing, a ponytail contest, a demonstration of an ethanol-powered vehicle, an art exhibit, a reggae concert, or a sheep show with judges squeezing the animals' sides like rolls of Charmin (to feel for the ribs; it's legit, but it looks funny). Be sure to bring some cash for all the good junk food—this is the place to forget about fat and calories for a few hours and snarf some corn dogs, cotton candy, and other tasty-but-naughty stuff; you can take an extra walk around the block tomorrow. The kids will probably beg for some tacky souvenirs, too, and your life will be easier if you plan to fork over a couple bucks and indulge them a little.

The Old State Capitol was the statehouse from 1839 until 1876, when the state offices were moved to the capitol that is still in use today. The Old Capitol was the first statehouse in Springfield, following the legislators' vote to move the capital there from Vandalia. It also was the first capitol building in Illinois to house all three branches of state government together—the executive (the governor, treasurer, secretary of state, and other officers), the legislative (the House of Representatives and the Senate), and the judicial (the Supreme Court). After the government moved to the new capitol, the Old Capitol was used for other purposes until 1961, when the governor signed legislation allowing the state to buy and renovate the Greek Revival building. It was totally dismantled in 1966 and then put back together three years later, after a below-ground parking ramp and offices were added and the walls rebuilt. It was restored to look the way it did in Abraham Lincoln's time. The House, where Lincoln served his final term as a representative in 1840–41, has a coat and top hat placed at the seat he probably occupied. He returned to this very chamber in 1858 for his famous "House Divided" speech, and his body lay in state here before burial at the Lincoln Tomb. The Senate chamber is more ornate, with a chandelier hanging from the high ceiling. White pillars stand in a semicircular arc across the back to support a gallery where the women sat. (Women didn't win the right to vote until the Nineteenth Amendment was passed in 1920, so they certainly were not allowed to run for elected office, and they were not allowed on the floor with the men.) They made their opinions clearly known by clapping their hands in approval or stomping their feet in disapproval. Behind a railing at the back of the main floor, called a *lobby,* stood people who shouted to their senator and tried to persuade him to vote their way. Such people came to be known as *lobbyists,* and they're still at it today, although in subtler ways. On Fridays and Saturdays between 10 A.M. and 4 P.M., visitors are taken on a 45-minute tour by costumed interpreters who speak as characters from the 1850s. The quality of these volunteers' performances varies; some are engaging, while one in particular gets a bit long-winded. Younger children are apt to get bored with the presentation, and you're better off coming at another time when you can just wander around.

NELSON RECREATIONAL CENTER (all ages)

1601 North Fifth Street, Springfield 62702; (217) 753–2800. The pool is open from Memorial Day through Labor Day, from 1 to 8 P.M. daily. Admission costs $3.50 for anyone age 13 or older and $3 for kids age 4 through 12; tots age 3 or younger get in free. The indoor ice rink is open year-round from 6 to 8 P.M. Friday and 3 to 5 P.M. Saturday. Additional summer hours are 12:30 to 2 P.M. Monday, Wednesday, and Friday. Admission costs $3.50 per person, all ages, and includes skate rental.

If you're ready for something more active after all that downtown culture, head north to the Nelson Recreational Center in Lincoln Park. You can take a dip in the pool during summer or go ice-skating year-round. The ice rink was remodeled in 1998. The park grounds also have a picnic area, a playground, and a pond.

ADVENTURE VILLAGE (ages 2 to 12)

Sangamon Avenue and Peoria Road, Springfield 62702; (217) 528–9207. Hours are 5:30 to 9 P.M. Friday and 1 to 6 P.M. Saturday and Sunday; all closing times are a bit negotiable, so show up earlier for maximum enjoyment. There's no charge to walk in and look around. A wrist ticket allowing unlimited rides costs $10.

Adventure Village is an active option especially appropriate for younger children. This family amusement park with about a dozen rides is located just inside the main gate of the Illinois State Fairgrounds. Choose from among the regular-size Ferris wheel, merry-go-round, Tilt-a-Whirl, or YoYo or the kid-size Himalaya, Spider, helicopters, or little duckies. There are a couple of attractions that kids can bounce around in, one inflated and the other filled with plastic balls, and a miniature train travels the perimeter of the park (but seats can accommodate adults as well). Some rides have height restrictions: For example, children must be at least 36 inches tall for one but not more than 48 inches tall for another.

LINCOLN TOMB (age 7 and up)

1500 Monument Avenue, off North Grand Avenue in Oak Ridge Cemetery, Springfield 62702; (217) 782–2717. Open from 9 A.M. to 5 P.M. daily from March through October and 9 A.M. to 4 P.M. daily from November through February. It is closed New Year's, Martin Luther King, Presidents', Veterans, general election, Thanksgiving, and Christmas days. Admission is **Free**.

Here you'll find the 117-foot-tall Lincoln Tomb. Bronze statuary groups flank the four corners at the base of the granite obelisk, and a statue of the president stands in front. Below, outside the entrance to the tomb, is a bronze bust of Lincoln; his nose is a shiny gold from all the visitors who have rubbed it for good luck. Abraham and his wife, Mary Todd Lincoln, plus three of their four sons, Eddie, Willie, and Tad, are in crypts here. (Fourth son Robert Todd Lincoln is buried in Arlington National Cemetery with his wife and son.) Construction of the tomb began in 1869, four years after the president's assassination, and it was dedicated in 1874. Reconstructions were done in 1899 and 1930. Today you can go inside the cool marble tomb and walk in a circular path past bronze statues of Lincoln at various stages of his life to the chamber in back where the family is interred. A rectangular red marble headstone marks the spot where the president is buried. There is a simple elegance and dignity to this place.

ILLINOIS VIETNAM VETERANS MEMORIAL (age 7 and up)

In Oak Ridge Cemetery near the Walnut Street entrance, Springfield 62702; (217) 782–2717. The memorial is open the same hours as the cemetery itself, 8 A.M. to 8 P.M. daily from the first Sunday in April through the last Sunday in October and 8 A.M. to 5 P.M. daily the rest of the year. **Free**.

The Illinois Vietnam Veterans Memorial is about half a mile west of the Lincoln Tomb. Modeled after the national monument, this one features slanted black marble slabs fanning out from a white circular memorial to the various branches of the armed forces. Each of the slabs is engraved with the names of Illinois service personnel who died in or are still missing from the Vietnam War (1957–1975), a total of 2,970 lives sacrificed. Words on paper do not do justice to how moving this memorial is. It is a worthwhile stop for families: The Vietnam

War is recent enough to have touched many parents' lives in some way, and a visit here is more valuable than a chapter in a history book in spurring discussion of this controversial war and its continuing repercussions.

WASHINGTON PARK BOTANICAL GARDENS (all ages)

In Washington Park, accessible from both South Grand Avenue and Chatham Road; (217) 753–6228. Mailing address: P.O. Box 5052, Springfield 62705. Open year-round, from noon to 4 P.M. Monday through Friday and noon to 5 P.M. Saturday and Sunday; closed Christmas Day. Admission is **Free***, although there is a donation box should you wish to support upkeep of the gardens. No smoking in the conservatory.*

Because of its domed conservatory, the Botanical Gardens are open year-round. The conservatory contains tropical plants, and outside gardens are filled with roses and perennials during the temperate months.

THOMAS REES MEMORIAL CARILLON (age 2 and up)

In Washington Park, accessible from both South Grand Avenue and Chatham Road; (217) 753–6219. Mailing address: P.O. Box 5052, Springfield 62705. The carillon is open from noon to 8 P.M. Tuesday through Sunday during June, July, and August and noon to dusk on weekends only during spring and fall; closed during winter. No charge to look around outside or in the room at the base; two-part tour including video presentation and elevator ride to see the bells costs $2 per adult and $1.50 per child.

Washington Park and Lincoln Park are the largest of Springfield's 30 parks. The most obvious attraction in Washington Park rises above the treetops—the Thomas Rees Memorial Carillon. Free concerts ring out every Sunday afternoon from the 66 bronze bells that span a range of five and a half octaves. The bells, cast in the Netherlands, have a total weight of nearly 74,000 pounds, with the smallest a mere 22 pounds and the largest a whopping 15,000 pounds. The carillon was dedicated in 1962 and renovated in 1987. Visitors can watch a short video presentation in a room inside the base of the carillon, then ride an elevator up to the bell tower. A small gift counter in the base of the tower offers souvenirs, including small bells.

WHITE OAKS MALL (all ages)

2501 West Wabash Avenue (corner of Wabash Avenue and Veterans Parkway), Springfield 62704; (217) 787–8560. Hours are 10 A.M. to 9 P.M. Monday through Saturday and noon to 6 P.M. Sunday.

Serious shoppers will want to head to White Oaks Mall, where the slogan is, "Shop like you mean it." Anchored by department stores Bergner's, Famous-Barr, and Sears, this two-story enclosed mall contains a variety of specialty stores. Kids will like the gadgets in Babbages and the toys in Kay-Bee and the Disney Store. Aladdin's Castle features arcade games. The food court has a McDonald's and also offers pizza, hot dogs, ice cream, and cookies, among other taste treats. The White Oaks Cinema shows first-run movies.

JUNGLE O FUN (age 2 and up)

3031 Koke Mill Road, Springfield 62704; (217) 787–0707. Open from 10 A.M. to 6 P.M. Monday, 10 A.M. to 9 P.M. Tuesday through Saturday, and 11 A.M. to 6 P.M. Sunday. Admission costs $6.50 for kids age 5 through 16 and $3.50 for children age 2 through 4; babies age 1 or younger and parents accompanying their children get in free.

About a quarter mile west of the mall, this indoor children's playground has an unusually large "play apparatus"—21 feet high—with slides, ball pits, bounce area, and all the good stuff you expect from this type of facility. There's a game room, too, plus a concession area where you can sit down for a cold soft drink or a meal of pizza or hot dogs.

KNIGHT'S ACTION PARK AND CARIBBEAN ADVENTURE (age 6 and up)

1700 Recreation Drive (Highway 36 south bypass and Chatham Road), Springfield 62707; (217) 546–8881. Open from 9 A.M. to 11 P.M. daily from April through October; water attractions start in mid-May and end on Labor Day. Rates are based on height rather than age: anyone more than 4 feet tall pays $16.50, and anyone 4 feet tall or shorter pays $12 for all the water attractions. For an extra $2 you can play miniature golf or ride a go-kart (prices are $4.50 and $3.75, respectively, if you purchase them without the water pass). Kids must be at least age 12 to ride a go-kart. Other land attractions are priced separately. Internet: www.knightsactionpark.com.

This sprawling complex has both wet and dry activities to keep the family busy. The water attractions include swimming pools, water slides, bumper boats, pedal boats, and the Caribbean Wild River action ride. A wave pool was added in 2000. The miniature golf course includes a green dragon peering out over a stone wall as you putt. Older kids may enjoy go-karts and laser tag. You can spend even more money in the batting cages or the arcade game room. Come only if you're prepared to drop a bundle and spend the better part of the day here to get the maximum bang for your buck. It's not the best value for little kids, who tire more quickly and can't handle all the offerings, but you'll probably have to drag your teenager out at the end of the visit.

HENSON ROBINSON ZOO (all ages)

1100 East Lake Drive, Springfield 62707; (217) 753–6217. From mid-April through November 1, the zoo hours are 10 A.M. to 5 P.M. Monday through Friday and 10 A.M. to 6 P.M. Saturday and Sunday. During June, July, and August, the closing time is extended to 8 P.M. on Wednesday. Admission costs $2.50 for anyone age 13 through 61, $1.25 for adults age 62 or older, and $1 for kids age 3 through 12. Children age 2 or younger get in free. Stroller rental costs $2. The building and grounds are accessible for strollers and wheelchairs. Internet: www.hensonrobinsonzoo.org.

You'll have a scenic drive skirting Lake Springfield to get to the Henson Robinson Zoo. This facility was expanded and renovated in 1996, and the building through which you enter has a classroom, a gift shop and concession area, and clean rest rooms with changing tables and low sinks. Walkways are paved with smooth asphalt that's great for strollers and wheelchairs. The general atmosphere here is relaxed and pleasant. Spider monkeys frolic on an island in the middle of a pond, and free-roaming fowl wander the grounds, the more unusual specimens being a turkey and a pure-white peahen. An American desert exhibit contains American kestrels, a burrowing owl, and sand tortoises. (It used to have a roadrunner, too, but that's been moved to the bird section.) Cacti dot the pen's landscape, and a painted mural across the back wall re-creates the colors of the American Southwest. A number of exhibits are labeled Vanishing Animals, including the blackfooted penguin, Asiatic black bears, and Galapagos tortoises. Other highlights are the prairie dog colony, the prowling cheetah, the majestic bald eagle, and the fruit bats in the nocturnal animals exhibit. One new element that shows mixed results is the Zoo Key, a plastic tab that you can buy or rent and which is inserted into a slot on an electronic box at various points around the grounds to elicit additional information, quizzes, and songs—wonderful for children in the 2 to 6 age range. The problem is that there's also a button you can push that simply plays a little tune urging you to go get a "zoo-key, zoo-key," in the same sort of syrupy-sweet tone as the songs on the *Barney* TV show. Naturally, preschoolers love this ditty and will go around pushing the button on every box they see; after a while, it will drive everyone else bananas.

Where to Eat

Saputo's. *801 East Monroe; (217) 544–2523.* Open from 11 A.M. to 11 P.M. Monday through Friday, 5 to 11 P.M. Saturday, and 4 to 10 P.M. Sunday. This downtown restaurant has been owned and operated since 1948 by "Springfield's first family of Italian cooking." Pasta dishes reflect the specialties of southern Italy: ravioli, rigatoni, mostaccioli, manicotti, fettucine Alfredo, and linguine with clam sauce, for example. Steaks and seafood also appear on the menu. Smoking is allowed in one section. $$

The Old Lux. *1900 South 15th Street, between Laurel and Ash; (217) 528–0503.* Open from 4:30 to 9:30 P.M. Tuesday through Saturday and 4:30 to 9 P.M. Sunday; closed Monday. This downtown establishment dates back to 1941 and boasts that it was "voted best filet in Springfield"—as in filet mignon. Steaks, chicken, and seafood entrees dominate the menu, which also features sandwiches. Be sure to check on the nightly specials. $$

Red Lobster. *2696 South Dirksen Parkway; (217) 529–6900.* Hours are 11 A.M. to 10 P.M. Sunday through Thursday and 11 A.M. to 11 P.M. Friday and Saturday. See Restaurant Appendix for description. $$

Gallina's Pizza. *3133 South Dirksen Parkway; (217) 529–0649.* In Capitol City Shopping Center, near Hampton Inn. Hours are 11 A.M. to 11 P.M. Monday through Thursday and 11 A.M. to 12:30 A.M. Friday and Saturday; closed Sunday. This casual, family-operated eatery serves a hot, cheesy, thin-crust pizza that is *delizioso!* Deep-dish pizza, pasta dinners, and sandwiches are also on the menu. Blowups of family snapshots in Italy line the brick walls, and half the selections in the jukebox are in Italian, the other half assorted American classic rock. $

Rock 'n' Roll Hardee's. *2501 Stevenson Drive; (217) 529–1331.* Hours are 5 A.M. to 11 P.M. Sunday through Thursday and 5 A.M. to midnight Friday and Saturday. The roast beef sandwiches, burgers, fried chicken, tasty breakfast biscuits, and other reasonably priced menu offerings are the same as those at most Hardee's, but the red-white-and-black decor is filled with neon, chrome, and such nostalgic features as an authentic Texaco gas pump and a Wurlitzer jukebox (not original—it plays CDs). $

Old Country Buffet. *2733 Veterans Parkway; (217) 787–2202.* Hours are 10:30 A.M. to 8:30 P.M. Monday through Friday, 8 A.M. to 9 P.M. Saturday, and 8 A.M. to 8:30 P.M. Sunday. Serving breakfast, lunch, and dinner. See Restaurant Appendix for description. $

Where to Stay

Despite being in the Land of Lincoln, you're not likely to find many log cabins for lodging. Most of the motel chains are on the east side of the city, clustered along I-55, with another clump on the west along Highway 4.

Best Inns of America. *500 North First Street; (217) 522–1100 or (800) 237–8466.* There are 91 rooms at this economy chain motel. There is an outdoor pool. "Special K breakfast" (Special K cold cereal, milk, juice, coffee, doughnuts, and toast) is included in the room rate. $$

Comfort Inn. *3442 Freedom Drive; (217) 787–2550 or (800) 228–5150.* This property has 67 rooms and an indoor swimming pool. The room rate includes complimentary continental breakfast. Dogs are allowed. $$

Days Inn. *3000 Stevenson Drive; (217) 529–0171 or (800) 325–2525.* This two-story chain property has 153 rooms. There is an outdoor swimming pool. Pets are allowed. The room rate includes free breakfast. $$

Fairfield Inn. *3446 Freedom Drive; (217) 793–9277 or (800) 228–2800.* This 63-room economy member of the Marriott family has an indoor swimming pool and whirlpool. Continental breakfast is included in the room rate. $$

Hampton Inn. *3185 South Dirksen Parkway; (217) 529–1100 or (800) 426–7866.* This four-story, 123-room hotel has comfortable rooms with coffeemaker and cable TV. Amenities include heated indoor pool and whirlpool. Free cookies and lemonade are available in the lobby in the afternoon. The room rate includes a generous continental breakfast. $$

Super 8 East. *1330 South Dirksen Parkway; (217) 528–8889 or (800) 800–8000.* This four-story mock Tudor hotel has 65 rooms with cable TV. No pool. Pets allowed. $

For More Information

Springfield Convention & Visitors Bureau, *109 North Seventh Street, Springfield 62701; (217) 789–2360 or (800) 545–7300. Internet: www.springfield-illinois.com.*

Decatur

Population: 83,885. About an hour's drive east of Springfield (I–72 and U.S. Highway 36 are the same road on this stretch) is Decatur. Incorporated as a city in 1836, it became a rail hub for the Great Western and Illinois Central Railroad starting in 1854. In 1900 R. R. Montgomery reportedly invented the fly swatter in Decatur. In 1920 the Decatur Staleys became a charter member of the National Football League. Coached by George Halas, the team later would become the Chicago Bears. Throughout the 1900s affluent Decatur families adopted a variety of architectural styles for their homes. Today the city's Historic District features Gothic Revival, Second Empire, Italianate, Queen Anne, Classic Revival, Romanesque Revival, and Frank Lloyd Wright's Prairie styles. But many of the ordinary citizens here live in basic bungalows.

SCOVILL CHILDREN'S ZOO (all ages)

71 South Country Club Road, Decatur 62521; (217) 421–7435. Open from 10 A.M. to 8 P.M. daily between Memorial Day and Labor Day. From mid-April to Memorial Day and from Labor Day to mid-October, hours are 10 A.M. to 4 P.M. Monday through Friday and 10 A.M. to 6:30 P.M. Saturday and Sunday. Admission costs $2 for anyone age 13 through 61, $1.50 for adults age 62 or older, and $1 for children age 2 through 12. Babies age 1 or younger get in free. Internet: www.decatur-parks.org/html/zoo.html.

This local zoo is small but quite nice. A real effort has been made to integrate indigenous plant life into the animal exhibit areas, and multicolored flower beds brighten the well-tended grounds. The collection of about 500 animals includes kangaroos, a capybara, emus, Chilean flamingos, toco toucans, Amazon parrots, ring-tailed lemurs, a ring-tailed coati, bobcats, and a whole "town" of prairie dogs. A petting zoo contains goats, donkeys, piglets, a calf, ducklings, and chicks. For an extra $1 for adults or 50 cents for kids or seniors, you can ride a little train that's a one-quarter-scale replica of an 1863 C.P. Huntington steam engine. The train even has a wheelchair lift.

PROJECT PLAYGROUND (ages 2–12)

71 South Country Club Road, Decatur 62521, next to the zoo. Hours are 6 A.M. to 10 P.M. daily, year-round. **Free**.

Since it's right next door to the zoo, you can count on this sprawling, wooden outdoor playground to add at least half an hour to your visit. It has towers, bridges, ladders, slides, swings, you name it.

CHILDREN'S MUSEUM OF ILLINOIS (all ages)

55 South Country Club Road, Decatur 62521; (217) 423–5437. Open from 9:30 A.M. to 4:30 P.M. Monday through Friday, 10 A.M. to 5 P.M. Saturday, and 1 to 5 P.M. Sunday. Admission costs $3.50 for anyone age 17 through 54 and $3 for young people age 3 through 16 or adults age 55 or older. Children age 2 or younger get in free. Wednesday is two-for-one admission day for kids. Through the summer a school-age kid who brings in a final report card gets in **Free**, *regardless of what the grades on it are. The museum is within walking distance of the zoo. You can park your car in the zoo lot and walk over if the museum lot is full; parking is free in both lots.*

You'll easily spot this two-story white building with red and green trim. Little children will have a good time just pointing out the squares, triangles, and diamond shapes in the facade. The most unique feature at this children's museum is the "shadow wall," a wall covered with

Lincoln's New Salem About 20 miles northwest of Springfield, up Highway 97, is Lincoln's New Salem Historic Site, a reconstruction of the village of New Salem, where Abraham Lincoln lived and worked for six years as a young man during the 1830s. You can stroll down the "main drag" and stop to look into the cabin-style shops and houses on either side of the street; the total distance is about three quarters of a mile. If your toddler (or you) can't make it that far, you can hitch a free ride in a horse-drawn wagon, which will save you some steps. Perhaps you can walk in and ride out, or vice versa. The Onstot Cooper Shop is the only original building. The others were rebuilt during the 1930s by the Civilian Conservation Corps at the original sites. All are filled with authentic furnishings and artifacts of the 1830s. Guides in period costumes are posted in many of the two dozen buildings to help explain what went on there. Sometimes you'll see a demonstration of craftwork or music. Hours are 9 A.M. to 5 P.M. daily from March through October and 8 A.M. to 4 P.M. daily from November through February; closed some holidays. Days and hours of operation are subject to change, however, especially during winter months, so call (217) 632–4000 to double-check before driving out there. Admission is **Free**, with a suggested donation of $2 per adult and $1 per child. You can watch a free 10-minute orientation film in the Visitor Center auditorium before setting off. The climate-controlled center also contains exhibits and rest rooms. Souvenirs are in another nearby building, along with a McDonald's.

phosphorescent (glow-in-the-dark) vinyl opposite a black wall with a bright flashlight at the top—the only light in the room. You stand up against the vinyl wall, striking a pose if you like, and when the flash goes off, your body blocks the light behind it on the wall, creating the appearance of a dark shadow against the lightened wall. Definitely cool. The museum also has giant bubble makers, whisper disks, a plasma sphere, a tandem bike with a skeleton rigged up as the second rider, a fire truck, and a toddler play area with blocks. A kid-size bank offers a chance to role-play. In the "handicapped area," able-bodied kids can experience firsthand the challenge of getting around on crutches or in a wheelchair. Lucky's Climber is a two-story climbing structure lined with carpeting and including sturdy nets. This museum is a lot of fun for the young and the young at heart.

ROCK SPRINGS CENTER FOR ENVIRONMENTAL DISCOVERY (all ages)

3939 Nearing Lane, Decatur 62521; (217) 423–4913. Open year-round. Visitor center hours are 9 A.M. to 4 P.M. Monday through Friday and 10 A.M. to 4 P.M. Saturday and Sunday. Homestead Prairie Farm is open from 1 to 4 P.M. Saturday and Sunday from May through October. The bike trail is open from 8 A.M. to dusk daily. Admission to all areas is **Free**, *although donations are accepted. There are fees for some special events.*

This conservation education complex has numerous features to enhance the relationship between human beings and nature. The visitor center and museum are a good place to start. From there, head outside to the Homestead Prairie Farm, a farmstead that has been restored to represent the lifestyle of the 1860s. Gaze over the expansive grounds from the lookout tower. There are ponds for fishing and numerous trails, one a 10-foot-wide trail accessible to wheelchairs as well as hikers and bicyclists. A bikeway originating on the property goes across a 224-foot-long bridge over the Sangamon River.

HICKORY POINT MALL (all ages)

I–72 at U.S. Highway 51; (217) 875–0080. Mailing address: U.S. Highway 51, Forsyth 62535-1006. Hours are 10 A.M. to 9 P.M. Monday through Saturday and noon to 5 P.M. Sunday.

A modernistic building houses this indoor mall anchored by Von Maur, JCPenney, Kohl's, Sears, and Bergner's department stores. Kay-Bee Toys and Waldenkids stores will be of interest to children.

Where to Eat

Taters Family Grill. *2981 North Main Street; (217) 877–1111.* Open from 10 A.M. to 11 P.M. Monday through Thursday, 10 A.M. to midnight Friday and Saturday, and 10 A.M. to 10 P.M. Sunday. Baked-potato soup is the specialty here. Among the entrees are steaks, pork chops, meat loaf, and chicken and noodles. The menu includes pictures and tidbits of local history along with the food listings. $$

Old Country Buffet. *3194 North Water Street; (217) 875–0525.* Hours are 11 A.M. to 8 P.M. Monday through Thursday, 11 A.M. to 9 P.M. Friday, 8 A.M. to 9 P.M. Saturday, and 8 A.M. to 8 P.M. Sunday. See Restaurant Appendix for description. $

Where to Stay

Holiday Inn Conference Hotel. *U.S. Highway 36 and Wycles Road; (217) 422–8800 or (800) 465–4329.* This four-story property contains 383 guest rooms, and it has a banquet room that can hold 2,000 people. Amenities include a Holidome with indoor swimming pool, whirlpool, fitness center, and games. Pets are allowed. There is a restaurant on the premises. Breakfast is not included in the room rate. $$$

Ramada Limited. *355 Hickory Point Road; (217) 876–8011 or (800) 272–6232.* Opened in 1997, this property has 62 rooms with cable TV, coffeemaker, and hair dryer. Amenities include an indoor swimming pool and whirlpool. Roll away bed available at extra charge. Continental breakfast is included in the room rate. $$

For More Information

Decatur Area Convention & Visitors Bureau, *202 East North Street, Decatur 62523; (217) 423–7000 or (800) 331–4479. Internet: www.decaturcvb.com.*

Bloomington

Bloomington and Normal are like Minneapolis and St. Paul—you can hardly mention one without the other, and the two communities indeed seem as one when you're driving around in them. Roughly an hour's drive from Peoria (I-74 from the northwest), Springfield (I-55 from the southwest), Decatur (Highway 51 from the south), or Champaign-Urbana (I-74 from the southeast; another linked pair we'll be exploring later in this chapter), it is easy to combine a stop here with a visit to other cities in the area.

Bloomington (population 51,972) is on the western side. It is home to Illinois Wesleyan University and has some interesting family attractions. Unfortunately, the Nestlé-Beich candy factory is no longer giving tours, but there are still other fun things to do in town.

CHILDREN'S DISCOVERY MUSEUM (ages 2–11)

716 East Empire Street, Bloomington 61701; (309) 829–6222. Hours are 10 A.M. to 4 P.M. Tuesday and Wednesday, 10 A.M. to 8 P.M. Thursday, and 10 A.M. to 5 P.M. Friday and Saturday; closed Sunday and Monday. Admission costs $3 for anyone age 2 or older; children age 1 or younger get in free. The facility is accessible for wheelchairs.

This children's museum has a dozen "discovery centers" that will delight children with varying interests. The artistic types can paint on a wall or make an artwork out of recycled materials, which they can take home. Railroad buffs can assume the role of conductor in the area with the Brio train. Children who like to play doctor can check out the medical and dental center. Bookworms can hole up in the reading loft. You'll also find kid-size models of a grocery store, a post office, a radio station, and a farm, plus a real car to play in. Toddler Town is the place especially geared toward the youngest visitors.

MILLER PARK (all ages)

Off South Morris Avenue, Bloomington 61701; (309) 823–4260. The park is open from sunrise to sunset daily, and admission is **Free**. *The public beach is open from 1 to 5 P.M. Saturday and Sunday only, during summer. Beach admission costs $3 for adults age 19 or older and $2 for young people age 3 through 18; children age 2 or younger get in free.*

Miller Park has an old locomotive on display that you can climb up into, a band shell, and a concession booth as well. When you add these attractions to the beach, the zoo (see next entry), and the miniature golf course (see subsequent entry) that are situated here, you can easily spend a whole summer day at this one park.

MILLER PARK ZOO (all ages)

1020 South Morris Avenue, Bloomington 61701; (309) 434–2250. Hours are 10 A.M. to 5 P.M. daily; closed Christmas Day. Admission costs $3 for anyone age 13 through 59 and $2 for adults age 60 or older and children age 3 through 12; children age 2 or younger get in free. Take Veterans Parkway to Morris Avenue and turn north; brown signs will help direct you. The zoo is nestled among the Miller Park grounds.

Well-paved pathways make it easy for strollers to navigate this small, well-established zoo. It opened in 1891, but only the lion house looks anywhere near that old, and it's in good shape. The big cats have large, rock-walled and fenced outdoor pens connected to the house, so they are in open air during temperate weather. Alas, the last of the zoo's lions have died, but Miller Park claims to be the only zoo in Illinois with Sumatran tigers. These are majestic felines, yet when you see one lolling in a doze on its back with its paws up, it looks just like an oversize house cat. The zoo also has beautiful snow leopards. You'll find sun bears in this area as well. Glass cases containing amphibians and other small animals are placed low enough for little kids to see into them easily. An indoor tropical rain forest exhibit is small but pleasant. Goats and sheep roam the contact area for youngsters to pet. Feeding schedules are posted at the entrance if you want to pick a time when you can watch the animals eat. They definitely perk up then; for example, the two lemurs go ape when the staffer comes in with their tray of fresh fruit and veggies.

The Miller Park Zoo has a number of unusual specimens in its collection: a reindeer; an endangered red wolf; a forest genet, a mammal that looks like a cat but is related to the mongoose and civet; and, from Papua New Guinea, a singing dog whose name is earned from its melodic howl. The Wallaby Walkabout is a fenced-in area visitors can stroll through (staying on the pathway, mind you) to see free-roaming wallabies and other small creatures from the Land Down Under. Zoo Lab, which opened in 1999, has hands-on activities and a butterfly garden. The gift shop here is especially good, with jewelry and high-quality stuffed animals—including such offbeat ones as lemurs and platypuses—at prices that aren't totally outrageous.

CHUCKIE'S CADDY CLUB (age 3 and up)

In Miller Park, Bloomington 61701; (309) 434–2651. Open from 10 A.M. to 8 P.M. daily during summer. Cost for players of all ages is $3 per person for the first game, $2.50 for the second game, and $2 for each subsequent game.

Decorated with flowers and a little wishing well, this miniature golf course is rather plain and straightforward, making it popular with kids. The prices are fairly reasonable, so it won't break the bank to stay and play a while. The Bloomington Park District has plans to remodel the course in summer 2001.

GRADY'S FAMILY FUN CENTER (age 3 and up)

1501½ Morrissey Drive (Highway 150, Bloomington 61701; (309) 662–3332. Hours are 11 A.M. to 10 P.M. daily. A round of miniature golf costs $4.50 for anyone age 7 or older and $4 for kids age 6 or younger. Bumper boats cost $3.50 per individual rider, or $1.50 for a child age 3 or older who rides with a bigger person; tots age 2 or younger are not allowed in the boats, and drivers must be at least 44 inches tall. Go-karts cost $4.50 per person; you must be at least 12 years old and 58 inches tall to drive, and at least 4 years old and 50 pounds to be a passenger. Kiddie carnival rides cost $1.50 apiece. Batting cages cost 50 cents for eight pitches; you must be at least 8 years old or 54 inches tall. Grounds are accessible for strollers and wheelchairs.

There's something for everyone here. There's no charge to get in; you pay only for what you play. A sign also gives fair warning to potential troublemakers, who are noticeably absent: GRADY'S IS A FAMILY FUN PARK.

NO DRUGS, ALCOHOL, PROFANITY, PETS OR LOITERING. UNRULY BEHAVIOR WILL NOT BE TOLERATED. The facility is clean, colorful, and well lit. The 18-hole miniature golf course features a Statue of Liberty, a working windmill, and a barn, all the proper scale, and the holes aren't so tricky as to frustrate younger players. An arcade adjacent to the minigolf course has the usual sorts of video games, plus genuine pinball machines for those who love the physical satisfaction of leaning forward and pumping the flippers; you get three balls for a quarter. At seven minutes the bumper-boat ride is longer than usual for this type, and nearly two dozen boats can be in the water with space left over. Life jackets are provided for the kiddies. In the batting cages you can choose from among fast- or slow-pitch softball or slow-, medium-, or fast-pitch baseball. You of course are expected to wear a helmet (provided free along with the bat). Tiny tots will get a kick out of the kiddie carnival, a collection of eight junior-size rides, such as Ferris wheel, airplanes, Himalaya, and choo-choo.

APPLE BARN (all ages)

Rural Route 4, 1650 North County Road, Bloomington 61702; (309) 963–5557. About 5 miles west of Bloomington. Open from 8 A.M. to 6 P.M. Monday through Friday from July through December; Saturday and Sunday hours from 9 A.M. to 5 P.M. are added from August through December.

This commercial orchard was started in 1918. This is not a pick-your-own sort of place, but you can see the grounds and buy some fresh apples or cider and pies made from them. Harvest Days takes place the first full weekend in October. You also can take a wagon ride to the fields in October to select your Halloween pumpkin.

PRAIRIE AVIATION MUSEUM (age 4 and up)

At Bloomington-Normal Airport, Illinois Highway 9 East, Bloomington 61702; (309) 663–7632. Hours are 5 to 8 P.M. Tuesday (April through November only), 11 A.M. to 4 P.M. Friday and Saturday, and noon to 4 P.M. Sunday. Admission is Free.

Here you'll find two old airplanes—a 1942 Douglas DC-3 and a 1963 Corsair—that you can examine up close. Go into the cockpit and imagine yourself as the pilot. Also part of the outdoor and hangar displays are a 1958 Cessna 310B, a Marine Corps Sea Cobra helicopter, a huge UH-1 "Huey" helicopter, and other aircraft. Indoors the main museum has a flight simulator and displays of model airplanes, real engines, an escape capsule, old uniforms, and memorabilia from the now defunct Ozark Airlines, which operated flights around the Midwest.

Maybe you're old enough to remember that carrier or even (like this author) flew on one of its planes.

Where to Eat

Lucca Grill. *116 East Market Street (corner of Market Street/Highway 9 and Highway 51 North); (309) 828–7521.* Open from 11 A.M. to 1 A.M. Monday through Saturday and 3 to 10 P.M. Sunday. Serving lunch, midafternoon sandwiches, and dinner. This casual little Italian restaurant is loaded with atmosphere, from the ornate ceiling to the memorabilia-covered walls to the dumbwaiter in the back that brings food down from the second-floor kitchen. It's noisy, so you won't have to worry about your kids getting too loud, and it can get pretty crowded, so try to come before or after the main dinner hour if you don't want to wait for a table. The thin-crust pizza is cheesy and delicious. The thick, spicy meat sauce available for the assorted pasta dishes makes them taste almost like goulash (which is good or bad, depending on how you feel about goulash). You can get marinara or Alfredo sauce instead, if you prefer. Pasta entrees come with salad and bread. Steaks, chicken, and seafood dishes also appear on the menu. One caveat for parents of wee babes: The rest rooms are tiny, each barely big enough for a toilet and a sink—forget about trying to change a diaper here. $$

Bakers Square. *321 Veterans Parkway; (309) 454–5555.* Open from 6 A.M. to 11 P.M. daily. See Restaurant Appendix for description. $

Where to Stay

Days Inn West. *1707 Market Street; (309) 829–6292 or (800) 329–7466.* Off I-55/74 at Market Street exit. This economical chain property has 58 rooms. Amenities include an indoor heated pool with spa. Pets are allowed in smoking rooms only. Continental breakfast is included in the room rate. $$

Best Inns of America. *1905 Market Street; (309) 827–5333 or (800) 237–8466.* This 107-room budget property has an outdoor pool, allows pets, and includes a "Special K breakfast" (cold cereal, milk, juice, coffee, doughnuts, and toast) in the price of the room. This motel also has a special parking lot for trucks, but the rooms are fairly well insulated against the interstate traffic. $$

For More Information

Bloomington-Normal Area Convention and Visitors Bureau, *210 South East Street, Bloomington 61702; (309) 829–1641 or (800) 433–8226. Internet: www.visitbloomingtonnormal.org or www.normal.org.*

Normal

Population: 40,023. Normal lies to the east of Bloomington and is the home of Illinois State University. Among its other attractions, it has two malls, which can be comfortable places to push the stroller around for a couple hours, and lots of eateries.

ILLINOIS STATE UNIVERSITY PLANETARIUM (age 5 and up)

School Street and College Avenue, Normal 61761; (309) 438–5007. Show days and times vary, typically Monday and Wednesday evenings during summer. Tickets cost $2 for anyone age 13 through 59, $1.50 for kids age 5 through 12 or adults age 60 or older, and $1 for children age 3 or 4. Not recommended for those age 2 or younger.

The white-domed Illinois State University Planetarium, at the east end of Femley Hall on the ISU campus, offers public programs while the university is in session. During fall and spring sessions, shows are given on weekends. During the summer session both weekday and weekend shows are offered. The Spitz A-3P star projector can beam more than 2,300 stars onto a 30-foot dome, and the shows are designed to appeal to kids. Tickets may be purchased at the door beginning 15 minutes before the show. Use your best judgment about whether your preschooler is ready for this kind of show—you don't want your child to get scared or bored and thus be turned off to this fascinating science before ever giving it a fair chance.

ECOLOGY ACTION CENTER (age 5 and up)

202 West College Avenue, Normal 61761; (309) 454–3169. Hours are 1 to 6 P.M. Monday through Saturday. Admission is Free.

An old house is home to this small facility opened in 1995 and dedicated to environmental education. Free tours take 15 to 30 minutes, and visitors learn about recycling, composting, and saving energy. Recycled products are on display in one room; another room features live fish and a nature mural. The center hosts many school groups and community workshops.

NORMAL THEATRE (age 3 and up)

209 North Street, downtown Normal 61761; (309) 454–9722 or 454–9720. Movie tickets cost $4 per person, all ages. Call for current schedule of films and other entertainment.

This restored art deco movie house originally opened in 1937 and reportedly was the first theater in Bloomington-Normal built specifically for sound films. Today it shows "classic" (that is, old) movies, some of which are suitable for families, as well as live theatrical and musical performances.

ILLINOIS BASKETBALL COACHES ASSOCIATION HALL OF FAME (age 8 and up)

8 Traders Circle, in the Holiday Inn North, Normal 61761; (815) 452–2903. Open all day, every day. **Free**.

This exhibition room honors coaches, players, and other people related to basketball. It probably wouldn't be of much interest to little children, but older kids who've played the game or followed a team may enjoy a brief visit, especially if you're staying in the motel anyway.

FAIRVIEW PARK POOL (all ages)

800 North Main Street, Normal 61761; (309) 454–9540. Open from Memorial Day through Labor Day. Hours are 1 to 9 P.M. Monday through Thursday and noon to 9 P.M. Friday through Sunday. Admission costs $4 for anyone age 16 or older and $3 for kids age 3 through 15. Children age 2 or younger get in free.

There are actually two swimming pools at this facility. The "activity pool" is the better one for families with young children. It is zero-depth along one edge, with water sprays, arched water jets, a water "mushroom" fountain, and a polar bear slide. A 5-foot-deep area at the other end has six lanes for lap swimming. The "plunge pool" has much deeper water, a 1-meter diving board, and two drop slides. Sand volleyball and a concession area round out the amenities.

COLLEGE HILLS MALL (all ages)

Off Veterans Parkway at College Avenue, Normal 61761; (309) 454–1300. Open from 10 A.M. to 9 P.M. Monday through Saturday and noon to 5 P.M. Sunday.

Covering both ends of the economic spectrum, the posh Von Maur and the budget-minded Target are the anchor department stores at this one-story indoor shopping mall. There's no food court, but throughout the mall you'll find a bagel place for a snack, A&W for frosty root beer and sandwiches, and Old Country Buffet for a hearty lunch or dinner.

EASTLAND MALL (all ages)

Off Veterans Parkway at Empire Street, Normal 61761; (309) 663–5361. Open from 10 A.M. to 9 P.M. Monday through Saturday and noon to 6 P.M. Sunday.

This one-story indoor shopping mall is anchored by Sears, JCPenney, Kohl's, and Bergner's. Gap Kids features children's clothing. Electronics Boutique stocks video games among its inventory. Snacks and light meals can be purchased in the food court.

Where to Eat

Old Country Buffet. *In College Hills Mall; (309) 454–6755.* Open from 11 A.M. to 8 P.M. Monday through Thursday, 11 A.M. to 9 P.M. Friday and Saturday, and 8 A.M. to 8 P.M. Sunday. See Restaurant Appendix for description. $

Sirloin Stockade. *Along Veterans Parkway near the malls; (309) 862–1007.* Hours are 11 A.M. to 9 P.M. Monday through Friday and 11 A.M. to 10 P.M. Saturday and Sunday. Choose your cooked-to-order steak and then go through a buffet to pick out lots of stuff to go with it. $

Bakers Square. *321 South Veterans Parkway near the malls; (309) 454–5555.* Hours are 7 A.M. to 11 P.M. daily. See Restaurant Appendix for description. $

Bob Evans. *Along Veterans Parkway near the malls; (309) 663–5131.* Open from 6 A.M. to 10 P.M. daily. See Restaurant Appendix for description. $

Red Lobster. *Along Veterans Parkway near the malls; (309) 663–9405.* Hours are 11 A.M. to 10 P.M. Sunday through Thursday and 11 A.M. to 11 P.M. Friday and Saturday. See Restaurant Appendix for description. $$

Where to Stay

Jumer's Chateau. *1601 Jumer Drive; (309) 662–2020 or (800) 285–8637.* Off Veterans Parkway, near College Hills Mall in Normal. This beautiful four-story hotel does indeed look like a château, and the Old World opulence within is typical of Jumer Hotels. The chain was founded in 1960 by D. James Jumer, and each property is in a similar vein but with its own unique features. This one opened in 1988. It has 180 guest rooms and suites, each elegantly furnished. Amenities include indoor swimming pool, whirlpool, saunas, and game room. The level of refinement here is not appropriate for little children, who would not appreciate it, but a Jumer's visit makes a memorable treat for older grade-schoolers and teens with taste. Breakfast is not included in the room rate. Breakfast, lunch, dinner, and room service are provided by the restaurant Le Radis Rouge (literally, The Red Radish—sounds swankier in French, doesn't it?). Be sure to ask about package deals and discounts for AAA; you may be able to keep the price below $100. $$$$

Motel 6. *1600 North Main Street; (309) 452–0422.* At the opposite end of the economic spectrum from Jumer's, this budget property has 98 rooms and an outdoor pool. Pets are allowed. $

Super 8. *2 Traders Circle; (309) 454–5858.* Exit at Business 51 south off I-55. This budget property has 52 rooms with cable TV. Pets are allowed at extra charge. Room rates include continental breakfast. $

Holiday Inn North. *8 Traders Circle; (309) 452–8300 or (800) 465–4329.* At I-55 and U.S. Highway 51. This five-story hotel has 160 rooms. Amenities include a Holidome with indoor pool, hot tub, sauna, exercise room, and game room. $$$

Best Western University Inn. *6 Traders Circle; (309) 454–4070 or (800) 528–1234.* This two-story brick motel received a three-diamond rating from AAA. It has 102 rooms plus indoor swimming pool and video games. You can also go fishing at this property. Pets are allowed. Continental breakfast is included in the room rate. $$

Champaign

Champaign-Urbana, our other twin city in Central Illinois, is roughly an hour's drive southeast of Bloomington-Normal via Interstate 74 or Highway 150. From Decatur it's less than an hour's drive northeast on Interstate 72. Coming from the north or south, Interstate 57 will be the fastest route. Champaign-Urbana has a combined population of about 100,000, not counting the student body at the University of Illinois—another 36,000 people. The U of I campus straddles the boundary between Champaign and Urbana and is a dominant presence in the life of the community. For general information about the university and its offerings, call (217) 333-4666. Let's look first at some family activities on the Champaign side.

MARKETPLACE (all ages)

2000 North Neil Street (at I–74), Champaign 61820; (217) 356–2700. Open from 10 A.M. to 9 P.M. Monday through Saturday and 11 A.M. to 6 P.M. Sunday. Stroller and wheelchair rentals are available.

This one-story indoor shopping mall is the biggest and best in the area. With white walls and ceilings, it's not the most colorful mall you've ever seen, but skylights augment the artificial lighting to make it bright and airy. The marble-look floors provide a smooth rolling surface for strollers or wheelchairs. Two fountains, one in front of JCPenney and the other in front of Sears, add pleasing ambient noise and visual appeal. Those two department stores plus Bergner's are the anchors, and the floor plan is roughly cross-shaped. (A Kohl's store is nearby but not attached to the mall.) A number of stores here are of particular interest to kids. Those on a hunt for the newest Beanie Babies can check in either of two Hallmark stores, Kirlin's or Marian's. Hat World carries an amazing inventory of caps bearing the logos of professional sports teams and schools. At World of Science, you can buy experiment kits with biology or dinosaur themes, or a Make Your Own kit for soap, hot sauce, or a medieval clock. The store carries a fascinating array of toys, games, puzzles, and books, and it even has a music listening station. Grade-schoolers especially will think World of Science is really cool. There is an arcade called Tilt lit in yellow and orange neon, but it caters more to teens and adults than children. The mall has no food court, but there's one pizza place, and you can buy a bunch of sweets to snack on: caramel corn, cookies, chocolates, and other candy.

ORPHEUM CHILDREN'S SCIENCE MUSEUM (all ages)

346 North Neil Street, Champaign 61820; (217) 352–5895. Hours are 1 to 5 P.M. Wednesday through Sunday. Admission costs $1 for anyone age 3 or older; children age 2 or younger are free. Internet: www.m-crossroads.org/orpheum.

Housed in a 1914 theater building, this museum opened in the late 1990s and underwent further expansion in 2000. Inside are a variety of hands-on exhibits that make learning about science fun. For example, kids can walk a 14-foot plank or operate a block and tackle to experience the amazing scientific principles of such simple machines as the lever and the pulley, which enable people to lift objects much heavier than their own weight. The Bernouilli Blower suspends a ball in midair, and the Ghost Images exhibit plays tricks with light. Younger children will be drawn to the plastic human torso model, the cardboard blocks, and the PVC pipe organ. In the outdoor Dino Dig area, visitors use paleontologists' tools to unearth mock dinosaur bones.

WILLIAM M. STAERKEL PLANETARIUM (age 5 and up)

2400 West Bradley Avenue, Champaign 61821; (217) 351–2568. Open year-round on Friday and Saturday evenings. Tickets for one show cost $3 per person for adults and $2 for kids age 2 through 12, students with ID, and seniors. Children age 1 or younger are admitted free, but the show is not recommended for children that young. You can attend two consecutive shows for $4.50 per adult and $3 per kid, student, or senior. Light shows cost $4 per person, all ages, and are not recommended for preteens; children age 5 and under will not be admitted to a light show. Internet: www.parkland.cc.il.us/coned/pla.

You'll have stars in your eyes after a visit to the planetarium, viewing projections of heavenly bodies onto the interior dome to create a night sky indoors. Each year there are special shows geared toward children;

the 2000 titles included "Teddy's Quest," "Larry Cat in Space," "Rusty Rocket's Last Blast," and the mystery-themed "Planet Patrol: Solar System Stake-Out and Star Stealers." Younger children may get scared of the dark or simply bored, so don't rush them into a planetarium show at too early an age; use your best parental judgment in determining whether your youngster is ready for this fascinating medium. For teens and adults there is also a "light show" that blasts loud rock music and throws in all sorts of special effects—flashing lights, fog, video-style pictures—for a total sensory overload. Popular light shows have featured Pink Floyd, The Who, Led Zeppelin, U2, and others.

PUTT-PUTT (age 3 and up)

815 Dennison Drive, Champaign 61821; (217) 356–6121. Off Prospect Avenue, 1 block north of Bradley Avenue. Summer hours are 10 A.M. to midnight Monday through Saturday and 11 A.M. to midnight Sunday. The hours are cut back in fall, and the place closes after the last weekend in September, reopening in late spring. The basic price is $4 per person per game, all ages. The facility offers a three-game ticket for $6, but it may be used by only one person. For example, to play only one game, a family of three must buy three single-game tickets at $4 apiece, a total of $12; they can't each use one game on a $6 three-game ticket. You don't have to play all the games in one night, however; these tickets have no expiration date. Internet: www.puttputtcu.com.

This is not the most exciting course in the world, but it's the only game in town if you want to play miniature golf in Champaign. There are actually two courses, one a bit more difficult but more fun than the other and still possible to make par. Each green is framed in bittersweet orange metal trim. Any skill you have at shooting pool will come in handy on some holes where you'll need to carom the ball off the metal borders (which makes an amusing "doink" sound) to get around obstacles such as wooden blocks or steel posts and reach the cup. Some of the greens have rolling hills that make the shot a bit trickier. But there are no moving parts and no tunnels, and the decor and landscaping are fairly minimalist—a full-size giraffe statue on one course, a baby elephant on another, a few yellow daylilies, and a lot of grass. There's a pop machine but no concession stand.

ANTS IN THEIR PANTS (ages 2–12)

247 South Mattis Avenue, Champaign 61821; (217) 351–2687. At the south end of a strip of stores in the Country Fair Shopping Center, just south of University Avenue. Hours are 3:30 to 7:30 P.M. Monday through Thursday, 3:30 to 8:30 P.M.

Friday, 9 A.M. to 9 P.M. Saturday, and noon to 5 P.M. Sunday. Admission costs $3 per person age 3 through 17 and $1 for children younger than 3; accompanying adults get in free. Tokens cost 25 cents each. Kids must wear socks (available for $1.50 per pair).

You won't have to worry about the weather if you take the kids to this indoor amusement center. The biggest attraction is a giant play apparatus with tubes, slides, nets, and clear-bubble observation ports. The thing is a riot of color—it has a padded purple metal framework, with other plastic parts in pink, yellow, orange, blue, and green. Nearby is a smaller apparatus in black and white. Within a square metal framework, two layers of bouncy elastic webbing crisscross above a ball pit. Kids have a blast playing spider in it. This contraption is not as safe as the other, however. The frame is not padded, and there are metal screws exposed. There are fun things to do here that are less dangerous, however. For example, there are two rows of arcade games for varying ability levels. For the littler kids there are a couple of "bop" games that elicit giggles. Grade-schoolers go for basketball, Bozo buckets, the Barbie-and-Ken surf race, and youth-oriented video games. And everybody likes Skeeball. Most games cost only one token (25 cents) to play. Ditto the little horsie, helicopter, and choo-choo for the tots. The Ninja Turtles amusement park ride costs two tokens, but it goes up and down and around and around. Kids who are at least 4 feet tall can ride the bumper cars for four tokens. At no extra charge is the toddler play area for those age 3 or younger. Enclosed by a 2-foot-high wall, it has a padded slide, a shallow, open ball pit, and an assortment of Little Tikes cars, shopping carts, and kitchen appliances. The rest rooms are clean and have changing tables. Concession fare includes sodas and juice and snack foods like popcorn, chips, cookies, and crackers for under $1. Nachos, hot dogs, and pizza are available in the $2 to $4 range.

CENTENNIAL PARK (all ages)

Off Mattis Avenue between Sangamon Drive and Kirby Avenue, Champaign 61821; (217) 398–2550. Open daily from 8 A.M. to 11 P.M. **Free** *admission.*

Centennial Park is a good place for outdoor relaxation. Here you can have a picnic, hike a fitness trail, or release the kids on the playground. The Sholem Pool and the Prairie Farm are both in this park, too (see next two entries).

SHOLEM POOL AND WATERWORKS WATERSLIDE (all ages)

2200 Sangamon Drive, Champaign 61821; (217) 398–2581. At the north end of Centennial Park. Open from Memorial Day weekend through Labor Day. Hours are

11 A.M. to 8 P.M. Monday through Friday and 1 to 5 P.M. and 7 to 9 P.M. Saturday and Sunday. Admission costs $3.50 for anyone age 13 or older and $2.50 for kids age 12 or younger. The water slide is inside the pool complex, but you have to pay extra for it; you buy a wristband that includes both a specified number of trips down the slide and admission to the pool. Wristband prices start at $5 for two slides and go up from there. If the members of your family want to share a wristband, one person pays the wristband price and the others pay pool-only admission, and then the wristband is punched for the number of sliders going down each time.

Enter the pool complex at the sandy brick building with pink and yellow flower beds in front. There is a huge rectangular pool for regular swimming. It has a diving well with boards off to the side at one end. Children age 6 or younger, accompanied by parents, can swim in the separate kiddie pool. Depth is about 1 to 2 feet all the way around, so parents of toddlers should stay within arm's reach at all times. The water slide is in a separate area connected by a gate. Long wooden staircases lead up and up and up to a platform at the top of two long, twisting white flumes. Kids must be at least 3 feet tall and able to swim one width of the pool to be allowed on the slides, the latter requirement a wise precaution. Remember, it costs extra to go on the slide, so make sure you've purchased the required wristband before the kids climb up all those stairs. The pool can get temporarily crowded during the week with busloads of day campers who get an hour or two to swim. The concession area has tables with umbrellas where you can enjoy a Pepsi (75 cents to $2.50) and a snack such as chips, candy, ice cream, nachos, or a hot dog (60 cents to $1.50).

PRAIRIE FARM (ages 1–8)

Mattis and West Kirby Avenues, Champaign 61821; (217) 398–2550. At the south end of Centennial Park; parking is along Kirby Avenue. Open from Memorial Day through Labor Day. Hours are 1 to 7 P.M. daily. Admission is **Free**, *although there is a cute donation box that looks like a miniature barn if you feel like contributing to the upkeep. Paths are paved and accessible for strollers and wheelchairs. No smoking allowed.*

This small, simple facility is especially appealing for younger children. There are little red barns and pens with pigs, cows, horses, and chickens to look at. If the tots want a more hands-on experience, they can go in the fenced-in petting area and get acquainted with goats, ponies, and a calf. A pop machine is the only concession on-site, but you can bring a picnic basket and enjoy your own food at one of several picnic tables (which is a better deal for toddlers anyway). There are a couple of old wooden wagons on the grounds that add atmosphere but are not for playing on. Big shade trees keep the area comfortable on a warm, sunny day.

CURTIS ORCHARD (all ages)

3902 South Duncan Road, Champaign 61821; (217) 359–5565. East of I–57 and south of I–72. Open from August 1 through mid-December. Hours are 9 A.M. to 5:30 P.M. Monday through Saturday and noon to 5 P.M. Sunday. Admission is **Free**, *but naturally you would be expected to pay for the apples you pick.*

South of town is this family-oriented orchard with 4,000 trees from which you can pick your own apples. You can also tour a working farm that produces corn and soybeans. Kids can play in the barn or visit goats, bunnies, and chicks in the petting farm. The sales area has delicious cobbler, pies, and doughnuts plus bags of fruit you can buy if you don't feel like picking it yourself. The orchard sells Halloween pumpkins and Christmas trees, too.

Where to Eat

Round Barn Steakhouse. *1900 Round Barn Road, off Mattis Avenue; (217) 359–9800.* Across the street from Ants in Their Pants. Hours are 11 A.M. to 2 P.M. and 4 to 9 P.M. Monday through Friday, noon to 10 P.M. Saturday, and 11 A.M. to 8 P.M. Sunday. Serving lunch, dinner, and Sunday brunch. This eye-catching restaurant lives up to its name. The adult menu contains a wide variety of steaks, including prime rib, plus chicken and shrimp entrees for diners who aren't into red meat. The children's menu at about $3 includes french fries and drink with an entree such as hamburger, chicken, grilled cheese, or macaroni and cheese. $$

Aunt Sonya's. *220 West Kirby Avenue; (217) 352–8156.* A mile or 2 east of Centennial Park Prairie Farm. Hours are 6 A.M. to 9 P.M. Sunday and Monday, 6 A.M. to 11 P.M. Tuesday through Thursday, and 6 A.M. to midnight Friday and Saturday. Breakfast is served all day long and is the specialty here, but you can get burgers and other sandwiches for lunch or a "home cookin'" entree like Swiss steak or chicken and noodles for dinner. The kids' menu features pancakes, grilled cheese, spaghetti, burgers, fish sticks, and chicken fingers; prices range from $2 to $3, including drink. $

Bob Evans. *1813 North Neil Street; (217) 356–1006.* Hours are 6 A.M. to 10 P.M. daily. See Restaurant Appendix for description. **$**

TGIFriday's. *101 Trade Center Drive; (217) 352–5595.* Hours are 11 A.M. to 11 P.M. Monday through Thursday, 11 A.M. to midnight Friday and Saturday, and 11 A.M. to 10 P.M. Sunday. See Restaurant Appendix for description. $$

Where to Stay

Comfort Inn. *305 Marketview Drive; (217) 352–4055 or (800) 228–5150.* There are 67 comfortable rooms in this two-story motel. It has an indoor pool with whirlpool. Continental breakfast is included in the room rate. $$

Fairfield Inn. *1807 Moreland Boulevard; (217) 355–0604.* This three-story property has 65 rooms and an indoor heated pool and spa. The room rate includes continental breakfast. $$

Super 8. *202 Marketview Drive; (217) 359–2388 or (800) 800–8000.* This economy property has 61 rooms with cable TV. Pets are allowed. $$

For More Information

Champaign-Urbana Convention and Visitors Bureau, *1817 South Neil Street, Suite 201, Champaign 61820-7234; (217) 351–4133 or (800) 369–6151. Internet: www.cupartnership.org/cvb.*

Urbana

The Urbana half of Champaign-Urbana is more closely connected with the university and has fewer attractions of interest to families with young children. Keep an eye out in the future for the university's new Spurlock Museum of World Cultures, which is scheduled to open in 2001. Possibly the best attraction in town is a hotel: Jumer's Castle Lodge. It's located downtown in an area rich in historic architecture. Next door is the First United Methodist Church with its Gothic bell tower. Behind it is the sand-colored brick post office, which dates back to 1911, and across the street from that is the orange-brick courthouse building. The whole area makes you feel as though you've taken a step back in time to a romanticized era of refinement.

JUMER'S CASTLE LODGE (age 8 and up)

209 South Broadway Avenue, Urbana 61801; (217) 384–8800 or (800) 285–8637. Rates vary, but you may be able to get a room for just under $100, especially if you have AAA. Rates do not include breakfast. Internet: www.jumers.com.

This ornate Tudor palace has opulent interiors reminiscent of a more elegant period. The lobby decor is all dark wood and lush burgundy, softly lit with wrought-iron chandeliers and filled with antique furnishings such as a grandfather clock, a piano, and bronze and porcelain statuary. The rooms are equally fancy: carpeting patterned after an antique oriental rug, beds framed in tasseled drapes, a brick floor in the bathroom. (The stately armoire, however, hides a thoroughly modern TV set, with cable.) You'd think the place was 100 years old, but the guest rooms on the upper floors actually date only from 1977. That was the year that D. James Jumer bought the old Urbana-Lincoln Hotel, which was built in the early 1920s, and remodeled it in this Old World European style. Even the indoor pool area maintains the Tudor theme, with a high ceiling and tall, arched windows in front. A door in front opens onto a sundeck, which unfortunately overlooks the parking lot. The room has a good combination of air and water temperatures, so you can take a refreshing swim and then rest comfortably on a chaise lounge afterward. There's a whirlpool in the corner if you want to warm up a bit more. Breakfast is served in the Library, which has thousands of real hardcover books in custom-crafted oak cases lining the walls. (There's a 1926 edition of Jane Austen's 1816 novel *Emma,* for example.) On the wall inside the doorway is a collection of moose and deer heads. The prices are in the $5 to $8 range, not including beverages, and there's no children's menu.

If you're willing to eat dinner before 6 P.M., you can get a real bargain in the Great Hall restaurant. This high-ceilinged room has imported German wall tapestries and velvet draperies. Portraits of English nobles also grace the walls. Classical music plays in the background. Guests sit in high-back chairs that lend an air of privacy, and of course the tables are set with cloth napkins, fine silverware, and crystal glasses. Yet, in this dignified atmosphere, early-bird entrees are only about $10, including bread, salad, potato, and vegetable. The portions are filling, too, although not so large that you can't find room for one of the scrumptious desserts that the waiter will display for you on a silver tray. You'll want to linger over dessert and coffee anyway, just to soak up the atmosphere.

The Jumer's experience is almost like living in a fairy tale, and your older grade-schooler will love it and remember it for a long time. But, please, please, don't waste your time and money—and spoil the atmosphere for the rest of the guests—by bringing little children who are too young to appreciate it. One of the things that makes the experience so special is the peaceful lack of crying babies and fussing toddlers.

CRYSTAL LAKE PARK AND POOL (all ages)

Broadway and Park Streets, Urbana; (217) 367–1536. The park is open year-round, from sunrise to 11 P.M. daily. Park admission is **Free**. *Pets must be kept on leashes, and alcoholic beverages are not allowed. The pool is open during summer only, from 1 to 8 P.M. daily. Pool admission is $3.50 for anyone age 13 or older, $2.50 for kids age 2 through 12, and free for children age 1 or younger.*

Crystal Lake Park is a nice place to relax and enjoy the great outdoors here in Urbana. It's the biggest park in the Champaign-Urbana area and the only one with a lake. You can fish for largemouth bass, channel catfish, bluegill, and redear from shore or from one of several overlook decks. If you want to go out onto the lake, you can rent a rowboat, canoe, or paddleboat for $3.50 per half hour or $5 per hour. Arrange the rental at the Lake House, where you can also find soft drinks and light snacks. The Lake House Cafe is open from 11 A.M. to 6 P.M. daily from late April through early September. The T-shaped swimming pool also has a concession area. Or you can have a picnic at the park using the picnic tables and grills scattered throughout the grounds. You can take a hike along the nature trails, or turn the kids loose on the playground. If you're here in July, you may catch the Annual Blues Festival. You can skate on the frozen lake for some winter fun.

Where to Eat

Garcia's Pizza. *803 South Lincoln Avenue; (217) 359–1212.* Open from 11 A.M. to 11 P.M. Sunday through Thursday and 11 A.M. to midnight Friday and Saturday. This campus-area pizza place is a favorite of students. Both thick- and thin-crust types are offered. If your kids are the type who'll eat anything, try the "gut-buster" with the works. (There are several Garcia's outlets in Champaign as well.) $

Cracker Barrel. *2101 Kenyon Road; (217) 344–9087.* Hours are 6 A.M. to 10 P.M. Sunday through Thursday and 6 A.M. to 11 P.M. Friday and Saturday. See Restaurant Appendix for description. $

Where to Stay

Eastland Suites. *1907 North Cunningham (I–74 and Highway 45); (217) 367–8331.* Despite its name, this property has about 150 regular hotel rooms, each with microwave and minifridge, as well as several types of suites. A $2 million renovation in 2000 gave the place a nearly brand-new look. Amenities include indoor pool and exercise room. Pets are allowed. Full breakfast buffet is included in the room rate. $$$

Hampton Inn. *1200 West University Avenue; (217) 337–1100.* This 92-room property has an exercise room but no swimming pool. Continental breakfast is included in the room rate. $$

Monticello

Population: 4,549. About 18 miles west of Champaign-Urbana is the town of Monticello. You'll find a couple of pleasant family attractions here.

MONTICELLO RAILWAY MUSEUM (all ages)

Off I–72 at exit 63, Monticello 61856; (217) 762–9011. Open only weekends and holidays from May 1 through October 31. Board at 12:30, 2, or 3:30 P.M. Saturday or Sunday at the museum's restored Illinois Central Depot or at 2:30 or 4 P.M. Saturday or Sunday at the restored 1899 Wabash Depot in downtown Monticello. Rides cost $6 for anyone age 13 through 61 and $4 for kids age 4 through 12 and adults age 62 or older. Children age 3 or younger ride free with an adult. Internet: www.prairienet.org/mrm.

Here you'll see historic railroad cars and equipment on display, including both steam engines and electric railcars. You can take a 50-minute train ride through the countryside in one of the museum's vintage coaches or cabooses. A uniformed conductor will punch your ticket and remain on hand to answer any questions you may have.

ALLERTON PARK (all ages)

Near the railway museum, about 4 miles southwest of Monticello—look for signs; (217) 762–2721. Open daily from 8 A.M. to sunset. Admission is **Free**. *A visitor center on the grounds is open from 8 A.M. to 5 P.M. daily.*

This lovely 1,500-acre park features flower gardens, greenhouses, sculpted hedges, and statues and sculptures from Cambodia, Thailand, and China. The park has been named a National Natural Landmark.

Where to Eat

Sage City. *On Charter Street, along the west side of the town square downtown; (217) 762–7454.* Open from 7 A.M. to 9 P.M. Tuesday through Thursday, 7 A.M. to 10 P.M. Friday and Saturday, and 8 A.M. to 2 P.M. Sunday; closed Monday. Steak is the specialty, but there are also nightly specials. The children's menu items are $3 to $5, not including drink. Kids can choose hamburger, hot dog, chicken tenders, grilled cheese sandwich, pizza, or spaghetti. $$

Pizza Hut. *777 West Bridge; (217) 762–8585.* Hours are 11 A.M. to 10 P.M. Sunday through Thursday and 11 A.M. to 11 P.M. Friday and Saturday. See Restaurant Appendix for description. $

Where to Stay

Best Western Monticello Gateway Inn. *I–72 at exit 166; (217) 762–9436 or (888) 331–4600. Fax (217) 762–3202.* This 41-room property is just a quarter mile south of the railway museum and about 5 miles from Allerton Park. Amenities include indoor swimming pool, hot tub, and exercise room. Continental breakfast is included in the room rate. $$

For More Information

Monticello Chamber of Commerce, *Old Wabash Depot, P.O. Box 313, Monticello 61856; (800) 952–3396. Internet: www.monticello.net.*

Piatt County Tourism Council, *P.O. Box 324, Monticello 61856; (217) 762–7912 or (800) 952–3396.*

Tuscola

Population: 4,155. This town bills itself as "Your First Stop in Amish Country." You won't see many buggies until you get a bit farther south, but there are several attractions here for the family to enjoy.

FACTORY STORES OF TUSCOLA (all ages)

I–57 at U.S. Highway 36, Tuscola 61953; (217) 253–2282 or (888) 746–7333. Open from 10 A.M. to 9 P.M. Monday through Saturday and 11 A.M. to 6 P.M. Sunday. Internet: www.charter-oak.com/tuscola.

This outdoor factory outlet mall has more than 60 stores. The triangular design of the main sign is repeated along the rooftops of the strip. OshKosh B'Gosh and Carter's Childrenswear have cute children's clothes, and older kids can pick out brand-name sneakers at bargain prices at the Reebok store. The Kay-Bee Toy Outlet may be tempting. Samsonite Company Store can provide luggage for your next family vacation. You'll find burgers, tacos, and pizza among the food offerings.

DOUGLAS COUNTY MUSEUM (age 8 and up)

700 South Main Street, Tuscola 61953; (217) 253–2535. Hours are 9 A.M. to 4 P.M. Monday through Saturday; closed Sunday. Admission is **Free**.

This small museum emphasizes local history through its changing exhibits. For example, a recent display featured old vacuum cleaners as part of the exhibit *The Pride and Pain of Housework: Washing, Ironing, Cooking, Cleaning and Stitching. Every Day Should Be Veterans Day* featured World War II memorabilia. Because many of the glass display cases contain books and papers, young visitors will find it more interesting if they are able to read. Special events include demonstrations of cross-stitch crafts.

PRAIRIELAND PRIDE PLAYGROUND (ages 1–12)

In Ervin Park, off Main Street, Tuscola 61953; (800) 441–9111. Open during park hours, 7 A.M. to 9 P.M. daily. Admission is Free.

The community built this magnificent outdoor playground in the late 1990s. Kids of all ages, but especially the younger ones, will love to run and jump and climb all over this wooden apparatus that has towers, bridges, and slides.

Where to Eat

Liga's Steak and Pasta House. *U.S. Highway 36 at Main Street; (217) 253–2155.* Open from 11 A.M. to 9 P.M. Tuesday through Thursday, 11 A.M. to 10 P.M. Friday and Saturday, and 11 A.M. to 8 P.M. Sunday; closed Monday. Serving lunch, dinner, and Sunday buffet. The name should tip you off about what kind of food to expect at this local favorite. A children's menu for those age 10 or younger includes spaghetti, ravioli, tortellini, pizza, burgers, and chicken strips, at prices ranging from $3.50 to $4.50, not including drink. $$

1871 Luncheonette. *103 West Sale, downtown; (217) 253–6406.* Open from 10 A.M. to 3 P.M. Monday through Friday, 10 A.M. to 4 P.M. Saturday, and 11 A.M. to 2 P.M. Sunday. This charming lunch spot offers sandwiches and soups, but the best part is the homemade desserts. $

Where to Stay

AmeriHost Inn. *1006 Southline Drive (I–57 at U.S. Highway 36); (217) 253–3500. Fax (217) 253–2773.* Near Factory Stores of Tuscola. The inn has 59 rooms with in-room coffeemaker and cable TV. Amenities include heated indoor pool and whirlpool. Continental breakfast is included in the room rate. $$

Holiday Inn Express. *1201 Tuscola Boulevard; (217) 253–6363 or (800) 465–4329.* Near Factory Stores of Tuscola. There are 82 rooms at this three-story motel. Amenities include indoor heated pool and whirlpool. The room rate includes continental breakfast bar. $$

Super 8. *I–57 at U.S. Highway 36; (217) 253–5488 or (800) 800–8000.* Near Factory Stores of Tuscola. This budget property has 66 comfortable rooms with cable TV. No pool. $

For More Information

Tuscola Visitors Center, *502 Southline Road (U.S. Highway 36), Tuscola 61953; (800) 441–9111.*

Arcola

Population: 2,678. Near the intersection of U.S. Highway 45 and Illinois Highway 133 is Arcola. This town lies at the eastern edge of an area known as Illinois Amish Country, which stretches to the west for 10 to 15 miles, extending north as far as Highway 36 and south roughly to the border between Douglas and Coles Counties. This area contains numerous homes and businesses belonging to members of the Old Order Amish, a Protestant religious group (part of the Pennsylvania Dutch) that believes in living a simple life separate from the rest of the world. The Amish are easy to recognize by appearance: Men wear wide-brimmed hats and typically dress in black or blue, the married ones sporting a beard but no mustache, while women wear plain, solid-color long dresses and white bonnets called prayer caps. Amish clothes are

The Big Cheese in Arthur The biggest concentration of Amish, about 3,500 people, is in and around the town of Arthur, west of Arcola along Highway 133. Here you'll find shops specializing in handmade wood furniture, custom-built cabinets, upholstery, textiles, health foods, and baked goods. (You can also get horseshoes, leather harnesses, or wagon repair services if you happen to have a horse and buggy.) Special events are scheduled throughout the year. If you're here in early September, you can see a 1,000-pound cheese wheel at the Amish Country Cheese Festival. Flea markets, a dog show, a petting zoo, and buggy rides are also part of the two-day celebration. Contact Amish Country Information Center, 106 East Progress Street, Arthur 61911; (800) 722-6474. Internet: www.illinoisamishcountry.com.

fastened with straight pins—no buttons, zippers, or snaps. Amish rules forbid the use of electricity and telephones, and they do their plowing with animals rather than machines. They usually travel in horse-drawn black buggies.

In reality, it's hard to live completely separated from the rest of the world, and Amish businesses do serve non-Amish patrons as well as members of their own community. But don't plan to visit if you just want to gawk and take pictures—save that for the zoo. No person appreciates being stared at as an oddity, and it is *against Amish religious beliefs to be photographed.* Just exercise the golden rule and treat them with the same respect and courtesy with which you would want others to treat you. With that attitude, you probably will find the Amish quite hospitable. (You also will find some telephones and electrical service in the area; not everyone around here is Amish.)

The **Historic Depot,** a redbrick building in downtown Arcola, has helpful tourist information provided by friendly people. Redbrick streets add a quaint touch to the 3-block-long downtown. Main Street is lined with interesting shops selling crafts, antiques, and memorabilia. The Amish are famous for their handmade brooms, and there is an annual Broom Corn Festival in mid-September, featuring crafts, entertainment, food, and a parade highlighted by the Lawn Rangers, a drill team with lawn mowers.

If you notice quite a bit of Raggedy Ann memorabilia around here, there's a good reason. You can see the gravestone of Johnny Gruelle, author of the charming children's books, near the depot. The Johnny Gruelle Raggedy Ann and Andy Museum is downtown. An annual festival honors the floppy celebrities the weekend before Memorial Day weekend.

JOHNNY GRUELLE RAGGEDY ANN AND ANDY MUSEUM (all ages)

110 East Main Street, Arcola 61910; (217) 268–4908. Hours are 10 A.M. to 5 P.M. Tuesday through Saturday and 1 to 4 P.M. Sunday; closed Monday. Admission is free, but there is a suggested donation of $1 per person age 12 or older. The building is wheelchair accessible. Internet: www.raggedyann-museum.org.

Johnny Gruelle was born in Arcola in 1880. In 1915 he created and patented Raggedy Ann, a rag doll with black button eyes and red yarn hair. He published *Raggedy Ann Stories* in 1918 and continued to write books about Raggedy Ann and later Raggedy Andy until his death in 1938 in Miami Beach. This museum opened in 1999, although building and expansion are expected to continue through about 2005. There are three permanent installations so far. Johnny's Studio is a re-creation of the author's Miami Beach workshop of the early 1930s. Marcella's Room is an imagined interpretation of a bedroom used by Gruelle's daughter,

Marcella, from about 1908 to 1912, based on Gruelle's drawings in *Raggedy Ann Stories.* The third exhibit area contains 10 display cases highlighting the chronological development of the Raggedy Ann dolls and story characters. If you and your kids grew up loving Raggedy Ann and Andy, you won't want to miss this treasure trove of memorabilia.

ROCKOME GARDENS (all ages)

125 North County Road 425E, Arcola 61910; (217) 268–4106 or (800) 549–7625. Season begins in late April and runs through mid-October. Days of operation are somewhat limited until the peak season, late May through early September, when the facility is open daily. Be sure to call ahead if you plan to visit during the off-peak times. The gardens are open from 9 A.M. to 5:30 P.M. Shops are open from 10 A.M. to 5 P.M. Monday through Friday and 10 A.M. to 5:30 P.M. Saturday and Sunday. Admission costs $8.50 for anyone age 13 through 59, $7.50 for adults age 60 or older, and $6.50 for kids age 4 through 12. Children age 3 or younger get in free. Admission is half-price on Sunday. Most parts of the park are accessible for strollers and wheelchairs, but there are a few places reachable only by stairs. Internet: www.rockome.com.

Arcola's most famous attraction is Rockome Gardens. Formerly an Amish farm and homestead, in 1958 it became a sprawling complex of rock and flower gardens, craft and food shops, and entertainments. The original farmhouse was preserved and is presented as a museum showing how the Amish live. With their prohibition on electricity, the Amish use wood or gas cookstoves, gas-operated refrigerators, and propane gas to heat their homes. Rooms are plainly furnished.

If you're willing to spend an extra $1.75 per person, you can take a tour of the grounds in a genuine horse-drawn Amish buggy. The friendly driver will point out the attractions and answer questions as you clop along. The ride offers a good overview so that you can decide which parts you want to walk back to later. The grounds are large enough that youngsters' feet may tire, so set your priorities at the beginning (looking at the rocks and flowers may not be the most thrilling thing for them, so save that for farther down the list). There is also a "train" ride on a wheeled wagon that goes out into the cornfields rather than around the grounds. Newer attractions include a wooden "tree house," reachable by stairs, and an interesting model train layout. Some of the older attractions have perennial appeal. The Haunted Cave, where things pop out at you accompanied by spooky voices and sound effects, is fun but a bit too scary for younger or more nervous children. Just about everybody likes the dancing chicken and the piano-playing duck. These two attractions feature live birds, each in a specialized glass-walled cage with one section where they sit and another where they perform. Drop a quarter in the slot to get some action. The chicken goes in and pecks a selection on a tiny jukebox and then scratches around to the tinkly music. The duck pulls a chain to turn on a light above its toy piano, then whacks on the keys with its bill. At the end of each performance, a handful of corn pours out a chute, and the bird gobbles up its reward. Animal-rights activists might have some objections to this kind of entertainment, but it amuses visitors of all ages.

A unique attraction for kids in the 3-to-12 age range is the horse-powered sawmill. It costs $1, but it's worth it. The kid sits atop a horse whose harness is attached to an elaborate network of gears and belts to power a rotating sawblade about 10 feet away. As the kid rides the horse around in a circle, the gears turn and the sawblade whirs away to slice a half-inch-thick round off the end of a log. Then the kid goes to the blacksmith shop, where, for 10 cents per letter, the young smithy will use a glowing-hot iron to emblazon the kid's name into the wood. This personalized keepsake makes a great souvenir.

Antique farm implements are on display in one barn, room displays with period furnishings in another. Craft shops feature quilts, dolls, candles, and jewelry. If you want a snack, you'll have to forget about fat and calories to indulge in Amish-made sausage, cheese, fudge, ice cream, or a rich, buttery-tasting iced cinnamon roll.

Where to Eat

Dutch Kitchen Family Restaurant. *127 East Main Street, downtown; (217) 268–3518.* Open from 7:30 A.M. to 7 P.M. daily. Amid decor with country charm, you can eat a sandwich, a plate lunch, or a full dinner. Save room for the homemade pie. $

Rockome Family-Style Restaurant. *At Rockome Gardens; (217) 268–4106 or (800) 549–7625.* Open from 11 A.M. to 7 P.M. on days when Rockome Gardens is open. "Family-style" means that food at each table is served from communal bowls and platters. $$

Where to Stay

Budget Host Amish Country Inn. *I–57 and Illinois Highway 133; (217) 268–3031 or (800) 283–4678.* This small motel has comfortable, modern rooms with telephone and electricity. There is an outdoor swimming pool. The room rate includes "deluxe" continental breakfast. If you stay for two nights, you get one pair of free tickets per room for Rockome Gardens. $

Comfort Inn. *610 East Springfield Road; (217) 268–4000 or (800) 228–5150.* The 41 rooms in this chain property have cable TV and recliners. No pool. Pets allowed. Continental breakfast is included in the room rate. $$

Arcola Camper Stop. *472 Davis Street; (217) 268–4616.* A quarter mile west of I-57 off exit 203. Open year-round, but more limited service in winter. This RV park has water and electrical hookups, hot showers, rest rooms, pay phone, and dump station. $

For More Information

Arcola Depot Welcome Center, *135 North Oak Street, Arcola 61910; (800) 336–5456. Internet: www.arcola-il.org.*

Mattoon

Population: 18,441. I-57 skirts this town, and several other throughfares pass through it: U.S. Highway 45 and Illinois Highways 121 and 16. The main drag is Broadway Avenue, which parallels Route 16 a block north. This Broadway doesn't quite live up to its New York namesake, however. The marquee of the old downtown movie theater no longer lights up because the cinema is closed. (The Showplace 8 between Mattoon and Charleston handles the movies nowadays.) Still, there are a few family-oriented spots around town, plus baseball and softball tournaments each summer and Bagelfest in July.

PETERSON PARK (all ages)

Broadway Avenue east of North Sixth Street, Mattoon 61938. Open from 5 A.M. to 11 P.M. daily. Free *admission.*

You can have a picnic in the park. There are picnic tables, or you could spread out a blanket on the grass. A vintage army tank makes an interesting conversation piece. Children will enjoy the newer playground equipment made of sturdy plastic in bright colors. You can play a round of miniature golf, too (see next entry).

PLA-MOR GOLF (age 3 and up)

In Peterson Park, Mattoon 61938; (217) 235–9711. Open from noon to 9 P.M. daily during summer. Cost is $2 per game for adults and $1.50 per game for kids age 12 or younger.

This 18-hole miniature golf course features red, yellow, and blue borders around each of the greens, and a working stoplight adds another flash of color. Some of the holes are a little tricky, but fun. You'll try to drive the ball between the blades of a windmill, under some dangling bowling pins, and around a loop-the-loop.

LYTLE PARK POOL (all ages)

3320 Western Avenue, in Lytle Park, Mattoon 61938; (217) 258–9801. Open from 1:30 to 8 P.M. daily in the summer. Admission costs $3 for anyone age 13 or older and $2 for kids age 4 through 12; children age 3 or younger get in free.

This local swimming hole claims to be the largest outdoor public pool in the state, holding a million gallons of water. Water levels range from zero-depth to 10 feet. The pool has water slides and diving boards. The surrounding park has playground equipment and basketball and tennis courts.

CROSS COUNTY MALL (all ages)

I–57 and Illinois Highway 16, Mattoon 61938; (217) 235–3432. Open from 10 A.M. to 9 P.M. Monday through Saturday and noon to 5 P.M. Sunday.

This indoor mall has more then 30 stores. The anchor department stores are JCPenney, Sears, and Elder Beerman.

Where to Eat

McHugh's Double Drive Thru. *South Eighth Street and Charleston Road (Route 16); (217) 234–7565.* Open year-round. Hours are 10 A.M. to 10 P.M. Monday through Thursday, 10 A.M. to 11 P.M. Friday and Saturday, and 10:30 A.M. to 10 P.M. Sunday. This burger joint decorated in a red-and-white checkerboard design has been in business since the early 1990s. Yes, it does have *two* drive-through lanes, but there also are six round tables with umbrellas outside if you want to eat on the premises during summer. Burgers are cooked to order and look like McDonald's but taste better. The fries look and taste much like Mickey D's. Be sure to ask about the day's special flavor of milk shake; the blackberry is delicious! Or you can stick with vanilla, chocolate, or strawberry. $

Lee's Famous Recipe Chicken. *South Eighth Street and Charleston Road (Route 16); (217) 235–3731.* Hours are 10 A.M. to 9 P.M. Sunday through Thursday and 10 A.M. to 9:30 P.M. Friday and Saturday. While McHugh's across the street challenges McDonald's, Lee's gives KFC a run for the money. Choose your chicken fried or baked, and a dinner comes with two side items. The already reasonable prices are even lower on Tuesdays. $

A Lincoln Site to See The **Lincoln Log Cabin State Historic Site** in Lerna preserves the last home of Thomas and Sarah Bush Lincoln, Abraham Lincoln's father and stepmother. The site is accessible off Illinois Highway 130 (between Charleston and Greenup) or I–57 (between Mattoon and Effingham). Thomas Lincoln purchased the farm in 1840 and worked the land, using traditional methods to grow corn, oats, and wheat. The family also raised livestock, including hogs, sheep, milk cows, chickens, and geese. Their own food garden included potatoes and other vegetables. Today an accurate replica of the Lincolns' cabin, reconstructed from old photographs and affidavits, stands on the original site. (The original cabin had been moved to Chicago in 1892 for the World's Columbian Exposition and was subsequently lost—and don't ask how you can lose a whole cabin.) A garden, orchard, and crop field have been planted with varieties from the 1800s. During summer the site becomes even more of a living-history farm, with costumed interpreters playing the roles of the Lincoln family and their neighbors. They work in the fields, do housework, and (for the kids) play games of the period, and they speak in the Southern Upland dialect used on the farm (yes, it's still English). Food is prepared using recipes from 1840s cookbooks.

Adjacent to the Lincoln farm on the historic site is the **Sargent Farm,** a reconstruction containing the original frame house purchased in 1840 by the Lincolns' more prosperous neighbor, Stephen Sargent. Whereas the Lincolns practiced traditional subsistence farming, Sargent was considered a "progressive" farmer who took advantage of the latest agricultural innovations. By 1850 his holdings included 400 acres of land and more than 165 head of livestock. His farm was originally located 10 miles east of the Lincoln farm but was moved to the Lincoln Log Cabin State Historic Site in 1985 to allow visitors to observe in closer proximity the contrast between the two farming styles.

The **Reuben Moore Home,** 1 mile north of the Lincoln log cabin, was the home of Abe Lincoln's stepsister, Matilda Hall, who married Reuben Moore and moved with him into the house in 1856. Lincoln was a dinner guest at this frame house.

The Lincoln Log Cabin State Historic Site is open daily from 8 A.M. to dusk, with costumed interpreters on site from 9 A.M. to 5 P.M.; closed New Year's, Thanksgiving, and Christmas days. Admission is Free. Special events are held throughout the year. For more information contact Site Manager, Lincoln Log Cabin State Historic Site, Rural Route 1, Box 172A, Lerna 62440; (217) 345–6489. Information is also available from the Web site, www.lincolnlogcabin.org.

Lake Shelbyville Area Southwest of Amish Country along Illinois Highway 16 is the 11,000-acre Lake Shelbyville. The United States Army Corps of Engineers began construction of this artificial lake on the Kaskaskia River in 1963, and water was impounded to begin filling it in 1970. Several towns that border the lake have related attractions of interest to families, including Findlay, Sullivan, Windsor, and the lake's namesake, Shelbyville.

The **Lake Shelbyville Visitor Center,** on Dam Road just east of Shelbyville, is open year-round. Hours between Memorial Day and Labor Day are 9 A.M. to 4:30 P.M. daily. Days of operation are more restricted the rest of the year. Call (217) 774–3951 for details.

The Army Corps of Engineers offers **Free** tours of the **Lake Shelbyville Dam,** which is visible off Illinois Highway 16, just east of Shelbyville. Call the Visitor Center for the current schedule, and take one of the tours if you can–it goes right under the sluice gates. If you can't be there at tour time, the Spillway East Recreation Area, just off the highway below the dam, has picnic tables and grills, a playground for the kids, and rest rooms. You'll likely see someone fishing in the waters beyond the spillway.

Two state parks, Eagle Creek and Wolf Creek, offer a variety of outdoor activities year-round. For both parks you can contact Superintendent, Eagle Creek State Park, Route 1, P.O. Box 6, Findlay 62534; (217) 756–8260.

For more information about the area, contact the Shelby County Office of Tourism, 315 East Main Street, Shelbyville 62565 (217) 774–2244. Internet: www.lakeshelbyville.com.

Cracker Barrel. *1101 Charleston Avenue East; (217) 234–9091.* Hours are 6 A.M. to 10 P.M. Sunday through Thursday and 6 A.M. to 11 P.M. Friday and Saturday. See Restaurant Appendix for description. $

Where to Stay

All three of these economical chain properties opened in the mid-1990s and are located just off I–57 at exit 190B.

Fairfield Inn. *206 McFall Road; (217) 234–2355 or (800) 228–2800.* The inn has an indoor pool and whirlpool. Continental breakfast is included in the room rate. $$

Hampton Inn. *1416 Broadway Avenue East; (217) 234–4267 or (800) 426–7866.* Winner of the Symbol of Excellence award for top-quality Hampton hotels as rated by guests throughout the chain, this 61-room property features an indoor pool. Room rates include continental breakfast bar. $$

Super 8. *205 McFall Road; (217) 235–8888 or (800) 800–8000.* This basic budget motel has 61 rooms with cable TV and recliners. Pets are allowed. No pool. Continental breakfast is included in the room rate. $$

For More Information

Mattoon Chamber of Commerce, *1701 Wabash Avenue, Mattoon 61938; (217) 235–5661. Internet: www.advant.net/mattooncommunity.*

Mattoon Welcome Center, *500 Broadway, Mattoon 61938; (217) 258–6286 or (800) 500–6286.*

Other Things to See and Do in Central Illinois

January: Central Illinois Jazz Festival, Decatur; (217) 422-8800

February: Lincoln's Birthday Open House, Mount Pulaski; (217) 732-8930

March: Home, Lawn & Garden Expo, Decatur; (217) 422-7300

April: Community Wide Yard Sale, Carlinville; (217) 854-2141

May: Springfest, Oblong; (618) 592-4355

June: Heritage Days, Farmer City; (309) 928-2676

Moweaqua Pow Wow Days; (217) 768-3418

Strawberry Fest, Newton; (618) 783-3399

Balloon Classic at Vermilion County Airport, Danville; (800) 383-4386

July: Bagelfest, downtown Mattoon; (217) 258-6286 or (800) 500-6286

Olde Tyme Family Farm Equipment Show, Hillsboro; (217) 532-3711

Most communities have a Fourth of July celebration, and many county fairs are in July and August.

August: U.S. National Hot Air Balloon Championships, Rantoul; (217) 893-9955

Fairbury Fair; (815) 692-3899 or Internet: www.fairburyil.org

September: Casey Popcorn Festival; (217) 932-5951

Apple and Pork Festival, Clinton; (217) 935-6006

National Sweetcorn Festival, Hoopeston; (217) 283-7108

Honey Bee Festival, Paris; (217) 465-4179

October: Harvest Bluegrass Festival, Tuscola; (800) 441-9111

Pumpkinfest, Decatur; (217) 422-7300

November: Victorian Splendor Parade and Light Festival, Shelbyville; (800) 874-3529

December: Festival of Trees, Jacksonville; (800) 593-5678

Holiday Open House, Bement; (217) 678-8184

Pontiac Holiday Basketball Tournament; (815) 844-6692

Southern Illinois

You'll know you're heading down into Southern Illinois when you begin to notice the flat stretches of central prairie giving way to a gentle undulation of wooded hills and valleys. Forests cover about 10 percent of the state, and most of them are here (the Shawnee National Forest spans the width of far Southern Illinois, stretching for about 70 miles). Get ready to slow down and enjoy the natural beauty that surrounds you. For information about this part of the state, you can contact the **Southernmost Illinois Tourism Bureau,** P.O. Box 278, Ullin 62992; (800) 248-4373.

Effingham

Population: 11,851. OK, so Effingham isn't Rome, but it sure seems like all roads lead here. Interstates 57 and 70, U.S. Highways 40 and 45, and State Highways 32 and 33 all converge in this town. It is estimated that 25,000 vehicles a day pass through Effingham. Amtrak and Greyhound stop here, too. However you arrive, you'll find some attractions of interest for families in this area.

The biggest attraction in the area is **Lake Sara,** located 5 miles northwest of Effingham along Highway 32/33; take exit 160 off I-57/70. Along the 27 miles of picturesque shoreline you'll find a swimming area with water slide, sandy beach, and modern bathhouse (217-868-2964), an 18-hole golf course (217-868-2860), campgrounds (217-868-2964), and two marinas, Lake Sara Marina (217-868-2791) and Ridge Runners Cove Marina (217-868-2329). Buy an Illinois state fishing license and get a boat permit from the Effingham Water Authority (217-347-7333) and you're ready to fish for black bass, bluegill, crappie, walleye, and channel catfish.

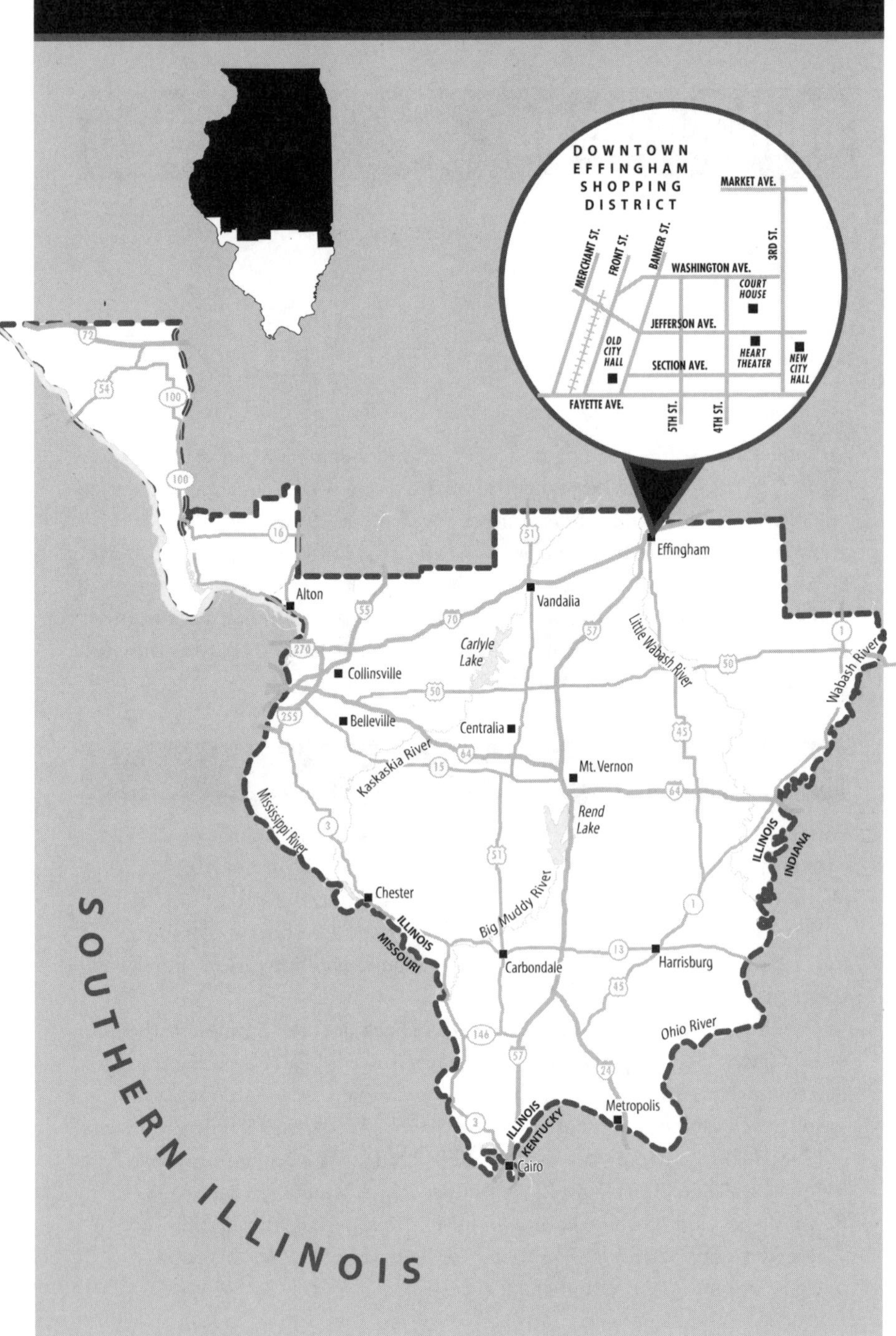
DOWNTOWN EFFINGHAM SHOPPING DISTRICT
MARKET AVE.
MERCHANT ST.
FRONT ST.
BANKER ST.
3RD ST.
WASHINGTON AVE.
COURT HOUSE
JEFFERSON AVE.
OLD CITY HALL
HEART THEATER
NEW CITY HALL
SECTION AVE.
FAYETTE AVE.
5TH ST.
4TH ST.
Effingham
Alton
Vandalia
Carlyle Lake
Little Wabash River
Collinsville
Belleville
Centralia
Kaskaskia River
Mt. Vernon
Rend Lake
Wabash River
Mississippi River
ILLINOIS
INDIANA
Chester
Big Muddy River
ILLINOIS
MISSOURI
Carbondale
Harrisburg
Ohio River
Metropolis
ILLINOIS
KENTUCKY
Cairo
SOUTHERN ILLINOIS

Effingham's lively downtown is well maintained and attractive, with neat awnings in blue, red, and green overhanging brick storefronts. The two-story redbrick Effingham County Courthouse stands in the center, at Jefferson Avenue and Third Street. Effingham, reportedly named after a British lord who refused to fight against the colonists during the American Revolution, has been the county seat since 1859.

You'll feel as though you're farther west than Illinois if you visit Effingham during a three-day period in June—that's when students from around the state converge here for the Illinois High School Rodeo Association State Rodeo Finals. You'll see these gutsy teenagers compete in such events as roping, steer wrestling, and bull and bronco riding.

K BOWL (age 4 and up)

1208 North Keller Drive (North Highway 32), Effingham 62401; (217) 342–4145. Regular hours are noon to 10 P.M. Sunday through Thursday and noon to midnight Friday and Saturday. Cost is $1 per game Monday through Thursday and $2 per game Friday through Sunday, plus $1 per person for shoes.

This 32-lane bowling alley is under the same roof as TGIFriday's (see Where to Eat) and an off-track betting parlor (not for families). It has automatic computerized scoring, and gutter bumpers are available for families with younger children. A game room has video games and pool tables. Carryout pizza is available at K Bowl, or you can hold out for a full meal at Friday's next door.

GOLFLAND (age 3 and up)

Keller Drive at Avenue of Mid-America, Effingham 62401; (217) 342–9173. Behind K Bowl. Open daily from June through August and Friday through Sunday only during May and September; closed from October through April. Hours are 5 to 10 P.M. Monday through Friday and noon to 10 P.M. Saturday and Sunday. Cost is $2 per game, all ages.

A white split-rail fence encloses this cute little 18-hole miniature golf course. The holes aren't too tricky, and the course is populated by colorful animal statues: a blue seahorse, a yellow lion, a gray seal, a brown bear. A tower and a well are other features. Nearby is a batting cage for baseball and softball sluggers.

K SQUARE OUTLET MALL (all ages)

1100 Avenue of Mid-America, Effingham 62401; (217) 342–4343. Take exit 160 off I–57/70 and then head north a mile or 2 on Keller Drive. Turn right, heading east, at Avenue of Mid-America and follow the signs to the mall. Open from 10 A.M. to 9 P.M. Monday through Saturday and 11 A.M. to 6 P.M. Sunday.

This outdoor outlet mall, a semicircular strip of brick storefronts, houses more than 20 manufacturers. Kids 4 Less has girls' and boys' clothing from infant through size 7. Collector's Dream has Beanie Babies, dolls, and other collectibles. Fannie May can satisfy a sweet tooth with chocolates and other candies. Other stores have clothing, housewares, and books. An indoor center section has a food court offering pasta, deli sandwiches, and yogurt. Rest rooms and pay phones also are located here. The Court Gallery has some amusing caricature portraits to look at, and artist Joan Ellis Lutz will draw one of your family for a price.

EVERGREEN HOLLOW PARK (all ages)

Off Evergreen Avenue, Effingham 62401; (217) 342–4415. Off I–57/70, take exit 160. Turn south onto Keller Drive and then almost immediately east onto Evergreen Avenue. Open from 5:30 A.M. to 11 P.M. daily. **Free** *admission.*

Here's a good place for a picnic on a nice day. There's a playground for the kids, too. The park covers 27 acres and also includes four tennis courts that are lit at night, a flag football field, and three baseball and softball diamonds.

KLUTHE MEMORIAL SWIMMING POOL (all ages)

On Evergreen Avenue, in Evergreen Hollow Park, Effingham 62401; (217) 342–6870. Off I–57/70, take exit 160. Turn south onto Keller Drive and then almost immediately east onto Evergreen Avenue. Open from Memorial Day through Labor Day. Hours are 12:30 to 8:30 P.M. daily. Admission costs $3.50 for anyone age 16 or older and $3 for those age 15 or younger.

There are actually two pools here, one for swimming laps and one for just hanging out. The latter is great for wee ones, with a zero-depth end and a 4-foot maximum on the other end, plus a play area with frog slide. Older kids and teens will enjoy the big water slide. Pop and snacks are available from vending machines.

EVERGREEN MINI GOLF (age 3 and up)

On Evergreen Avenue, in Evergreen Hollow Park, Effingham 62401; (217) 342–2544. Off I–57/70, take exit 160. Turn south onto Keller Drive and then almost immediately east onto Evergreen Avenue. Open from April through September. Hours are 11 A.M. to 10 P.M. Monday through Thursday, 11 A.M. to 11 P.M. Friday and Saturday, and noon to 9 P.M. Sunday. Opening time changes to 4 P.M.

on school days. Cost is $3.50 per game for anyone age 13 or older and $2.50 per game for kids age 12 or younger.

This 18-hole miniature golf course benefits from its setting in Evergreen Park. The course includes a waterfall (which doesn't always work), a wishing well, and assorted animals. Soft drinks and snacks are offered at the concession counter.

HEART THEATRE (age 3 and up)

133 East Jefferson Avenue, Effingham 62401; (217) 342–6161. Call for current show titles and times. Tickets cost $4.50 for anyone age 12 or older and $3 for kids age 11 or younger.

This downtown theater stands across the street from the county courthouse. Its big, brightly lit marquee spells out tonight's first-run feature film. Buy your ticket at the booth outside, open the beveled glass doors, and walk into this art deco palace. They just don't make 'em like that anymore.

VILLAGE SQUARE MALL (all ages)

U.S. Highway 45 South, Effingham 62401; (217) 347–0623. Take exit 160 off I–57/70. Open from 9 A.M. to 9 P.M. Monday through Saturday and noon to 5 P.M. Sunday.

Effingham's only indoor mall is very basic: one rectangular strip with stores on both sides. But the fact that it has few frills—no boutique carts or potted plants—makes its open aisles great for strollers and wheelchairs. Bring along a few quarters, and your tot can ride on a tiny motorcycle, Noah's Ark, or merry-go-round. JCPenney anchors the mall at one end. Merchandise for sale in 30 stores includes clothing, shoes, music, and gifts; a Hallmark store sells Beanie Babies. The Play Land arcade has mostly video games geared toward older kids. There's no food court, so don't plan on a meal; an ice-cream cone will tide you over.

SILVER DOLLAR LANES (age 4 and up)

2300 South Banker, off U.S. Highway 45 South, Effingham 62401; (217) 342–3939. Near Village Square Mall. Call for current open bowling hours and prices. Cosmic Bowling from 8 to 11 P.M. Saturday.

This nondescript building has 24 lanes. For families with young children, there are lightweight balls, small shoes, and bumpers to fill the gutters. A game room has five pool tables.

Where to Eat

A&W. *1700 Avenue of Mid-America; (217) 342–0332.* Open from 10:30 A.M. to 9 P.M. Sunday through Thursday and 10 A.M. to midnight Friday and Saturday. This casual family eatery has a motif that's combination art deco and giant jukebox. The burgers and chicken strips are cooked to order and tasty, but the star attraction is the famous A&W root beer with that frosty-mug taste. Get it straight from the fountain in an iced glass mug, or order a root beer float or shake. Yum. $

Bobber Cafe. *In the Bobber Auto Truck Plaza on north Highway 32/33; (217) 347–7161.* Open 24 hours a day. As you might expect with all the roads crisscrossing Effingham, the town has a number of truck stops. They can be surprisingly good places to eat, serving hearty meals and often pies and other desserts with a homemade taste. Bobber Cafe is one of the most well known. $

Cracker Barrel. *1101 Avenue of Mid-America; (217) 347–7130.* Near the K Square Outlet Mall and Budgetel Inn. Hours are 6 A.M. to 10 P.M. Sunday through Thursday and 6 A.M. to 11 P.M. Friday and Saturday. See Restaurant Appendix for description. $

Pizza Man. *604 West Jefferson Avenue; (217) 347–7766.* West of downtown. Hours are 11 A.M. to 10 P.M. Monday through Saturday and 4 to 10 P.M. Sunday. This place is a local favorite. If you have a really big family, there's a *28-inch* pizza on the menu. $

TGIFriday's. *1208 North Keller Drive (Illinois Highway 32/33); (217) 342–9499.* In the same building as K Bowl lanes. Open from 11 A.M. to 10 P.M. Sunday through Thursday and 11 A.M. to midnight Friday and Saturday. See description in Restaurant Appendix. $$

Where to Stay

Anthony Acres Resort. *Beach Road; (217) 868–2950.* Off Highway 32, turn south at the Amoco station onto Lake Sara Road and continue about half a mile. Turn west onto Moccasin Road and continue about 1.5 miles, and then turn south onto Beach Road, a gravel road, and follow the signs to the resort office. If you'd like to stay in something more comfortable than a tent, you can rent a furnished "cabin" in a long row of peach-colored cinder-block units at this casual resort that's right next to the lake—great for fishing. Each cabin has a fully equipped kitchen, so you can cook up all those fish you catch, along with other food you bring along (hot dogs are a handy backup when the fish aren't biting). The resort has a little sand beach and small roped-off swimming area, a playground, a hiking area, and boat docks. The grounds are tidy, and the accommodations very basic but nice. $$$

AmeriHost Inn. *1304 West Evergreen Drive; (217) 342–5050.* Off I–57/70 at exit 160. This property has 61 rooms, some of them "deluxe whirlpool rooms" (at higher rates, of course), all with cable TV. Amenities include indoor pool, hot tub, sauna, and exercise room. Pets allowed. Continental breakfast is included in the room rate. $$

Baymont Inn & Suites. *1103 Avenue of Mid-America; (217) 342–2525 or (800) 301–0200.* Within walking distance of the K Square Factory Outlet Mall. This three-story hotel has 122 rooms, each with a coffeemaker and cable TV. Amenities include indoor pool and health club. Pets allowed. Room rate includes continental breakfast delivered to your room. $$

Best Inns of America. *1209 North Keller Drive (Illinois Highway 32/33); (217) 347–5141 or (800) 237–8466.* Across from Avenue of Mid-America. This chain property has 83 rooms with cable TV and an outdoor pool. Pets allowed. Special services offered for the hearing impaired. Room rate includes Special K breakfast of cold cereal, milk, juice, coffee, and toast. $

Econo Lodge. *1205 North Keller Drive (Illinois Highway 32/33); (217) 347–7131 or (800) 553–2666.* Across from Avenue of Mid-America. This property has 74 rooms with cable TV. It features an indoor pool, sauna, whirlpool, and exercise room. Pets allowed. Breakfast is included in the room rate. $

Keller Ramada Inn. *Keller Drive (Illinois Highway 32/33); (217) 342–2131 or (800) 535–0546.* This property, near K Bowl and Golfland, has 169 rooms and is the biggest motel in town. Amenities include both an indoor and an outdoor pool, a fitness center, and an on-site restaurant, Thelma's. Pets allowed. Room rate includes continental breakfast. $$$

For More Information

Greater Effingham Chamber of Commerce and Industry, *508 West Fayette Avenue, Effingham 62401; (217) 342–4147. E-mail: chamber@effingham.net. Internet: www.effingham.net/chamber.*

Vandalia

Population: 6,114. From Effingham, keep going west about 30 miles along Highway 40 or I–70 to where they intersect with Highway 51 and you'll reach Vandalia. This lovely town was the Illinois state capital from 1819 to 1839, before the capital moved to Springfield. It was in Vandalia that Abraham Lincoln was enrolled as a practicing attorney and assumed the first statewide office of a political career that eventually took him to the White House. Even before that, Vandalia was the western terminus of the nearly 600-mile-long

Cumberland Road, the main route taken by pioneers from the East to the West in the 1800s. The marble *Madonna of the Trail* statue, a memorial to the pioneer mothers of covered wagon days, stands on the northwest corner of the Vandalia Statehouse square to mark the spot where the Cumberland Road ended.

VANDALIA STATEHOUSE (age 5 and up)

315 West Gallatin Street, at the corner of Kennedy (U.S. Highway 51), Vandalia 62471; (618) 283–1161. About 1 mile south of I–70 on Highway 51. Open daily from 9 A.M. to 5 P.M. from March through October and 9 A.M. to 4 P.M. from November through February. Closed Thanksgiving, Christmas, and New Year's Day. Admission is **Free**, *but there is a clear plastic box for donations, with a suggested amount of $2 per adult and $1 per child. Accessible for wheelchairs in all areas except the rest rooms. No smoking inside the building.*

The white, Federal-style Vandalia Statehouse is the oldest existing capitol building in Illinois, dating back to 1936. The two-story building has legislative chambers on the upper floor and state offices on the lower floor. The cross-shaped interior design allows for great cross breezes with the doors open in milder weather. Friendly guides in period costume will gladly give you a personal tour, or you can just wander at leisure. Some original furnishings remain, along with other period pieces. (Explain a spittoon and watch your kid's face for the "ewwww!" reaction.) The guides may let your children sign their names with a quill pen on a piece of paper for a memorable souvenir. While all ages are admitted, a historical site such as this one will be of limited interest to kids who haven't yet started school and begun to hear about Abe Lincoln, thus the recommended minimum age of 5.

This statehouse was actually Vandalia's third capitol. The first, a two-story frame structure, was destroyed by fire in 1823. The second, hurriedly erected in 1824 so that the capital would not be moved to another town, was poorly constructed and by 1834 suffered from hazardously sagging floors and bulging walls. It was there that newly elected state legislator Abraham Lincoln first took his seat in 1834. The building was abandoned after the legislature adjourned in 1835. With workers salvaging what they could from the second building, the third capitol was constructed quickly (over a period of four months) but carefully and was opened in time for the legislative session that convened in December 1836, Lincoln's second term as a state representative. In 1837 Lincoln made his first protest against slavery here, a relatively mild statement asserting that "the institution of slavery is founded on both injustice and bad policy." The slavery issue was further debated by legislators, however, most notably Lincoln and Stephen Douglas. Amid charges of corruption (some things never change), the legislature in 1837 voted to move the capital to Springfield in 1840. And so it remains to this day. The Vandalia Statehouse served as the Fayette County Courthouse until 1933. Restoration from the 1930s through the 1970s brought the capitol back to its appearance during Lincoln's time.

FAYETTE COUNTY MUSEUM (age 8 and up)

Main Street at Kennedy Boulevard, Vandalia 62471; (618) 283–4866 or (616) 283–1534. Behind the Vandalia Statehouse, half a block north. Open from 10 A.M. to 4 P.M. Monday through Saturday and noon to 4 P.M. Sunday. Admission is **Free***, although donations in any amount are welcome.*

This brick building with bell tower was the First Presbyterian Church a hundred years ago, but now the pews are gone, and its roomy interior is a museum chock-full of Lincoln-era and other historical memorabilia. Two items actually used by Lincoln are here: his letter cabinet and an ax with his initials carved into the head. A mural painted across one wall shows what Vandalia looked like during Abe's time as a state legislator. There are shackles that were once used to restrain American slaves, a rusted testament to the degradation forced upon one group of human beings by another. Then there are farm implements and kitchen gadgets from everyday life in the mid-1800s, many of which are curiosities to us today. If you'd like an explanation of what some of these things are, a volunteer guide will be glad to provide explanations and show you around. If you're visiting in summer, you'll be glad to know that air-conditioning was installed in the museum in 1998. This museum will fascinate older kids, but it's too small to navigate a stroller through, and there are too many delicate items on open display that would pose a temptation for younger children to grab without any appreciation of their historical significance, thus the recommended minimum age of 8.

VANDALIA BOWL (age 4 and up)

2605 VanTran Avenue, Vandalia 62471; (618) 283–9294. Open bowling hours vary; call ahead to check. Cost is $2 per person per game for regular or bumper bowling. Shoes cost $1 per person.

This cozy bowling alley refurbished its 12 lanes in the summer of 1998, so your ball is likely to have a smooth roll toward the pins. For families it's helpful to have the gutters blocked with the soft bumpers (*everyone's* score improves that way!). There's no computerized score-keeping, however, so make sure someone in your group knows how to keep track of the strikes and spares.

VANDALIA LAKE (all ages)

North of town off Illinois Highway 185, Vandalia 62471; (618) 283–2728. Open from sunup to sundown daily. **Free** *admission for fishing or picnicking, $10 per day for a boating pass. Public beach for swimming (618–283–0081) is open in summer from 11:30 A.M. to 6 P.M. Monday through Thursday, 4 to 7 P.M. Friday, 10 A.M. to 7 P.M. Saturday, and 10 A.M. to 6 P.M. Sunday; admission fee charged.*

This 660-acre lake north of town was constructed in 1967. Visitors can walk in the woods that border the lake's 12 miles of shoreline or go fishing for largemouth bass, bluegill, and channel catfish. There is a marina for boaters. You can swim at the public beach or have a home-packed lunch at one of the picnic tables nearby. There's a campground if you'd like to stay the night.

Where to Eat

McDonald's. *820 VanTran Avenue; (618) 283–2711 or (800) 359–3080.* Accessible off I-70. Open from 6 A.M. to 11:30 P.M. Sunday through Thursday and 6 A.M. to 12:30 A.M. Friday and Saturday. Here you'll find the burger chain's usual fast-food fare, but this particular eatery is worth mentioning because it has an indoor playground for the kids. $

Pizza Hut. *1620 North Eighth Street; (618) 283–0530.* Hours are 11 A.M. to 10 P.M. Sunday through Thursday and 11 A.M. to 11 P.M. Friday and Saturday. See description in Restaurant Appendix. $

Ponderosa Steakhouse. *I–70 and U.S. Highway 41; (618) 283–4559.* Take exit 61 off I-70. Open from 11 A.M. to 9 P.M. Monday through Thursday, 11 A.M. to 10 P.M. Friday, 7 A.M. to 10 P.M. Saturday, and 7 A.M. to 9 P.M. Sunday. Lunch and dinner daily featuring steaks, of course, plus chicken, seafood, and sandwiches. Entrees include salad bar and buffet of hot side dishes. Breakfast buffet served Saturday and Sunday only. $

Where to Stay

Days Inn. *I–70 and U.S. Highway 51 North; (618) 283–4400.* Take exit 63 off I-70. This motel has 95 rooms with cable TV and an outdoor pool. Restaurant on premises. Room rates include deluxe continental breakfast. $$

Ramada Limited. *709 East Vine Street; (618) 658–6300 or (800) 272–6232.* This property has 42 rooms with cable TV. Amenities include an indoor swimming pool. Room rates include continental breakfast. $$

Travelodge. *I–70 and U.S. Highway 51 North; (618) 283–2363 or (800) 255–3050.* Take exit 63 off I-70. You'll recognize this 45-room property by the mock St. Louis arch out front. Rooms have cable TV and coffeemakers. There's also an outdoor pool and playground. Pets welcome. Room rates include continental breakfast. $

For More Information

Vandalia Chamber of Commerce Tourist Information Center, *1408 North Fifth Street, Vandalia 62471; (618) 283–2728.*

Internet: www.vandalia.net (community-sponsored, unofficial Web site).

Now let's take a look at the southern area along the Mississippi River, starting with Grafton.

Grafton

Population: 918. Founded in the 1800s, Grafton is reportedly the oldest town in Jersey County. A record flood in 1993 caused a great deal of destruction, but Grafton has kept on going. The Shafer Wharf Historic District has a variety of shops and historic buildings. Probably the biggest claim to fame here, however, is Pere Marquette State Park.

PERE MARQUETTE STATE PARK (all ages)

Illinois Highway 100, also called Great River Road, Grafton 62307; (618) 786–3323. Open from 7 A.M. to 9 P.M. daily. Admission is **Free**.

This scenic 7,900-acre park is the largest state park in Illinois. It was named after the French missionary priest Jacques Marquette (*père* is the French word for "father"), who accompanied the French-Canadian explorer Louis Jolliet on a canoe trip down the Mississippi in 1673. Today the park has 12 miles of hiking trails and 12 miles of equestrian trails that you can use to conduct your own expedition. To rent a mount, call Pere Marquette Riding Stables at (618) 786-2156. The park also has picnic areas and a boat dock. Interpretive programs are available, and there are concessions. Overnight accommodations are available in the park at the lodge or at a campground for tents and RVs.

RAGING RIVERS WATER PARK (all ages)

100 Palisades Parkway (just off Illinois Highway 100/Great River Road), Grafton 62037; (618) 786–2345. Open from late May through mid-September. Hours are 10:30 A.M. to 7 or 8 P.M. daily, the earlier closing time applying *at the beginning and end of the season. Admission costs $15.95 for anyone age 9 through 59, $12.95 for children age 3 through 8, and $8.95 for seniors age 60 or older. Tykes age 2 or younger get in free. Parking costs an additional $4 per vehicle. No glass containers or alcoholic beverages allowed. Internet: www.ragingrivers.com.*

White-water rapids and 1,000-foot-long body flumes earn this sprawling complex its name. There's a wave pool, too, which is a fun experience but not recommended for small children. Ditto the swishing Swirlpool. Tots can play instead in the Itty Bitty Surf City pool area with small water slides. The Tree House Harbor is like a playground in the water—but watch out for the giant water bucket that will tip over and dump its contents on anyone standing below. Visitors of all ages can float on an inner tube along Trickle Creek.

Where to Eat

Fin Inn. *Highway 100/Great River Road; (618) 786–2030.* Open from 11 A.M. to 9 P.M. daily. This restaurant specializes in river fish. You can also get steaks, seafood, and chicken. Twenty-three of the tables are alongside viewing windows that allow diners to peek in at river fish and turtles swimming in four 2,000-gallon aquariums. $$

O'Jan's Fish Stand. *101 West Main Street; (618) 786–2229.* Open year-round. Hours are 11 A.M. to 7 P.M. Monday through Thursday and 11 A.M. to 7:30 P.M. Friday and Saturday, although it may close as early as 5:30 or 6 P.M. in winter. This casual eatery overlooks the river. Sit outside on the open deck if the weather permits. Otherwise, there are about 10 tables inside, but the room is glassed in to retain the view. The food is mainly fish, of course. $

Where to Stay

Pere Marquette Lodge. *Illinois Highway 100, also called Great River Road; (618) 786–2331.* You can stay overnight in the state park in its spacious lodge, which has a 700-ton stone fireplace in the main hall. There are 50 rooms in the main lodge, plus 22 guest cabin rooms. Don't let the rustic look fool you, though—you'll also find an indoor pool with sauna and Jacuzzi and a restaurant that serves steaks, seafood, fried chicken, and a Sunday buffet, so you won't exactly be roughing it. $$$

For hotels and motels, see subsequent entry for Alton.

Alton

Population: 32,905. Illinois Highway 100 continues south along the Mississippi River from Grafton to Alton, a historic river town founded in 1818. If you're driving along during fall, keep your eyes open for the 200 to 400 bald eagles that spend the winter in the area each year. Around Alton the state highways also carry street names. As you may already know, Highway 100 is Great River Road. Highway 3 is Homer Adams Parkway or Beltline, Highway 140 is College Avenue, and Highway 143 is Berm Highway.

Along Highway 143, which parallels the Mississippi River, you'll find the **Melvin Price Lock & Dam No. 26.** Stop here and watch barges pass through; it's Free. Farther south, where Highway 143 intersects Highway 67, the Clark Bridge looms. This cable-stay bridge spanning the Mississippi looks like a giant pair of silver inverted Vs. There's no charge to drive across.

SAM VADALABENE BIKE TRAIL (all ages)

Along Great River Road between Alton and Grafton; (800) 258–6645. Open from sunrise to sunset daily. Free.

If you start at the Alton end, about 1 mile northwest of town, there's a free parking area. This paved trail extends along the Great River Road and ends at Pere Marquette State Park.

ALTON MUSEUM OF HISTORY AND ART (age 6 and up)

2809 College Avenue, Alton 62002; (618) 462–2763. Hours are 10 A.M. to 4 P.M. Monday through Friday and 1 to 4 P.M. Saturday and Sunday. Admission is $2 per adult and 50 cents per child.

This museum has a fine display on the Underground Railroad, the network of hiding places used by runaway slaves on their passage north to freedom. Alton was a key station for slaves who escaped from St. Louis while en route to auction. Local citizens hid the slaves in their attics, cellars, or barns, or even in local caves, to keep them safe from the trackers and bounty hunters who pursued them. (The Visitors Bureau offers a guided tour of some of these sites; call 800-258-6645.) Another museum exhibit of interest to kids concerns Robert Wadlow, known as the "Gentle Giant," whom the *Guiness Book of World Records* cites as the tallest man in history. Wadlow was born in 1918 and reached an adult height of 8 feet, 11.1 inches—just shy of 9 feet!—before his death in 1940. Even today's tallest NBA players would have had to look up to him. A life-size bronze statue of Wadlow stands outdoors across the street from the museum.

ALTON SQUARE MALL (all ages)

Alton Square Mall Drive at Homer Adams Parkway, Alton 62002; (618) 465–5500. Hours are 10 A.M. to 9:30 P.M. Monday through Saturday and noon to 6 P.M. Sunday. The mall is accessible for strollers and wheelchairs, but there are no ramps from one level to the other; you must use elevators in the department stores.

This two-story indoor shopping mall is anchored by JCPenney and Sears department stores and has numerous specialty shops. Kids are most likely to be interested in Kay-Bee Toys or the novelties in Spencer Gifts and Kirlin's Hallmark. Teens will find plenty of clothing and music stores. A food court features pizza, pasta, cookies, and ice cream.

Where to Eat

Midtown Restaurant. *1026 East Seventh Street (at Center Street); (618) 465–1321.* Open from 11 A.M. to about 10 P.M. Tuesday through Friday, 4 to about 11 P.M. Saturday, and 11:30 A.M. to about 10 P.M. Sunday. "We're a restaurant serving spirits, not a tavern serving food" is the philosophy at this cheerful local establishment run by Dorothy and Bob Metzger. The atmosphere—piano sing-alongs and friendly ambience—is as much a draw as the food, the specialty of which is fried chicken. There are "heart-healthy" options on the menu, too. $

Pizza Hut. *3096 Homer Adams Parkway; (618) 465–6600.* Hours are 11 A.M. to 11 P.M. Monday through Thursday, 11 A.M. to midnight Friday and Saturday, and noon to 11 P.M. Sunday. See Restaurant Appendix for description. $

Red Lobster. *170 Homer Adams Parkway; (618) 465–6554.* Hours are 11 A.M. to 9 P.M. Sunday through Thursday and 11 A.M. to 11 P.M. Friday and Saturday. See Restaurant Appendix for description. $$

Steak 'n Shake. *80 Homer Adams Parkway; (618) 466–7006.* Open 24 hours a day. See Restaurant Appendix for description. $

Where to Stay

Comfort Inn. *11 Crossroads Court; (618) 465–9999 or (800) 228–5150.* This comfortable chain property has 62 rooms and a heated indoor pool. Pets are allowed. Continental breakfast is included in the price of the room. $$

Holiday Inn. *3800 Homer Adams Parkway; (618) 462–1220 or (800) 465–4329. Fax (618) 462–0906.* This four-story hotel has 137 rooms. Amenities include Holidome recreation center with indoor pool, whirlpool, sauna, and fitness center. Ask about the package deal including Raging Rivers Water Park. $$$

Days Inn. *1900 Homer Adams Parkway; (618) 329–7466 or (800) 329–7466.* This 118-room property features indoor swimming pool and fitness center. Pets are allowed. $$$

For More Information

Greater Alton/Twin Rivers Convention and Visitors Bureau, *200 Piasa Street, Alton 62002; (618) 465–6676 or (800) 258–6645. Fax (618) 465–6151. Internet: www.altoncvb.org.*

Collinsville

Population: 22,446. Along Highway 159 south of I–55/70, you'll come to Collinsville. Look for the "World's Largest Catsup Bottle," a 170-foot-tall steel water tank and tower. It was built in 1949 and restored in 1995. If you arrive in early June, you'll be just in time for the International Horseradish Festival. Maybe you'll want to enter the root toss or the horseradish-eating (on hot dogs) contest. You'll also find the more typical crafts and a petting zoo at this free event. Another popular celebration in Collinsville is the Italian Fest in mid-September; there's no admission charge for that one, either. Probably the most famous attraction in the Collinsville area—and one you shouldn't miss—is Cahokia Mounds.

CAHOKIA MOUNDS (all ages)

Collinsville Road, Collinsville 62234; (618) 346–5160. Take I–255 south from I–55/70 (or north from I–64) to the Collinsville Road exit. Head 2 miles west on Collinsville Road to the Interpretive Center, which is open daily from 9 A.M. to 5 P.M. Admission is by donation; the suggested rate is $2 for adults and $1 for kids. A free picnic area on the grounds is open daily from 8 A.M. to dusk. The site is closed New Year's Day, Martin Luther King Jr. Day, Presidents Day, Veterans Day, general election day, Thanksgiving, and Christmas. If you can, try to visit around the end of September during the Heritage America festival, which celebrates Native American cultures with craft demonstrations and dance and music performances. Internet: medicine.wustl.edu/~mckinney/cahokia/cahokia.html.

This state historic site, which covers nearly 4,000 acres, contains the remains of the central section of what is reportedly the only prehistoric Indian city north of Mexico. The area was first inhabited around A.D. 700 and reached a population of nearly 20,000 at its peak in 1100 before declining over the next couple of centuries and finally being abandoned by the 1400s. Scholars don't know exactly why this once-thriving walled city with temples, plazas, rows of thatch-roofed houses, and sprawling agricultural fields died out; theories include disease, war, social unrest, and a climatic shift in the 1200s that could have reduced crop production and depleted resources needed to sustain the population. When French explorers arrived in the late 1600s, they found the Cahokia Indians, a subtribe of the Illini, living there and named the region after them. In 1982 Cahokia Mounds was designated a United Nations World Heritage Site for its importance in the study of North American prehistory, joining the illustrious company of such other World Heritage Sites as the Great Wall of China, the Taj Mahal, the Egyptian Pyramids, and the City of Rome.

The prehistoric earthen mounds were built in platform, conical, and ridgetop formations, the shape and size depending on the mound's intended use. The larger, flat-topped platform mounds served as bases for ceremonial buildings and homes for the wealthy elite. The other two kinds were used as markers or as burial plots for prominent people. Although the buildings are long gone, 68 of the original 120 mounds have been preserved, as has Woodhenge, a 410-foot-diameter circular sun calendar akin to England's Stonehenge. Little kids will like the open spaces, while students can mentally re-create the great cultures that once existed at the very spot on which they stand.

SPLASH CITY FAMILY WATERPARK (all ages)

10 Gateway Drive, off Illinois Highway 157 in Eastport Plaza, Collinsville 62234; (618) 346–4571. Open daily from late May through mid-August and Friday, Saturday, and Sunday only from mid-August through Labor Day; hours are 11 A.M. to 7 P.M. Admission costs $8.50 for adults and $6 for young people age 2 through 17. Children age 1 or younger get in free. All children age 7 or younger must be accompanied in the water by an adult. Nonswimming adults supervising older children may pay a $3 "just watching fee" in lieu of regular admission. Internet: www.collinsvillerec.com.

This new facility features two twisting water slides, a "lazy 8 river" for inner-tube floating, several swimming areas, a wet sand play area, and concessions. The zero-depth area has water jets, slide, and playhouse. A separate baby pool is enclosed by a gate. On a clear day, you can see the St. Louis Gateway Arch.

Where to Eat

Bob Evans. *600 North Bluff Road; (618) 344–1131.* Hours are 6 A.M. to 10 P.M. daily. See Restaurant Appendix for description. $

Wendy's. *401 North Bluff Road; (618) 345–7999.* Open from 10 A.M. to midnight daily. See Restaurant Appendix for description. $

Where to Stay

Best Western Heritage Inn. *2003 Mall Road; (618) 345–5660 or (800) 528–1234.* This tan, two-story motel has 81 rooms. Amenities include indoor swimming pool and Jacuzzi. Continental breakfast is included in the room rate. $$

Drury Inn. *602 North Bluff Road; (618) 345–7700.* This 123-room property has an indoor pool. It also allows pets. The room rate includes continental breakfast. $$

Holiday Inn. *1000 Eastport Plaza Drive; (618) 345–2800 or (800) 465–4329.* This huge chain property has 230 rooms. Amenities include indoor pool, sauna, and fitness center. Room rate includes continental breakfast. $$$

Motel 6. *295A North Bluff Road; (618) 345–2100.* This no-frills chain property has 86 rooms and an outdoor pool. $

For More Information

Collinsville Convention & Visitors Bureau, *One Gateway Drive, Collinsville 62234; (618) 345–4999. Internet: ci.collinsville.il.us.*

Fairview Heights

Population: 14,351. This town reportedly is one of the fastest-growing communities in southwestern Illinois. And where there's growth, there are families.

RECREATION STATION PLAYLAND (all ages)

Longacre Drive at South Ruby, in Longacre Park, Fairview Heights 62208; (618) 489–2040. Open year-round from 8 A.M. to sunset daily. **Free**.

At 16,000 square feet, this outdoor wooden playground structure is one of the biggest in the United States. In addition to the usual slides and ladders, it has a castle and a sunken pirate ship.

ST. CLAIR SQUARE (all ages)

I–64 at Illinois Highway 159 East, Fairview Heights 62208; (618) 632–7566. Hours are 10 A.M. to 9:30 P.M. Monday through Saturday and noon to 6 P.M. Sunday. Internet: www.stclairsquare.com.

This two-story indoor shopping mall has more than 140 stores, anchored by JCPenney, Sears, Dillard's, and Famous-Barr department stores. Parents can buy clothing for their young children at Children's Place and Gymboree. The mall has a food court.

Where to Eat

Old Country Buffet. *10850 Lincoln Trail, in Crossroads Center; (618) 398–4702.* Hours are 10:30 A.M. to 8:30 P.M. Monday through Thursday, 10:30 A.M. to 9 P.M. Friday, 8 A.M. to 9 P.M. Saturday, and 8 A.M. to 8:30 P.M. Sunday. See Restaurant Appendix for description. $

Olive Garden. *25 Ludwig Drive; (618) 397–8727.* Hours are 11 A.M. to 10 P.M. Sunday through Thursday and 11 A.M. to 11 P.M. Friday and Saturday. See Restaurant Appendix for description. $

Where to Stay

Best Western Camelot Inn. *305 Salem Place; (618) 624–3636 or (800) 528–1234.* Near the mall, this two-story tan motel has 55 rooms with cable TV. Amenities include indoor swimming pool and game room. $$

Fairfield Inn. *140 Ludwig Drive; (618) 398–7124 or (800) 228–2800.* This 63-room chain property in the Marriott family has an indoor pool. Continental breakfast is included in the room rate. $$

For More Information

Fairview Heights Chamber of Commerce, *10003 Bunkum Road, Fairview Heights 62208; (618) 397–3127. Internet: www.fairviewheights.com.*

Southwestern Illinois Tourism, *10950 Lincoln Trail, Fairview Heights 62208; (800) 442–1488.*

Belleville

Population: 42,785. This community traces its roots to the mid-1800s, when more than 6,000 German immigrants came to the area. Every day, so the story goes, the baker's wife walked around town delivering gingerbread and other baked goods from a basket balanced on her head. Today Belleville celebrates that heritage with the annual "Gingerbread Walk" festivities between Thanksgiving and New Year's Day.

ECKERT'S COUNTRY STORE AND FARMS (all ages)

3101 Greenmount Road, Belleville 62220; (618) 233–0513. Open from late May through October 31. Hours are 8 A.M. to 7 P.M. Monday through Saturday and 9 A.M. to 6 P.M. Sunday.

At this farmstead you can pick your own fruit, including strawberries in spring, peaches in summer, and apples in fall. Pumpkins are available in October. You'll get to ride out to the fields in a farm wagon. For the kids there's a small petting zoo on the grounds. You can have a light meal in the restaurant and buy jams and jellies in the Country Store.

FUN SPOT (age 5 and up)

1400 West Boulevard, Belleville 62220; (618) 234–4502. Tuesday session from 7 to 9 P.M. costs $1.50 per person. Friday or Saturday session from 7:30 to 11 P.M. costs $4 per person. Saturday afternoon sessions are from 1 to 3 P.M. and 3 to 5 P.M.; cost is $2.50 per person for either session or $3.50 for both. A Wednesday session from 1 to 3 P.M. is added in June; admission costs $2.50 per person. Closed in July. Skate rental for all sessions costs $1.25 for regular skates and $2.50 for in-line or speed skates.

This family-oriented roller rink's name says it all. If it doesn't run past your kids' bedtime, the Tuesday evening session—called "Cheapskate Night"—is a bargain.

Carlyle Lake Carlyle Lake is the largest artificially created lake in Illinois. The 15-mile-long lake covers about 26,000 acres within an area bordered by I-70 and U.S. Highway 40 to the north, U.S. Highway 51 to the east, U.S. Highway 50 to the south, and Illinois Highway 127 to the west. Seven recreation areas and two state parks are clustered around its shores. There are swimming beaches, nature trails, picnic areas, camping areas, and boat ramps and rentals. Call (618) 594–2484 for details.

SKYVIEW DRIVE-IN (all ages)

5700 North Belt West, Belleville 62220; (618) 233–4400. Open from spring through fall. First show starts around sunset. Call for current schedule of films and show times. Admission costs $6 per person age 13 or older and is free for the first two kids age 12 or younger in each vehicle; additional kids pay $2 each.

Have some old-fashioned fun by taking the family to the drive-in for a movie—or two. Each of the two screens plays a double feature of first-run films. Pay attention to the ratings, however, because sometimes the PG movie you want to see is paired with an R-rated second feature that you should skip.

Where to Eat

Ryan's Family Steakhouse. *4850 North Illinois Street; (618) 236–0579.* Hours are 10:45 A.M. to 9:30 P.M. Sunday through Thursday and 10:45 A.M. to 10:30 P.M. Friday and Saturday. In addition to the specialty steaks, the highlight here is the Megabar, a buffet of carved meats, salad, vegetables, and other side dishes. The Megabar alone is plenty for some diners. $

Pizza Hut. *605 Carlyle Road; (618) 235–6565.* Hours are 11 A.M. to 10 P.M. Monday through Thursday, 11 A.M. to 11 P.M. Friday and Saturday, and 11:30 A.M. to 10 P.M. Sunday. See Restaurant Appendix for description. $

Where to Stay

Days Inn. *2120 West Main Street; (618) 234–9400 or (800) 624–9288.* This two-story chain property has 80 rooms with color TV. There is an outdoor swimming pool. Pets are allowed. Room rate includes continental breakfast. $

For More Information

Belleville Tourism, *216 East A Street, Belleville 62220; (800) 677–9255.*

Centralia

Population: 14,274. Centralia was named by the Illinois Central Gulf Railroad for its location at about midpoint in south-central Illinois. During the 1990s downtown development around the intersection of U.S. Highway 51 and Illinois Highway 161 and a $1.6 million streetscape improvement project gave the city a face-lift. There's a story behind the Egyptian motif you may notice on some of the buildings: Back in 1831 a late spring and an early killing frost left many northern Illinois counties with virtually no corn to harvest. Milder weather in the south left that region with plenty, so northerners "went down to buy corn in Egypt," a reference to the biblical Genesis story with Joseph and his brothers. So if you hear people around these parts talking about Egypt, they probably don't mean the country in Africa.

CENTRALIA CARILLON (all ages)

114 North Elm, Centralia 62801; (618) 533–4381. Tours are available upon advance request and conducted between 8 A.M. and 5 P.M. Monday through Friday. Cost is $1.50 for adults and $1 for children. The bell tower can be reached only by stairs. Internet: www.members.accessus.net/~carlo.

The most prominent feature of Centralia's refurbished downtown is the Centralia Carillon. Built during the early 1980s, it stands 160 feet tall and has 65 bells, which you can see through the clear glass windowpanes that enclose the belfry. Nearly all the bells are inscribed on their outer surface. The smallest weighs 20 pounds and has a diameter of 8 inches; the largest weighs 5½ tons and measures nearly 80 inches in diameter; the total bell weight is 30½ tons. The bells are played by a local carillonneur who climbs 173 steps to reach the 7½-foot, 5½-octave keyboard. Tunes range from classical to pop. There's a small museum in the base of the tower. A small park with a fountain surrounds the carillon.

FOUNDATION PARK (all ages)

Private Park Driveway, off East McCord Street (Illinois Highway 161), Centralia 62801; (618) 533–0001. Open year-round from dawn to sunset daily. Admission is **Free**. *Alcoholic beverages are prohibited.*

On the east side of the city is a 235-acre nature park called Foundation Park. It has a picnic area, a fitness trail, two stocked ponds for fishing, and a wintertime ice rink. Engine 2500, a preserved classic steam engine, is on display in the park. You might catch an outdoor concert in the Joy Bowl, a 5,000-seat amphitheater. There's no admission charge to the park—unless you visit during the Annual Balloon Fest in mid-August. Then it costs $2 per adult and $1 per student age 7 through college (age 6 or younger free) to get in, plus another $2 for parking. But you'll probably think it's worth it to see more than 40 hot air balloons making a mass ascension each morning and evening. A few unusual ones show up, too—one year they included a three-tier birthday cake, a clown, a jester, a bald eagle, and Tony "They're GRRRREAT!" the Tiger. Artisans demonstrate such skills as woodworking and dulcimer playing, and you can choose from among about two dozen concessionaires if you get hungry. Fireworks top off the festivities. The crowd ranges from 50,000 to 75,000, so you'll have company.

FAIRVIEW PARK POOL (all ages)

Off West McCord Street between Brooks Avenue and Buena Vista Terrace, Centralia 62801; (618) 533–7676. The park is open year-round, and park admission is **Free**. *The swimming complex is open daily during summer from noon to 5 P.M. and 6 to 8 P.M. Admission to the pools costs $2 for adults and $1.50 for young people age 3 through 17; children age 2 or younger get in free.*

Another park in Centralia is Fairview Park, which has a swimming complex with three pools. The main swimming pool measures 60 feet by 80 feet and is 4 to 5 feet deep; the wading pool is 30 feet by 50 feet and 1 to 2 feet deep; and the diving pool has 1- and 3-meter boards and is 13 feet deep. There are bleachers where you can watch the action.

Where to Eat

The Family Table. *405 West Noleman; (618) 532–9711.* Hours are 5 A.M. to 8 P.M. Monday through Saturday and 5 A.M. to 2 P.M. Sunday. Serving breakfast, lunch, and dinner. Steaks, catfish, and specials such as meat loaf or roast beef will fill you up for dinner. Children get smaller portions and $1 off the price of entrees on the main menu. $

JJ's Buffet. *123 North Locust; (618) 532–3663.* Open from 10:30 A.M. to 9 P.M. Monday through Saturday and 10 A.M. to 8 P.M. Sunday. Choose from a half dozen entrees and serve yourself from the big salad bar. The price is for all you can eat, including desserts and drinks. $

Pizza Hut. *725 West Broadway; (618) 532–2782.* Hours are 11 A.M. to 10 P.M. Monday through Thursday and 11 A.M. to 11 P.M. Friday, Saturday, and Sunday. See Restaurant Appendix for description. $

Where to Stay

Bell Tower Inn. *200 East Noleman; (618) 533–1300.* This local lodging half a block from the carillon has 58 rooms and an indoor pool. Pets are allowed. $

For More Information

Greater Centralia Chamber of Commerce, *130 South Locust, Centralia 62801; (618) 532–6789. Internet: www.centraliail.com.*

Mount Vernon

Population: 16,988. Southeast of Centralia is Mount Vernon, which, like Effingham, lies at the crossroads of numerous thoroughfares: I–57 and I–64 and Illinois Highways 15, 37, 142, and 148. Mount Vernon was established in 1819 and is the seat of Jefferson County.

CEDARHURST (age 3 and up)

Richview Road, west off Highway 37, Mount Vernon 62864; (618) 242–1236. Hours are 10 A.M. to 5 P.M. Tuesday through Saturday and 1 to 5 P.M. Sunday; closed Monday and all national holidays. General admission is **Free**, *but donations are appreciated. There are fees for the craft fair and for some special programs and special events.*

One of the most interesting places in town is the Cedarhurst cultural facility. Cedarhurst displays paintings by American artists from the late 19th and early 20th centuries. Its Children's Gallery offers changing exhibitions and special programs and activities. Outdoors you can wander among 30 artworks in the Sculpture Park or stroll the half-mile Juniper Ridge Nature Trail. The popular Cedarhurst Craft Fair takes place here the first weekend after Labor Day.

HISTORICAL VILLAGE (all ages)

North 27th Street, Mount Vernon 62864; (618) 246–0033. Open from 10 A.M. to 4 P.M. Saturday and 1 to 4 P.M. Sunday. Admission is **Free**.

Structures dating from 1873 to the 1920s stand here. They include log cabins, a one-room schoolhouse, a church, a blacksmith's shop, and a general store featuring antique tools.

WHEELS THROUGH TIME (all ages)

1121B Veterans Memorial Drive, Mount Vernon 62864; (618) 244–4118. Open from 9 A.M. to 5 P.M. Monday through Friday and 9 A.M. to 4 P.M. Satuday; closed Sunday. Admission is **Free**.

Located behind the Harley-Davidson Motorcycle Shop, this museum has vintage bicycles, racing motorcycles, and cars on display.

Rend Lake Area Due south of Mount Vernon is Rend Lake, a huge recreation spot and a habitat for great blue herons and assorted other waterfowl and shorebirds. With 19,000 acres of water contained within 162 miles of shoreline, it is the second largest artificially created lake in Illinois; only Carlyle Lake is bigger. The Army Corps of Engineers operates six major recreation areas around Rend Lake, with campgrounds, beaches, picnic and wildlife areas, and a marina. Facilities and fees vary, so for detailed information write: Management Office, U.S. Army Corps of Engineers, Rural Route 3, Benton 62812, or call the Rend Lake Visitor Center at (618) 724–2493. Internet: www.rendlake.com.

A good place to start your trip to the area is at the **Rend Lake Environmental Learning Center,** at the east end of Main Dam Road; (618) 439–7430. A must-see attraction in the Rend Lake area is the **National Coal Museum** near West Frankfort; (618) 937–2625. Visitors are taken into a real coal mine, 600 feet underground.

Where to Eat

Cracker Barrel. *4425 Fairfax Drive; (618) 242–9110.* Hours are 6 A.M. to 10 P.M. Sunday through Thursday and 6 A.M. to 11 P.M. Friday and Saturday. See Restaurant Appendix for description. $

Lone Star Steakhouse. *122 Outlet Avenue, off I–57; (618) 244–7827.* Hours are 11 A.M. to 10 P.M. Sunday through Thursday and 11 A.M. to 11 P.M. Friday and Saturday. Steaks are the obvious specialty at this family-oriented chain restaurant. $$

Pizza Hut. *3519 Broadway; (618) 244–3848.* Open from 11 A.M. to midnight Sunday through Thursday and 11 A.M. to 1 A.M. Friday and Saturday. See Restaurant Appendix for description. $

Where to Stay

Holiday Inn. *I–57/I–64 and Route 15; (618) 244–7100 or (800) 243–7171.* This five-story hotel has 236 rooms with cable TV. Amenities include indoor pool and whirlpool. Pets are allowed. $$

Motel 6. *333 South 44th Street (I–57 and Route 15); (618) 244–2383 or (800) 466–8356.* This budget chain motel has 78 rooms and an outdoor pool. Pets are allowed. $

Villager. *I–57 and Route 15; (618) 244–3670.* This former Ramada Inn was remodeled in 2000. It has 188 rooms and an indoor pool. Pets are allowed. $$

For More Information

Mount Vernon Convention and Visitors Bureau, *I–57 and I–64, P.O. Box 2580, Mount Vernon 62864; (800) 252–5464. Internet: www.southernillinois.com/tourism.*

Carbondale

Population: 27,033. Carbondale sits atop the upper edge of the Shawnee National Forest along Illinois Highway 13. U.S. Highway 51 runs straight south through town. Carbondale has a number of historic homes, many of them still private residences, dating back to the turn of the 20th century. Drive along Poplar, Walnut, and Main Streets to catch a glimpse of some. If you're into architecture, look for Victorian, Italianate, and Queen Anne styles.

Carbondale is the home of Southern Illinois University. The SIU mascot is the *saluki,* a breed of dog, so don't be surprised if you see that word crop up in the names of stores and restaurants. Call (618) 453-2121 for information on university-related attractions and events.

A Really Big Show The Egyptian Drive-Inn on Illinois Highway 148 just off Illinois Highway 13 boasts the "world's largest screen (12 stories high)." It opened in 1948 and is still drawing patrons to its nightly summer double features. Gates open at 7 P.M.; the first show starts around 8:30 P.M. Admission is $4 for anyone age 13 or older and free for kids age 12 or younger. Call (618) 988-8116 to hear what's playing.

WOODLAWN CEMETERY (all ages)

405 East Main Street, Carbondale 62901; (800) 526–1500. Open daily; **Free**.

The first Memorial Day service was observed in Carbondale's Woodlawn Cemetery in 1866. The cemetery has more than 60 graves of Civil War soldiers, and it is on the National Register of Historic Places. You can stop by anytime to pay your respects.

POPLAR CAMP BEACH (all ages)

At Cedar Lake, off U.S. Highway 51 south of Carbondale; (800) 526–1500. Open during summer. Hours are 9:30 A.M. to 5:30 P.M. Monday through Friday and 9:30 A.M. to 7 P.M. Saturday and Sunday. Admission costs $1.50 for anyone age 5 or older; children age 4 or younger get in **Free**.

Here's a lovely place for a day at the beach. In addition to the lake, the area has rest rooms, picnic tables, and concessions. Lifeguards are on duty in case of emergencies. Away from the beach area, Cedar Lake is also a popular spot for fishing. Anglers go after bass, bluegill, crappie, and catfish.

UNIVERSITY MALL (all ages)

1235 East Main Street, Carbondale 62901; (618) 529–3681. Hours are 10 A.M. to 9 P.M. Monday through Saturday and noon to 5:30 P.M. Sunday. The mall is accessible for wheelchairs and strollers.

This one-story indoor shopping mall is anchored by JCPenney, K's, and Famous-Barr department stores. It has about 100 shops. Kids are drawn to the Science Center. The mall has a food court. From time to time the mall features special exhibits.

JEFFERSON COUNTY STAGE COMPANY (age 3 and up)

101 North Washington, Carbondale 62901; (618) 549–5466. Box office hours are 5 to 7 P.M. Monday through Friday and noon to 4 P.M. Saturday. Call for the current schedule.

Plays for children are presented occasionally by this nonprofit organization of amateur actors from the community.

Where to Eat

Denny's. *1915 West Sycamore; (618) 457–7196.* Open 24 hours a day, serving breakfast, lunch, and dinner. $

Lone Star Steakhouse. *3160 East Main Street; (618) 529–2556.* Open from 11 A.M. to 10 P.M. Sunday through Thursday and 11 A.M. to 11 P.M. Friday and Saturday. Adults can enjoy such beef cuts as rib eye, filet mignon, and prime rib. Fried chicken, fajitas, and other items are available for those who don't want red meat. The $4.95 children's menu price includes beverage and ice cream along with the main dish; entrees include chicken tenders and grilled cheese. $$

Steak 'n Shake. *1365 East Main Street; (618) 457–1668.* Open 24 hours a day. See Restaurant Appendix for description. $

Where to Stay

Best Inns of America. *1345 East Main; (618) 529–4801 or (800) 237–8466.* This 86-room motel has an outdoor pool and allows pets. The room rate includes a "Special K breakfast" of cold cereal, milk, juice, coffee, and toast. $

Holiday Inn. *800 East Main Street; (618) 529–1100 or (800) 465–4329.* This property has 95 rooms. Amenities include the Holidome, with an indoor swimming pool and a Jacuzzi and games. Pets are allowed. The motel's Saluki Cafe is a full-service restaurant that also serves a Sunday brunch. The room rate includes continental breakfast. $$$

Comfort Inn. *1415 East Main; (618) 549–4244 or (800) 228–5150.* This 64-room property has an indoor pool. Continental breakfast is included in the room rate. $$

Devil's Kitchen Lake Campground. *1625 Tacoma Lake Road, about 12 miles south of town; (618) 457–5004.* Open from early March through late November. Bringing your own gear, you'll pay $15 per night for a spot with electric and water hookup or $10 for one without electricity. You can rent an RV at the lake for $30 to $55 per night. RV rentals must be reserved in advance. Campers and day visitors can rent a canoe or kayak. The rate is $10 per boat for the first hour, $3 for each additional hour. $

For More Information

Carbondale Convention and Tourism Bureau, *1245 East Main Street, Suite A-32, Carbondale 62901; (800) 526–1500. Internet: www.cctb.org.*

Chester

Population: 8,194. Along Illinois Highway 3, at the junction with Illinois Highway 150 near the Mississippi River, is the town of Chester. This historic river town was established in 1819. Elzie C. Segar, creator of the cartoon character Popeye, was a native son whose legacy lives on with the **Elzie C. Segar Memorial Park** downtown. You'll recognize it because of the giant Popeye statue. The Popeye's Picnic festival is held during early to mid-September, featuring a parade, a carnival, food stands, a flea market, music, and fireworks.

Four miles northeast of Chester on Highway 150 is **Mary's River Covered Bridge,** which was built in 1854 and has a 90-foot span. It was originally part of a planked road between Chester and Bremen.

SPINACH CAN COLLECTIBLES (all ages)

1001 State Street, Chester 62233; (618) 826–4567. Hours vary; call ahead. Internet: www.midwest.net/orgs/ace1. E-mail: spinach@midwest.net.

Located inside Chester's historic 1875 Opera House building, this is the place to be for all things Popeye. The store sells Popeye merchandise, is the headquarters of the Official Popeye Fan Club, and houses the

Mini Popeye Museum full of Popeye collectibles from around the world. You can buy other kinds of collectibles here, too, including trading cards and comic books.

RANDOLPH COUNTY MUSEUM AND ARCHIVES (age 7 and up)

1 Taylor Street, Chester 62233; (618) 826–5000. Open from 12:30 to 3:30 P.M. Monday, Thursday, and Friday. Admission is **Free**.

For a sampling of French colonial and Civil War memorabilia, check out the Randolph County Museum and Archives. The museum building itself is a piece of history, built in 1864. It is staffed entirely by volunteers, many of whom are retirees with personal stories to share about the area. Next door is the Randolph County Courthouse, whose glassed-in observation deck affords a panoramic view of the Mississippi River Valley. The county commemorated its bicentennial in 1995.

RANDOLPH STATE FISH AND WILDLIFE AREA (all ages)

Off U.S. Highway 150, 5 miles northeast of Chester; (618) 826–2706. Open year-round, from sunrise to about 10 P.M. daily. Admission is **Free**. *Pets must be kept on leashes at all times.*

Randolph County Lake, an artificially created clear-water lake completed in 1961, is the centerpiece of this fish and wildlife area. The lake is stocked with bass, bluegill, channel catfish, rainbow trout, redear, and walleye, and several other kinds of game fish also have found their way in. Bring your own gear or rent tackle and buy bait at the on-site concession stand. You can also rent a boat there or bring your own; the lake has a boat ramp. Six picnic areas feature shelters, tables, grills, and water fountains, and there's a small playground. Hiking trails wind through the woods for visitors on foot, and there are 8 miles of equestrian trails if you have a horse. Campsites are available for overnight guests. Strictly regulated small-game hunting is allowed for properly licensed visitors who check in at the park office.

Where to Eat

Reids' Harvest House Smorgasbord. *2440 State Street; (618) 826–3034.* Open from 7 A.M. to 8:30 P.M. Tuesday through Thursday and Sunday and 7 A.M. to 9 P.M. Friday and Saturday; closed Monday. About half a mile down the road from the motel is this restaurant serving buffet-style breakfast, lunch, and dinner. $

Where to Stay

Best Western Reids' Inn. *2150 State Street; (618) 826–3034 or (800) 528–1234.* This two-story brick motel has 46 rooms with cable TV. Amenities include indoor hot tub and outdoor swimming pool. Room rate includes continental breakfast. $$

For More Information

Randolph County Tourism Committee, *1 Taylor Street, Chester 62233; (618) 826–5000.*

Metropolis

Population: 6,734. U.S. Highway 45 will take you to Metropolis. As you might guess, Superman is a big deal here—literally. A 15-foot-tall statue of the Man of Steel stands guard in front of the Massac County Courthouse on Superman Square downtown.

SUPER-MUSEUM (age 3 and up)

On Superman Square, downtown Metropolis 62960; (618) 524–5518. Open daily from 9 A.M. to 6 P.M. Admission costs $3 per person age 6 or older and is free for children age 5 or younger.

You can learn more about the caped hero in the Super-Museum. Its collection spans 60 years and is worth $2.5 million. The museum is housed within a gift shop full of souvenirs.

FORT MASSAC STATE PARK (all ages)

1308 East Fifth Street, Metropolis 62960; (618) 524–9321. The park is open year-round from 7 A.M. to 10 P.M. daily. Museum hours are 10:30 A.M. to 5:30 P.M. daily. Admission is **Free** *for both.*

Besides Superman, the other prime attraction in the area is Fort Massac State Park on the banks of the Ohio River, south off U.S. Highway 45. Dedicated in 1908 as the first Illinois state park, it features a reconstructed timber fort that's a replica of one originally built in 1794. The park's museum has a collection of uniforms and equipment used by soldiers who were stationed at the fort. You can enjoy the 1,450 acres of parkland for picnicking, hiking, boating, and camping.

The third weekend in October at the park is reserved for the Fort Massac Encampment, two days of reenactments of battles and military maneuvers from the period 1750–1812. Food is cooked over open fires, and crafts are handmade the old-fashioned way.

ELIJAH P. CURTIS HOME (age 8 and up)

405 Market Street, Metropolis 62960; (618) 524–5120. Open from April through September, by appointment only. Admission is **Free**, *but donations are welcome.*

This historic home with unusual woodwork was built in 1870 and belonged to Major Elijah P. Curtis, who served in the Civil War. The Massac County Historical Society operates the home as a museum and includes it in home tours around Christmastime.

BOB'S BOWLING AND RECREATION CENTER (age 4 and up)

Route 45 East, Metropolis 62960; (618) 524–9900. Open from 5 P.M. to 1 A.M. Monday through Friday and 2 to 10 P.M. Saturday and Sunday. Cost is $2.25 per person per game, plus 50 cents per person for shoes.

This local bowling alley has 16 lanes. It also features pool tables, video games, and a snack bar.

Shawnee National Forest Sprawling across the far southern portion of Illinois, from the Mississippi River border on the west to the Ohio River border on the east, is the massive and beautiful Shawnee National Forest. The national forest encompasses many state parks, including Cave-in-Rock, Dixon Springs, Giant City, and Horseshoe Lake, and the Trail of Tears State Forest. Lake Thunderhawk and Little Grassy Lake also lie within it. You'll find hiking trails and spots for picnicking, fishing, and camping in these areas. Shawnee National Forest features such natural wonders as the Pomona Natural Bridge, the Burden Falls waterfall, and the Garden of the Gods. The Crab Orchard National Wildlife Refuge is also nestled within Shawnee National Forest. The Golconda Marina draws many boaters who come to enjoy the Ohio River Recreation Area. For a complete listing of Shawnee National Forest attractions—plus detailed information on hiking, backpacking, camping, and picnicking—contact the Shawnee National Forest Headquarters, 50 Highway 145 South, Harrisburg 62946; (618) 253-7114. A really useful, complete guide to the state parks can be obtained by writing to the Illinois Department of Conservation, Lincoln Tower Plaza, 524 South Second Street, Springfield 62701-1787.

BREMER'S ORCHARD (all ages)

5446 Orchard Road, Metropolis 62960; (618) 524–5783. Open from 7 A.M. to 7:30 P.M. daily in season. Call ahead to check availability.

This peach orchard is on a family farm. It's not a pick-your-own place, however, and it doesn't have any other amenities, so come here if you just want to buy a box of fresh fruit to take home with you.

Where to Eat

Montego's. *1201 East Eighth Street; (618) 524–4059.* Across from Fort Massac State Park, on U.S. Highway 45. Hours are 11 A.M. to 10 P.M. Sunday through Thursday and 11 A.M. to 11 P.M. Friday and Saturday. This local restaurant features a pizza buffet on Thursday, Saturday, and Sunday nights and an all-you-can-eat catfish fry Friday night. At other times you can order steaks, ribs, and pizza off the menu and nibble from the salad bar. $

Farley's Cafeteria. *613 Market Street; (618) 524–7226.* Open from 3:30 to 7 P.M. Wednesday through Saturday; closed Sunday through Tuesday. Walk through the buffet line and select your preferred combination of entree, side dish, salad, dessert, and beverage. Prices are a la carte, so don't let your eyes be bigger than your stomach. $

Pizza Hut. *Highway 45 at I–24; (618) 524–3820.* Hours are 11 A.M. to 11 P.M. Sunday through Thursday and 11 A.M. to midnight Friday and Saturday. See Restaurant Appendix for description. $

Hardee's. *601 Ferry Street; (618) 524–2536.* Hours are 6 A.M. to 11 P.M. daily. The flavorful biscuits are great for breakfast, and the big roast beef sandwich makes a tasty meal. $

Where to Stay

Best Inns of America. *2055 Fifth Street; (800) 237–8466.* This motel has 63 rooms and an indoor pool. It allows small pets. The room rate includes a "Special K breakfast" of cold cereal, milk, juice, coffee, and toast. $

Best Western Metropolis Inn. *U.S. Highway 45 at I–24; (618) 524–3723.* This 56-room property has an indoor pool and allows pets. Room rate includes continental breakfast. $$

Comfort Inn. *2118 East Fifth Street; (618) 524–7227 or (800) 228–5150.* Take exit 37 off I-24. This chain motel has 52 rooms with cable TV. Amenities include an indoor heated pool. Continental breakfast is included in the room rate. $$

For More Information

Massac County Chamber of Commerce and Tourism, *610 Market Street, P.O. Box 188, Metropolis 62960; (618) 524–2714 or (800) 949–5740.*

Cairo

Population: 4,846. If you head south on U.S. Highway 51 to the southern tip of the state, you'll reach Cairo, the end of the line for Illinois. The name of this town is pronounced *KAY-roh,* not like its larger namesake in Egypt. Cairo was established in 1857.

U.S. CUSTOM HOUSE (age 7 and up)

Fourteenth and Washington Avenues, Cairo 62914; (618) 734–1019. Hours are 10 A.M. to noon and 1 to 3 P.M. Monday through Friday. Admission is **Free***, although donations are welcome. The first floor is accessible for wheelchairs.*

Check in at the U.S. Custom House. Completed in 1872 and preserved and placed on the National Register of Historic Places 101 years later, the building once held a U.S. post office and a federal court. Today it's a museum with historical artifacts on the first floor. You can see the desk used by General Ulysses S. Grant while he was headquartered in Cairo during the Civil War.

FORT DEFIANCE STATE PARK (all ages)

U.S. Highway 51, 2 miles south of Cairo 62914; (618) 734–2737. Open year-round from 9 A.M. to 10 P.M. daily. Admission is **Free**.

Fort Defiance State Park overlooks the confluence of the Mississippi and Ohio Rivers. The fort is the post that General Grant commanded. You can have a picnic here, but camping is not allowed. The Cairo Riverboat Days Festival is held here in early October.

Where to Eat

Andy's Drive-In. *2308 Sycamore; (618) 734–4361.* Open from 9 A.M. to 8 P.M. Monday through Friday and 10 A.M. to 8 P.M. Saturday; closed Sunday. You can eat in your car, but you have to go get the food yourself—there are no carhops here. There is a dine-in area, however. The fare is burgers, fries, and typical drive-in food. $

Shemwell's Barbecue. *1102 Washington; (618) 734–0165.* Hours are 8 A.M. to 8:30 P.M. Monday through Thursday, 8 A.M. to 9 P.M. Friday and Saturday, and 10 A.M. to 9 P.M. Sunday. This is one of several spots in town that serve barbecue. $

Where to Stay

Days Inn. *Rural Route 1; (618) 734–0215 or (800) 325–2525.* This two-story chain property has 38 rooms and an outdoor pool. Pets are allowed. $

For More Information

Cairo Chamber of Commerce,
Cairo 62914; (618) 734–2737.

Other Things to See and Do in Southern Illinois

January: American Bald Eagle Tours, Alton; (800) 258-6645

February: Living History Weekend at Fort Massac State Park, Metropolis; (618) 524-9321

Business Showcase, Godfrey; (618) 467-2280

March: March Madness Archery Shoot, Eddyville; (618) 672-4316

April: Great Grafton Westfest Weekend; (618) 786-2315

Mid-America Morel Mushroom Festival, Jonesboro; (618) 833-8697

May: Herbfest, Dongola; (800) 635-0282

Mayfest, Cobden; (618) 893-2557

June: Superman Celebration, Metropolis; (800) 248-4373

Rendezvous at Fort de Chartres, Prairie du Rocher; (618) 284-7230

Route 66 Festival, Edwardsville; (800) 442-1488

July: Massac County Youth Fair, Metropolis; (800) 248-4373

Most communities have a Fourth of July celebration, and many county fairs are in July and August.

August: Olden Days, Brighton; (800) 226-6632

Cobden Peach Festival; (800) 248-4373

Ste. Genevieve Jour de Fete; (618) 826-2477

September: Effingham Transportation Celebration; (800) 772-0750

Past to Present Festival, Harrisburg; (618) 252-8391

Murphysboro Apple Festival; (618) 684-6421

October: Annual Fall Festival and Cookout, Alto Pass; (618) 893-2344

Riverboat Days, Cairo; (618) 734-2735

Kampsville Old Settler's Days; (618) 653-4563

Oktoberfest, Maeystown; (800) 442-1488

November: Veterans Day Parade, Anna; (618) 833-5182

Deer Festival, Golconda; (618) 683-6246

December: Old Fashioned Christmas, Vandalia; (618) 283-1161

Christmas Stroll and House Tour, Okawville; (800) 442-1488

Restaurant Appendix

You'll find a number of chain restaurants throughout Illinois. These are detailed descriptions of some that are most appropriate for families. While most restaurants in a chain are similar, there may be slight variations among individual restaurants.

BAKERS SQUARE

This chain started out many years ago as Poppin' Fresh Pies, serving mainly pie and light soup-and-sandwich meals. Over the years it changed its name to Bakers Square and broadened both its menu and its hours. Now most locations serve both light and hearty fare for breakfast, lunch, and dinner. The kids' menu is $1.99, not including drink or pie, and has such entrees as burgers, chicken strips, macaroni and cheese, and roast turkey. *Locations include:*

Alsip
Bloomington
Bourbonnais
Bradley
Burbank
Crystal Lake
Chicago
Cherry Valley
Deerfield
Downers Grove
Elk Grove Village
Glendale Heights
Gurnee
Hanover Park
Hoffman Estates
Homewood
Joliet
LaGrange
Lansing
Libertyville
Matteson
Melrose Park
Mount Prospect
Naperville
Niles
Normal
Orland Park
Palatine
Palos Heights
Rolling Meadows
Springfield
St. Charles
Villa Park
Westmont
Wheaton
Willowbrook
Wilmette

BOB EVANS

Internet: www.bobevans.com

Maybe you've seen his sausage in the supermarket. That's how ol' Bob began back in 1946. He started making his own recipe to serve at his truck stop in Ohio. Eventually he built a restaurant to serve the famous sausage, and other things, and then another, and another. There are now more than 400 Bob Evans restaurants in 20 states. They share a sort of red-barnish facade with the name emblazoned in yellow, and inside the decor is folksy. Sausage remains the centerpiece of the breakfast menu, surrounded by such hearty accompaniments as biscuits and gravy, eggs, or hotcakes. The lunch and dinner menus feature burgers and other sandwiches, and country-cookin' entrees such as chicken and noodles, meat loaf, turkey and dressing, and country fried steak. Sandwiches fall in the $4 to $4.50 range, entrees in the $6 to $9 range. Only nonalcoholic beverages are served. The children's menu costs about $2, not including drink, and features pizza, hot dog, spaghetti, cheeseburger, chicken nibbles, and a turkey dinner. *Locations include:*

Alsip
Bloomington
Bolingbrook
Champaign
Collinsville
Danville
Decatur
East Peoria
Fairview Heights
Joliet
Lansing
Marion
Naperville
Normal
Pekin
Peoria
Peru
Schaumburg
Springfield

BOSTON MARKET

Internet: www.boston-market.com

This chain offers sit-down food at close to fast-food speed and prices. The most expensive individual meal shouldn't cost more than $6, not including the drink, and you can buy a family-style meal that drives the per-person cost down a bit more. Marinated rotisserie chicken is the specialty, but ham, turkey, and meat loaf are other meat options. Side dishes include potatoes, various tasty vegetables, stuffing, pasta, and a plethora of salads. Children's meals are junior versions of the adult choices, with smaller portions and smaller prices. Best of all, the entire chain is smoke-free. *Locations include:*

Arlington Heights
Aurora
Bolingbrook
Bradley
Buffalo Grove
Calumet City
Chicago
Countryside
Crestwood

Crystal Lake
Deerfield
DeKalb
Elgin
Elk Grove Village
Elmhurst
Fairview Heights
Geneva
Glendale Heights
Glenview
Gurnee
Hanover Park
Homewood
Joliet
Lake Zurich
Lombard
Melrose Park
Morton Grove
Mount Prospect
Naperville
Norridge
Oak Lawn
Orland Park
Oswego
Palatine
Park Ridge
River Forest
Round Lake Beach
Schaumburg
Skokie
Waukegan
Westchester
West Dundee
Westmont
Wheaton

CHUCK E. CHEESE'S

Internet: www.chuckecheese.com

This family-friendly chain is known more for its entertainment value than its food. But people don't usually come for the food, they come to *play!* Small children enjoy a playground of tubes, slides, and ball pits. Grade-schoolers will have a good time feeding tokens into all the arcade and skill games. And when you do sit down to eat, there is entertainment in the form of 6-foot-tall robotic puppets gathered on a stage to sing and play music for you. Head cheese Chuck E. is a big gray mouse, and if there's a birthday party, someone in costume will deliver the cake to the birthday girl or boy. Regular coupons in the newspapers can save you money if you buy a package deal with pizza, pitcher of pop, and game tokens. Redeem your arcade prize tickets for a plastic doodad at the souvenir stand. *Locations include:*

Arlington Heights
Batavia
Chicago
Darien
Fairview Heights
Joliet
Matteson
Melrose Park
Naperville
Oak Lawn
Peoria
Rockford
Skokie
Springfield
Streamwood
Tinley Park

CRACKER BARREL

Internet: www.crackerbarrelocs.com

People come to this chain for the atmosphere as much as the food. Subtitled the Old Country Store, the restaurant also has a gift shop full of crafts and other items. Each restaurant is designed with a front porch where there are oak rocking chairs to sit in and wait for your name to be called. (They don't take reservations, and the place is pretty popular, so there may be a wait at mealtimes.) The restaurant serves breakfast, lunch, and dinner, all hearty country-style fare. Most dinner entrees are less than $10. There is a children's menu with the usual assortment of choices. *Locations include:*

Bloomington
Bourbonnais
Caseyville
Decatur
Effingham
Elgin
Gurnee
Joliet
Lincoln
Marion
Matteson
Mattoon
Morton
Mount Vernon
Naperville
Ottawa
Rockford
Romeoville
Springfield
Tinley Park
Troy
Urbana

GIORDANO'S

Internet: www.giordanos.com

This chain has been around since 1974 and is famous for its stuffed pizza, a thick concoction in which cheese and other ingredients of your choice are placed upon a layer of crust and then covered over with another layer of crust and tomato sauce. The menu also includes lasagna, fettucine Alfredo, mostaccioli, ravioli, spaghetti, chicken dishes, and a variety of sandwiches and salads. Entrees are in the $7 to $9 range. Beer and wine are offered in addition to soft drinks. *Locations include:*

Buffalo Grove
Chicago
Downers Grove
East Hazel Crest
Elk Grove Village
Evanston
Glen Ellyn
LaGrange
Lake Zurich
Morton Grove
Naperville
Niles
Oakbrook Terrace
Oak Forest
Oak Lawn
Oak Park
Orland Park
Palos Heights
Rosemont
Schaumburg
Streamwood
Rockford
Westchester
Willowbrook

HOMETOWN BUFFET AND OLD COUNTRY BUFFET

Internet: www.buffet.com

At HomeTown and Old Country, two sister chains, you pay one price up front and then take whatever you want from several buffet tables. Even drinks (nonalcoholic) and desserts are included. The adult price for dinner is about $8, and kids age 10 or younger typically pay 50 cents multiplied by their age. The salad bar has lettuce salads, macaroni, cottage cheese, all sorts. At least two kinds of soup are offered, too. Hot food includes beef, ham, fried and broiled chicken, fried and broiled fish, pasta, various types of potatoes, corn, carrots, and other vegetables, plus various types of breads and rolls. Desserts include ice cream, puddings, cobbler, and other sweets. It's a good value for the money. *Locations include:*

Arlington Heights
Bloomingdale
Bradley
Champaign
Chicago
Chicago Ridge
Countryside
Crystal Lake
Decatur
Deerfield
Downers Grove
Fairview Heights
Ford City
Forest Park
Forsyth
Joliet
Lansing
Lincolnwood
Lombard
Matteson
Moline
Naperville
Niles
Normal
Peoria
Rockford
Rolling Meadows
Springfield
Streamwood
Tinley Park
Vernon Hills
West Dundee

IHOP (INTERNATIONAL HOUSE OF PANCAKES)

Internet: www.ihop.com

Most IHOPs are open around the clock, serving breakfast anytime and lunch and dinner at their appropriate times. Of course breakfast features pancakes, but you can get bacon and eggs, French toast, waffles, and other things as well. Lunch and dinner include a variety of sandwiches and meat-and-potatoes sort of entrees under $10. Children's menu prices fall in the $2 to $3 range. Frequent newspaper coupons make IHOP a bargain. *Locations include:*

Arlington Heights
Aurora
Bolingbrook
Bridgeview
Buffalo Grove
Chicago
Crestwood
Crystal Lake
East Hazelcrest
Elgin
Evanston
Glendale Heights
Gurnee
Hoffman Estates
Joliet
LaGrange
Lansing
McHenry
Melrose Park
Niles
Oak Park
Orland Park
Schaumburg
Skokie
Vernon Hills
Westchester
Wheaton

MCDONALD'S

Internet: www.mcdonalds.com

The fast-food giant merits a brief mention here for its family-friendly atmosphere. Locations with a PlayPlace are especially helpful when traveling, because they provide a relatively safe environment for young children to work off some pent-up energy before getting back in the car. The food is familiar and consistent, and kids' Happy Meals with toys remain a bargain at $2 to $3. High chairs are usually available. *Locations throughout Illinois.*

NANCY'S PIZZERIA

Internet: www.nancyspizza.com

This Chicago-area chain's claim to fame is stuffed pizza: cheese and other ingredients of your choice placed upon a layer of crust and then covered over with another layer of crust and tomato sauce. Nancy's also offers sandwiches and pasta dishes—all less than $10—along with appetizers, salads, and desserts. Some locations are sit-down restaurants, others strictly carryout. Call ahead to check. *Locations include:*

Alsip
Aurora
Bolingbrook
Bourbonnais
Burbank
Chicago
Des Plaines
Elmhurst
Highland Park
Lake in the Hills
Lemont
Lisle
Lockport
Mokena
Naperville
Niles
Oak Forest
Oak Lawn
Palatine
Rolling Meadows
Roselle
Schaumburg
Tinley Park
Westmont
Woodridge
Worth

OLD COUNTRY BUFFET

See previous listing for HomeTown Buffet.

OLIVE GARDEN

Internet: www.olivegarden.com

This chain of sit-down restaurants is good for families whose children are at least in grade school, because you do have to wait for your order to be taken, cooked, and delivered. Pasta entrees include such traditional favorites as lasagna, ravioli, and fettucine Alfredo, but the specials often provide variations on those themes to great success. There are some chicken and seafood entrees on the menu as well. Entree prices range from about $8 to $13, including a big communal bowl of salad from which you can take as many servings as you like. Children can order pasta or their own minipizza for about $4. *Locations include:*

Arlington Heights
Bloomingdale
Bloomington
Burbank
Champaign
Downers Grove
Fairview Heights
Lansing
Lincolnwood
Matteson
Naperville
North Riverside
Peoria
Rockford
Schaumburg
Springfield
St. Charles
Vernon Hills
Waukegan
West Dundee

PIZZA HUT

Internet: www.pizzahut.com

This chain provides consistent quality in thin-crust, hand-tossed, and thick pizzas. Sit-down locations also typically offer salads and pasta dishes. Beverages are all nonalcoholic. Coupons can cut the cost a bit; check your Sunday newspaper. *Locations throughout Illinois.*

POPEYES CHICKEN

Internet: www.popeyes.com

"Love That Chicken from Popeyes!" That's the company's slogan, and the Schuldt family agrees with it wholeheartedly—Popeyes is our favorite fried-chicken chain. The flavorful chicken (mild or spicy) is crispy on the outside and juicy inside, and the buttery buttermilk biscuits melt in your mouth. Most Popeyes restaurants have both sit-down and carryout service. The chain started in New Orleans in 1972, and its menu reflects the cuisine of that region: You can get Cajun rice or red beans and rice in place of french fries, and some restaurants also offer Cajun crawfish. Popeyes was named after Gene Hackman's Popeye Doyle character in the film *The French Connection*, but Popeye the Sailor Man is featured in the advertising. *Locations include:*

Alton
Arlington Heights
Aurora
Berwyn
Bloomingdale
Blue Island
Bolingbrook
Bridgeview
Burbank
Cahokia
Calumet City
Chicago

Cicero
Crest Hill
Darien
East St. Louis
Effingham
Elgin
Evergreen Park
Fairview Heights
Granite City
Harvey
Joliet
Maywood
Melrose Park
Midlothian
Morton Grove
Mount Prospect
Mount Vernon
North Chicago
Oak Park
Palatine
Park Forest
South Holland
Springfield
Tinley Park
Villa Park
Washington Park
Waukegan

PORTILLO'S

This casual Chicago-area chain offers burgers, hot dogs, and other sandwiches such as chicken or Italian beef, typically in a two-story restaurant with all sorts of interesting memorabilia and mannequins to look at. The prices are low enough that no children's menu is offered. *Locations include:*

Addison
Arlington Heights
Batavia
Bloomingdale
Bolingbrook
Chicago
Crestwood
Downers Grove
Elk Grove Village
Elmhurst
Forest Park
Glendale Heights
Naperville
Niles
Northlake
Rolling Meadows
Schaumburg
Streamwood
Summit
Tinley Park
Vernon Hills
Villa Park

RED LOBSTER

Internet: www.redlobster.com

This sit-down restaurant chain offers reasonable-quality seafood at reasonable prices. Dinners are served with crisp lettuce salad and hot, garlicky biscuits. You can Create Your Own Platter of two or three seafood choices. Entrees run about $9 to $18. Items on the children's menu cost about $3.50, including drink; among them are popcorn shrimp, chicken planks, and spaghetti. Smoking and nonsmoking sections usually are fairly well separated, sometimes by a small bar in the middle of the restaurant. *Locations include:*

Alton
Aurora
Bloomingdale
Bloomington
Bradley
Champaign

Chicago
Danville
Decatur
DeKalb
Downers Grove
Fairview Heights
Gurnee
Joliet
Lincolnwood
Marion
Marion
Matteson
Normal
Norridge
Oak Lawn
Orland Park
Peoria
Peru
Rockford
Schaumburg
Springfield
West Dundee

STEAK 'N SHAKE

Internet: www.steaknshake.com

If you're looking for some atmosphere in an economical choice, Steak 'n Shake restaurants are done up in black-and-white ersatz art deco. The chain began in 1934 in Normal and for many years remained concentrated in central, western, and southern Illinois, but it began to reach northward into the Chicago suburbs in the late 1990s. The menu offers "steakburgers" (like hamburgers, only allegedly made with better-quality beef) and other sandwiches accompanied by thin french fries, salads, and other assorted side dishes. The dessert menu is heavy on mouthwatering ice-cream concoctions. Most Steak 'n Shake restaurants are open twenty-four hours a day, seven days a week, serving breakfast as well as lunch and dinner. *Locations include:*

Alton
Aurora
Belleville
Bloomington
Bolingbrook
Bourbonnais
Carbondale
Champaign
Collinsville
Danville
Decatur
DeKalb
Downers Grove
East Peoria
Edwardsville
Effingham
Elgin
Fairview Heights
Forsyth
Galesburg
Glendale Heights
Gurnee
Hoffman Estates
Jacksonville
Joliet
Lake in the Hills
Lincoln
Marion
Mattoon
McHenry
Moline
Mount Prospect
Mount Vernon
Naperville
O'Fallon
Oswego
Pekin
Peoria
Peru
Quincy
Rockford
Rosemont
Springfield
Tinley Park
Urbana

TGIFRIDAY'S

Internet: www.tgifridays.com

Here is a sit-down restaurant where you can bring the kids and not have to worry about them getting too loud. Chances are, the place is already loud. The restaurant exudes a party atmosphere, but the place also tries to seem homey and old-fashioned. A raised section in the center of the restaurant houses a bar. Smoking is allowed in certain sections, which usually are not well separated; beware if you are allergic or highly sensitive. High chairs and booster seats are generally available. The menu is almost a book, it has so many pages. Sandwiches cost about $5 to $8 and are typically served with french fries. Entrees, most served with soup or salad, potato, and sometimes vegetables, fall in the $8 to $12 range for pasta, chicken, fish, and shrimp, and in the $12 to $18 range for steaks and ribs. The children's menu entrees for either lunch or dinner cost about $3, *not including drinks.* Open for lunch and dinner. *Locations include:*

Batavia
Bedford Park
Bloomingdale
Bourbonnais
Carpentersville
Champaign
Cherry Valley
Chicago
Darien
Effingham
Fairview Heights
Glenview
Gurnee
Hoffman Estates
Joliet
Lombard
Moline
Naperville
Oak Park
Rockford
Schaumburg
Springfield
Vernon Hills

WENDY'S

Internet: www.wendy's.com

Serving lunch and dinner; some locations are open late into the evening. No smoking in most restaurants. High chairs and booster seats are generally available. Wendy's is one of the best fast-food buys around. The value menu features a variety of items for only 99 cents, so you can have a feast for only two or three bucks per person. There are kid meals with little prizes, if you want to go that route, for $2 to $2.60. Most adult combos with burger, fries, and drink are under $5. The hearty stuffed pitas fall in the $2 to $3 range. Most Wendy's restaurants tend to be clean and well lit. *Locations throughout Illinois.*

Lodging Appendix

The following is a list of some of the more family-oriented hotel and motel chains. Individual listings in each town include information on a particular property's size, amenities, and price category (prices do vary by location; for example, Downstate properties are typically cheaper than those in the Chicago metro area). You'll take some of the anxiety out of your trip if you make your reservations in advance. Rates may vary by season, usually being higher in summer. At most of these chains, kids stay free in the same room with their parents, but the age cutoff may be 12 at one place and 18 at another, so check the specifics when you make your reservation. Be sure to ask about any special rates or package deals that are sometimes available. You'll also save money by staying at a hotel or motel that includes breakfast in the room rate. Note the following terms:

Continental breakfast: At least coffee and some sort of bread or pastry. Exactly what you get varies from one property to another. Many also include juice, milk, and cold cereal.

Full or American breakfast: Hot food such as bacon and eggs or pancakes. Rarely included in the price of a room at any hotel or motel.

*An asterisk indicates that there is a listing for a specific hotel or motel in that town's Where to Stay entry.

BAYMONT INN

(800) 301–0200; Internet: www.baymontinns.com

Formerly Budgetel, most of these properties are three- or four-story rectangular concrete blocks. They have comfortable, nicely furnished rooms inside, and all that cement seems to help muffle outside noise. Rooms have coffeemakers and cable TV. Some Baymont Inns also have suites. Only a few of the Baymont Inns in Illinois have a swimming pool, but those that do are indoor pools. None of the Illinois properties has a restaurant on the premises, but there is usually one within walking distance, often next door. Nearly all the Illinois properties accept "small pets." It's best to check with the specific one you want to stay at to determine what they consider "small." All are willing to make special accommodations for nonsmokers or persons with disabilities. There's all sorts of stuff for business travelers, too. *Locations include:*

*Alsip
Champaign
Decatur
East Peoria
*Effingham
*Elgin
Glenview
Gurnee
Hoffman Estates
Litchfield
Matteson
Rockford
Springfield
*Tinley Park
Willowbrook

BEST INNS OF AMERICA

(800) 237–8466; Internet: www.bestinn.com

Properties vary in appearance, but they usually are two stories high and located near an interstate or highway. Often truck parking is available, so you might hear some noise from the big rigs. On the other hand, some kids get a kick out of seeing a parked 18-wheeler up close. The rooms are basic but comfortable, and you can request a nonsmoking one. All the Illinois properties have an outdoor swimming pool. (Rockford's is an indoor.) None has a restaurant on the premises, but there's usually one nearby. A "Special K breakfast" of cold cereal, milk, juice, coffee, and toast or pastries is included in the room rate. *Locations include:*

*Bloomington
*Carbondale
Caseyville
*Effingham
Libertyville
Marion
*Metropolis
Mount Vernon
Rochelle
Rockford
*Springfield
Waukegan

BEST WESTERN

(800) 528–1234 English, (800) 332–7836 Spanish, (800) 634–9876 French, (800) 528–2222 TDD; Internet: www.bestwestern.com

Best Westerns are independently owned and operated, so there is a much greater variation in appearance, amenities, and quality than with many other chains. Most of the ones in Illinois are two-story motels, although there are a few high-rise hotels. Some have an indoor or outdoor swimming pool. Some allow pets. Some have a restaurant on the premises. Some include breakfast in the room rate. Some of the properties are beautiful and well maintained, some so-so, and a few downright divey. If you can, visit the particular motel you want before you book a room there. If that's not feasible, try to get the chain's current *Travelers' Guide & Road Atlas,* a detailed list for each location. At all U.S. Best Westerns, children age 12 or younger stay free in the same room with a paying adult. *Locations include:*

Altamont
Antioch
Arlington Heights
*Aurora
Burbank
Burr Ridge
Calumet Park
Charleston
*Chester
*Chicago
*Collinsville
Danville
Decatur
DeKalb
Des Plaines
Dixon
Effingham
*Elk Grove Village
*Fairview Heights
*Freeport
*Galena
Glen Ellyn
Grayville
Greenville
Homewood
Joliet
La Grange
*Lansing
Libertyville
Litchfield
Marion
*Metropolis
*Moline
*Monticello
Morris
Morton Grove
Nashville
*Normal
Pontoon Beach
Rantoul
Robinson
*Rockford
Romeoville
Rosemont
*St. Charles
Savoy
Springfield
Ullin
*Waukegan
Westmont

COMFORT INN

(800) 228–5150; Internet: www.comfortinn.com

Properties vary in appearance, but most are rectagular, light-colored buildings two to six stories high. Rooms are comfortable, most with cable TV. There are a few Comfort Suites, which feature partially divided living and sleeping areas (no door between them) and a coffeemaker and small refrigerator. Among the approximately 50 properties in Illinois, more than half have an indoor swimming pool; a few have an outdoor pool, and some have no pool at all. Be sure to check for the one you're interested in. Policies regarding pets also vary. A few Comfort Inns have a restaurant on the premises, but most do not. All include continental breakfast in the room rate. *Locations include:*

*Alton
*Arcola
*Aurora (Suites only)
Bloomington (Suites also)
Bolingbrook
*Carbondale
Casey
*Champaign
*Chicago
Collinsville
Danville
*Des Plaines
Dixon
*Downers Grove
Edwardsville
Effingham (Suites only)
*Elk Grove Village
Forsyth
Franklin Park
Galesburg
*Gurnee (Suites also)
Harvey (Suites only)
*Joliet
Lansing (Suites only)
Lincoln
Litchfield
Lombard (Suites only)
Manteno
Marion (Suites also)
Mattoon (Suites only)
Mendota
*Metropolis
*Moline
*Morris
Morton
Mount Vernon
Oakbrook Terrace (Suites only)
O'Fallon
Orland Park
Ottawa
Palatine
*Pekin
Peoria (Suites only)
Peru
Pontiac
Princeton
*Quincy
*Rockford (Suites also)
Salem
*Springfield (Suites also)
Waukegan

DAYS INN

(800) 329–7466; Internet: www.daysinn.com

The size and shape of the buildings varies, and so do the amenities offered. Some have an indoor heated pool, some have an outdoor pool, and some have no pool. Some have an on-site restaurant. Some include continental breakfast in the room rate. The main thing they have in common is comfortable rooms at economical prices. *Locations include:*

Addison
*Alton
*Barrington
*Belleville
Benton
*Bloomington
*Cairo
Carbondale
Caseyville
Champaign
Charleston
Chicago

Clinton
Collinsville
Danville
Decatur
East Hazel Crest
Effingham
*Elgin
*Elk Grove Village
El Paso
Farmer City
Gilman
Granite City
Kankakee
Lansing
Macomb
Marion
*Melrose Park
Metropolis
Morton
Mount Vernon
Muddy
Naperville
Niles
North Chicago
Oglesby
*Peoria
Princeton
Quincy
Rantoul
Richmond
Schiller Park
Sheffield
Shorewood
*Springfield
*St. Charles
*Vandalia
Waukegan
Westmont
Woodstock

FAIRFIELD INN

(800) 228–2800; Internet: www.fairfield.com

The building is two to four stories high. Fairfield Inn is the economy-class member of the Marriott family. Rooms have simple, comfortable furnishings and cable TV. All the Illinois inns have a heated swimming pool, most an indoor one with spa as well. All properties in the chain include continental breakfast in the price of the room. *Locations include:*

Bedford Park
*Bourbonnais
*Champaign
Collinsville
Danville
*Fairview Heights
Forsyth
*Galesburg
Glenview
*Gurnee
Joliet
Lansing
*Mattoon
*Moline
Naperville
Normal
*Peoria
Peru
Quincy
Rockford
*Springfield
Tinley Park
Willowbrook

HAMPTON INN

(800) 426–7866; Internet: www.hampton-inn.com

The inn is usually a white building, three to five stories high. Amenities include coffeemakers, irons and ironing boards, dataports, and a free movie channel on the TV. Nearly all of the more than 30 Hampton Inns in Illinois have a swimming pool, about half an indoor one. Room rates include a complimentary breakfast bar. *Locations include:*

Bedford Park
Bloomington
*Bourbonnais
Carbondale
Chicago
Collinsville
Countryside
*Crestwood
East Peoria
Effingham
*Elgin
Elk Grove Village
Fairview Heights
Forsyth
*Gurnee
Hoffman Estates
Joliet
Lincolnshire
*Lombard
Marion
Matteson
*Mattoon
Moline
Morton
Mount Vernon
Naperville
Quincy
*Rockford
*Schaumburg
Schiller Park
South Holland
*Springfield
Tinley Park
*Urbana
Westchester

HOLIDAY INN

(800) 465–4329; Internet: www.holiday-inn.com

Properties vary in appearance but usually have nicely furnished rooms, an indoor or outdoor pool, and a restaurant on the premises. They are pretty reliable in terms of cleanliness and competent staff. Typically breakfast is available in the restaurant or through room service, but the cost is not included in the room rate. The newer Holiday Inn Express properties are generally smaller and do not have an on-site restaurant (usually there's an independent restaurant nearby), but they typically do include a continental breakfast and unlimited local telephone calls in the room rate. They may or may not have a pool; it's best to double-check. Those with suites have a separate living room area, and usually there's a door between it and the bedroom area. *Locations include:*

*Alton
Arlington Heights
Bolingbrook
*Bourbonnais
Cahokia
*Carbondale
Carlinville
*Carol Stream
*Chicago
*Collinsville
Countryside
*Crystal Lake
*Decatur
*Downers Grove
Elgin
*Elk Grove Village
Elmhurst
Evanston
Galesburg
*Glen Ellyn
Gurnee
Harvey
Highland
Hillside
Itasca
Jacksonville
Joliet
Lincoln
Macomb
Marion
Markham
Matteson
Metropolis
Moline
*Morris
Morton
*Mount Vernon
Mundelein
*Naperville

*Normal
Oak Lawn
Oglesby
Ottawa
Palatine
Pekin
*Peoria
Pontiac
*Quincy
Rock Falls
*Rockford
Rolling Meadows
Rosemont
Salem
Schaumburg
Skokie
Springfield
*St. Charles
Sycamore
*Tuscola
Urbana
Waukegan
Willowbrook
Woodstock

MOTEL 6

(800) 466–8356; Internet: www.motel6.com

This budget chain offers low-cost lodging. The rooms may not be the largest or quietest you've ever stayed in, but they're usually reasonably clean and comfortable. About half the properties have an outdoor swimming pool. There are no meals included in the room rate, and only a few properties have a restaurant on-site, but food of some sort is nearby. *Locations include:*

Arlington Heights
*Aurora
*Bourbonnais
Caseyville
*Chicago
*Collinsville
East Peoria
Elk Grove Village
Glenview
Joliet
Marion
Moline
*Mount Vernon
*Normal
Palatine
Rolling Meadows
Schiller Park
Springfield
Urbana
Villa Park

QUALITY INN

(800) 228–5151; Internet: www.qualityinn.com

Properties vary in appearance. A cousin of Comfort Inn, Quality Inn is geared more toward the economy-minded business traveler, but families can sometimes find a bargain on the weekend, when many business travelers have gone home. About half the Illinois properties have an indoor or outdoor swimming pool. A few have a restaurant on the premises, and those that do not have one include breakfast in the price of a room. *Locations include:*

Bloomington
Caseyville
Champaign
Chicago
Effingham
Lombard
Peru

RAMADA INN

(800) 272–6232; Internet: www.ramada.com

The typical Ramada Inn has nicely furnished rooms, an indoor or outdoor pool, and a restaurant on the premises. Breakfast usually is available in the restaurant or through room service and is not included in the room rate, but some properties do include a continental breakfast. Ramada Limited properties have been cropping up—smaller motels that offer a continental breakfast with the room. *Locations include:*

Bolingbrook
Carbondale
*Chicago
Collinsville
Danville
*Decatur
*Effingham
*Elgin
Fairview Heights
Flora
*Freeport
Galesburg
Glendale Heights
Harvey
Joliet
Mattoon
McHenry
Mount Prospect
Mundelein
O'Fallon
*Pekin
Peru
Pontoon Beach
Rockford
Rosemont
Springfield
Troy
Urbana
*Vandalia
Vienna
*Waukegan

RED ROOF INN

(800) 843–7663; Internet: www.redroof.com

This is a fairly economical chain that offers clean, comfortable rooms. It's fine if you're just looking for a place to sleep. But if you want to hang out at the motel, this chain may not be your best choice because most have few amenities of interest to kids. None of the Illinois properties has a swimming pool or an on-site restaurant; only the Troy property offers breakfast with the room. About half the inns allow pets; call ahead to check. *Locations include:*

Arlington Heights
Champaign
*Downers Grove
Hoffman Estates
Joliet
Lansing
Naperville
Northbrook
Peoria
Rockford
South Holland
Springfield
Troy
Willowbrook

SLEEP INN

(800) 753–3746; Internet: www.sleepinn.com

A cousin of Comfort Inn, Sleep Inn is more of a budget chain, with comfortable rooms and few amenities in one- or two-story buildings. Most of the Illinois properties do not have a swimming pool or a restaurant on the premises. All do include continental breakfast in the room rate. *Locations include:*

Bedford Park
Harvey
Lake Bluff
Lansing
*Naperville
O'Fallon
Peoria
Rockford
Springfield
Urbana

SUPER 8

(800) 800–8000; Internet: www.super8.com

This South Dakota–based budget chain continues to expand. Rooms tend to be clean and comfortable, the amenities minimal, although a few have a swimming pool. All offer free coffee in the lobby each morning, and some include continental breakfast in the room rate. Some of the properties allow pets. *Locations include:*

Altamont
Alton
Aurora
Beardstown
Belleville
Benton
Bloomington
Bourbonnais
Bridgeview
Calumet Park
Canton
Carbondale
*Champaign
Chenoa
Chicago
Chillicothe
Collinsville
*Crystal Lake
Danville
Decatur
*DeKalb
Dixon
DuQuoin
Dwight
*East Moline
East Peoria
Effingham
Elgin
Elk Grove Village
El Paso
Fairview Heights
Freeport
Galesburg
Geneseo
Gilman
Greenville
Harrisburg
Jacksonville
Jerseyville
Joliet
*Kewanee
Lansing
LeRoy
Lincoln
Litchfield
Macomb
Marion
Marshall
*Mattoon
McHenry
McLean

Mendota
Mokena
Monee
Monmouth
Morris
Mount Vernon
Mundelein
Murphysboro
*Normal
Okawville
Olney
Ottawa
Paris
Pekin
Peoria
Peru
Pontiac
Pontoon Beach
Princeton
Quincy
Rantoul
River Grove
Rochelle
Rock Falls
Rockford
Romeoville
Salem
*Springfield
Staunton
*St. Charles
Taylorville
Troy
*Tuscola
Washington
Waterloo
Watseka
Waukegan
Wenona
Woodstock
Yorkville

TRAVELODGE

(800) 578–7878; Internet: www.travelodge.com

and THRIFTLODGE

(800) 525–9055; Internet: www.thriftlodge.com

Travelodge and Thriftlodge properties are a good choice for families on a budget. The properties are usually two-story buildings with 50 to 100 clean, comfortable rooms. The Broadview, Des Plaines, Effingham, Libertyville, Quincy, and Springfield locations also offer the Sleepy Bear's Den guest room for families, which has bear decor and a VCR with kids' videos. Most of the Illinois properties have an outdoor swimming pool. About half the properties allow pets; check ahead of time. All the Illinois properties either have a restaurant on the premises or are located near one. A few of the properties include continental breakfast in the room rate. *Locations are Travelodge unless otherwise indicated and include:*

Broadview
Chicago
*DeKalb
*Des Plaines
East Hazel Crest
Effingham
Franklin Park (Thriftlodge)
Glen Ellyn
Libertyville
Mokena
Naperville
Niles (Thriftlodge)
Ottawa
Quincy
Springfield
Urbana
*Vandalia
Waukegan (Thriftlodge)

General Index

Activities Index

AMUSEMENT CENTERS, INDOOR PLAYGROUNDS, AND THEME PARKS

CHILDREN'S MUSEUMS

MINIATURE GOLF

PARKS

PLAYGROUNDS (OUTDOOR)

TRAINS

WATER PARKS, SWIMMING POOLS, AND BEACHES

ZOOS AND ANIMAL ATTRACTIONS

Free Attractions

There is no admission charge for the following attractions, although some of them have donation boxes for optional contributions.